COLLECTOR'S GUIDE TO CHILDREN'S BOOKS

1850 TO 1950
VOLUME TWO

IDENTIFICATION & VALUES

Diane McClure Jones & Rosemary Jones

COLLECTOR BOOKS
A Division of Schroeder Publishing Co.,

D1511439

—— ⋯⊨◎ *Searching For A Publisher?* ◎⊨⋯ ——

Cover design: Beth Summers
Book design: Joyce Cherry
Book layout: Karen Smith

COLLECTOR BOOKS
P.O. Box 3009
Paducah, Kentucky 42002-3009

Copyright © 1999 by
Diane McClure Jones & Rosemary Jones.

Printed in the U.S.A. by Image Graphics Inc., Paducah KY

⟶ ⇥ *Contents* ⇤ ⟵

⸺ ⋆⇒ *Acknowledgments* ⇐⋆ ⸺

We would like to thank the friendly folks at Seattle Book Center, Shorey Books, Westside Story Books, all located in Seattle; Book Stop in Poulsbo, Washington; Suzanne and Truman Price of Monmouth, Oregon; the nice people who put together the Anacortes Book and Paper Show; and the many helpful dealers at the Seattle Antiquarian Book Fair.

Hugs to Margaret Beagle, our most enthusiastic cheerleader, and to our generous friends, Sabrina Urquhart, Kris Walberg, Yvonne Walberg, Lynn Beltz, and Kirk Stines, who once again loaned us books from their private collections to use for the illustrations.

And a special thanks to readers of the first volume who shared their knowledge, including some great series information from Christopher Cuomo and a couple of wonderful pop-ups from Patricia Davenport of Angelique Books in Kalamazoo, Michigan.

Introduction

As we stated in the introduction to the first volume of *Collector's Guide to Children's Books*, there simply wasn't room to list every book ever published. We had to make some hard choices on what to include and what to leave for later price guides.

Volume 2 adds completely new price listings for many authors and series not covered in Volume 1. Once again, these listings cover approximately 100 years of publishing for children, 1850 to 1950, and are divided into two main sections: books listed by author and books listed by series. A bonus section, Play Books, was also added, which features books meant to be played with, such as paint books, animation books, pop-ups, and other one-of-the-kind publishing experiments.

Again, we gave priority to editions that we saw in other collections or in various shops and at antiquarian book fairs. This let us confirm with our own eyes the details of a particular edition. When this wasn't possible, we relied on recent auction records, dealer's catalogs, and the many new Internet databases linking bookstores across America.

We tried to confine our listings to books that were written primarily for children's entertainment. Some books were originally written for adult entertainment, such as the Tarzan series, but evolved into childhood favorites. We have added those, even though you may not always find them shelved in the children's section of a used bookstore.

Since so many of our readers enjoyed the illustrators' biographies in Volume I, we added new biographies as well as expanded listings for certain illustrators.

Fans of picture books will find many more listings dealing with these delightful books created for the youngest readers.

So that Volume 2 can be used as a companion book for Volume 1, we have added title indexes for both Volume 1 and Volume 2, and also an author index for Volume 1, as well as a revised section including more Internet resources, some addresses for newsletters and fan clubs, and a glossary.

At the conclusion of the introduction to Volume 1, we asked for collectors' suggestions for future books. The resulting correspondence has been truly wonderful. We appreciate all the time and trouble taken by our readers to send us information on books in their collections or to identify other authors and illustrators that would be of interest to collectors.

We have included on the next pages some commonly asked questions and our answers. We welcome your suggestions for future price guides. Please address your comments to Rosemary Jones, 600 W. McGraw #2, Seattle WA 98119, e-mail: lostlvs@aol.com. For those mailing their questions, please include a self-addressed stamped envelope for reply.

Question: I am enclosing a description of a book I found, and all it has is the date 1903 on the back of the title page. Can you tell me if it is really that old?

Answer: Without actually seeing the book, it's very hard to judge the age. Many publishers, like Grosset & Dunlap, often used the original copyright date rather than the actual date of publication. Look at the illustrations and dust jacket. Illustrations showing modern dress or hairstyles can be good clues that the book was published later than indicated by the copyright date. Dust jackets may list other books written by the author or printed by the publishers. The last title listed can be a clue, and if these titles were written after 1903, this may identify when your book was published. Also, a close examination of cover materials and paper can help date a book.

Question: You list all these great Internet resources, but I don't own a computer! How can I use these?

Answer: If you don't have a computer at home, check with your local library to see if they can help you do research. Many libraries now offer Internet connections for their patrons and often give free classes about using computers. You'll also find cybercafes in larger cities, where you can interact with newsgroups, search Web sites, and sip your favorite espresso drink. Finally, if you're trying to buy a copy of a certain book, many used book dealers now offer search services for their customers.

Question: I have a very old copy of PRINCE AND THE PAUPER that is in nice condition. Is it worth something?

Answer: If a book is not a first edition or is not a hard-to-find text, then age alone doesn't add to the value. Because Mark Twain's books have been reprinted so many times, the value usually depends on the presentation of the text and the illustrator. An elaborate binding, color illustrations, or a well-known illustrator certainly adds to the value.

Question: If a book sells for $500 at an auction, does that mean that all the copies of that title are worth the auction price?

Answer: Auction prices are one indication of the desirability of a title, but these prices can often be inflated by the circumstances of an auction, such as a famous former owner of the book, or a lot of media attention driving up the prices. Sometimes a really high price may be just a "spike" in the market, not to be repeated any time soon. A well-publicized auction may raise the prices as people become more aware of a book. It also can inspire more people to sell their copies of the book, raising the availability of a title and lowering the price. Also, the auction price reflects only the desirability of that particular copy, such as a first edition or limited edition, or a signed copy, rather than all copies of that particular title.

Question: In Volume 1, you listed about four different versions of my favorite book, but not the one I have. Why not?

Answer: We probably had not seen your version at the time of publication. Due to space restrictions, we often cut out duplicate titles if we hadn't actually seen the book. Also, some extremely popular titles, such as *Heidi*, came out in dozens of editions, and we haven't found all of them.

Question: Are only first editions worth something?

Answer: While first editions may be worth more than later editions, price is often determined by other factors. If this is an exceptionally hard-to-find book, and one sought by many collectors, then any edition may command a good price. For some books, only one or two editions were ever published, but if it is not a "desired" book by collectors, the edition makes very little difference to the price.

Question: *All I can remember about my favorite childhood book is that it was about a girl named Betsy who had a pet frog. Any way that I might find the author or title?*

Answer: If you have a book dealer specializing in children's books in your town, try asking them. Children's librarians can also be a great help. On the Internet, the newsgroup called "rec.arts.books.children" does discussions like this every day, and the participants are truly wonderful at identifying books from bits and pieces of the plot.

Question: *How scarce are the books marked RARE in your Guide? What are they worth?*

Answer: In Volume 1 and Volume 2, the term RARE was used to distinguish those books highly desirable to collectors which do not come to market very often, and whose prices often exceeded $1000 at auction. In most cases, these are first editions of very famous books, such as *Alice In Wonderland*, where the original print runs were very small or very few copies are known to be in existence today. Certain picture books, although they had large print runs, simply did not survive the abuse of toddlers and thus are very scarce today in any edition.

Question: *I have this little Victorian book with short stories and a couple of black-and-white pictures. I've never seen this title before and can't find it listed anywhere. It is more than 100 years old, so is it valuable?*

Answer: Age alone does not determine price for books. For collectors, the desirability of children's books is often linked to their favorite reading as children. Many children's books from the late Victorian era (1880 to 1900) are selling for much less than popular picture books from the 1930s simply because they are unknown to today's collectors.

Question: *I am trying to find a book that my grandmother used to read to me, and I know the title but not the author. How can I find the author's name?*

Answer: In the new sections at the back, you'll find the books described in Volumes 1 and 2 listed by title. Many of the databases available on the Internet, including the Library of Congress, also include searches by title.

Explanation of Pricing

Prices of collectible books vary dramatically, due to changes in popularity of items. The revival of interest in an old novel for any reason, such as the production of a film based on the story, can create or increase demand.

We have based our prices on suggested prices received from a number of antiquarian book dealers.

All quoted prices are for books in good condition but without dust jackets. When dust jacket pricing information is available, it is included and identified.

Good condition means clean, sound cover and spine without breaks or furred edges, clean undamaged pages, all pages and illustrations tightly attached. Price adjustments should be made for fingerprints, small tears, loose pages. Large reductions are made for broken and seriously damaged covers, loose and missing pages, torn pages, water stains and mold. In the case of children's books, other common damage found includes pencil and crayon marks.

Illustrations are a major factor in determining the price of a children's book. The illustrator is the major factor; the number and condition of the illustrations is the secondary factor.

First editions are noted. First state and other specific variations that dramatically alter the price of a particular volume have not been considered. This type of information is so specific and detailed that it needs to be obtained by the collector from a source specializing in a particular collection, such as a dealer or a club for collectors of a specific category.

Rare books are designated as such in the listings and not priced. A rare book is one that is extremely difficult to find, and the price is usually determined at the time of the sale. It will often depend solely on how much an individual collector wants the book. Auction prices can go into the thousands of dollars for a particular sale to a particular customer, but that price may never be paid again for an identical volume and is therefore not a reliable guide to pricing.

Investments: Because of the fragile nature of paper and the "well-handled" condition of most children's books, most collectors collect children's books for the joy of finding and owning them. Some of them may be excellent investments. Some may lose value. As we cannot guess which books will increase in value and which will decrease, we have in our own collections books that we acquired and love for their content rather than their potential monetary value.

Explanation of Dust Jackets

"Children's book jackets, of course, give maximum opportunity for color, gay effects and inventive design. Their varied shapes invite the designer and the picturesque material with which they usually deal delights his picture making soul."

Henry Pitz, *A Treasury of American Book Illustration,* 1947

History

Dust jackets, also called book jackets or dust wrappers, were a relatively late invention of book publishers. The earliest jackets lacked the design, color, and illustration that we normally associate with dust jackets.

Nineteenth century books often had elaborate covers, sometimes made completely of leather, more often, in the case of children's books, made of cloth-covered boards. The decorations and lettering were often impressed and embellished with gilt. To protect these beautiful covers from dust, light, and handling while in the bookstore, the books were sometimes covered with paper wrappers which were fairly plain, containing title and author's name only. These paper forerunners of the dust jacket were usually thrown away by the buyer.

Around the turn of the century, publishers began to use the wrappers as an advertising tool, listing additional books by the author or adding information about other books in a series. The cover of the book was still heavily decorated. Cover decoration included gilt lettering, pictures printed in gilt ink, or color plates pasted-on to the cover. The pictures on the cover or on the frontispiece of the book were often used as the dust jacket art.

By the 1920s, most books were sold in dust jackets. During this time, the dust jackets for children's books developed the elaborate original designs that we associate with them today, while the covers of the books became plainer and plainer. By the mid-twentieth century, many book covers had only the title and the author's name printed on them.

As publishers realized the marketing value of dust jackets, they added features to the jacket that were not available within the book. During the late 1920s, the Bobbsey Twins, an often re-printed series, featured a dust jacket with two paper dolls printed on the back. The dust jackets for Ruth Plumly Thompson's Oz books featured commentaries on the novels by Thompson, a bonus for her fans!

Sometimes, the jacket design was designed by a different artist than the artist who did the interior illustrations, and the jacket artist's reputation can make the dust jacket as desirable a collectible as the book. George T. McWhorter, curator of the Burroughs Memorial Collection at the University of Louisville, calls a first edition of an N.C. Wyeth designed dust jacket "the rarest Burroughs collectible." The jacket was adapted from a *New Story Magazine* illustration for the dust jacket of *The Return of Tarzan.* For collectors of Tarzan as well as N.C. Wyeth, the first edition version of the jacket has become an elusive Holy Grail, worth almost any price to the serious collector.

Ranks, Clipping, Marrying, and Color Copies

Dealers' catalogs use a variety of rankings for dust jackets, ranging from poor to fine. Like all systems of ranking, these listings are meant only as a guide for the buyer and are subject to the dealer's own values or experience. There is not a universal standard for dust jacket conditions.

In general, a fine dust jacket is one in near mint condition. No rips, tears, or other markings mar the jacket. The fine jacket should appear as if it was rarely or never handled. A good dust jacket shows normal wear, such as whitening at the top and bottom of the spine, that a jacket develops over several years of use, but the illustration or graphic design is still bright, clear, and attractive to the eye.

We've done our pricing based on dust jackets in good condition. However, in some cases, such as the N.C. Wyeth jacket mentioned earlier, an original dust jacket, even badly ripped or marred, still makes the book highly desirable.

Many collectors also want to check for the clipping of a jacket. A normal practice for gift givers is to clip the price from a jacket. This small triangular cut usually occurs in the upper right hand corner of the inner flap. A price clipped dust jacket is fairly common, and if the rest of the jacket is in good condition, this may make little difference in price or collectibility.

A second type of clipping occurs when the words "Book Club Edition" are removed from the dust jacket. This clip resembles the price clip but is usually located on the lower right hand corner of the front flap or the lower left hand corner of the back flap. For some collectors, book club editions have no value at all, and their dust jackets are similarly despised. For others, just getting a copy of the book with a good-looking cover, clipped or not clipped, is worthwhile. For those purchasing with the desire to eventually resell the books, book club editions are not viewed as desirable collectibles and are usually priced as nice reading copies.

"Marrying" occurs when someone puts a dust jacket from one book on a different book. For example, a collector may find two copies of a first edition Nancy Drew. One copy has a clean dust jacket, but the book itself is damaged. The other book has no dust jacket, but is in good condition. The collector may buy both books and then switch the jacket to the better book to gain a more desirable item. Since this switch occurs on the same edition of the book, this really does improve the collectibility of the book.

However, sometimes you will find jackets married to different editions of a book, such as a first edition book with a second edition dust jacket. Sometimes, these odd marryings occurred at the printers. There have been many documented instances of the first editions of the later Oz books being originally sold with different edition dust jackets as an attempt by the publisher to use up existing stock. At other times, these marryings were made by collectors who simply wanted a nice dust jacket on their book. These books are not as desirable to serious collectors as a true first edition with a true first edition jacket.

If the combination of a certain edition of a dust jacket and a certain edition of a book make an enormous difference in price, such as raising a book's worth from $400 to $4000, the careful collector should deal only with a bookseller whom they trust with their money and make every attempt to verify the "points" of the jacket and book. Most highly collectible books, such as the Oz books and Burroughs books, have inspired very specific reference works which can be extremely helpful to the collector. Also helpful are clubs devoted to a specific author, where information can be shared. Auction catalogs from well documented collections can also help in this type of research.

Finally, with the advent of better color copiers, we've seen a rise in color copies of dust jackets wrapped around books. A color copy of a jacket should not add to the price to the book. They should be simply viewed as a pretty way to protect the book and add no value in the resale market beyond their printing cost, a few dollars at most.

Color copies are fairly easy to spot. The paper feels different than regular dust jackets, and the copy often shows the rips and tears of the original jacket as large white spots.

Dust Jacket Styles

For nineteenth century books with heavily decorated covers, surviving plain dust jackets are rare. However, the lack of a jacket makes little difference in the desirability of these books for collectors. The plain dust jackets may add a small amount of novelty value to the price simply because they are difficult to find, but the lack of a wrapper does not seriously lessen the value of the book.

Individually illustrated hardcovers with same-as-cover dust jackets became popular in the early 1900s. These books usually had cloth-over-board covers with paste-on-pictorials, and the jacket matched the pictorial, as in the Washington Square series. In the 1930s and 40s, children's picture books began to have color illustrated paper-over-board covers, and the dust jackets were identical to the covers. Examples of this type of book are Lindman's *Snipp, Snapp, Snurr,* and the Dr. Seuss books. In both cases, the jackets were often discarded as they did not make the book more attractive on the shelf. However, because these dust jackets are pretty, as well as protective of the cover, a clean, sturdy jacket does add to the price of the book.

The exact value of a matching dust jacket heavily depends on the collectibility of the book. These dust jackets fall into a troubling middle ground for collectors who must balance the rarity against the fact that the same illustration already exists on the book. Examples of valuable jackets are the original dust jackets on the early Oz books. Their value is high in proportion to the difficulty of finding them. Later Oz books are more apt to have jackets, and so the jackets add less value to the price. The highly collectible early Volland editions of the Raggedy Ann books were boxed in matching boxes which gave the same protection as a jacket, and those boxes

Washington Square – individually illustrated hardcover with same-as-cover dust jackets.

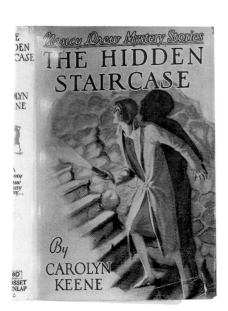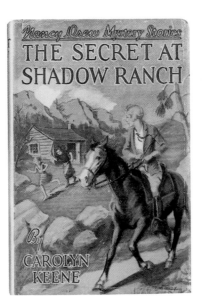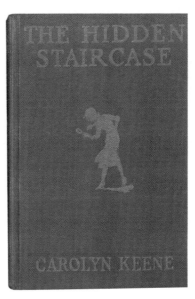

Nancy Drew – individually illustrated dust jacket over a plain hardcover.

double the price. On the low end of this group are the Washington Square Series types of books. These books are in limited demand, the price remains fairly low, and the books are generally collected as reading copies. Also, the dust jackets on this series are of poorer quality printing and add less than 20% increase to the price because buyers do not want to pay extra for a dust jacket.

Individually illustrated dust jackets over plain covers are valued for the quality of the illustration.

For children's books with plain covers under bright dust jackets and for books with little or no interior illustrations, dust jackets can make a great difference in price. These dust jackets may represent the only color illustration of the story. Often the books themselves are easy to find, and this is

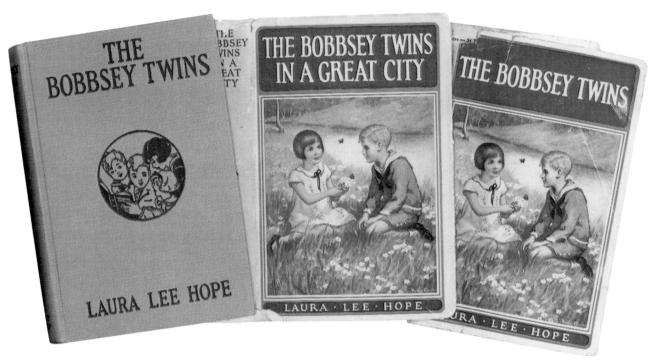

Bobbsey Twins – one-illustration-for-series dust jacket that matches all other dust jackets in the series.

especially true of many of the children's series books, but the dust jackets have been lost.

With highly collectible books, the effect on price can be dramatic, as with the Tarzan books. Because the covers are plain and the wraparound illustrated dust jackets are highly decorative, a mint dust jacket of a first edition of Tarzan increases the value by ten times, so that a $400 first edition may leap in value to $4,000 for the same book with jacket.

Early Nancy Drew books with plain blue hardcovers, and original Russell Tandy illustrated dust jackets, and early Judy Bolton books with plain brown covers, and original Pelagie Doane illustrated dust jackets are generally triple the value of copies without dust jackets.

One-illustration-for-series dust jackets that match all the other dust jackets in the series, with only the title changed, were also commonly used from the 1920s through the 1940s. The Bobbsey Twins series were often packaged this way. The dust jacket usually adds 20% to 50% to the price.

You'll also find series books with one illustration that appears on both the book covers and the dust jackets. The Bobbseys were packaged this way, too. These dust jackets have the least value of series covers because the illustration already exists on the book, and all the book covers and dust jackets are identical except for the change in title.

A non-matching individually illustrated dust jacket over a hardcover with a colorful plate illustration is another puzzling combination for collectors. The value here depends on the quality of the cover compared to the dust jacket. Usually the dust jacket is brighter and therefore is desired by collectors. An odd example of the reverse is the Windemere Series, where the black cloth-over-board covers are dramatically trimmed in silver, and the paste-on-pictorials are bright. These hardcovers are much more attractive than the somewhat pale dust jackets. Most collectors prefer the Windemere Series hardcover left uncovered on their shelves, and so the dust jacket adds little or no value.

The examples listed are for series books because the value of their dust jackets is more uniform. The value of dust jackets on individual books varies widely, depending on the rarity of the book, the rarity of a good condition jacket, the contrast between book cover and jacket, the popularity of the artist who designed the dust jacket, and other factors.

Dust Jacket Prices

Many readers of our first volume asked us to include dust jacket prices in this volume.

Therefore, throughout the listings the price shown is for the book itself, without dust jacket, but whenever we have been able to verify the price for a book with a good condition, original dust jacket, we have also included this information.

Examples of Book Cover Styles

The following illustrations show some of the popular materials and styles used to make book covers for children's books in the nineteenth and early twentieth centuries.

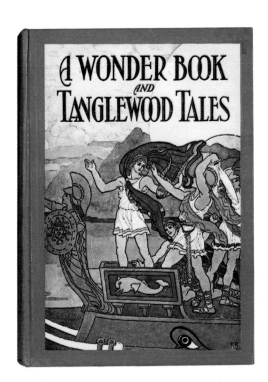

Andersen's Fairy Tales, gilt on cloth-over-board.

Voyage of the Mary Adair, half-cloth with paper-over-board.

Wonder Book paste-on-pictorial.

Captain January with paste-on-illustration.

The most commonly used combination of materials was heavy cardboard covered with colored cloth. The undated edition of *Andersen's Fairy Tales and Stories* is a good example of nineteenth century decoration, combining pattern, pictures, color and gilt, all applied directly to the cloth covering. Also popular in this era was the delicately illustrated paper-over-board half-cover with a cloth margin and spine, frequently used for small books such as Crompton's *Voyage of the Mary Adair*.

To add brighter illustrations to cloth covers without the expense of printing directly on the cloth, paste-ons were used. The 1930 edition of Hawthorne's *Wonder Book and Tanglewood Tales* has a paste-on-pictorial cover, with the paper covering almost all the book cover and including printed matter. The smaller pasted-on paper illustration added to the cover of the 1924 Baby Peggy edition on Richards' *Captain January* is called a paste-on-illustration, because it only included the illustration, covers only a portion of the front of the book, and the lettering is on the cloth-over-board cover, not on the paper.

Sari's *Jeanne-Marie Goes to Market*, 1938, has a full paper-over-board cover, popular for children's books both for the ease of printing the illustration and for production cost reductions.

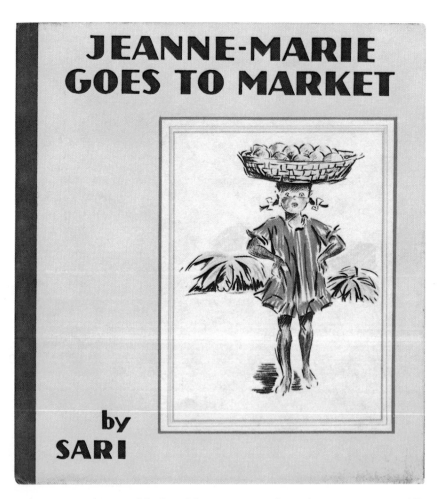

Jeanne-Marie with paper-over-board cover.

Prices are for books in good condition but without dust jackets, except when noted. See section on pricing for further explanation. Dates preceding publisher's name refer to the date of publication of the particular edition described. (Dates in parentheses indicate year of first copyright or first publication.)

A

ABBOTT, Eleanor Hallowell
Being Little in Cambridge When Everyone Else Was Big, 1936 Appleton first edition, green cloth-over-board cover with gilt, 280 pages. $50.00

ABBOTT, Jacob
Franconia Stories, edited by Margaret Armstrong, 1923 Putnam, blue cloth-over-board cover with gilt lettering and paste-on-pictorial, 321 pages, color frontispiece, 4 b/w plates by Helen Armstrong. $25.00

ABC BOOKS
See FRISKEY, Margaret, GAG, Wanda, LEAR, Edward, WINTER, Milo.
Also, see the PLAY BOOK section.

ADAMS-ACTION, Mrs.
Six Bold Babes, or *The Adventures of a Perambulator,* undated ca. 1903 Routledge, blue cloth-over-board cover with gilt, small, 255 pages, 12 b/w illustrations by M. E. Edwards. $20.00

ADSHEAD, Gladys L.
Brownies Hush Fair, 1938 Oxford, illustrated hardcover, illustrations by Elizabeth Orton Jones. $20.00
What Miranda Knew, 1944 Oxford, small square easy-read picture book, color illustrations throughout by Elizabeth Orton Jones. $20.00

AESOP, ca. 500 BC
Aesop's Fables and Picture Fables, undated ca. 1900 edition Routledge, London, cloth-over-board cover in red and brown design with gilt lettering, about 335 pages, including b/w woodcuts and 10 color plate illustrations. $35.00

ALCOTT, Louisa May, see Series, LOUISA MAY ALCOTT LIBRARY.
Jack and Jill, (1880) 1925 Little Brown, cloth-over-board cover. $25.00
Jo's Boys and How They Turned Out, (1886) 1912 Little Brown, cloth-over-board cover with gilt, 365 pages. $35.00

Pansies and Water Lilies, (1888) 1902 edition, beige cloth-over-board cover with decoration, small, b/w illustrations. $40.00

ALDEN, Joseph
Burial of the First Born, a Tale for Children, 1866 Tilton, green cloth-over-board cover, illustrated. $20.00
Rupert Cabell and Other Tales, ca. 1850 Gates and Stedman, small, cloth-over-board cover with gilt, b/w illustrations. $20.00

ALDIN, Cecil, see Series, HAPPY FAMILY.
Dog Day or the Angel in the House, 1902 Russell, first American edition, small, illustrations by Aldin. $125.00
Dozen Dogs or So, 1928 edition Scribners, first American edition, oversize, tan cloth-over-board hardcover, 12 color plates plus b/w illustrations by author. $110.00
Mongrel Puppy Book, undated ca. 1900 Humphrey Milford, London, oversize, illustrated paper-over-board cover, 12 color plates by Aldin. $250.00

ALEXANDER, Elsie, see Series, SUNNYBROOK.

ALLEN, Betsy, see Series, CONNIE BLAIR

ALLEN, Captain Quincy, see Series, OUTDOOR CHUMS.

ALLEN, Gladys
Dig Here!, 1938 Goldsmith, blue cloth-over-board cover, 252 pages. ($15.00 with dust jacket) $6.00

ALLEN, Merritt Parmelee
Battle Lanterns, 1949 Longmans, cloth-over-board cover, illustrated endpapers, b/w illustrations by Ralph Rey Jr. $10.00
Black Rain, 1939 Longmans, cloth-over-board cover, illustrated endpapers, b/w illustrations by James MacDonald. $15.00
Green Cockade, 1942 Longmans, cloth-over-board cover, illustrated endpapers, b/w illustrations by Henry Gillette. $10.00

ALLEN, Willis
Kelp, Story of the Isles of Shoals, 1888 Lothrop,

green cloth-over-board cover with gilt, small, 242 pages, b/w illustrations. $20.00

ALMOND, Linda

Peter Rabbit and the Little Boy, 1935 Platt Wee Books, small, 62 pages, cloth-over-board cover, color illustrations signed J. L. G. $35.00

Peter Rabbit and the Little Girl, 1935 Platt Wee Books, small, cloth-over-board cover, color plates. $35.00

Peter Rabbit and the Tiny Bits, 1935 Platt Wee Books, small, cloth-over-board cover, color plates. $35.00

Peter Rabbit Goes A-Visiting, 1921 Altemus, illustrated hardcover, illustrations signed J.L.G. $45.00

A.L.O.E., see Tucker, Charlotte.

AMES, Esther Merriam

Twistum Tales, 1929 Rand McNally, color paste-on-illustration on cloth-over-board cover, b/w and full-page color illustrations by Arnold Lorne Hicks. $40.00

Young Andy, a Story of a Hundred Years Ago, 1932 Gabriel, cloth-over-board cover with paste-on-pictorial, color and b/w illustrations. ($75.00 with dust jacket) $20.00

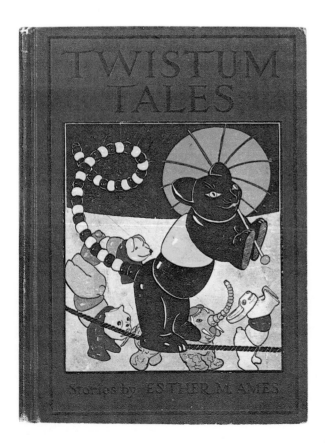

AMSDEN, Dora

Macaroni Tree, 1927 Hebberd, maroon decorated cover, oversize, blue tinted plates by Joseph Paget-Fredericks. $40.00

ANDERSEN, Hans Christian 1805–75, also see PEAT, Fern Bisel

Andersen's Fairy Tales and Stories, undated ca. 1900 edition Routledge, London, cloth-over-board cover in red, green, and brown design with gilt, about 335 pages, including b/w woodcut illustrations. $25.00

Little Mermaid, 1939 Macmillan, first thus edition, blue cloth-over-board cover with illustration and gilt, illustrated endpapers, four color plates plus b/w illustrations by Dorothy Lathrop. $80.00

ANDERSON, C. W.

Horses are Folks, 1949 Harper, oversize oblong, cloth-over-board cover, illustrated endpapers, 90 pages, b/w illustrations by author. ($50.00 with dust jacket) $35.00

Thoroughbreds, 1942 Macmillan, lithograph illustrations by author. ($50.00 with dust jacket) $35.00

Tomorrow's Champion, 1946 Macmillan first edition, oversize oblong, 74 pages, lithograph illustrations by author. $35.00

ANDERSON, Robert Gordon

Eight O'Clock Stories, 1923 Putnam, oversize, 269 pages, illustrated blue cloth-over-board cover with gilt lettering, full-page color illustrations by Dorothy Hope. $55.00

Half Past Seven Stories, ca. 1922 Putman, cloth-over-board cover, 251 pages, color frontispiece, two-tone plates. $35.00

Little Chap, 1919 Putnam, brown cloth-over-board cover with gilt, small, 43 pages, color frontispiece. $20.00

Over the Hill Stories, 1925 Putnam, blue cloth-over-board cover, oversize, illustrations by Nina Ralston Jordon. $30.00

ANDREWS, Mary Raymond Shipman

Eternal Masculine, 1916 Scribners, green cloth-over-board cover with color and gilt decoration, 8 b/w plates by Philip Goodwin and F. C. Yohn. $15.00

ANDREWS, Virginia

High Up in a Penthouse, 1938 Harper, 38 pages, oversize, color illustrated paper-over-board cover, illustrated endpapers, b/w illustrations by author. ($35.00 with dust jacket). $25.00

ANTHONY, Edward
Every Dog Has His Say, 1947 Watson-Guptill first edition, oversize, 44 pages, illustrations by Morgan Dennis. $30.00

ANTHONY, Edward and Joseph
Fairies Up-to-Date, 1923 Little Brown, hardcover with paste-on-pictorial, 189 pages, illustrations by Jean de Bosschere. $65.00

APPLETON, Carolyn T.
Cocky Cactus, 1946 Van Kampen, first edition, oversize, 44 pages, color illustrations by author. $25.00

APPLETON, Victor, see Series, DON STURDY, MOVING PICTURE BOYS.

ARASON, Steingrimur
Golden Hair, 1946 Macmillan, 223 pages, map endpapers, b/w illustrations by Gertrude Howe. $15.00

ARNETT, Anna Williams
Takamere and Tonhon, Two Little Red Children in their Prairie Home, 1932 Beckley-Cardy, small, 136 pages, color illustrations by Dorothy Saunders. $20.00

ARNOLD, Maj. Henry, see Series, BILL BRUCE AVIATOR SERIES.

ARTHUR, T. S.
Cedardale, or The Peacemakers, 1884 edition Lippincott, purple cloth-over-board cover with gilt, small, 208 pages, b/w illustrations. $25.00

ASHMUN, Margaret, see Series, ISABEL CARLETON SERIES.
No School Tomorrow, 1925 Macmillan, 215 pages, blue cloth-over-board cover with gilt, brown/b/w frontispiece, 3 b/w plates by A. Williamson. $15.00
School Keeps Today, 1926 Macmillan, 235 pages, blue cloth-over-board cover, 4 b/w plates by A. Williamson. $15.00

ASQUITH, Cynthia, editor
Flying Carpet, 1925 Scribner, first American edition, anthology, tan cloth-over-board cover, 200 pages, oversize, color illustrations by Earnshaw, H. M. Brock, Pearse, Atwell, plus b/w illustrations. $30.00

ATWATER, Emily Paret
How Sammy Went to Coral-Land, 1902 Jacobs, impressed cover illustration, small, 112 pages, b/w illustrations. $20.00
Trixsey's Travels, 1905 Jacobs, small, cloth-over-board cover, 138 pages, b/w illustrations. $20.00

AULT, Norman
Dreamland Shores, poems, 1920 Milford, London, oversize, 83 pages, printed illustration on cover, map endpapers, 8 color plates plus b/w illustrations by author. $250.00

AUNT ELLA
Wonderful Fan, 1882 Dutton, color illustrated paper-over-board cover, oversize, 96 pages, b/w illustrations. $35.00

AUSTIN, Margot
Barney's Adventure, 1941 Dutton, oversize picture book, illustrations by author. ($50.00 with dust jacket) $20.00
Manuel's Kite String, 1943 Scribner, small, 112 pages, b/w illustrations by author. $20.00
Willamette Way, 1941 Scribners, illustrated tan cloth-over-board cover, oversize, 42 pages, color illustrations by author. $35.00

AVERY, Kay
Wee Willow Whistle, 1947 Knopf first edition, oversize, illustrated paper-over-board cover, color illustrations by Winifred Bromhall. $25.00

B

BABYLAND Editors
Our Little Men and Women, 1894 Lothrop, illustrated cloth-over-board cover with gilt, oversize, 296 pages, photos and b/w illustrations. $40.00

BAILEY, Carolyn
Little Hannibal, 1938 Platt Munk first edition, hardcover with pictorial plate, b/w illustrations. ($85.00 with dust jacket) $30.00
Stories from an Indian Cave, 1935 edition Whitman, green cloth-over-board cover with paste-on-pictorial, 217 pages, color and b/w illustrations by Joseph Dash. $25.00

BAILEY, Margery
Seven Peas in the Pod, 1919 Little Brown, illustrated cloth-over-board cover with gilt, 8 b/w/green plates and numerous b/w line drawings by Alice Bolan Preston. $35.00

BAKER, Charlotte
House on the River, 1948 Coward first edition, 128 pages, charcoal illustrations by author. $15.00

BAKER, Margaret
Dunderpate, 1938 Dodd, cloth-over-board cover, silhouette illustrations by Mary Baker. $40.00
Four Times Once Upon a Time, 1926 Duffield, silhouette illustrations on colored paper by Mary Baker. $40.00
Little Girl Who Curtsied, 1926 Duffield 2nd edition, cloth-over-board cover, silhouette illustrations by Mary Baker. $40.00
Three for an Acorn, 1935 Dodd, cloth-over-board cover, silhouette illustrations by Mary Baker. $40.00
Water Elf and the Miller's Child, (1928) 1930 Duffield 3rd edition, oblong picture book, cloth-over-board cover, silhouette illustrations by Mary Baker. $45.00

BAMFORD, Mary E.
Denby Children at the Fair, 1904 Cook, small, impressed cover design, b/w illustrations. $10.00
My Land and Water Friends, 1886 Lothrop, oversize, tan cloth-over-board cover with black lettering and gilt, 223 pages, b/w illustrations by L. J. Bridgman. $20.00
Ti, a Story of San Francisco's Chinatown, undated ca. 1900 Cook, cloth and marbled paper-over-board cover. $50.00

Up and Down the Brooks, 1889 Riverside Library edition, blue cloth-over-board cover, 222 pages, illustrated. $30.00

BANCROFT, Laura (L. Frank Baum), see Series, TWINKLE TALES
Bandit Jim Crow, ca. 1906 Reilly Britton, Twinkle Tales series, small, illustrated cloth-over-board cover, approx. 62 pages, color illustrations by Maginel Wright Enright. $85.00

BANNERMAN, Helen, see PEAT, Fern
Story of Little Black Quasha, 1908 Nisbet, London, small, 111 pages, 28 full-page color illustrations by author, presentation copy signed to her brother, one of a kind, dealer's catalog price $2,800.00

BANNING, Nina
Pit Pony, 1947 Knopf first edition, b/w illustrations by author. $15.00

BARKSDALE, Lena
First Thanksgiving, 1942 Knopf, hardback, illustrated by Lois Lenski. ($40.00 with dust jacket) $20.00
That Country Called Virginia, 1945 Knopf, hardcover, illustrated by Harry Roth. $15.00
Treasure Bag Stories and Poems, 1947 Knopf

first edition, oversize, 159 pages, color illustrated paper-over-board cover, illustrated endpapers, color illustrations throughout by Maurice Brevannes. $35.00

BARNABY, Horace, see PEAT, Fern

BARRIE, James
Little Minister, 1898 Russell, hardcover, Maude Adams edition with b/w plates, including paintings and photos, 375 pages. $30.00

BARRIS, Anna Andrews
Red Tassels for Huki in Peru, 1939 Whitman first, oversize, 64 pages, b/w/orange paste-on-pictorial cover, b/w/orange endpapers and illustrations by Iris Beatty Johnson. ($60.00 with dust jacket) $45.00

BARROWS, Marjorie
Ezra the Elephant, 1936 Grosset, illustrated endpapers, color and b/w illustrations by Nell Smock. $45.00

Fraidy Cat, a Glowing-Eye book, 1942 Rand McNally, illustrated paper-over-board cover with holes throughout for mounted glow-in-the-dark "eyes," 22 pages, illustrations by Barbara Maynard. $50.00
JoJo, a Glowing-Eye book, 1944 Rand McNally, paper-over-board cover with cutout throughout illustrated pages for JoJo's face, instructions: "hold JoJo close to a lightbulb...take into dark-

ened room...JoJo's eyes shine!" B/w/brown/blue illustrations by Clarence Biers. $50.00
One Hundred Best Poems for Boys and Girls, collected by author, 1930 Whitman, hardback. $35.00
Organ Grinders' Garden, 1938 Rand McNally, first edition, oversize, illustrated by Helen and Alf Evers. $25.00
Sukey, You Shall Be My Wife and Other Stories, 1944 Lowe, hardback, illustrated by Ann Elizabeth. ($30.00 with dust jacket) $15.00
Timothy Tiger, a Glowing-Eye book, 1944 Rand McNally, paper-over-board cover with cutout throughout illustrated pages for Tiger's face, color illustrations by Keith Ward. $50.00
Waggles, Glow-in-Dark book, 1945 Rand McNally, paper-over-board cover with cutout throughout illustrated pages for dog's face, color illustrations by Clarence Biers. $50.00

BARRY, Ethelred
Miss De Peyster's Boy, 1902 Crowell, red cloth-over-board cover with gilt, small, 82 pages, b/w illustrations by author. $15.00

BARTRUG, C. M.
Blacky, 1939 McLoughlin, small, illustrated paper-over-board cover, illustrated by Charles Bracker. $35.00
Mother Goose Health Rhymes, 1942 Whitman, small oblong, 32 pages, illustrated endpapers, b/w illustrations by Marjorie Peters. $35.00

BARZINI, Luigi
Little Match Man, 1917 Penn, cloth-over-board cover with paste-on-pictorial, 164 pages, color plates by Hattie Longstreet. $50.00

BASSETT, Sara Ware
Carl and the Cotton Gin, 1924 Little Brown, cloth-over-board cover, 264 pages, plates. $20.00
Christopher and the Clockmakers, 1925 Little Brown, cloth-over-board cover, 246 pages, plates. $20.00
Paul and the Printing Press, 1920 Little Brown, cloth-over-board cover, 218 pages, plates. $20.00
Steve and the Steam Engine, 1921 Little Brown, cloth-over-board cover, 253 pages, plates. $20.00
Ted and the Telephone, 1922 Little Brown, cloth-over-board cover, 223 pages, plates. $20.00
Walter and the Wireless, 1923 Little Brown, cloth-over-board cover 256 pages, plates. $20.00

BEAUMONT, Cyril W.
Sea Magic, 1928 John Lane, London, color illustrated boards, design by Wyndham Payne. $25.00
Toys, 1930 London, first edition, hardcover, decorations by Eileen Mayo. $40.00

BECHDOLT, Jack
Trusty, Story of a Police Horse, 1947 Dutton first edition, cloth-over-board cover, b/w illustrations by Decie Merwin. ($25.00 with dust jacket.) $15.00
Vanishing Hounds, 1941 Oxford, hardback, b/w illustrations by Decie Merwin. $15.00

BEDFORD, Francis
Visit to London, verses by Edward Verrall Lucas, ca. 1900 Brentano's, first American edition, oversize, 118 pages, illustrated cover, color plate illustrations by Bedford. $175.00

BEESON, Helen, see NEWTON, Ruth

BELASCO, David, and BYRNE, Chas.
Fairy Tales Told by Seven Travelers at the Red Lion Inn, 1907 Baker, blue cloth-over-board cover with white impressed illustration, illustrated endpapers, 179 pages, b/w illustrations by George Bleekman. $25.00

BELLOC, Hilaire
Moral Alphabet in Words of One to Seven Syllables, 1899 Arnold, London, square, 63 pages, illustrations by "B. B." (Basil Blackwood), first edition presentation copy signed by Belloc. $800.00

BENEDICT, Emma
Happy Time Fancies, verse, 1893 Lee & Shepard, pictorial boards, cloth spine, small, 13 pages. $15.00

BENNETT, Dorothy
Golden Almanac, 1944 Simon & Schuster, first edition, oversize, 96 pages, color and b/w illustrations by Masha. $25.00

BENNETT, John
Pigtail of Ah Lee Ben Loo, 1930 Longmans first edition, orange cloth-over-board cover, silhouette illustrations by author. $65.00

BENNETT, Rowena
Around Toadstool Table, 1930 Rockwell, small, 109 pages, cloth-over-board cover with color paste-on-pictorial, b/w illustrations by Lucille Holling. $35.00
Runner for the King, 1944 Follett, oversize, cloth-over-board cover, 48 pages, color plates by Fiore Mastri. $25.00
Teddy's Sailboat and Other Stories, 1942 Rand McNally, small, illustrated paper-over-board cover, illustrations by Mastri. $15.00

BERGERGREN, Ralph
Jane, Joseph and John, 1918 Atlantic Monthly, oversize picture book, green cloth-over-board cover with paste-on-pictorial, 62 pages, b/w illustrations and decorations by T. B. Hapgood, 6 color plates by Maurie Day. $85.00

BERNARD, Florence Scott
Through the Cloud Mountain, ca. 1924 edition Lippincott, large, cloth-over-board cover with paste-on-pictorial, gilt lettering, 8 color plates by Gertrude Kay. $40.00

BERRY, Erick
Cynthia Steps Out, 1937 Goldsmith, cloth-over-board cover. $15.00
Girls in Africa, 1928 Macmillan first edition, 128 pages, color frontispiece and b/w illustrations by author. $50.00
Nancy Herself, 1938 Goldsmith, cloth-over-board cover, 250 pages. $15.00

BERTAIL, Inez
Time for Bed, 1939 Doubleday, small oblong picture book, color endpapers, b/w and color illustrations by Ninon MacKnight. $25.00

BESKOW, Elsa
Sun-Egg, 1933 Harper, oversize oblong picture book, color illustrated paper-over-board cover, color plates by author. $65.00

BESTON, Henry
Firelight Fairy Book, 1919 Little Brown, printed illustration on cloth-over-board cover, b/w illustrations by Maurice Day. $20.00

BIALIK, H. N.
Far Over the Sea, 1939 Am. Hebrew Congress first edition, hardcover, poems and music. $15.00

BIANCO, Pamela
Sing a Song of Journeys, 1937 edition Grosset, paper-over-board cover, illustrated by author. $25.00

BIGHAM, Madge A.
Bad Little Rabbit and Other Stories, 1927 edition Little Brown, cloth-over-board cover, 155 pages, color illustrations. $30.00
Merry Animal Tales, (1906) 1922 edition Little Brown, illustrated yellow boards, 200+ pages, illustrations by Clara Atwood. $30.00
Overheard in Fairyland, 1909 Little Brown, green cloth-over-board cover with illustra-

tion, gilt lettering on spine, 238 pages, frontispiece, color illustrations throughout by Ruth S. Clements. $60.00

Sonny Elephant, 1930 Little Brown, cloth-over-board cover, color illustrations by Berta and Elmer Hader. $45.00

Within the Silver Moon, 1911 Little Brown, pictorial boards, illustrated by Elizabeth Otis. $20.00

BINGHAM, Clifton
All Sorts of Comical Cats, 1902 Lister, oversize, cloth spine, pictorial paper-over-board cover, chromolith frontispiece and two-color illustrations throughout by Louis Wain. Hard-to-find. $450.00

BIRLEY, Caroline
We Are Seven, 1881 Dutton, red cloth-over-board cover with gilt, small, 136 pages, 8 color illustrations by T. Pym. $25.00

BLAIR, Matilda, editor
Little Plays for Little Players, 1907 McLoughlin, green cloth-over-board cover, small, color illustrations. $15.00

BLANCH, Josephine Mildred
Compilation of Cradle Songs, 1907 Murdock Press, gray hardcover, oversize, 62 pages . $35.00

BLAND, R. Nesbit
Bunny Tales, ca. 1880 Nister, cloth cover, small, 64 pages, color and b/w illustrations by Edith Cubitt. $45.00

BLODGETT, Mabel F.
Magic Slippers, 1917, small, illustrated cloth-over-board cover, color and b/w illustrations by author. $35.00

BLYTON, Enid, see Series section, FAMOUS FIVE
Enid Blyton's Treasury, 1947 Evans Brothers, published for Boot's Pure Drug Co., cloth-over-board cover, oversize, color and b/w illustrations. $35.00

Little Girl at Capernaum, 1948 Lutterworth, first edition, color and b/w illustrations by Elsie Walker. ($30.00 with dust jacket) $15.00

Silver and Gold, undated Nelson ca. 1927, hardcover with paste-on-pictorial, 8 color plates by Ethel Everett. $35.00

BONTEMPS, Anna and CONROY, Jack
Slappy Hooper, the Wonderful Sign Painter, 1946 Houghton, oversize oblong, 44 page picture book, color endpapers and color illustrations throughout by Ursula Koering. $25.00

BOOTH, Maud Ballington
Sleepy-Time Stories, (1899) 1905 edition Putnam, cloth-over-board cover with impressed gilt design, 17 b/w plates by Maud Humphrey. $40.00

Twilight Fairy Tales, 1906 Putnam, gilt page edge, 16 color plates by Amy Carol Rand. $40.00

BOSWELL, Hazel
French Canada: Pictures and Stories, 1938 Viking, cloth-over-board cover, small oblong, 82 pages, illustrated endpapers, 24 full-page color illustrations by author. $25.00

BOWEN, Sidney, see Series section, RED RANDALL

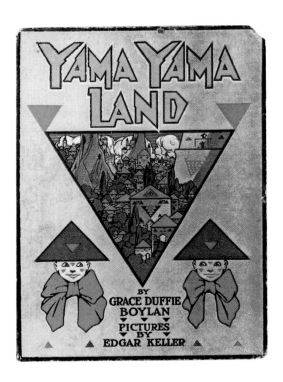

BOYLAN, Grace Duffie
Yama Yama Land, 1909 Reilly Britton, b/w and full color illustrations including 2 double page color plate illustrations by Edgar Keller. $100.00

Young Folk's Uncle Tom's Cabin, 1901 Jamieson-Higgins, cloth-over-board cover, illustrations by Ike Morgan. $100.00

Young Folk's Uncle Tom's Cabin, 1928 edition Albert Whitman, green cloth-over-board cover with paste-on-pictorial, color illustrated endpapers, b/w illustrations by Ike Morgan. $45.00

BOYLE, Eleanor Vere, illustrator
Beauty and the Beast, 1875 edition Sampson Low, London, oversize, 57 pages, 10 chromolithographs designed by Boyle. $300.00

BOYLE, Kay
Youngest Camel, 1939 Little Brown, first edition, cloth-over-board cover, illustrations by Fritz Kredel. $35.00

BRADDELL, Maurice
Little Gorky of the Black Swans, 1947 Jonathan Cape, London, first edition, hardback, 263 pages. $25.00

BRADEN, James, see Series section, BOYS' INDIAN

BRADLEY-BIRT, F. B.
Bengal Fairy Tales, 1920 John Lane, London, oversize, cloth-over-board cover with gilt, 209 pages, 6 color plates by Abanindranath Tagore. $50.00

BRANDT, Carl
Bob Hazard, Dam Builder, 1916 Reilly Britton, blue cloth-over-board cover, oversize, illustrated. $20.00

BRECKENRIDGE, Gerald, see Series section, RADIO BOYS

BREWSTER, Frances Stanton
Song Stories and Song for Children, 1898 American Book, first edition, hardcover. $20.00

BRIDGES, William
Wild Animals of the World, 1948 Garden City, oversize, cloth-over-board cover with gilt, 268 pages, color and b/w illustrations by Mary Baker. ($35.00 with dust jacket) $25.00

BRIGHAM, S. J.
Under Blue Skies, ca. 1886 Worthington, oversize, pictorial boards, color plates and tinted decorations throughout. $65.00

BRILL, George Reiter
Rhymes of the Golden Age, 1908 Stern, green cloth-over-board cover with paste-on-pictorial, illustrated endpapers, 121 pages, color and b/w illustrations by author. $20.00

BRINE, Mary D.
Mother's Little Man, 1906 Altemus, color pictorial boards with cloth spine, small, b/w illustrations. ($50.00 with dust jacket) $25.00
Mother's Song, 1886 Cassell, flowered cloth-over-board cover with gilt illustration, 48 pages, decorated endpapers, heavy paper, b/w illustrations by C. Northam. $25.00

BRISLEY, Joyce, see Series section, MILLY-MOLLY-MANDY

BROCK, Emma
Birds' Christmas Tree, 1946 Knopf, hardback, color illustrations by author. $35.00
Hen That Kept House, 1933 Knopf, red decoration on yellow cover, 40 pages, illustrations by author. $40.00
Kristie and the Colt and the Others, 1949 Knopf first edition, hardback, color illustrations and b/w illustrations by author. ($55.00 with dust jacket) $40.00
Runaway Sardine, 1929 Knopf, hardback, color illustrations by author. $40.00
Then Came Adventure, 1941 Knopf, green cloth-over-board cover, 184 pages, Lake Superior/Gooseberry Bay map endpapers, b/w illustrations throughout. $40.00
Three Ring Circus, 1950 Alfred Knopf, yellow cloth-over-board cover. $20.00
Topsy-Turvy Family, 1943 Knopf first edition, hardcover, color illustrations by author. $20.00

BRONSON, Wilfred
Chisel-Tooth Tribe, 1939 Harcourt, cloth-over-board cover, illustrated endpapers with map, color frontispiece, color plates and b/w illustrations by author. $25.00
Starlings, 1948 Harcourt, small square, illustrated cloth-over-board cover, illustrated endpapers, b/w illustrations by author. ($25.00 with dust jacket) $15.00

BROOKE, L. Leslie
House in the Wood, (1909) 1947 edition Warne, cloth-over-board cover, illustrations by author. $25.00

BROOKS, Amy, see Series section, PRINCESS POLLY

BROOKS, E. S.
Boy of the First Empire, 1895 Century, green cloth-over-board cover with gilt, 320 pages, b/w illustrations by Ogden. $25.00

BROOKS, Edward
Story of the Faerie Queene, (based on Spenser), 1902 Penn, blue cloth-over-board cover with decoration, small, 418 pages, b/w illustrations. $15.00

BROOKS, Noah
Boy Emigrants, (1876) 1900 edition Scribner, gray with gilt illustration, small, 309 pages, b/w illustrations by Moran and Sheppard. $20.00
Boy Settlers, Story of Early Times in Kansas, (1891) 1899 edition Scribners, gray cloth-over-board cover with black/silver decoration, small, 16 b/w illustrations by Rogers. $20.00

BROTHERTON, Alice Williams
What the Wind Told to the Treetops, 1887 Putnam, cloth-over-board cover with gilt, 54 pages, b/w illustrations. $25.00

BROWN, Beth
Universal Station, 1944 Regent House, cloth-over-board cover. ($15.00 with dust jacket) $10.00

BROWN, Jeanette Perkins
Little Book of Bedtime Stories, 1947 Abingdon, cloth-over-board cover, 28 pages, b/w illustrations by Decie Merwin. $20.00

BROWNE, Frances
More editions of *Granny's Wonderful Chair:*
Granny's Wonderful Chair, 1924 edition Dutton, green cloth-over-board cover with gilt, 280 pages, b/w illustrations signed Dora Curtis. $20.00
Granny's Wonderful Chair, 1932 edition Winston, cloth-over-board cover with printed illustration, color frontispiece, illustrated endpapers, b/w illustrations by Mabel Dodge Holmes. $20.00
Wonderful Chair and the Tales It Told, 1900 edition Heath, school edition with instructions for teachers, small, cloth-over-board cover, 192 pages, pen illustratons by Clara Atwood. $30.00

BROWNE, G. Waldo, see Series section, WOODRANGER TALES

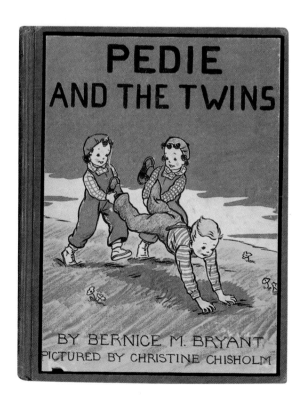

BRYANT, Bernice M.
Pedie and the Twins, 1942 Whitman, brown cloth-over-board cover with paste-on-pictorial, illustrated endpapers, 32 pages, color illustrations by Christine Chisholm. ($25.00 with dust jacket) $20.00

BRYANT, Lorinda Munson
Children's Book of Animal Pictures, 1931 Century, cloth-over-board cover, oversize, b/w photo illustrations. $30.00
Children's Book of Celebrated Pictures, 1922 Century, maroon cloth-over-board cover, 101 pages, b/w illustrations. $40.00

BUFF, Mary and Conrad
Hurry-Skurry and Flurry, 1944 Viking, oversize, cloth-over-board cover, illustrated. ($40.00 with dust jacket) $20.00

BULFINCH
Book of Myths, 1942 Macmillan, first thus edition, gray cloth-over-board cover, oversize, color and b/w illustrations by Helen Sewell. ($85.00 with dust jacket) $45.00

BULLOCK, L. G.
Children's Book of London, 1948 Warne, oversize, illustrated paper-over-board cover, full-color maps and b/w illustrations by author. $35.00

BURBANK, Addison
Cedar Deer, 1940 Coward McCann, red cloth-over-board cover. ($25.00 with dust jacket) $10.00

BURGESS, Thornton W., see Series section, BEDTIME STORY-BOOK SERIES, GREEN FOREST, NATURE STORIES
Thornton Burgess Animal Stories, 1942 edition Platt Munk, orange cloth-over-board cover, 8x7 inches, illustrated endpapers, color and b/w illustrations throughout by Harrison Cady. ($40.00 with dust jacket) $20.00
Tommy and the Wishing Stone, (1915 Little Brown) 1923 edition Little Brown, green hardcover with paste-on-pictorial, small, 109 pages, 8 b/w plates by Harrison Cady. $15.00
Tommy and the Wishing Stone, (1915 Little Brown) undated ca. 1930s-40s Grosset edition, hardcover, illustrated endpapers, b/w illustrations by Harrison Cady. First of the three Wishing-Stone books. ($20.00 with dust jacket) $10.00

BURGLON, Nora
Children of the Soil, 1932 Doubleday, cloth-over-board cover, illustrations by E. P. D'Aulaire. $20.00

BURKE, Stella M. (also listed as Stella Burke May)
Chico's Three-Ring School, 1929 Appleton, red cloth-over-board cover, color illustrated endpapers, b/w illustrations by Bernice Oehler. $30.00
Children of Japan, 1936 Rand McNally, small oblong with illustrated paper-over-board cover, 66 pages. $30.00
Men, Maidens and Mantillas, 1923 New York Century, cloth-over-board cover. $20.00

BURNETT, Carolyn, see Series section, BLUE GRASS SEMINARY SERIES

BURNETT, Frances
Editha's Burglar, 1888 Jordan, cloth-over-board cover with gilt, photo frontispiece, b/w plates by Henry Sandham. $45.00
Editha's Burglar, 1925 Page, hardcover, Baby Peggy photoplay editions with b/w photo illustrations from the movie. ($40.00 with dust jacket) $30.00
Little Princess, 1905 Warne, lst edition in rewritten book form (originally serialized in St. Nicholas Magazine), gilt decorations on cover, 8 color plate illustrations by Harold Piffard. $300.00
Piccino and Other Child Stories, 1894 Scribner, illustrated cloth-over-board cover, b/w illustrations by Reginald Birch. $50.00
Piccino and Other Child Stories, 1904 McClure, bordered pages, decorations by Jessie Wilcox Smith. $65.00
Two Little Pilgrims' Progress, 1895 Scribner, cloth-over-board cover, b/w illustrations by Reginald Birch. $85.00

BUTTERWORTH, Hezekiah, see Series section, ZIGZAG JOURNEYS

BURLEIGH, Cyril, see Series section, HILL TOP BOYS

BURROUGHS, Edgar Rice, see Series section, MARS, TARZAN

BURTIS, Thomson
Flying Blackbirds, 1932 Grosset, illustrated endpapers, illustrations by J. Clemens Gretta. ($35.00 with dust jacket) $20.00
Four Aces, 1932 Grosset, illustrated endpapers and frontispiece by J. Clemens Gretta. $20.00

BUSCH, Wilhelm
Max and Moritz, originally written in German, ca. 1865, following are English translations:
Max and Maurice, (author's name listed as William Busch on this translated edition), 1898 edition Little Brown, small, cloth-over-board cover with impressed illustration, 56 pages, verse, b/w illustrations. $60.00
Max and Moritz: a Story of Seven Tricks, 1925 edition Braun & Schneider, cloth spine, illustrated paper-over-board cover, 56 pages, illustrations by author. $40.00

BUTLER, Elinor
Diamond Spider, 1910 Alice Harriman Co, cloth-over-board cover, small, b/w illustrations by C. M. Dowling. $20.00

BUTLER, Ellis Parker
Confessions of a Daddy, 1907 Century, small, 107 pages, red/white/black cloth-over-board cover, b/w illustrations by Fanny Cory. $30.00
Incubator Baby, 1906 Funk & Wagnalls, cloth-over-board cover with design, small, 111 pages, color illustrations by May Preston. $30.00

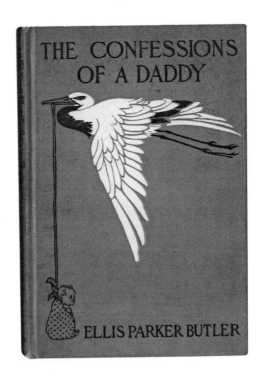

BUTTERWORTH, Hezekiah
Boyhood of Lincoln, 1893 Appleton, lst edition, illustrated green cloth-over-board cover, b/w illustrations by Winthrop Peirce. $20.00
Brother Jonathan, 1909 Appleton, hardcover, 246 pages, b/w illustrations. $20.00
History of the United States, 1904 edition Saalfield, small, blue hardcover, 692 pages, b/w illustrations and maps. $20.00
In the Days of Audubon, 1901 Appleton first edition, cloth-over-board cover. $65.00

Knight of Liberty, 1895 Appleton, rust cloth-over-board cover with gilt. $20.00

Log Schoolhouse on the Columbia, 1890, hardcover. $45.00

Over the Andes, 1897, cloth-over-board cover, 370 pages, b/w illustrations by Henry Sandham. $20.00

Pilot of the Mayflower, 1898 Appleton, red cloth-over-board cover with gilt. $20.00

Poems for Christmas, Easter and New Year's, 1885 Estes, green cloth-over-board cover with gilt, 153 pages, text illustrations. $20.00

Songs of History, 1887 New England Publishing Co., cloth-over-board cover. $25.00

True to his Home, 1897 Appleton, hardcover. $15.00

Wampum Belt, (ca. 1896) 1902 edition Appleton, red cloth-over-board cover, b/w illustrations. $25.00

Young Folks History of America, 1882 Estes, hardcover, 150 engravings. $25.00

Young Folks History of Boston, 1881 Estes, green cloth-over-board cover with gilt, engravings. $25.00

Young McKinley, 1905 Appleton first edition, red cloth-over-board cover, hardback, 307 pages. $25.00

BYINGTON, Eloise

Doll Land Stories, 1923 Whitman, illustrated hardcover, small, 75 pages, color illustrations by Uldene Shriver. $20.00

Wishbone Children, 1934 Whitman, blue cloth-over-board cover with paste-on-pictorial, illustrated endpapers, color illustrations by Kathleen Frantz. ($50.00 with dust jacket) $25.00

CAMPBELL, Helen L.

Story of Little Konrad: the Swiss Boy, 1903 Educational Publishing, cloth-over-board cover, b/w photo illustrations. $10.00

CAMPBELL, Julie, see Series section, GINNY GORDON

CANNON, Cornelia James

Fight for the Pueblo, 1934 Houghton, cloth-over-board cover, 204 pages, illustrated endpapers, b/w illustrations by Marian Cannon. $25.00

Lazaro in the Pueblos, 1931 Houghton, cloth-over-board cover, 197 pages, illustrated endpapers, b/w illustrations by Marian Cannon. $25.00

Pueblo Girl, 1929 Houghton, cloth-over-board cover, 174 pages, color frontispiece and b/w illustrations by Olive Rush. $40.00

CARMER, Carl

Hurricane's Children, 1937 Farrar first edition, cloth-over-board cover, 175 pages, b/w illustrations by Elizabeth Black Carmer. $30.00

CARR, Annie Rowe, see Series section, NAN SHERWOOD

CARR, Mary Jane

Children of the Covered Wagon, a Story of the Old Oregon Trail, 1946 printing Crowell, blue cloth-over-board cover. $15.00

Top of the Morning, 1941 Crowell, small oblong, cloth-over-board cover, verse, two-color illustrations by Henriette Jones. $25.00

CARROLL, Lewis

Alice's Adventures in Wonderland, 1922 edition Dodd Mead, cloth-over-board cover with gilt illustration, 12 color plates plus two-color spot illustrations, tissue overlays, illustrations by Gwynedd Hudson. $160.00

Alice's Adventures in Wonderland, ca. 1924 edition Lippincott, large, cloth-over-board cover with paste-on-pictorial illustration, gilt lettering, Tenniel drawings plus color plates by Gertrude Kay. $100.00

Alice's Adventures in Wonderland, 1920 Harrap, green cloth-over-board cover with paste-on-pictorial, 8 color plates and b/w illustrations by Bessie Pease. $150.00

Alice's Adventures in Wonderland, ca. 1920 Ward Lock, cloth spine with illustrated boards, 24 color plates by Margaret Tarrant. $150.00

Hunting of the Snark, 1876 Macmillan, illustrated boards, 83 pages, gilt edged, illustrations by Henry Holiday. $285.00

Hunting of the Snark, 1903 Harper, paper-over-board cover with gilt, 248 pages, 24 b/w plates by Peter Newell, text page decorations by Robert Murray. $225.00

CARRYL, Charles E.

Admiral's Caravan, 1920 edition Houghton, cloth-over-board cover, illustrations by Reginald Birch. ($30.00 with dust jacket) $15.00

Davy and the Goblin, (1884) 1928 edition Houghton, Riverside Bookshelf, cloth-over-board cover with paste-on pictorial, illustrated endpapers, color frontispiece, 6 color plates and b/w illustrations by Bensell and Bacharach. (There are many editions of this book and price depends on illustrations.) $45.00

Syndicate And Other Stories, 1899 Harper, cloth-over-board cover, 297 pages. $25.00

CARTER, Herbert, see Series section, BOY SCOUTS

CARY, Alice and Phoebe
Ballads for Little Folk, (1873) 1877 Hurd Houghton, green cloth-over-board cover with gilt and paste-on-pictorial, 189 pages, b/w illustrations. $20.00
Clovernook Children, 1885 Ticknor first edition, small, blue cloth-over-board cover with gilt. $40.00

CASSERLEY, Anne
Barney and the Donkey, 1938 Harper first edition, small, cloth-over-board cover, silhouette illustrations by author. $25.00
Brian of the Mountain, 1931 Harper first edition, small, cloth-over-board cover, silhouette illustrations by author. $25.00
Roseen, 1929 Harper first edition, small, cloth-over-board cover, silhouette illustrations by author. $25.00
Whins of Knockattan, 1928 Harper first edition, small, cloth-over-board cover, silhouette illustrations by author. $25.00

CASTLEMON, Harry (C. A. Fosdick), see Series section, CASTLEMON SERIES
Under the pseudonym Castlemon, Fosdick wrote numerous series for boys as well as individual titles. Price is usually based on condition, and with paste-on-pictorial covers priced higher than plain covers.
Camp in the Foothills, 1893 Coates, cloth-over-board cover. $10.00
Haunted Mine, 1902 edition Coates, cloth-over-board cover. $10.00
Julian Mortimer, 1901 edition Burt, gray cloth-over-board cover with impressed illustration. $15.00
Rebellion Dixie, undated edition Winston ca. 1915, hardcover, illustrated endpapers. $10.00
Steel Horse, or Rambles of a Bicycle, 1888 Winston, color paste-on pictorial cover, illustrated endpapers. $20.00
Struggle for a Fortune, 1905 edition Donohue, cloth-over-board cover. $10.00
Two Ways of Becoming a Hunter, 1892 Coates, cloth-over-board cover, small, b/w illustrations. $10.00
Winged Arrow's Medicine, 1901 edition Donohue, printed illustrated cover by W. H. Fry. $15.00

CATHER, Katherine Dunlap
Pan and His Pipes and Other Tales for Children, 1916 Victor, pictorial tan boards, small, 80 pages, brown/white illustrations, ads for Victor phonograph records of songs. $20.00

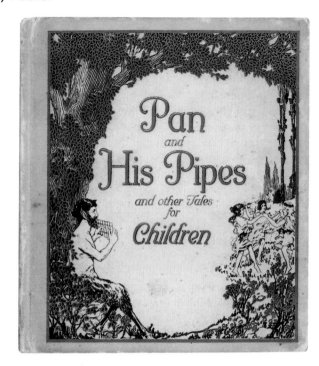

CATHERWOOD, Mary Hartwell
Story of Tonty, (1889) 1901 McClurg, orange cloth-over-board cover, small, 225 pages, b/w illustrations by Enoch Ward. $20.00

CAUDILL, Rebecca
Happy Little Family, 1947 Winston first edition, small, 116 pages, tan cloth-over-board cover, illustrated endpapers, b/w illustrations by Decie Merwin. ($30.00 with dust jacket) $20.00
Schoolhouse in the Woods, 1949 Winston first edition, small, 120 pages, green cloth-over-board cover, illustrated endpapers, b/w illustrations by Decie Merwin. ($30.00 with dust jacket) $20.00
Up and Down the River, 1951 Winston first edition, small, 115 pages, blue cloth-over-board cover, illustrated endpapers, b/w illustrations by Decie Merwin. ($30.00 with dust jacket) $20.00

CAUTLEY, Marjorie
Building a House in Sweden, 1931 Macmillan, small, hardback, 40 pages, brown/white illustrations by Helen Sewell. $20.00

CAVANAH, Frances
Children of the White House, 1936 Rand McNally, red/white/blue illustrated paper-over-board cover, 35 pages, b/w illustrations by Genevieve Foster. $25.00
Marta Finds the Door, 1941 Grosset, color illustrated paper-over-board cover, 118 pages, color frontispiece, b/w illustrations by Harve Stein. $15.00

Private Pepper, 1945 Whitman, color illustrated paper-over-board cover, 32 pages, illustrated endpapers, two-color illustrations by Diana Thorne. ($20.00 with dust jacket) $15.00

Private Pepper Comes Home, 1947 Whitman, color illustrated paper-over-board cover, 32 pages, illustrated endpapers, 2-color illustrations by Diana Thorne. ($20.00 with dust jacket) $15.00

Sandy of San Francisco, McKay, color illustrated paper-over-board cover, illustrated endpapers, color illustrations by Pauline Jackson. $15.00

CAVANNA, Betty

Girl Can Dream, 1948 Winston, blue cloth-over-board cover, 189 pages, b/w illustrations by Harold Minton. ($20.00 with dust jacket) $10.00

CHAFFEE, Allen

Adventures of Twinkly Eyes, the Little Black Bear, 1919 Milton Bradley, decorated cloth-over-board cover,183 pages. $25.00.

Brownie Flat Tail Builds a House, 1937 McLaughlin, red hardcover, 116 pages, frontispiece by Paul Bronson, decorated pages. $20.00

Fuzzy Wuzz, 1922 Milton Bradley, decorated cloth-over-board cover, 4 b/w illustrations by Peter Da Ru. $20.00

Fuzzy Wuzz Meets the Ranger, 1937 McLoughlin, hardback, 256 pages, b/w frontispiece illustration. $20.00

Sitka the Snow Baby, 1923 Milton Bradley, hardback, 116 pages, b/w illustrations by Peter Da Ru. $20.00

Sully Joins the Circus, 1926 Century, cloth-over-board cover, small, 270 pages, b/w illustrations by Albert Carmen. $15.00

Tawny Goes Hunting, 1937 Random House, cloth-over-board cover, b/w illustrations by Paul Bransom. ($50.00 with dust jacket) $25.00

CHAFFEY, M. Ella

Adventures of Prince Melonseed, 1916 Briggs first edition, blue cloth-over-board cover, illustrations by Margaret Chaffey. $60.00

CHALMERS, Audrey

Birthday of Obash, 1937 Oxford, small, hardcover, yellow paper illustration pages, b/w illustrations by author. $20.00

Fancy Be Good, 1941 Viking, oversize, orange cloth-over-board cover, 46 pages, b/w illustrations by author. ($20.00 with dust jacket) $15.00

Hundreds and Hundreds of Pancakes, 1942 Viking, oblong cloth-over-board cover, b/w illustrations by author. ($25.00 with dust jacket) $20.00

I Had a Penny, 1944 Viking, cloth-over-board cover, 44 pages, b/w illustrations by author. $20.00

Kitten's Tale, 1946 Viking, cloth-over-board cover, 45 pages, b/w illustrations by author. $20.00

Parade of Obash, 1939 Oxford, small, 78 pages, b/w illustrations by author. $20.00

Poppadilly, 1945 Viking, cloth-over-board cover, 40 pages, b/w illustrations by author. $20.00

Topple's Wish, 1948 Viking, oblong, cloth-over-board cover, 36 pages, b/w illustrations by author. ($20.00 with dust jacket) $15.00

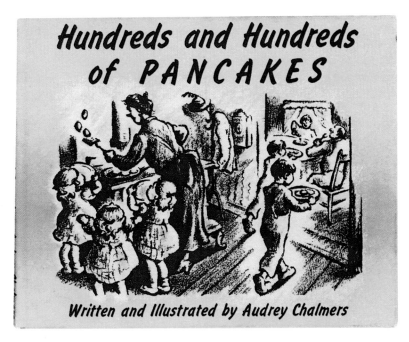

Hundreds and Hundreds of PANCAKES

Written and Illustrated by Audrey Chalmers

CHAMBERLIN, Ethel C.
Shoes and Ships and Sealing Wax, 1928 Volland, color illustrated paper-over-board cover, illustrated endpapers, color and b/w illustrations by Janet Lee Scott. $50.00
Shoes and Ships and Sealing Wax, Saalfield, hardcover, color and b/w illustrations by Janet Lee Scott. $20.00

CHAMBERS, Robert W.
Cardigan, 1930 Harper, cloth-over-board cover, 423 pages, b/w illustrations by Henry Pitz. ($30.00 with dust jacket) $15.00

CHAN, Chih-Yi and Plato
Good-Luck Horse, 1943 Whittlesey House, small oblong, green cloth-over-board cover, illustrated endpapers, two-color illustrations by Plato Chan. ($20.00 with dust jacket) $10.00

CHANNING, Blanche M.
Winifred West, 1901 Wilde, gray cloth-over-board cover, small, 271 pages, b/w illustrations by Chase Emerson. $15.00

CHAPMAN, Allen, see Series section, DAREWELL CHUMS

CHAPPELL, George S.
Rollo in Society, 1922 Putnam, (satire of the 19th-century Abbott books), small, cloth-over-board cover with paste-on-pictorial, b/w illustrations by William Hogarth. $20.00

CHASE, Mary
Book of Ruth, 1946 edition by Limited Edition Club, oversize hardback with vellum spine, gilt, illustrated boards, illustrated frontispiece, 8 mounted color plates by Arthur Syzk, 1,950 copies signed by Syzk. ($300.00 with slip-case) Without slip-case $150.00
Book of Ruth, 1946 Heritage Press edition, hardback, color plates by Arthur Syzk. ($40.00 with slipcase) $20.00

CHAUCER, Geoffrey
Canterbury Tales, modern verse translation by Frank Ernest Hill, 1946 Limited Edition Club, oversize hardback with vellum spine, illustrated frontispiece, full-page color plates by Arthur Syzk, 1500 copies signed by Syzk. ($300.00 with slip-case) Without slip-case $150.00
Canterbury Tales, modern verse translation by Frank Ernest Hill, 1946 Heritage Press edition, 550 pages, hardback, full-page color plates by Arthur Syzk. $35.00

CHEEVER, Harriet
King Charles, 1900 Dana Estes, red cloth-over-board cover with gilt lettering, paste-on-pictorial. $15.00
Little Mr. Van Vere of China, 1898 Estes, cloth-over-board cover, 243 pages. $20.00
Pony Dexter, 1911 Estes, green cloth-over-board cover with paste-on-pictorial, small, 88 pages, b/w illustrations by Marlowe. $10.00

CHELEY, F. A.
Campfire Stories, 1942 Greenberg, tan cloth-over-board cover, 329 pages, frontispiece, 6 sepia plates. ($30.00 with dust jacket) $20.00

CHERUBINI
Pinocchio in Africa, 1911 Ginn Once-Upon-A-Time Series, small, print illustrated cloth-over-board cover, 152 pages, b/w illustrations by Charles Copeland. $20.00

CHIESA, Carol Della
Puppet Parade, 1932 Longmans first edition, cloth-over-board cover, 242 pages, map endpapers, b/w illustrations by Helene Carter. $20.00

CHILD, Maria
Adventures of Jamie and Jeannie, undated ca. 1900 Lothrop, red cloth-over-board cover with silver gilt, small, b/w illustrations. $15.00

CHRISTESON, H. M. and F. M.
Tony and His Pals, 1934 Whitman, cloth-over-board cover with photo paste-on-pictorial, b/w photograph illustrations of Tom Mix and his horse, Tony. $30.00

CHRISTIAN, George
Patch Pants the Tailor, 1947 John Martin's House, oversize picture book, illustrated paper-over-board cover, illustrated endpapers, color illustrations throughout by author. ($30.00 with same-as-cover dust jacket) $20.00

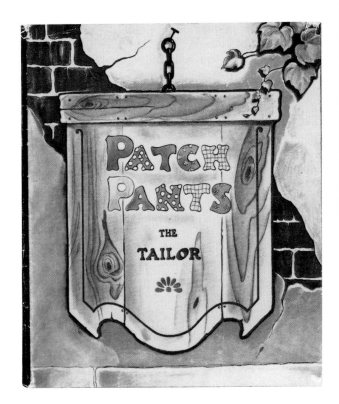

CHURCH, Peggy Pond
Burro of Angelitos, 1931 Suttonhouse first edition, oversize, cloth spine and illustrated boards, 42 pages, double-page color illustrations and line drawings by Gigi Johnson. ($65.00 with dust jacket) $50.00

CLARK, Ann Nolan
Little Herder in Spring, 1940 Indian School, oversize, bi-lingual reader, line art by Hoke Denetsosie. $25.00

CLARK, Dorothy
Peter on the Min, 1942 Lothrop, cloth-over-board cover, illustrated endpapers, 171 pages, two-color illustrations by Weda Yap. $20.00

CLARK, Imogen
Will Shakespeare's Little Lad, (1897) 1916 edition Scribner, small, 306 pages, cloth-over-board cover with paste-on-pictorial, 4 color illustrations by Reginald Birch. $20.00

CLARK, Joan, see Series section, PENNY NICHOLS

CLAUDY, Carl. H., see Series section, ADVENTURES IN THE UNKNOWN SERIES
Gold He Found, 1928 Appleton, cloth-over-board cover, illustrated. ($25.00 with dust jacket) $15.00
Partners of the Forest Trail, 1915 McBride, cloth-over-board cover, 225 pages, color plate illustrations. $20.00
Prize Winners' Book of Model Airplanes, 1931 Bobbs Merrill, cloth-over-board cover, 242 pages, includes folded plans in pockets. ($25.00 if plans are missing) $65.00
Tell-Me-Why Stories, ca.1914 McBride, cloth-over-board cover with print illustration, 8 color plates by Norman Rockwell. $50.00
Tell-Me-Why Stories About Animals, 1914 McBride, hardback. $20.00
Treasures of the Darkness, 1933 Doubleday Jr. Mystery Club book, cloth-over-board cover, 288 pages, color frontispiece. $30.00

CLEMENT, Marguerite
All the World is Colour, 1930 Farrar, oversize picture book, illustrated endpapers, two-color illustrations throughout by Pierre and Germaine L'Hardy. ($50.00 with dust jacket) $25.00

CLIFTON, Oliver, see Series section, CAMP FIRE BOYS

CLINTON, Althea
Treasure Book of Best Stories, 1933 Saalfield, oversize picture book, pictorial cover, b/w illustrations by Fern Bisel Peat, color plates by Eleanora Madsen. $50.00

CLYMER, Eleanor
Grocery Mouse, 1945 McBride, oversize, green

cloth-over-board cover, 96 pages, illustrations by Jeanne Bendick. ($30.00 with dust jacket) $20.00

Trolley Car Family, 1947 McKay, blue hardcover. ($35.00 with dust jacket) $25.00

CLYNE, Geraldine, see Play Book section, Pop-Up Books, Jolly Jump-Ups

COBB, Bertha (1867-1951) and Ernest

Allspice, the Adventures of Daddy Fox, Ginger Bear, the Miller and Anita, 1929 edition Arlo Publishing, small, cloth-over-board cover, 285 pages, b/w photos and b/w illustrations. $15.00

Andre, ca. 1930 Arlo Publishing, cloth-over-board cover. $15.00

Arlo, (1915) 1928 edition Arlo Publishing, small, cloth-over-board cover, illustrated endpapers, b/w illustrations. $15.00

Clematis, 1917 Putnam, cloth-over-board cover, illustrated endpapers, color frontispiece, b/w illustrations by Cram and Lewis. ($25.00 with dust jacket) $15.00

Dan's Boy, (1926) 1929 edition Putnam, cloth-over-board cover, illustrated endpapers, b/w illustrations by L. J. Bridgman. ($25.00 with dust jacket) $15.00

Miller's Wife, ca. 1925 Arlo Publishing, cloth-over-board cover. $15.00

Who Knows? a Book of Puzzle Stories, 1924 Arlo Publishing, cloth-over-board cover. 134 pages, illustrated. $15.00

COBB, Captain Frank, see Series section, AVIATOR SERIES, STARS AND STRIPES

COBLENTZ, Catherine

Scatter, the Chipmunk, 1946, hardback, illustrated endpapers, b/w/brown illustrations. $20.00

COBURN, Claire M.

Our Little Swedish Cousins, (1906) 1921 edition Page, small, illustrated cloth-over-board cover, plates by Bridgman and Woodberry. $15.00

COBURN, Walt

Ringtailed Rannyhans, 1927 Burt, cloth-over-board cover, 323 pages. $15.00

COLLE, Alfred and VAN ALSTINE, Lois

Chillee Um-Gum, 1938 Grosset, color illustrated paper-over-board cover, illustrated endpapers, oversize, color and b/w illustrations throughout. $25.00

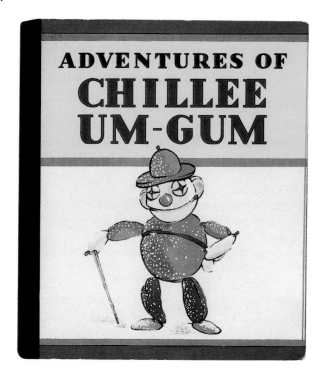

COLLINS, Archie Frederick, see Series section, JACK HEATON

COLOMA, Padre Luis

Perez the Mouse, translated by Lady Moreton, 1950 edition Dodd Mead, small, yellow cloth-over-board cover, 63 pages, glossy paper, color illustrations by George H. Vyse. ($35.00 with dust jacket) $15.00

COLTON, Matthew, see Series section, FRANK ARMSTRONG

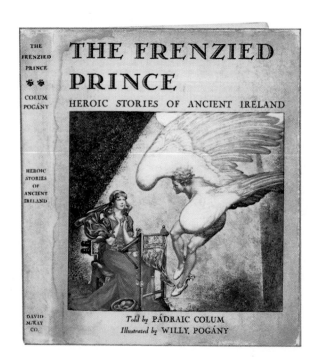

COLUM, Padraic
Frenzied Prince, 1943 McKay first edition, over-size, green hardcover, 196 pages, full-page color plus b/w illustrations by Willy Pogany. ($45.00 with dust jacket) $25.00

COMMAGER, Henry Steele
St. Nicholas Anthology, 1948 Random first edition, red cloth-over-board cover, 542 pages. ($25.00 with dust jacket) $15.00

COMSTOCK, Harriet
Princess Rags and Tatters, 1912 Doubleday, gray cloth-over-board cover with illustration, small, 112 pages, 4 color illustrations by E. R. Lee. $30.00
Tower or Throne, 1902 Little Brown, decorated blue cloth-over-board cover with gilt, 6 b/w plates by Harriet Roosevelt Richards. $20.00

CONNOR, Sabra
Quest of the Sea Otter, 1927 Reilly Lee, green cloth-over-board cover with gilt, map endpapers. $20.00

COOK, Canfield, see Series section, LUCKY TERRELL
Secret Mission, 1942 Grosset, cloth-over-board cover. $10.00

COOK, George C.
Roderick Taliaferro, 1903 Macmillan, green cloth-over-board cover with gilt, b/w illustrations by Seymour Stone. $20.00

COOKE, Donald
Nutcracker of Nuremberg, 1938 Winston, cloth-over-board cover, 148 pages, illustrated endpapers, b/w/orange and b/w/blue illustrations by author. $30.00
Pug Invades the Fifth Column, 1943 McKay, hardcover. $15.00

COOKE, Grace MacGowan
Gourd Fiddle, 1904 Altemus, small, illustrated red cloth-over-board cover, 118 pages, b/w illustrations by E. Lynn Mudge and E. B. Miles. $30.00

COOLIDGE, Florence Claudine
Little Ugly Face and Other Indian Tales, (1925) 1927 edition Macmillan, orange cloth-over-board cover with illustration, small, 181 pages, color illustrations by Maud and Miska Petersham. $30.00

COOLIDGE, Susan, see Series section, SUSAN COOLIDGE LIBRARY

In the High Valley, undated Blackie, cloth-over-board cover. ($25.00 with dust jacket) $10.00
Little Knight of Labor, 1899 Little Brown first edition, cloth-over-board cover, illustrated. (With hard-to-find dust jacket, price is about $200.00) $50.00
New Year's Bargain, (1881) 1901 Little Brown, green cloth-over-board cover, 231 pages, drawings by Addie Ledyard. $20.00
Round Dozen, 1883 Roberts, Boston, cloth-over-board cover, 298 pages, b/w illustrations. $15.00

COOPER, Frederick Tabor
Little Gold Nugget, 1928 Stokes, small, easy reader, hardback, 128 pages, two-color illustrations by Edna Potter. $20.00

CORSELIUS, Cornelia
Financie and Other Stories from Real Life, 1885 Register, blue cloth-over-board cover with gilt, small, 165 pages, b/w illustrations. $20.00

CORY, David, see Series section, LITTLE INDIAN, LITTLE JOURNEYS

CORY, Fanny, illustrator
Mother Goose, 1913 Bobbs Merrill, oversize picture book, illustrated hardcover with gilt, 73 pages, color plates by Cory. $175.00

COX, Palmer
Brownies Around the World, 1894 Century, first edition, oversize, color illustrated cover, illustrations by author $300.00
Brownies Through the Union, ca. 1895 Century, oversize, 144 pages, color illustrations and drawings by author. $150.00
Queer Stories About Queer Animals, 1905 National Publications, oversize, cloth-over-board cover with impressed color illustration and lettering, illustrated endpapers, brown/white and blue/white illustrations by author. $100.00

COX-McCORMACK, Nancy
Peeps, the Really Truly Sunshine Fairy, 1918 Volland, a Sunny Book, small, color cover illustration, color endpapers, color illustrations throughout by Katherine Sturges Dodge. $55.00

CRADDOCK, Charles Egbert
Champion, 1902 Houghton, small, 257 pages. $20.00
Down the Ravine, 1885 Houghton, small, 196 pages, b/w illustrations. $20.00

Phantoms of the Foot-Bridge and Other Stories, 1895 Harper, cloth-over-board cover, b/w illustrations. $25.00

Young Mountaineers, 1898 Houghton, 262 pages, b/w illustrations. $20.00

CRAIGIE, Mary

Once Upon a Time, 1876 Putnam, myths, green cloth-over-board cover with gilt, small, 127 pages, 4 b/w illustrations. $25.00

CRANCH, Christopher

Kobboltozo, Sequel to Last of the Huggermuggers, 1857 Phillips Sampson, orange cloth-over-board cover, 75 pages, b/w illustrations. $60.00

Last of the Huggermuggers, 1856 Phillips, cloth-over-board cover, b/w illustrations. $60.00

CRANE, Edith, and BURTON, Albert

Happy Days Out West, 1927 McNally, blue hardcover with paste-on-pictorial and gilt, small, 129 pages, 4 color plates by Dorothy Lake Gregory. $30.00

CREDLE, Ellis

Adventures of Tittletom, 1949 Oxford, cloth-over-board cover, b/w illustrations. $15.00

Down the Mountain, 1934 Nelson, cloth-over-board cover, two-color illustrations. $20.00

Flop-Eared Hound, 1940 Oxford, hardback, b/w photos. $20.00

CRICHTON, F. E.

Peep-in-the-World, 1931 edition Longmans, 258 pages, cloth-over-board cover, illustrated endpapers, b/w illustrations by Frank McIntosh. ($30.00 with dust jacket) $15.00

CROCKETT, S. R.

Red Cap Adventures, 1908 Adam, gray cloth-over-board cover with illustration, 411 pages, color illustrations by Allan Stewart. $40.00

Surprising Adventures of Sir Toady Lion, ca. 1897 Stokes, gray cloth-over-board cover with color illustration, 314 pages, 69 b/w illustrations by Gordon Browne. $25.00

CROCKFORD, Doris

Flying Scotsman, undated ca. 1937 Oxford University Press, oblong picture book, color illustrated paper-over-board cover with cloth spine, full-page color illustrations by Rachel Boger and Henry Cartwright. $35.00

CROMPTON, Frances E.

Voyage of the Mary Adair, undated ca. 1900 Dutton, small, half-cloth half paper-on-board pictorial cover, 48 pages, b/w illustrations credited to Evelyn Lance but signed "E. Nister." $25.00

CROSBY, Ernest

Captain Jinks, Hero, 1902 Funk & Wagnalls first edition, tan cloth-over-board cover with color decorations and gilt on spine, small, 393 pages, b/w illustrations by Dan Beard. ($75.00 with dust jacket) $20.00

CROSBY, Percy

Dear Sooky, 1929 Putnam, illustrated paper-over-board cover, 7 tipped in plates by author. $45.00

Dear Sooky, undated Grosset edition ca. 1932, title

Story & Pictures by Genevieve Cross

shown on cover as *Sooky*, but on title plate and copyright listing as Dear Sooky. Cloth-over-board cover with impressed illustration, 124 pages, 7 cartoon color plates mounted on plain pages, illustrations by author. $25.00

Skippy Rambles, 1932 Putnam first edition, cloth-over-board cover, b/w illustrations and photos. $45.00

CROSS, Genevieve

Little Heroes of Hartford, 1947 Cross Publications, cloth-over-board cover, illustrations by William Brigham. $15.00

Pop-Corn Lamb and the Peppermint Sticks, 1949 Cross Publications, oblong illustrated paper-over-board cover, illustrated endpapers, color illustrations throughout by author. $20.00

CROTHERS, Samuel McChord

By the Christmas Fire, 1908 Houghton, red cloth-over-board cover with gilt, small, 226 pages, b/w illustrations by Frances Comstock. $20.00

Children of Dickens, 1925 edition Scribner, oversize, 259 pages, black cloth-over-board cover with paste-on-pictorial, illustrated endpapers, 10 color plates by Jessie Willcox Smith. ($200.00 with dust jacket) $75.00

Children of Dickens, 1943 edition Scribner, oversize, 259 pages, black cloth-over-board cover, 10 color plates by Jessie Willcox Smith. $40.00

Miss Muffet's Christmas Party, (1902) 1930 edition Houghton, small, red cloth-over-board cover with gilt illustration and lettering, 106 pages, b/w illustrations by Olive Long. $25.00

CROWNFIELD, Gertrude

Catching Up with the Circus, 1926 Bouillon-Sanders, oversize oblong, color illustrated paper-over-board cover, illustrated endpapers, full-page 2-color illustrations by Ethel Pennewill Brown. $50.00

Traitor's Torch, 1935 Lippencott, cloth-over-board cover, 301 pages, color frontispiece, 3 b/w plates by Walter Pyle. ($25.00 with dust jacket) $15.00

CROWNINSHIELD, Mrs. Schuyler

Light-House Children Abroad, (1889) 1893 edition Lothrop, cloth-over-board cover with silver, b/w illustrations by Bridgman and others. $35.00

CRUMP, Irving

Boys' Book of Airmen, 1927 Dodd Mead, cloth-over-board cover, illustrated. ($25.00 with dust jacket) $15.00

Boys' Book of Cowboys, 1934 Dodd Mead, cloth-over-board cover, 232 pages, illustrated. $15.00

Boys' Book of Mounted Police, 1917 Dodd Mead, cloth-over-board cover, 232 pages, illustrated. $25.00

Mog, the Mound Builder, 1931 Grosset, orange cloth-over-board cover, 228 pages, illustrated endpapers, frontispiece by Remington Schuyler. ($20.00 with dust jacket) $15.00

Teen-Age Boy Scout Stories, 1948 Grosset Teen-Age Series, cloth-over-board cover. ($15.00 with dust jacket) $10.00

CRUMPTON, M. N.
Silver Buckle, 1899 Altemus, pictorial boards, 89 pages, b/w illustrations by Cornelia Bedford. $20.00

CUMMING, Lt. Col. Gordon
Wild Men and Wild Beasts, 1872 Scribner, brown cloth-over-board cover with gilt, small, 372 pages, b/w illustrations. $15.00

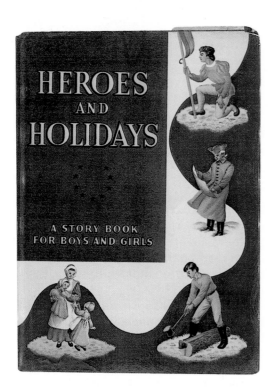

CUNNINGHAM, Virginia
Add-A-Rhyme, 1941 Garden City, oversize, color illustrations. $15.00
Heroes and Holidays, 1948 Whitman, easy reader, oversize, color illustrated hardcover, color illustrations throughout by the Granahams. ($20.00 with identical-design dust jacket) $15.00
One Hundred Animal Stories, 1947 Whitman, hardback, one-color illustrations. $20.00
Paul Laurence Dunbar and His Song, 1948 Dodd, hardback, b/w photo illustrations. $25.00
Stories of Animals, 1947 Whitman, color illustrated paper-over-board cover, b/w/brown illustrations by Dorothea Snow. $25.00

━✦ **D** ✦━

DALL, Caroline
From Boston to Baltimore, Patty Gray's Journey, 1869 See & Shepard, green cloth-over-board

cover with gilt illustration, small, 200 pages, b/w illustrations. $35.00

DALTON, William
White Elephant, or Hunters of Ava, undated ca. 1898 Griffith, blue cloth-over-board cover with gilt, small, 345 pages, b/w illustrations. $15.00

DANIELS, Elizabeth
Happy Hours, 1934 Rand McNally, small, 63 pages, photo cover illustration, full-page b/w photo illustrations on every other page, facing text page. $15.00

DARLINGTON, Edgar, see Series section, CIRCUS BOYS

DARTON, F. J., editor
Story of the Canterbury Pilgrims, 1914 Stokes, green cloth-over-board cover, 310 pages, 4 color plates by Maria Kirk. $30.00
Wonder Book of Beasts, undated, ca. 1909 Wells Gardner Darton, London, cloth-over-board cover with gold gilt, 403 pages, color frontispiece, b/w illustrations by Margaret Clayton. $35.00

DASKAM, Josephine
Memoirs of a Baby, 1904 Harper first edition, blue cloth-over-board cover, small 272 pages, b/w illustrations by Fanny Cory. $25.00

D'AULAIRE, Ingri and Edgar Parin

Magic Rug, 1931 Doubleday first edition, oblong picture book, color illustrations throughout by authors. $50.00

Nils, 1948 Doubleday first edition, oversize picture book, color illustrated paper-over-board cover, color and b/w illustrations throughout by authors. ($55.00 with same-as-cover dust jacket) $45.00

Ola and Blakken, 1933 Doubleday first edition, oversize picture book, color illustrated paper-over-board cover, color and b/w illustrations throughout by authors. $50.00

DAULTON, George

Helter Skelters, 1909 Stokes, decorated cloth-over-board cover, four-color illustrations by Maria Kirk. $30.00

DAUZET, Marceline, see PEAT, Fern

DAVIES, Mary Carolyn, poet

Little Freckled Person, 1919 Houghton, verse, cloth-over-board cover with printed illustration, 104 pages, color frontispiece, b/w plates by Harold Cue. $35.00

Penny Show, 1927 Harrison, cloth-over-board cover, full-page b/w illustrations by Herbert Fouts. $20.00

Skyline Trail, 1924 Bobbs, first, limited edition. $25.00

DAVIS, Julia

Stonewall, 1935 Dutton, cloth-over-board cover, illustrated by Cameron Wright. $35.00

DAVIS, Lavinia

Melody, Mutton Bone and Sam, 1948 Doubleday, 245 pages, hardcover, illustrations by Paul Brown. $15.00

DAWSON, Rosemary and Richard

Walk in the City, 1950 Viking, oversize picture book, color illustrated paper-over-board cover, map illustrated endpapers, 30 pages, color illustrations by authors. $30.00

DEAN, Graham, see Series section, HERB KENT

Riders of the Gabilans, 1944 Viking Jr. Literary Guild edition, cloth-over-board cover, illustrated endpapers, b/w illustrations by Wesley Dennis. ($25.00 with dust jacket) $15.00

Sky Trail, 1932 Goldsmith, tan cloth-over-board cover, 253 pages. ($20.00 with dust jacket) $8.00

DeANGELI, Marguerite

Elin's Amerika, 1941 Doran first edition, oversize, decorated cloth-over-board cover, 94 pages, litho illustrations by author. $85.00

Henner's Lydia, 1936 Doran first edition, oversize, 70 pages, litho illustrations by author. $85.00

Summer Day with Ted and Nina, 1940 Doubleday, small, illustrated endpapers, illustrated. ($85.00 with dust jacket) $50.00

Ted and Nina Go to the Grocery Store, 1935 Doubleday, small oblong, color illustrated paper-over-board cover, color illustrations by author. $45.00

DeBOSSCHERE, Jean

Beasts and Men, Folk Tales Collected in Flanders, 1918 Heinemann, oversize, cloth-over-board cover, illustrated endpapers, 12 color plates plus b/w illustrations by author. $120.00

Christmas Tales of Flanders, 1917 Dodd, leather and cloth-over-board cover with gilt, 12 color plates plus two-color and b/w illustrations by author. $200.00

Folk Tales of Flanders, 1918 Dodd, oversize, cloth-over-board cover with gilt, illustrated endpapers, 12 color plates plus b/w illustrations. $110.00

DEERING, Fremont, see Series section, BORDER BOYS

DEIHL, Edna

Aunt Este's Stories of Flower and Berry Babies, 1924 Whitman, tan cloth-over-board cover with color paste-on-pictorial, illustrated endpapers, illustrated. $40.00

Huffy Wants To Be A Pet, 1929 Gabriel, hardback, illustrations by A. E. Kennedy. $40.00

Little Black Hen, 1925 Whitman, blue cloth-over-board cover with paste-on-pictorial, 61 pages, illustrated endpapers, color illustrations by Sue Seeley. $25.00

Little Kitten That Would Not Wash Its Face, 1922 Gabriel, hardback, illustrated. $45.00

Little Rabbit that Would Not Eat, 1942 Gabriel, hardcover, color and b/w illustrations. $20.00

Mr. Blue Peacock, 1926 Whitman, cloth-over-board cover with color paste-on-pictorial, oversize, 63 pages, color illustrations by C. X. Shinn. $50.00

DeJONG, Dola

Level Land, 1943 Scribner, pictorial boards, 164 pages, b/w illustrations by Jan Hoowij. ($60.00 with dust jacket) $30.00

Picture Story of Holland, 1946 Reynal & Hitchcock, illustrations by Gerard Hordyk. $20.00

Sand for the Sandmen, 1946 Scribner, tan cloth-over-board cover, b/w/red illustrations by Natalie Norton. $15.00

DeLaMARE, Walter

Dutch Cheese, 1931 Knopf first edition, cloth-over-board cover, oversize, four color plates and b/w illustrations by Dorothy Lathrop. $60.00

Stuff and Nonsense, 1927 Constable, cloth-over-board cover, 110 pages, woodcut b/w illustrations by Bold. $45.00

DENNIS, Morgan

Morgan Dennis Dog Book, 1946 Viking, illustrated cover, 48 pages, full-page illustrations by author. ($30.00 with dust jacket) $15.00

DESCH, John

Midnight Revels, 1939 Sunset, cloth-over-board cover, 77 pages, b/w illustrations by X. Kraemer. $40.00

D'HARNONCOURT, Rene, see HARNONCOURT, Rene d'

DICKENS, Charles

Adventures of Oliver Twist, 1846 Bradbury and Evans, morocco and gilt cover, 24 etched copperplates by George Cruikshank, probably the first edition of this title bound in one volume. $500.00

Boots of the Holly-Tree Inn, 1928 edition Harper, red cloth-over-board cover, 44 pages, illustrated endpapers, color and b/w illustrations by Marie Lawson. $20.00

Children's Stories, Re-told by his granddaughter, 1900 Altemus, cloth-over-board cover with gilt, 64 pages, b/w illustrations. $20.00

Dombey and Son, retold by Alice F. Jackson, undated ca. 1900 Jack London, small, 143 pages, 8 color plate illustrations by F. M. B. Blaikie. $35.00

Holly-Tree, 1904 edition Altemus, cloth-over-board cover with gilt and illustration, illustrated endpapers, b/w illustrations. $30.00

DISNEY Studios

Little Red Riding Hood and the Big Bad Wolf, 1934 McKay, first edition, pictorial boards, full color illustrations from Disney Studios. $250.00

Thumper, 1942 Grosset, Disney color illustrations. (With dust jacket $125.00) $85.00

DITMARS, Raymond

Twenty Little Pets from Everywhere, 1943 Messner, first edition, two-color illustrations by Helene Carter. $20.00

DOANE, Pelagie, illustrator, see Illustrator section

Small Child's Book of Verse, 1948 Oxford, cloth-over-board cover with gilt lettering, oversize, 135 pages, illustrated endpapers, color and b/w illustrations by Doane. ($45.00 with dust jacket) $20.00

DODGE, Louis

Bonnie May, 1916 Scribners, b/w illustrations by Reginald Birch. $20.00

Children of the Desert, 1917 Scribner, gray cloth-over-board cover. $25.00

Sandman's Forest, (1918) 1920 edition Scribner, cloth-over-board cover with illustration, 293 pages, 6 color illustrations by Paul Branson. $45.00

DODGE, Mary Mapes
Hans Brinker, 1925 edition Winston, cloth-over-board cover with paste-on-pictorial, 325 pages, illustrated endpapers, 4 color plates by Clara M. Burd. $40.00

Land of Pluck, 1894 Century, first edition, cloth-over-board cover, gilt, b/w engraving illustrations. $45.00

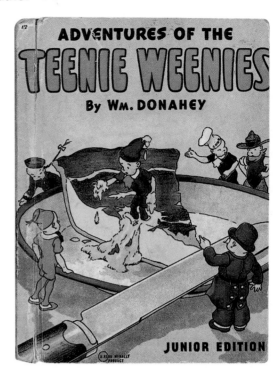

DONAHEY, William, author-illustrator, also, see Series section, TEENIE WEENIE SERIES

Adventures of the Teenie Weenies, (1920s) ca. 1940s Rand McNally Jr. Edition, color illustrated paper-over-board cover, small, color illustrations by author. $50.00

Children's Mother Goose, 1921 Reilly & Lee, oversize, illustrated hardcover, 12 color plate illustrations by Donahey. $125.00

Teenie Weenie Town, 1942 edition Whittlesey House, color illustrated paper-over-board cover, illustrated endpapers, 63 pages, 11 full color illustrations by author. $30.00

DOUGLAS, Amanda
How Bessie Kept House, 1903 Altemus, small, 121 pages, impressed cover illustration, b/w illustrations by L. R. Leopold. $15.00

DOW, Ethel C.
Diary of a Birthday Doll, 1908 Barse & Hopkins, cloth-over-board cover with paste-on-pictorial, color plates and b/w illustrations by Florence England Nosworthy and Louise Clark Smith. ($130.00 with dust jacket) $75.00

Mother's Hero, 1910 Stern, 122 pages, color paste-on-illustration on cloth-over-board cover, b/w illustrations by Isabel Lyndall, 4 color plates by S. Weber. $45.00

Proud Roxanna, 1909 Stern, green cloth-over-board cover with paste-on-pictorial, color plates and b/w illustrations by Eugenie Wireman. $50.00

DRAKE, Ensign Robert, see Series section, BOY ALLIES WITH THE NAVY

DRAYTON, Grace Gibbie Wiederseim, see Series section, BOBBY AND DOLLY

Dolly Dimples and Billy Bounce, 1931 Cupples and Leon, 86 pages, illustrated by author. $200.00

Tiny Tots: Their Adventures, (author name: Wiederseim, Grace G.), 1909 Stokes, illustrated paper-over-board cover, oversize, b/w illustrations and 12 full-page color illustrations by author. $125.00

DuBOIS, William Pene
Flying Locomotive, 1941 Viking, small oblong, illustrated paper-over-board cover, 48 pages, color illustrations by author. $35.00
Great Geppy, 1940 Viking, red/white striped cloth-over-board cover, color illustrations by author. $30.00

DUNBAR, Aldis
Sons O' Cormac, 1920 Dutton, green cloth-over-board cover with gilt, 233 pages. $20.00

DUNNE, J. W.
Jumping Lions of Borneo, ca. 1938 Holt, oversize, illustrations by Irene Robinson. $20.00
St. George and the Witches, 1939 Holt, cloth-over-board cover, 206 pages, b/w illustrations by Lloyd Coe. $15.00

DUPLAIX, Georges
Animal Stories, 1944 edition Simon Schuster, hardcover with illustrated boards, oversize, 92 pages, color illustrations by Feodor Rojankovsky. ($70.00 with dust jacket) $35.00
Animal Stories, 1946 edition Golden Books, oversize, illustrated white paper-over-board cover, 28 pages, Rojankovsky illustrations. $25.00
Big Brown Bear, 1947 edition Golden Books, oversize, illustrated paper-over-board cover, 28 pages, color illustrations by Gustaf Tenggren. $35.00
Gaston and Josephine, 1948 edition Little Golden Book, paper-over-board cover, small, color illustrations by Feodor Rojankovsky. $15.00
Gaston and Josephine in America, 1934 Oxford, color illustrated paper-over-board cover, oversize, color illustrated throughout by author. $95.00
Merry Shipwreck, 1942 Harper, oversize, paper-over-board cover, color illustrations by Tibor Gergely. $30.00
Pee-Gloo: A Little Penguin from the South Pole, 1935 Harper, hardcover, oversize, 40 pages, illustrated endpapers, illustrated by author. $75.00
Popo the Hippopotamus, 1935 edition Whitman, illustrated hardcover, 26 pages, illustrated endpapers, color illustrations by author. $95.00
Topsy-Turvy Circus, 1940 Harper first edition, oversize, illustrated paper-over-board cover with cloth spine, color illustrations throughout by Tibor Gergely. $100.00

DUPLAIX, Lily
White Bunny and his Magic Nose, 1945 Simon Schuster, oversize, paper-over-board cover with color illustration and flocked bunny, interior illustrations full-page color, with flocked characters, illustrations by Masha. ($50.00 with dust jacket) $30.00

DURANT, Nancy Miles
Oliver and the Crying Ship, 1915 Sherman French, blue cloth-over-board cover, small, 79 pages, b/w illustrations by Betancourt. $20.00

DURHAM, Victor, see Series section, SUBMARINE BOYS

DUVOISIN, Roger
They Go Out to Sea, 1943 Knopf, first edition, 171 pages, maps, 8 double page color and b/w illustrations by author. $40.00

DYER, Ruth O.
What Happened Then Stories, 1918 Lothrop, illustrated cloth-over-board cover with gilt, 270 pages, illustrated endpapers, 15 color plates by Florence Liley Young. $25.00

E

EASTMAN, Elaine Goodale
Yellow Star, 1911 Little Brown, light blue hardcover with printed illustration, 272 pages, 4 b/w

plates by Angel de Cora and William Lone Star. $15.00

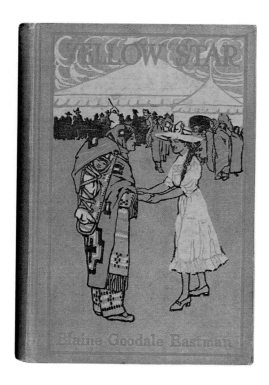

EDGERTON, Alice Craig
Queen Nature's Fairy Helpers, 1922 Lloyd, cloth-over-board cover, color frontispiece and b/w illustrations by Mabel Betsy Hill. $25.00

EDGEWORTH, Maria
Early Lessons, 1857 Routledge, marbled boards with leather spine, small, 427 pages, b/w illustrations by Birket Foster. $30.00
Harry and Lucy, Concluded, Vols. 3 and 4 (combined in one book),1861 Crosby, Nichols, Lee, cloth-over-board cover, small, 226 pages, b/w frontispiece. $30.00
Moral Tales For Young People, 1863 London, hardcover with gilt, engravings by Brothers Dalziel. $65.00
Simple Susan and Other Tales, 1929 edition Macmillan, red cloth-over-board cover, 216 pages, 4 color plates and 10 b/w illustrations by Clara Burd. $75.00

EDITH, Marchioness of Londonberry
Magic Ink-Pot, 1928 Macmillan, first edition, red cloth-over-board cover with gilt illustration, 208 pages, illustrations by author's daughter. $85.00

EDMONDS, Walter D.
Two Logs Crossing: John Haskell's Story, 1943

Dodd (1942 Newbery winner), illustrations by T. Gergely. $25.00

EDWARDS, Leo, see Series section, ANDY BLAKE, JERRY TODD, TRIGGER, TUFFY BEAN

EGGLESTON, Edward
Hoosier School Master, Memorial Edition, 1899 Thompson and Thomas, cloth-over-board cover with oval paste-on-pictorial, b/w plates by F. Opper, b/w illustrations by W. E. B. Starkweather. $10.00

EISGRUBER, Elsa, artist
Spin Top Spin, 1929 Macmillan, verse, author not identified, oversize picture book, color illustrated paper-over-board cover, color illustrations throughout by Eisgruber. $40.00

EL COMANCHO
Teepee Tales, 1927 Reilly & Lee, illustrated red cloth-over-board cover, 208 pages, illustrations by C.L. Bull. $15.00

ELDRIDGE, Ethel J.
Yen-Foh, a Chinese Boy, (1935) 1939 edition Whitman, illustrated paper-over-board cover, illustrated endpapers, color illustrations by Kurt Wiese. $25.00

ELIAS, E. L.
Young Folk's Book of Polar Exploration, (1928) 1929 Little Brown, beige cloth-over-board cover with paste-on-pictorial, map endpapers, 278 pages, color and b/w illustrations. $15.00

ELMSLIE, Theodora C.
His Lordship's Puppy, 1900 Penn, illustrated cloth-over-board cover, 205 pages, b/w frontispiece. $15.00

ELTING, Mary
Trains at Work, 1947 Garden City, illustrated paper-over-board cover, color and b/w illustrations by David Millard. $15.00

ELTON, Emily D.
Mince Pie Dream and Other Verses, 1897 E. R. Herrick NY, printed illustration on cloth-over-board cover, b/w/orange/green color plate illustrations by Blanche McManus. $70.00

ELY, Wilmer, see Series section, BOY CHUMS

EMERSON, Caroline
Father's Big Improvements, 1936 Stokes, orange

cloth-over-board cover, illustrated endpapers. $20.00

Hat-Tub Tale, 1928 Dutton, first edition, cloth-over-board cover, 185 pages, illustrated endpapers, b/w illustrations by Lois Lenski. $85.00

Merry-Go-Round of Modern Tales, 1927 Dutton, blue cloth-over-board cover, oversize, illustrated endpapers, b/w illustrations by Lois Lenski. $95.00

Old New York For Young New Yorkers, 1932 Dutton, cloth-over-board cover, illustrations by Alida Conover. $35.00

School Days in Disneyville, 1939 Heath first edition, hardback, illustrations by Disney Studios. $40.00

ENCKING, Louise F.
Toy Maker (Gerda Thelan), 1935 edition Whitman, oversize picture book, illustrated boards, 16 pages, color illustrations by F. Kukenthal. ($25.00 with cover-matched dust jacket) $20.00

ERSHOFF, Peter
Little Magic Horse, 1942 Macmillan, blue cloth-over-board cover, color illustrations by Vera Bock. $20.00

EULALIE, see Series section, PLATT MUNK
Famous Fairy Tales, Watty Piper, 1923 Platt, oversize, brown cloth-over-board cover with gilt lettering and paste-on-illustration, color illustrations throughout signed Eulalie. $70.00

My First Library: 8 Linenlike Books in A Box, 1931 Platt & Munk, Series, these are the linenlike small books in the 3100 series, titles include Chicken Little; Little Black Sambo; First Circus; Gingerbread Boy; Little Red Hen; Rooster, Mouse and the Little Red Hen; Tale of Peter Rabbit; Three Little Pigs. Complete set in original illustrated box. $150.00

EVANS, Florence A.
Jewel Story Book, 1903 Saalfield, green cloth-over-board cover with gilt, 102 pages, b/w illustrations by H. W. Fry. $20.00

EVERETT-GREEN, Evelyn
Sir Alymer's Heir, 1890 Nelson first edition, blue cloth-over-board cover with gilt, illustrated endpapers, small, 215 pages. $25.00

EVERS, Helen and Alf
Benny and His Birds, 1941 Rand McNally, oversize, hardback, 48 pages, illustrations by authors. ($40.00 with dust jacket) $30.00

Copy-Kitten, (1937) 1944 edition Rand McNally, square with illustrated paper-over-board cover, 46 pages, illustrations by authors. $30.00

Cry Baby Calf, 1943 Rand McNally, small, hardback, illustrations by authors. ($40.00 with dust jacket) $20.00

House the Pecks Built, 1940 Rand McNally, hardback, illustrations by authors. ($35.00 with dust jacket) $25.00

More About Copy-Kitten, (1940) 1945 edition Rand McNally, square with illustrated paper-over-board cover, 46 pages, illustrations by authors. $30.00

EWING, Juliana
Lob Lie-by-the-Fire, undated ca. 1880s edition London Society, hardcover, illustrated by Randolph Caldecott. $65.00

Lob Lie-by-the-Fire, 1913 edition George Bell, cloth-over-board cover, color plate illustrations by Alice Woodward. $40.00

FABRES, Oscar
Choo-Choo Train, 1946 John Martin, paper-over-board cover with spiral binding, color illustrations by author. $30.00

FAIRSTAR, Mrs. (R. H. Horne)
Memoirs of a London Doll Written by Herself,

(1846) 1922 edition Macmillan, blue cloth-over-board cover, b/w illustrations and color illustrations by Emma Brock. $25.00

FARJEON, Eleanor
Cherrystones, 1942 Lippincott, red cloth-over-board cover, b/w illustrations by Isobel and John Morton. ($20.00 with dust jacket) $15.00
Joan's Door, 1927 Stokes, red cloth-over-board cover with gilt, 127 pages, b/w illustrations by Will Townsend. $20.00
Kings and Queens, ca. 1935 Dutton, illustrated cover, 76 pages, 38 color plates by Thornycroft. $40.00
Miss Granby's Secret, 1941 Simon Schuster. ($20.00 with dust jacket) $10.00
Prayer for Little Things, 1945 Houghton, cloth-over-board cover, color illustrations by Elizabeth Orton Jones. ($25.00 with dust jacket) $15.00
Tale of Tom Tiddler, 1930 Stokes, light cloth-over-board cover with illustration, b/w illustrations by Tealby Norman. ($35.00 with dust jacket) $20.00
Ten Saints, 1936 Oxford, cloth-over-board cover, illustrations by Helen Sewell. ($40.00 with dust jacket) $20.00
World of Animals, 1945 Sylvan, London, oversize oblong, tan cloth-over-board cover with gilt, 31 pages, wood engraving by T. Stoney. $45.00

FARRAR, Frederic W.
Eric, or Little by Little, 1858 Black, Edinburgh, first edition, half leather, gilt and morocco cover, 394 pages, market stronger in Britain. $600.00

FARRAR, John
Songs for Johnny-Jump-Up, 1930 R. Smith, verse, small, cloth-over-board cover, 55 pages, line drawings by Rita Leach, printed in brown ink. $35.00

FAULKNER, Georgene
Flying Ship, 1931 Grosset, illustrated paper-over-board cover, illustrated endpapers, 2 color plates by Frederick Richardson, b/w illustrations by Charlotte Becker. $30.00
Gingerbread Boy, Fairy Tales from the World Over, 1931 Grosset, hardback, illustration by Milo Winter and Charlotte Becker. $20.00
Little Peachling, 1928 Wise-Parslow, green cloth-over-board cover, 91 pages, illustrated endpapers, color prints by Frederick Richardson. $40.00
Road to Enchantment, 1929 J.H. Sears, color illustrations by Frederick Richardson. $125.00.

FENN, G. Manville
Little Skipper, 1900 Altemus, beige cloth-over-board cover with gilt and illustration, 48 pages, 20 b/w illustrations. $15.00

FERRIS, Helen
Love's Enchantment (classic poems collected by Ferris), 1944 Doubleday, cloth-over-board cover with gilt, illustrated endpapers, 118 pages, color illustrations by Vera Bock. $20.00

FIELD, Ben, see Series section, WILDWOOD

FIELD, Eugene, see PEAT, Fern
In Wink-A-Way Land, 1930 edition Donohue, cloth-over-board cover with paste-on-pictorial, illustrated endpapers, 128 pages, b/w illustrations and 6 color plates. $25.00
Little Book of Tribune Verse, 1901 Grosset, blue-green cloth-over-board cover with gilt, 249 pages, b/w illustrations by Allyn Palmer. $15.00
Lull-aby Land, undated ca. 1925 edition Scribner, small, red cloth-over-board cover, 229 pages, b/w illustrations by Charles Robinson. $25.00
Wynken, Blynken and Nod, 1941 edition Whitman, oversize, color illustrated paper cover, 12 pages of full color illustrations by Margot Voigt. $40.00

FIELD, Louise A.
Peter Rabbit and His Ma, 1927 Saalfield, small, color illustrated paper-over-board cover, illus-

trated endpapers, full-page color illustrations by Virginia Albert. $35.00

Peter Rabbit and His Pa, 1916 Saalfield, small, color illustrated paper-over-board cover, illustrated endpapers, color illustrations by Virginia Albert. $35.00

FIELD, Mrs. E. M.
Mixed Pickles, 1900 Altemus, tan cloth-over-board cover, 212 pages, b/w illustrations. $20.00

FIELD, Rachel
All Through the Night, 1940 Macmillan, small, cloth-over-board cover, decorations throughout. $20.00

Hepatica Hawks, 1932 Macmillan first edition, cloth-over-board cover, small, illustrations by Allen Lewis. $40.00

Pointed People, 1930 edition Macmillan, cloth-over-board cover, b/w illustrations by author. $35.00

FILOSA, Dorothea
Susi, 1939 Garden City, color pictorial boards, oversize, color illustrations by author. $20.00

FINLEY, Jean, see Series section, BLUE DOMERS SERIES

FINLEY, Martha, see Series section, MILDRED

FISH, Helen Dean
Four and Twenty Blackbirds, 1937 Stokes, oversize, hardcover, illustrated endpapers, green/b/w illustrations throughout by Robert Lawson. $65.00

Pegs of History: A Picture Book of World Dates; 1943 Stokes, cloth-over-board cover, illustrations by Rafaello Busoni. ($30.00 with dust jacket) $15.00

FISHER, Dorothy Canfield and SCOTT, Sarah Fisher
On a Rainy Day, 1938 A. S. Barnes, orange hardcover with silhouette illustration, pencil illustrations throughout by Jessie Gillespie, printed on yellow background. ($35.00 with dust jacket) $20.00

FITZHUGH, Percy, see Series section, WESTY MARTIN

FLAHERTY, Frances
Sabu, the Elephant Boy, 1937 Oxford, wraparound photo illustration on paper-over-board cover, full-page photo illustrations facing page of text on each page. ($35.00 with same-as-cover dust jacket) $25.00

FLETCHER, Robert
Marjorie and Her Papa, 1904 Century, cloth-over-board cover, 20 b/w plates by Reginald Birch. $25.00

FLEXNER, Hortense
Chipper, 1941 Stokes, hardback. $15.00

North Window and Other Poems, 1943 Coward-McCann, blue cloth-over-board cover. $20.00

Wishing Window, 1942 Stokes, small picture book, b/w illustrations by Wyncie King. ($25.00 with dust jacket) $15.00

FLINTAN, Douglas L.
There Really Is a Father Christmas, 1938 Willett Clark, Chicago-NY, oversize, illustrated cover, b/w illustrations by Mary Jane Hoene. $20.00

FOA, Eugenie
Boy Artists: Sketches of the Childhood, 1877 Dutton, cloth-over-board cover. $30.00

Little Robinson Crusoe of Paris, translated by Julia Olcott,1925 Lippincott, cloth-over-board cover, 160 pages, illustrated endpapers, 8 color plates by Marion Mildred Oldham. $30.00

Strange Search, translated by Amena Pendleton, 1929 Lippincott, red cloth-over-board cover with gilt, illustrated endpapers, 8 color plate illustrations by Sherman Cooke. $40.00

FOLEY, Dorothy C.
When Our Ship Comes In, 1938 Saalfield, over-

size, picture book, color and b/w illustrations by Forrest Orr. $20.00

FOLLETT, Barbara Newhall
House Without Windows, 1927 Knopf first edition, cloth-over-board cover. $70.00

FORBES, Graham, see Series section, BOYS OF COLUMBIA HIGH, FRANK ALLEN

FORBES, Helen Cady
Apple Pie Hill, 1930 Macmillan, color and b/w illustrations by Eleanore Barte. $15.00
Araminta, 1927 Macmillan, small, color frontispiece by Paul Martin. $15.00
Mario's Castle, 1928 Macmillan, small, color and b/w illustrations by Marguerite de Angeli. $15.00
Mary and Marcia, Partners, 1927 Macmillan, map endpapers, b/w illustrations by Harrie Wood. $15.00

FORBUSH, William Byron
Wonder Book of Myths and Legends, 1928 Winston, blue cloth-over-board cover with paste-on-pictorial and gilt, 337 pages, illustrated endpapers, color and b/w illustrations by Frederick Richardson. $35.00

FORRESTER, Izola, see Series section, POLLY PAGE
Jack-O-Lantern, 1927 Macrae Smith, green cloth-over-board cover with paste-on-pictorial, small, 318 pages, illustrated by Harriet Longstreet Price. ($20.00 with dust jacket) $10.00

FORSTER, Frederick, see Series section, CLASSICS NEW AND OLD
Tippytoes Comes to Town, 1926 Rand McNally, oversize, 94 pages, cloth-over-board cover with paste-on-pictorial, color and b/w illustrations by Uldenne Trippe. $50.00

FOSTER, Elizabeth
Gigi, 1943 Houghton, oversize picture book, 118 pages, illustrated endpapers, color frontispiece, b/w illustrations by Ilse Bischoff. ($45.00 with dust jacket) $25.00

FOX, Charles Donald
Little Robinson Crusoe, 1925 Charles Renard, cloth-over-board cover with paste-on-pictorial, illustrated endpapers, illustrated with b/w photo plates from the Jackie Coogan movie, plus 7 photopages of Jackie doing his daily exercises. $65.00

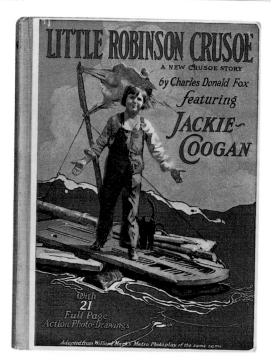

FOX, Frances Margaret, see Series section, LITTLE BEAR SERIES
Angeline Goes Traveling, 1927 Rand, first edition, green cloth-over-board cover with paste-on-pictorial, illustrated by Dorothy Lake Gregory. $30.00
Carlotta: A Story of the San Gabriel Mission, 1908 Page, hardback, illustrated by E. Ridgway. $25.00
Farmer Brown and the Birds, 1900 L. C. Page, Cosy Corner Series, illustrated by Etheldred B. Barry. $35.00
Janey, 1923 Rand McNally, hardback, illustrated by Dorothy Lake Gregory. $40.00
Little Mossback Amelia, 1939 Dutton, hardback, illustrated by Marion Downer. $25.00
Sister Sally, 1925 McNally, cloth-over-board cover with paste-on-pictorial, 105 pages, color and b/w illustrations by Dorothy Gregory. $40.00
Wilding Princess, 1929 Volland, cloth-over-board cover with gilt lettering, color plate illustrations by John Perkins. $55.00

FOX, Genevieve
Border Girl, 1939 Little Brown, b/w illustrations by George and Doris Hauman. $15.00
Green Treasure, 1941 Little Brown first edition, color frontispiece, b/w illustrations by Forrest W. Orr. $15.00
Lona of Hollybush Creek, 1940 Little Brown, color frontispiece, b/w illustrations by Forrest W. Orr. $15.00
Mountain Girl, 1932 Little Brown, color frontispiece, b/w illustrations by Forrest W. Orr. $20.00

Mountain Girl Comes Home, 1934 Little Brown, color frontispiece, b/w illustrations by Forrest W. Orr. $20.00

Susan of the Green Mountains, 1937 Little Brown first edition, illustrated endpapers, illustrations by Forrest W. Orr. $15.00

FOX, John Jr.
Little Shepherd of Kingdom Come, (1903) 1931 edition Scribner, oversize, impressed cover illustration, 14 color plate illustrations by N. C. Wyeth. $50.00

FRANCIS, J. G.
Book of Cheerful Cats and Other Animated Animals, 1903 edition Century, verse, small oblong, illustrated paper-over-board cover, 45 pages, b/w illustrations by author. $40.00

FRASER, W. A.
Outcasts, 1901 Scribner, green cloth-over-board cover with gilt decoration, illustrated endpapers, 138 pages, small, b/w illustrations by Arthur Heming. $15.00

FREDERICKS, J. Paget
Miss Pert's Christmas Tree, 1929 Macmillan, oversize, cloth-over-board cover with gilt, color and b/w illustrations by author. $35.00

FREEMAN, Ruth
Sparks and Little Sparks, 1940 Whitman, small oblong, print illustrated cover, b/w musical score on endpapers, b/w illustrations by Robert N. Blair. $10.00

FRENCH, Allen
Junior Cup, 1900 Century, b/w illustrations by Bernard Rosenmeyer. $15.00

Lost Baron, 1940 Mifflin, color and b/w illustrations by Andrew Wyeth. $20.00

FRENCH, Joseph Lewis, editor
Big Aviation Book for Boys, 1929 McLoughlin, oversize, 184 pages, photo illustrations. $25.00

FRIEND, Esther
Little Red Riding Hood, 1950 Rand McNally Junior Elf Book, color illustrated paper-over-board cover, color illustrations by Esther Friend. $15.00

FRISKEY, Margaret
Adventures for Beginners, 1944 Follett, an ABC, illustrated cover, oversize, 28 pages, color illustrations by Katherine Evans. $25.00

Chicken Little Count-to-ten, 1946 Children's, oversize, illustrations by Katherine Evans. $20.00

Scuttlebutt Goes to War, 1943 Wilcox and Follett, 32 pages, red/white/blue illustrated cover, red/white/black endpapers and illustrations by Lucia Patton. $25.00

Surprise on Wheels, 1945 Whitman, pictorial colored boards, color & b/w illustrations. $20.00

FROEBEL, Friedrich
Mother-Play and Nursery Songs, 1893 Lee & Shepard, edited by Peabody, 192 pages, red cloth-over-board cover, engraving illustrations. $50.00

FROST, Leslie
Not Really!, 1939 Coward McCann, small, b/w illustrations by James Reid. $15.00

FRY, Rosalie K.
Ladybug! Ladybug!, 1940 Dutton, 32 page picture book, three-color illustrations by author. $20.00

FRYER, Jane Eayer, see Series, MARY FRANCES

FULLER, Alice Cook
Gold for the Grahams, 1948 Messner, b/w illustrations by Dorothy Bayley Morse. $10.00

FULLER, Iola
Loon Feather, 1940 Harcourt, map endpapers. $10.00

FULLER, Muriel
Runaway Shuttle Train, 1949 McKay, first edition, oblong, red cover, illustrated endpapers, illustrated. $25.00

FULLER, O. Muiriel
Book of Dragons, 1931 McBride, cloth-over-board cover, illustrated endpapers, 181 pages, color frontispiece, b/w illustrations by Alexander Key. $30.00

FURLONG, May
Lost Log Cabin, 1938 Whitman, green cloth-over-board cover with paste-on-pictorial, illustrated endpapers, color illustrations by Elsa Goldy Young. $25.00

FYLEMAN, Rose
Forty Good-Morning Tales, 1929 Doubleday, color and b/w illustrations by Erick Berry. $25.00

G

GAG, Wanda
ABC Bunny, 1933 McCann, oversize picture book, color illustration on paper-over-board cover, red

lettering, b/w illustrations by author. ($85.00 with same-pattern dust jacket) $65.00

Snippy and Snappy, 1931 Coward McCann, oblong hardback. $65.00

Snow White and the Seven Dwarfs, 1938 Coward McCann, illustrated paper-over-board cover, small, 43 pages, b/w illustrations by author. $65.00

Snow White and the Seven Dwarfs, 1938 Hale library edition, hardcover, ex-library copy with pockets, etc., b/w illustrations by author. $20.00

GALE, Elizabeth
How the Animals Came to the Circus, 1917 Rand McNally, small, illustrated hardcover, 64 pages, color illustrations by Warner Carr. $25.00

GALE, Leah
Favorite Tales of Long Ago, 1943 Random, over-size picture book, illustrated paper-over-board cover, color illustrations by Miss Elliott. $35.00

GALLAGHER, Louise Barnes
Frills and Thrills, 1940 Dodd, hardcover, b/w illustrations by Jeva Cralick. $10.00

GARIS, Howard, see Series section, BUDDY, HAPPY HOME
Tuftoo the Clown, 1928 Appleton, mustard cloth-over-board cover, illustrated endpapers, 283 pages, 10 b/w illustrations by James Daugherty. $20.00

GARIS, Lilian C.
Joan: Just a Girl, a Gloria Book, 1924 Grosset, hardcover, illustrated by Thelma Gooch. $15.00

Let's Make Believe We're Soldiers, 1918 Dono-hue, illustrated cloth-over-board cover, 4 color plates. $35.00

GARIS, Roger, see Series section, OUTBOARD BOYS

GARLAND, Hamlin
Prairie Song and Western Story, 1928 Allyn & Bacon, small, 368 pages, b/w illustrations by Constance Garland. $10.00

GARNER, Elvira
Ezekiel, 1937 Holt, half-cloth cover with pictorial boards, 42 pages, color line drawings by author. ($110.00 with dust jacket). $60.00

Sara Faith Anderson: Her Book, 1939 Messner, color illustrations throughout by author. ($110.00 with dust jacket) $60.00

Way Down in Tennessee, 1941 Messner, color illustrations throughout by author. ($100.00 with dust jacket). $50.00

GARRARD, Philip
Banana Tree House, 1938 Coward McCann, illustrated endpapers, color and b/w illustrations by Berta and Elmer Hader. $35.00

Running Away With Nebby, 1944 McKay first edition, oversize, illustrated endpapers, color frontispiece, b/w illustrations by Willy Pogany. $25.00

GARRETT, Helen
Angelo the Naughty One, 1944 Viking, oversize picture book, color illustrations by Leo Politi. $30.00

Jobie, 1942 Messner, b/w illustrations by Connie Moran. $15.00

GARST, Shannon
Cowboy Boots, 1946 Abingdon, hardcover, b/w illustrations by Charles Hargens. $15.00

Wish on an Apple, 1948 Abingdon, hardcover, b/w illustrations by Jon Nielsen. $10.00

GARTH, John
Boy Scouts on the Trail, 1920 Barse, hardcover, b/w frontispiece. $25.00

GASKELL, Mrs.
Cranford, ca. 1890s Lovell Bros., hardcover, small, b/w illustrations. $25.00

GATES, Eleanor
Apron-Strings, 1917 Sully and Kleinteich, hardcover, 306 pages. $10.00

Rich Little Poor Boy, (1922 Appleton) 1937 edition Macaulay, hardcover, 419 pages. $10.00

GATES, Josephine
Sunshine Annie, 1910 Bobbs Merrill, cloth-over-board cover with color paste-on-pictorial, illustrations by Fanny Cory. $40.00

GAY, Romney
Cinder, 1934 Grosset Dunlap, colored boards. $25.00
Come Play with Corally Crothers, 1943 Grosset, easy reader, small, color illustration on paper-over-board cover, illustrated endpapers, color illustrations by author. $20.00
Five Little Playmates, a Book of Finger-play, 1941 Grosset Dunlap, illlustrated by Gay. $25.00.
Funny Noise, 1935 Grosset Dunlap, illustrated cover, 36 pages, decorated end papers, illustrated by Gay. $35.00
Picture Book of Poems, 1946 Grosset, oversize picture book, hardcover, illustrations by author. $35.00
Tale of Corally Crothers, 1932 Grosset, easy reader, small, color illustration on paper-over-board cover, illustrated endpapers, color illustrations by author. $30.00

GAYE, Selina
Little Cockney, a Story for Girls, 1907 Nelson, blue cloth-over-board cover, small, color frontispiece. $25.00

GEORGE, Lloyd and **GILMAN, James**
Air, Men and Wings, 1929 McBride, blue cloth-over-board cover, 263 pages, photos and drawings. $15.00

GERARD, Morice
Black Gull Rock, 1897 Thomas Nelson, small, 156 pages, hardcover with impressed design and gilt cover decoration, b/w frontispiece. $15.00

GERBER, Will
Gooseberry Jones, 1947 Putnam first edition, cloth-over-board cover, 96 pages, b/w illustrations by Dudley Morris. $50.00

GERE, Frances Kent
Once Upon a Time in Egypt, 1937 Longmans, oversize oblong, 71 pages, color endpapers, paper-on-board color illustrated cover, illustrations by author. $25.00

GERSON, Virginia
Happy Heart Family, (1907) 1939 Dodd 10th edition, oversize oblong picture book, paper-on-board illustrated cover, color plates and line drawings throughout by author. $50.00

GERSTAECKER, Frederick
Frank Wildman's Adventures on Land and Water, 1866 Crosby & Ainsworth, brown cloth-over-board cover, 312 pages, b/w illustrations. $30.00

GIBSON, Eva
Zauberlinda, the Wise Witch, 1901 Smith, decorated blue cloth-over-board cover, two-tone illustrations throughout. $120.00

GIBSON, Katharine, see PEAT, Fern
Goldsmith of Florence, 1936 Macmillan, oversize, printed illustration on cloth-over-board cover, illustrated endpapers, 205 pages, photo illustrations. $30.00

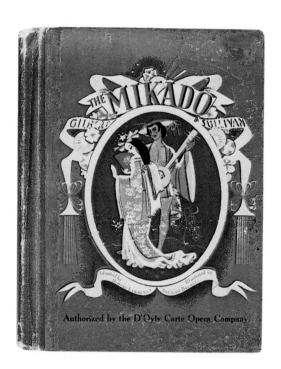

GILBERT AND SULLIVAN
Mikado, adapted by Robert Lawrence, authorized by the D'Oyly Carte Company, 1940 Grosset & Dunlap, small, 48 pages, paper-over-board cover with color illustration, b/w and color illustrations throughout by Sheilah Beckett. $15.00
Pinafore Picture Book, Story of the H.M.S. Pinafore, 1908 Macmillan, first American edition, narrative retelling for children of the operetta, written by Sir W. S. Gilbert, oversize, cloth-over-board cover with impressed illustration, 130 pages, illustrated endpapers, 16 color plates plus b/w in-text illustrations by Alice B. Woodward. ($135.00 with dust jacket) $55.00
Story of the Mikado, 1921 O'Connor, London, narrative retelling for children of the operetta,

written by Sir W. S. Gilbert, oversize, cloth-over-board cover with impressed illustration, 115 pages, illustrated endpapers, 6 color plates plus b/w in-text illustrations by Alice B. Woodward. ($95.00 with dust jacket) $35.00

GILBERT, Paul see Series section, BERTRAM
Egbert and His Marvelous Adventures, 1944 Harper first edition, b/w illustrations by H. A. Rey. $30.00
Elmer Buys a Circus, 1941 Grosset, pictorial cover and illustrated endpapers, illustrations by Anne Stossel. $30.00

GILCHRIST, Marie
Story of the Great Lakes, 1942 Harper, oversize, color illustrated paper-over-board cover, illustrated endpapers with map, lithograph color and b/w illustrations throughout by C. H. DeWitt, about 30 pages. $35.00

GILDER, Jeannette L.
Autobiography of a Tom-Boy, 1900 Doubleday, impressed cover illustration, 26 full-page b/w drawings by Florence Shinn. $25.00

GLADSTONE, Mrs. George
Sailing Orders, undated ca. 1888 Lothrop, red cloth-over-board cover with gilt, 144 pages, small, b/w illustrations. $20.00

GODOLPHIN, Mary, see Series section, IN WORDS OF ONE SYLLABLE
Sanford and Merton in Words of One Syllable, undated ca. 1900, hardcover. $35.00

GOLDSMITH, Cliff
Wisdom of Professor Happy, 1923 Metropolitan Life Ins., pictorial paper cover, 67 pages, small, b/w illustrations by Jessie Gillespie. $10.00

GORDON, Elizabeth, see Series section, LORAINE

GORDON, Frederick, see Series section, FAIRVIEW BOYS

GRAHAM, Mary Nancy, arranger
Book of Christmas Carols, 1938 Grosset Dunlap, illustrated endpapers, illustrations by Pelagie Doane. $25.00

GRAY, Louisa M.
Little Miss Wardlaw, 1899 Nelson, blue cloth-over-board cover with gilt, small, 445 pages, illustrated endpapers, frontispiece. $20.00

GREENWOOD, Grace
Stories from Famous Ballads, 1906 Ginn, red cloth-over-board cover with gilt, small, 100 pages, 1 color and 8 b/w illustrations by E. H. Garrett. $15.00

GRIDLEY, Marion
Indians of Yesterday, 1940 Donohue, oversize, 63 pages, 6 color plates by Lone Wolf. $60.00

GRIFFITH, Helen
Letty's Good Luck, 1914 Penn Publishing, hardcover. $15.00
Yes, Virginia!, 1928 Penn, small, 300 pages, color illustrated paste-on-pictorial cover, 3 b/w illustrations by Waunita Smith. $15.00

GRIMM Bros.
Hansel and Gretel and Other Stories, 1925 Doran, first American edition, oversize, red cloth-over-board cover with gilt, 12 color plates by Kay Nielsen. $400.00
Snowdrop and Other Tales, 1923 edition Doubleday, cloth-over-board cover with gilt, color and b/w illustrations by Arthur Rackham. $50.00

GROVER, Edwin Osgood
Just Being Happy, 1916 Algonquin, small, collection of quotations, illustrated. $15.00

GROVER, Eulalie Osgood
Mother Goose, see RICHARDSON, Frederick
Outdoor Primer, ca. 1904 Rand McNally, hardcover, 104 pages, illustrated with photos. $75.00
Robert Louis Stevenson: Teller of Tales, 1940 Dodd Mead, hardcover, illustrated by Marc Simont. $25.00
Sunbonnet Babies A B C Book, 1937 Rand McNally, pictorial board covers, small, illustrated in b/w and color by Bertha Corbett Melcher. $40.00
Sunbonnet Babies in Mother Goose Land, (1927) 1937 edition Rand McNally, pictorial boards, full-color and b/w illustrations by Bertha Corbett Melcher. $75.00

GRUBB, Mary B.
Our Alphabet of Toys, 1932 Harper, oversize, 28 pages, paper covers, b/w/color illustrations by Carolyn Ashbrook. $35.00

GRUELLE, Johnny
Gruelle's *Raggedy Ann* books are listed in Volume 1 of *Collector's Guide to Children's Books.*

Johnny Gruelle's Golden Book, 1929 edition Donahue, oversize, paper-over-board illustrated cover, 79 pages, collection of earlier works, color illustrations by author. $45.00

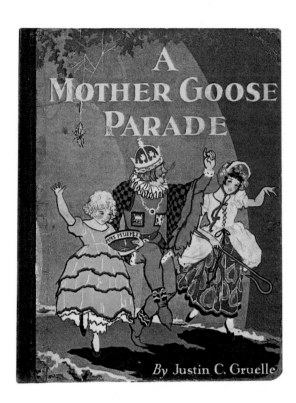

GRUELLE, Justin C.
Mother Goose Parade, 1929 Volland, oversize, rewritten Mother Goose poems by Justin Gruelle, color illustrated paper-over-board cover, color illustrations throughout by author. $100.00

Once Around the Sun, written by Elsa Titchenell, 1950 edition Theosophical University Press, blue cloth-over-board cover with paste-on-pictorial, oversize, 57 pages, color plates and b/w illustrations by Justin Gruelle. $35.00

Justin Gruelle, who was Johnny Gruelle's brother, also illustrated some of the *Raggedy Ann* books created from Johnny Gruelle's stories and published by the Johnny Gruelle Company, including:

Raggedy Ann and the Golden Butterfly, 1940 Johnny Gruelle Co., color illustrated paper-over-board cover, color illustrations throughout. $45.00

Raggedy Ann and Betsy Bonnet String, 1943 Johnny Gruelle Co., color illustrated paper-over-board cover, color illustrations throughout. $45.00

Raggedy Ann in the Snow White Castle, 1946 Johnny Gruelle Co., color illustrated paper-over-board cover, color illustrations throughout. $45.00

⇒ **H** ⇒

HABBERTON, John
Irrepressibles, 1877 Loring, cloth-over-board cover with gilt, small. $35.00

HADER, Berta and Elmer
Cricket, 1938 Macmillan, first edition, hardcover, illustrated by authors. $60.00.

Jamaica Johnny, 1935 Macmillan, first edition, square, green cloth-over-board cover, pictorial endpapers, illustrated by authors. $55.00

Little Appaloosa, 1949 Macmillan, oversize, green cloth-over-board cover, illustrated by authors. $50.00

Little Town, 1941 Macmillan first edition, red cloth-over-board cover, illustrations by authors. 50.00.

Midget and Bridget, 1934 Macmillan, orange cloth-over-board cover, illustrated by authors. $45.00

Old Woman and the Sixpence, 1928 Macmillan, hardcover, color illustrations by authors. $60.00

Rainbows End, 1946 Macmillan, hardcover, 169 pages, illustrations by authors. $25.00.

Skyrocket, 1946 Macmillan, first edition, gray cloth cover, illustrated. $35.00.

Smiths and Rusty, 1936 Scribner first edition, 118 pages, blue cloth-over-board cover, b/w illustrations. $60.00

Story of Pancho the Bull with the Crooked Tail, Macmillan, blue cloth-over-board cover, illustrated by Haders. $35.00

What'll You Be When You Grow Up?, 1929 Longmans first edition, small, color illustrated paper-over-board cover, illustrated endpapers, color throughout by authors. $55.00

HAEFNER, Ralph
Ted and Polly, a Home Typing Book for Younger Children, 1933 Macmillan, cloth-over-board cover, 107 pages. $20.00

HAILE, Ellen
Three Brown Boys and Other Happy Children, 1879 Cassell, impressed cover illustration with silver and gold gilt, b/w illustrations throughout, some by Kate Greenaway. $45.00

Two Gray Girls, 1880 Cassell, color paste-on-pictorial cover, 258 pages, b/w illustrations listed "by Kate Greenaway, M. E. Edwards and Others." $45.00

HALL, A. Neely
Outdoor Handicraft for Boys, 1938 Lippincott first edition, green cloth-over-board cover, 289 pages, b/w illustrations. $15.00

HALL, Edith King
Adventures in Toyland, What the Marionette Told

Molly, 1900 Altemus, tan cloth-over-board cover, small, 70 b/w illustrations by A. B. Woodward. $20.00

HALL, Eliza Calvert
Aunt Jane of Kentucky, (1898) 1907 edition Burt, impressed illustration on cloth-on-board cover, two-color frontispiece by Beulah Strong. $15.00
Land of Long Ago, 1909 Little Brown, small, pictorial hardcover, 295 pages, illustrated by G. Patrick Nelson and Beulah Strong. $25.00
Sally Ann's Experience, (1898) 1910 edition Little Brown, color illustrated cloth-over-board cover, small, 45 pages, color frontispiece by G. P. Nelson. $20.00

HALL, Esther Greenacre
Back to Buckeye, 1934 Jr. Literary Guild edition, hardcover, b/w illustrations by Lee Townsend. $15.00
College on Horseback, 1933 Random House, hardcover. $15.00
Haverhill Herald, 1938 Jr. Literary Guild edition, hardcover, b/w illustrations signed DeAragon. $15.00
Here-to-Yonder Girl, (1932) 1937 edition Macmillan, hardcover, b/w illustrations by Wilard Bonte. $15.00
Up Creek and Down Creek, 1936 Jr. Literary Guild edition, hardcover, b/w illustrations by Anna Braune. $15.00

HALL, May Emery
Jan and Betje, 1914 Merrill, small, hardcover,122 pages, b/w illustrations. $15.00

HALL, Ruth
In the Brave Days of Old, 1898 Houghton, gilt design on cover, b/w frontispiece. $15.00

HAMLIN, John
Tales of an Old Lumber Camp, 1936 Heath, printed illustration on cover, photo illustrations and line drawings by C. E. B. Bernard. $10.00

HAMLIN, Myra
Nan in the City, 1897 Roberts, red cloth-over-board cover, small, b/w illustrations by L. J. Bridgman. $20.00

HANCOCK, Irving, see Series section, GRAMMAR SCHOOL BOYS, HIGH SCHOOL BOYS, WEST POINT, YOUNG ENGINEERS

HARE, T. Truxton, see Series section, PHILIP KENT

HARK, Ann
Phantom of the Forest, 1939 Lippincott, hardcover, color frontispiece, b/w illustrations by Dorothy Bayley. $10.00
Story of the Pennsylvania Dutch, 1943 Harper, hardcover, oversize, illustrated by C.H DeWitt. $40.00
Sugar Mill House, 1937 Lippincott, hardcover, b/w illustrations by Marguerite de Angeli. $15.00

HARLAND, Marion
An Old-Field School-Girl, 1897 Scribner, impressed and gilt cover design, small, 208 pages, 12 b/w plate illustrations signed Keller. $15.00

HARNONCOURT, Rene d'
Hole in the Wall, 1931 Knopf, hardcover. $65.00

HAROLD, Childe
Child's Book of Abridged Wisdom, 1905 Elder, rope-hinged cover, small, double pages with color illustrations and decorations. $45.00

HARRADEN, Beatrice
Little Rosebud, 1890 Caldwell, small, 163 pages, gilt design and color paste-on-illustration on cover, color frontispiece, b/w illustrations by J. H. Bacon. $30.00
Master Roley, 1889 Warne, red cloth-over-board cover with gilt, small, 156 pages, b/w illustrations by Alfred Johnson. $35.00
Things Will Take a Turn, (1894) 1912 edition Scribner, small, 163 pages, impressed design on cover, b/w illustrations by J. H. Bacon. $20.00

HARRIS, Joel Chandler
Brer Rabbit Stories From Uncle Remus, 1941 Harper Parents Institute Edition, hardcover, 132 pages. $45.00
Chronicles of Aunt Minervy Ann, 1899 Scribners, tan illustrated cloth-over-board cover. $100.00
Little Mr. Thimblefinger and His Queer Country, (1894) 1898 edition Houghton, illustrated cloth-over-board cover, b/w illustrations by Oliver Herford. $70.00
Little Union Scout, 1904 McClure first edition, illustrated by George Gibbs. $100.00
Mr. Rabbit, 1895 McIlvaine first UK edition from the American sheets, illustrated tan cloth-over-board cover, 16 b/w plates by Oliver Herford. $75.00
Sister Jane: Her Friends and Acquaintances, 1896 Riverside Press, hardcover. $40.00
Tar Baby, 1904 edition Appleton, cloth-over-board cover with gilt, 190 pages, illustrated by Frost and Kemble. $150.00

Uncle Remus and his Legends of the Old Plantation, 1881 Bogue, London, 1st British edition, partial reprint of American version, small, illustrated cover, illustrations by Frederick S. Church and James Moser. $700.00

HARRIS, Leila and Kilroy
Blackfellow Bundi, 1939 Whitman, 63 pages, color paste-on-pictorial cover, color endpapers, b/w and color illustrations by Kurt Wiese. $50.00
Let's Read About Australia, 1950 Fideler, hardcover, 112 pages. $15.00.
Let's Read About Canada, 1949 Fideler, hardcover, Illustrated. $15.00

HART, William, see Series section, GOLDEN WEST BOYS

HARTWELL, James
Enchanted Castle, a Book of Fairy Tales from Flowerland, 1906 Altemus first edition, hardcover, illustrated endpapers, color illustrations by John Neill. ($200.00 with dust jacket) $95.00
Man Elephant, a Book of African Fairy Tales, 1906 Altemus, pictorial cloth-over-board cover. $35.00

HASTINGS, Howard L.
Animal Book, 1924 Cupples & Leon, green cloth-over-board cover with paste-on-pictorial, oversize, color plates and line drawings by Hastings. $25.00

HATHAWAY, Cynthia
Pretend Puppy, 1940 Garden City, color and b/w illustrations by Romney Gay. $20.00
Two Bridgets, 1944 Doubleday, color illustrated paper-on-board cover, color endpapers, color and b/w illustrations by Pelagie Doane. $20.00

HAWEIS, Mrs. H. R.
Chaucer for Children, 1882 Chatto, oversize, green cloth-over-board cover with decorations, 112 pages, 8 color plates by author. $85.00

HAWKES, Clarence
Field and Forest Friends, 1913 Browne, brown cloth-over-board cover, small, 207 pages, b/w illustrations by Charles Copeland. $15.00

HAWKSWORTH, Hallam
Clever Little People with Six Legs, 1924 Scribner, cloth-over-board cover, 294 pages, illustrations, index. $15.00

HAWLEY, Katherine
Cubby Bear, 1936 Whitman, a Stand-out Book with cut-out shape of bear glued to paper-over-board cover to create raised illustration, small square, 29 pages, illustrated endpapers, b/w/orange illustrations by Juanita Bennett. $25.00
Stories of the Quin-Puplets, 1935 Whitman, hardcover, illustrated. $20.00

HAWTHORNE, Nathaniel
Three Golden Apples, 1912 edition Constable, square pictorial boards, 4 color plates by Patten Wilson. $20.00
Wonder Book and Tanglewood Tales, 1930 edition Winston, red cloth-over-board cover with paste-on-pictorial, 399 pages, illustrated endpapers, 4 color plates and b/w illustrations by Frederick Richardson. $30.00

HAYES, Clair, see Series section, BOY ALLIES WITH THE ARMY, BOY TROOPERS

HAYES, Marjorie
Little House on Wheels, 1934 Little Brown, cloth-over-board cover, map endpapers, illustrations by George and Doris Hauman. $20.00

HAYS, Ethel, illustrator
Town Mouse and the Country Mouse, 1942 Saalfield, linen-like paper cover, oversize, book #476, full-page color illustrations throughout. $30.00

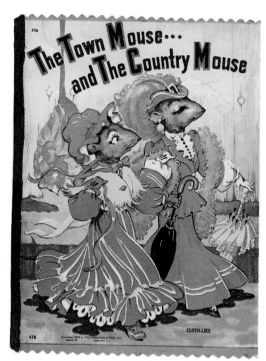

HAYS, Margaret
Kiddie Rhymes, 1911 Jacobs, oversize picture book, 29 pages, color plates and b/w illustrations by Grace Wiederseim (Grace Drayton). $60.00

HAYWOOD, Carolyn, see Series section, BETSY SERIES
Eddie and the Fire Engine, 1949 Morrow, cloth-over-board cover, illustrated by author. ($35.00 with dust jacket) $20.00
Little Eddie, 1947 Morrow, cloth-over-board cover, illustrated by author. ($35.00 with dust jacket) $20.00
Penny and Peter, 1946 Harcourt, red cloth-over-board cover, illustrated by author. ($25.00 with dust jacket) $15.00
Two and Two are Four, 1940 Harcourt, red cloth-over-board cover, illustrated by author. ($35.00 with dust jacket) $25.00

HEATH, Marian Russell
Margaret Tarrant's Christmas Garland, 1942 Hale Cushman, cloth-over-board cover with silver and paste-on-pictorial, tipped-in color plates by Tarrant. $65.00

HEGAN, Alice Caldwell
Mrs. Wiggs of the Cabbage Patch, (1901) 1909 edition Century, small, green cloth-over-board cover with impressed illustration and white lettering, 153 pages. $15.00

HEISENFELT, Kathryn, see NEWTON, Ruth

HELM, Clementine
Cecily (Elf Goldihair), translated by Elisabeth Stork, 1924 Lippincott, cloth-over-board with gilt lettering and paste-on-illustration, 298 pages, illustrated endpapers, 8 color plates by Gertrude Kay. $55.00

HELTON, Roy
Early Adventures of Peacham Grew, 1925 Penn, gray cloth-over-board cover, small, 117 pages, b/w illustrations by Edward Shenton. ($20.00 with dust jacket) $15.00

HEMINGER, I. N., editor
Animal Anecdotes, 1929 Dorrance, orange cloth-over-board cover, small, 182 pages, b/w illustrations by Howard Duff. $15.00

HENTY, George Alfred, (1832-1902)
    Henty's first boys' book was *Out of Pampas,* 1871 Griffith and Farran. He wrote 3 or 4 novels a year, both adult and juvenile. Many cross over, as his subject matter is action-adventure and appeals to both markets. During the height of Henty's popularity, his novels went through numerous editions and reprints. Reading copies are generally low priced. First editions and rare editions command high prices.
    The following books are undated and cannot be identified as firsts, and therefore are priced as good condition later printings.
Both Sides of the Border, undated Blackie, red illustrated boards. $20.00

Boy Knight, undated edition Burt, red cloth-over-board cover. $20.00

Captain Bayley's Heir, undated ca. 1904 edition Burt, illustrated cloth-over-board cover. $15.00

Dragon and the Raven, undated edition Hurst, green cloth-over-board cover with paste-on-pictorial, b/w illustrations. $20.00

Jack Archer, undated ca. 1900 edition Donohue, brown cloth-over-board cover. $10.00

Lion of St. Mark, ca. 1912 edition Blackie, half leather, gilt crest on cover, 384 pages. $15.00

Lost Heir, ca. 1900 Lupton, illustrated cloth-over-board cover. $35.00

Rujub the Juggler, 1893 edition Chattus & Windus, illustrated olive cloth-over-board cover, plates by Stanley Wood. $30.00

Tale of the Peninsular War, (1872) undated ca. 1890s edition Excelsior, khaki cloth-over-board cover with gilt, illustrated. $40.00

Through Russian Snows, ca. 1895 edition Scribner, cloth-over-board cover, 339 pages, b/w illustrations by Overend, map. $20.00

Through the Sikh War, ca. 1903 edition Scribner, cloth-over-board cover, b/w illustrations by Hurst. $20.00

Treasure of the Incas, ca. 1902 Scribner, cloth-over-board cover, 340 pages, b/w illustrations by Paget. $20.00

Under Drake's Flag, ca. 1900 edition Blackie, brown cloth-over-board cover with gilt illustration, sepia plates by Gordon Browne. $15.00

With Cochrane the Dauntless, ca.1896 edition Scribner, green cloth-over-board cover with gilt, 388 pages, b/w illustrations by Margetson. $30.00

With the Allies to Pekin, ca.1904 edition Blackie, green cloth-over-board cover with gilt, sepia plates by W. Paget. $40.00

With Wolfe in Canada, undated ca. 1907 edition Hurst, illustrated cloth-over-board cover. $30.00

Young Carthaginian, undated edition Hurst, cloth-over-board cover, b/w illustrations. $20.00

HERBEN, Beatrice Slayton, MD
Jack O'Health and Peg O'Joy, 1921 Scribner, cloth-over-board cover, 39 pages, color illustrations by Frederick Richardson. $65.00

HEWARD, Constance, see Series section, AMELIARANNE
Grandpa and the Tiger, 1924 Jacobs, cloth-over-board cover with paste-on-pictorial, small, 121 pages, illustrated endpapers, color and b/w illustrations by Lilian Govey. $35.00

HILL, Grace Brooks, see Series section, CORNER HOUSE GIRLS

HILL, Helen, see Series section, CHARLIE

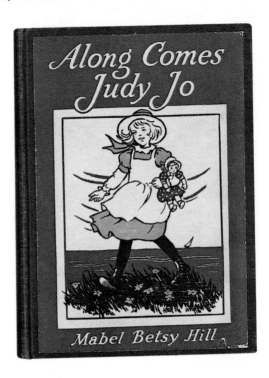

HILL, Mabel Betsy
Along Comes Judy Jo, 1943 Stokes, blue hardcover, paste-on-pictorial, b/w illustrations by author. $20.00

HILLYER, V. M.
Child's History of the World, 1924 Century, cloth-over-board cover with gilt, illustrations by Carle Boog. $50.00

HODGKINS, Mary D. H., editor
Atlantic Treasury of Childhood Stories, 1924 Atlantic Monthly Press, oversize green cloth-over-board cover with color paste-on-pictorial, illustrated endpapers, 409 pages, b/w illustrations by Beatrice Stevens. $25.00

HOFFMAN, Dr. Henry
Slovenly Peter, 1900 edition Winston, oversize, hardcover with gilt, "illustrations colored by hand after the original style," printed on title page. $65.00

Slovenly Peter, 1935 edition Harper, "translated by Mark Twain," original illustrations adapted by Fritz Kredel, color illustrated paper-over-board cover, color illustrations throughout. $45.00

HOFFMAN, Eleanor
Travels of a Snail, 1939 Stokes, hardcover, illustrations by Zhenya Gay. $25.00

White Mare of The Black Tents, 1949 Dodd, Mead, hardcover. $15.00

HOFFMAN, F., and **IRELAND, Mary**
Leo's Whaling Voyage, 1923 Augustana, illustrated boards. $20.00

HOLBERG, Ruth (author) and **Richard** (illustrator)
At The Sign of the Golden Anchor, 1947 Doubleday, cloth-over-board cover, illustrated by Jane Castle. $15.00
Bells of Amsterdam, 1940 Crowell, blue cloth-over-board cover, color and black and white illustrations $35.00
Gloucester Boy, 1940 Doubleday, color illustrated paper-on-board cover, illustrated endpapers, two-color illustrations. $20.00
Mitty and Mr. Syrup, 1935 Doubleday, pictorial paper-over-board cover, illustrated endpapers, color and b/w illustrations. $30.00
Mitty on Mr. Syrup's Farm, 1936 Doubleday, color illustrated paper-on-board cover, illustrated endpapers, color and b/w illustrations. $30.00
Oh Susannah, 1939 Doubleday, cloth-over-board cover. ($40.00 with dust jacket) $25.00
Tibby's Venture, 1943 Doubleday, green cloth-over-board cover, illustrations by Phyllis Cote. $30.00
Wee Brigit O'Toole, 1938 Doubleday, color illustrated paper-over-board cover, illustrated endpapers, color and b/w illustrations. ($30.00 with dust jacket) $20.00

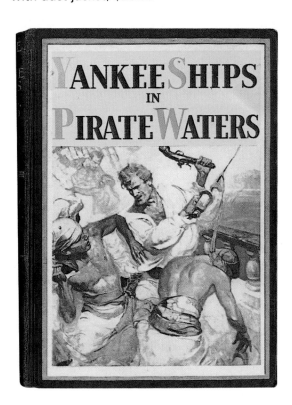

HOLLAND, Rupert Sargent
Arabian Nights, undated ca. 1930s Grosset, orange cloth-over-board cover, color frontispiece by W. H. Lister, illustrated endpapers. $15.00
Race for a Fortune, 1931 Lippincott, cloth-over-board cover, 266 pages, illustrated by Lyle Justis. $20.00.
Splendid Buccaneer: A Tale of the Atlantic Coast in Pirate Days, 1928 Lippincott, illustrated cloth-over-board cover, illustrations by Stafford Good. $30.00
Yankee Ships in Pirate Waters, 1931 Garden City, cloth-over-board cover with paste-on-illustration, 317 pages, illustrated endpapers, double page color illustrated title page, 3 color plates by Frank Schoonover. $35.00

HOLLING, Holling C.
Seabird, ca. 1948, oversize, 59 pages, illustrations by author. $20.00

HOLME, C. Geoffrey
Children's Toys of Yesterday, 1932 Studio, London, oversize, 128 pages, hundreds of photo illustrations plus 12 color plates. ($100.00 with dust jacket) $75.00

HOLMES, Oliver W.
Dorothy Q: Together with a Ballad of the Boston Tea Party and Grandmother's Story of Bunker Hill, 1893 Houghton, gray cloth-over-board cover with silver gilt, 131 pages, illustrations and decorations by Howard Pyle. $50.00
One Hoss Shay, With Its Companion Poems, 1892 edition Riverside Press, tan leather binding with dark brown inlays, small, 82 pages, b/w illustrations by Howard Pyle. $60.00
School Boy, 1879 Houghton, cloth-over-board cover with gilt, illustrated endpapers, 79 pages, b/w illustrations. $45.00

HONNESS, Elizabeth
Belinda Balloon and the Big Wind, 1940 Grosset, hardcover, illustrations by Pelagie Doane. $15.00
Flight of Fancy, 1941, hardcover, 44 pages, illustrations by Pelagie Doane. $15.00

HOPE, Laura, see Series section, BOBBSEY TWINS

HOOVER, Bessie
Pa Flickinger's Folks, 1909 Harper, gray cloth-over-board cover with decoration, small, 274 pages, b/w illustrations by Strothmann and Bertha Stuart. $15.00

HOPE, A. R.
Day After the Holidays, ca. 1875 Appleton, brown cloth-over-board cover with gilt,

small, 203 pages, b/w illustrations by G. P. Browne Jr. $30.00

HOROWITZ, Caroline
Treasury of Play Ideas for Tiny Tots, 1947 Hart, hardcover, illustrated endpapers, illustrations. $15.00

HUBBARD, Margaret Ann
Captain Juniper, 1947 Macmillan, hardcover, 257 pages. $15.00

HUEFFER, Ford H. Madox
Feather, 1892 Cassell Children's Library edition, small, patterned cloth-over-board cover, 212 pages, b/w illustrations by Ford Madox Brown. $25.00

HUNT, Clara Whitehall
About Harriet, 1916 Houghton, 150 pages, color illustrated paste-on-pictorial cover, color illustrations throughout by Maginel Wright Enright. $45.00
Little House in the Woods, 1918 Houghton, b/w illustrations by Mabel Betsy Hill. $25.00
Peggy's Playhouses, 1924 Houghton, color paste-on-pictorial cover, b/w illustrations by Gustaf Tenggren. $20.00

HUNT, Mabel Leigh
Peter Piper's Pickled Peppers, 1942 Stokes, small, 62 pages, printed illustration on cover, color illustrations throughout by Katherine Milhous. $20.00
Young Man of the House, 1944 Lippincott, hardcover, illustrated by Louis Slobodkin. $30.00

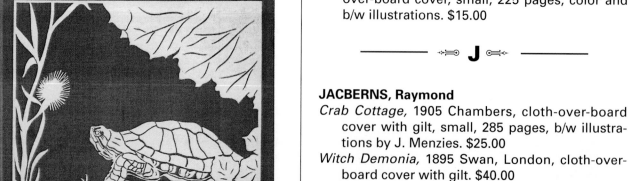

Let's Go Outdoors.

HUNTINGTON, Harriet E.
Let's Go Outdoors, 1939 Doubleday, picture book with photo endpapers and full-page photo illustrations by Preston Duncan. ($20.00 with dust jacket) $15.00
Let's Go to the Desert, 1941 Doubleday, picture book, illustrated with photographs. $15.00
Let's Go to the Seashore, 1949 Doubleday, square picture book, illustrated with full-page photographs. $15.00

HURD, Edith
Wreck of the Wild Wave, 1942 Oxford first edition, hardback, 247 pages, endpaper maps. $15.00

IRELAND, Mary E.
Hilda's Mascot, 1927 Saalfield, orange cloth-over-board cover, 332 pages. $15.00
Hilda's Mascot, Goldsmith edition, hardcover. ($20.00 with dust jacket) $7.00
Pixy's Holiday Journey, 1906 Saalfield, translated from German, color impressed illustration on cover, 250 pages, b/w frontispiece signed Haufler. $15.00

IRVING, Fannie Belle
Six Girls, 1884 Estes, elaborate color illustrated paper-on-board cover, illustrated endpapers, b/w engraving illustrations. $30.00

ISASI, Mirim
White Stars of Freedom, 1942 Whitman, hardcover, 302 pages, illustrations by Kurt Wiese. $15.00

IVES, Sarah Noble
Key to Betsy's Heart, 1916 Macmillan, green cloth-over-board cover, small, 225 pages, color and b/w illustrations. $15.00

———— →◈ **J** ◈← ————

JACBERNS, Raymond
Crab Cottage, 1905 Chambers, cloth-over-board cover with gilt, small, 285 pages, b/w illustrations by J. Menzies. $25.00
Witch Demonia, 1895 Swan, London, cloth-over-board cover with gilt. $40.00

JACKSON, Charlotte
Sarah Deborah's Day, 1941 Dodd first edition, illustrated paper-on-board cover, illustrated endpapers, b/w and three-color illustrations by Marc Simont. ($50.00 with dust jacket) $30.00

Tito the Pig of Guatemala, 1940 Dodd, illustrated paper-on-board cover, illustrated endpapers, b/w and three-color illustrations by Kurt Wiese. $20.00

JACKSON, Gabrielle
Dixie School Girl, undated Donohue, red cloth-over-board cover. $10.00
Peggy Stewart at Home, 1918 Goldsmith, hardcover. ($15.00 with dust jacket) $8.00
Wee Winkles at the Mountains, 1908 Harper, green cloth-over-board cover, illustrations by R. Robinson. $10.00

JACKSON, K. and **B.**
Farm Stories, 1946 Simon Schuster Giant Golden Book, oversize picture book, paper-over-board cover, color illustrations by Gustaf Tenggren. $25.00

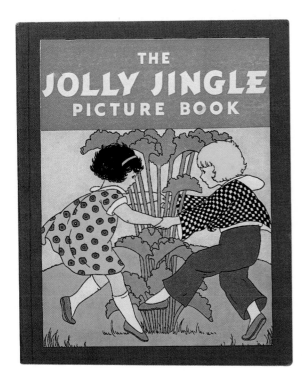

JACKSON, Leroy
Jolly Jingle Book, 1937 edition Rand McNally, (new edition of the 1926 Rimskittle Book), oversize hardcover with paste-on-pictorial, color illustrations throughout by Ruth Caroline Eger. $65.00

JACOBI, Elizabeth P.
Adventures of Andrus, 1929 Macmillan, 125 pages, printed illustration on cover, color frontispiece and b/w illustrations by Kata Benedek. $15.00

JACOBS, Caroline E.
Blue Bonnet Keeps House, written with Lela H. Richards, 1916 Page, cloth-over-board cover. $20.00

S.W.F. Club, 1912 Goldsmith, hardcover, 251 pages. ($15.00 with dust jacket) $7.00

JACOBS, Joseph
Johnny Cake, 1933 Putnam, cloth-over-board cover, illustrated by Emma Brock. $25.00

JAGENDORF, M.
In the Days of Han, 1936 Suttonhouse, hardcover, 168 pages, artwork by E. Neumann. $25.00
Merry Pranks, 1938 Vanguard, first American edition, gray cloth-over-board cover, two-color illustrations by Fritz Eichenberg. $60.00

JAMES, Winifred
Adventures of Luisa in Mexico, 1930 Dutton first edition, blue hardcover, small, 123 pages, b/w illustrations by Oliver Herford. ($25.00 with dust jacket) $15.00

JAMISON, Mrs. C. V.
Lady Jane, (1891) 1903 edition Century, b/w engraving plate illustrations signed Birch, Redwood, and others. $15.00
Toinette's Philip, (1894) 1917 edition Century, cloth-over-board cover with gilt, 236 pages, 26 b/w illustrations by Reginald Birch. $20.00

JANE WITHERS Books
Jane Withers, Her Life Story, written by Eleanor Packer, 1936 Whitman, oversize, color illustrated paper cover, 32 pages, b/w photo illustrations on every page. $35.00

JANVIER, Thomas A.

Aztec Treasure House, 1890 Harper, decorated cloth-over-board cover, small, illustrations by Frederic Remington. $30.00

Aztec Treasure House, 1918 edition Harper, 272 pages, b/w drawings and two-color plates by Ben Kutcher. $15.00

Santa Fe's Partner, 1907 Harper, decorated cloth-over-board cover, frontispiece, b/w plates by Arthurs. $30.00

Santa Fe's Partner, 1907 Harper, hardback, 237 pages, frontispiece, b/w illustrations, series edition. $20.00

JEANS, T. T., see Series section, THRILLING NAVAL STORIES

JEFFRIES, Richard

Wood Magic, (1895) 1899 edition Longmans, burgundy cloth-over-board cover, gilt edged, small, 379 pages, illustrated endpapers, b/w illustrations by Eleanor Vere Boyle. $20.00

Wood Magic, undated Collins, ca. 1890s, burgundy cloth-over-board cover with gilt, small, 320 pages, b/w illustrations by Lorna Steele. $20.00

JENKINS, Dorothy H.

Children Make a Garden, 1936 Doubleday, cloth-over-board cover, illustrated endpapers, 70 pages, green/white and b/w illustrations by Rhea Wells. $20.00

JENKS, Albert Ernest

Childhood of Ji-Shib the Ojibwa, 1900 Mentzer Bush, pictorial cloth hardcover, 130 pages, illustrated by author. $60.00

Childhood of Ji-Shib the Ojibwa, 1900 Mentzer Bush, small, 96 pages, impressed illustration on cover, b/w illustrations by Stacy H. Wood. $20.00

JENKS, Tudor

Boys' Book of Exploration, 1913 Doubleday, decorated cloth-over-board cover, 441 pages, plates and maps. $25.00

Century World's Fair Book for Boys and Girls, 1893 Century, illustrated cloth-over-board cover, oversize, illustrations, maps, photos. (Reprinted in several sizes and editions.) Marked first editions, $110.00, later editions, $40.00

Galopoff, the Talking Pony, 1901 Altemus, cloth-over-board cover. $15.00

Little Rough Rider, 1904 edition Altemus, small, 222 pages, impressed and gilt illustrated cover, 3 b/w plate illustrations by Reginald Birch. $20.00

Magic Wand, ca. 1905 Altemus, illustrated boards, small, 110 pages, illustrated endpapers, b/w illustrations by John Neill. $70.00

Magician for One Day, ca. 1905 Altemus, illustrated boards, small, 107 pages, illustrated endpapers, b/w illustrations by John Neill. $70.00

Photography for Young People, 1908 Stokes, brown cloth-over-board cover, small, 328 pages, b/w illustrations and photos. $40.00

Prince and the Dragons, ca. 1905 Altemus, illustrated boards, small, 101 pages, illustrated endpapers, b/w illustrations by John Neill. $70.00

Rescue Syndicate, ca. 1905 Altemus, illustrated boards, small, 110 pages, illustrated endpapers, b/w illustrations by John Neill. $70.00

Talking Pony, 1901 Altemus, cloth-over-board cover. $20.00

Timothy's Magical Afternoon, ca. 1905 Altemus, illustrated boards, small, 98 pages, illustrated endpapers, b/w illustrations by John Neill. $70.00

JERROLD, Walter

Nonsense Nonsense!, undated Stokes (with 1907 handwritten gift inscription), oversize, cloth-over-board cover with paste-on-pictorial, illustrated endpapers, color illustrations throughout by Charles Robinson. $250.00

JEWETT, Sarah Orne

Betsy Leicester's Christmas, (1894) 1922 edition Houghton, hardcover, small, 68 pages, 4 b/w plate illustrations by Anna Whelan Betts. $15.00

JOHNSON, Annie Fellows, see Series section, COSY CORNER

JOHNSON, Gaylord

Sky Movies, 1922 Macmillan, small, illustrated paper-over-board cover, illustrated endpapers, photo illustrations. $30.00

Star People, 1921 Macmillan, small, illustrated paper-over-board cover, illustrated endpapers, b/w illustrations. $30.00

JOHNSON, Ida Lee

Bluebird House, 1928 Augustana, small, 89 pages, paper-on-board photo illustrated cover. $20.00

Lost Slipper, 1928 Augustana, small, 89 pages, paper-on-board photo illustrated cover. $20.00

JOHNSON, Margaret

Gay, a Shetland Sheepdog, 1948 Morrow, cloth-over-board cover, b/w illustrations by author. ($20.00 with dust jacket) $10.00

Joey and Patches, a Tale of Two Kittens, 1947 Morrow, cloth-over-board cover, b/w illustrations by author. ($20.00 with dust jacket) $10.00

JOHNSON, Martha, see Series section, ANNE BARTLETT

JOHNSON, Siddie Joe
New Town in Texas, 1942 Longmans, b/w illustrations by Margaret Ayer. $20.00
Texas The Land of the Tejas, 1943 Random House, cloth-over-board cover. $15.00

JOHNSTON, Annie Fellows, see Series section, JOHNSTON JEWEL STORIES
Miss Santa Claus of the Pullman, 1913 Page, small, 172 pages, color frontispiece, 8 b/w plates by Reginald Birch. $30.00
Story of the Red Cross, (a Little Colonel-related book) 1918 Page, decorated cloth-over-board cover, small, 85 pages, 6 b/w illustrations by John Goss. $20.00

JOHNSTON, Eileen
Jamie and the Dump Truck, 1943 Harper, small picture book, illustrated paper-on-board cover, illustrated endpapers, two-color illustrations by Ora Brian Edwards. $20.00
Jamie and the Fire Engine, 1940 Harper, small picture book, illustrated paper-on-board cover, illustrated endpapers, illustrations by Mrs. Elliott. $20.00

JOHNSTON, Isabel M.
Jeweled Toad, 1907 Bobbs Merrill, illustrated cloth-over-board cover, 211 pages, color illustrations throughout by W. W. Denslow. Hard-to-find. $200.00

JORDAN, Mildred
Shoo-Fly Pie, 1944 Knopf, first edition, 118 pages, paper-on-board cover, illustrated endpapers, b/w and color illustrations by Henry Pitz. $25.00

JOSEPH, Alfred Ward
Sondo, a Liberian Boy, (1936) 1939 edition Whitman, picture book, 32 pages, paper-on-board cover, map endpapers, b/w illustrations by Bernice Magnie. $25.00

JUDD, Alfred
School on the Steep, undated ca. 1926 edition Nelson, London, small, 198 pages, b/w illustrations by H. M. Brock. $20.00

JUDSON, Clara Ingram
Billy Robin and His Neighbors, (1917) 1920 Rand McNally, illustrated cover, small, 76 pages, color and b/w illustrations by Warner Carr. $35.00
Pioneer Girl, 1939 Rand McNally, small, 80 pages, color paper-on-board illustrated cover, map endpapers, b/w/red illustrations by Genevieve Foster. $20.00

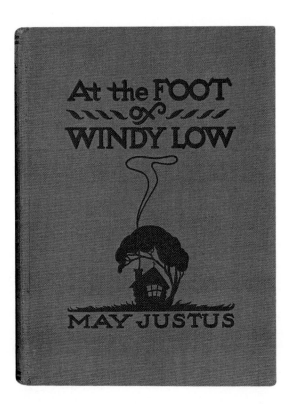

JUSTUS, May
At the Foot of Windy Low, 1930 Volland, 80 pages, green cloth-over-board cover with dark green print, full color endpapers and illustrations by Carrie Dudley. $45.00
Fiddler's Fair, 1945 Whitman, 32 page picture book, color illustrated paper-on-board cover, color endpapers, color illustrations by Christine Chisholm. $30.00
Gabby Gaffer, 1929 Volland first edition, 80 pages, green cover with gilt, 10 color plates by Carrie Dudley. $45.00
Jerry Jake Carries On, 1943 Whitman, hardback, illustrated by Christine Chisholm. $25.00

K

KAIGH-EUSTACE, Edyth
Jungle Babies, 1936 Rand McNally, Windermere edition, black cloth-over-board cover with paste-on-pictorial, color plates and b/w

illustrations by Paul Bransom and Don Nelson. $25.00

KAPLAN, A. O.
Baby's Biography, 1891 Brentano, oversize, cloth-over-board cover with gilt, 69 pages, color illustrations by Frances Brundage throughout. (Original box in good condition can double price.) $100.00

KARASZ, Mariska
See and Sew, Good Housekeeping Book, 1943 Stokes first edition, oblong, paper-over-board cover, illustrated endpapers, b/w/orange illustrations by Christine Engler. $15.00

KAUFFMAN, Andy and His Little Sister
Tigers and Things, 1929 Macmillan, small oblong picture book, color illustrated paper-over-cardboard cover, color illustrations by authors. $30.00

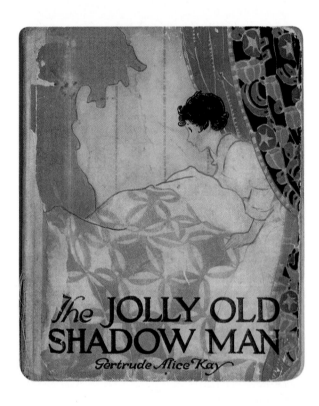

KAY, Gertrude, author-illustrator
Adventures in Geography, ca. 1930 Volland, oversize, orange cloth-over-board cover, illustrated endpapers, color illustrations by Kay. $40.00
Adventures in Geography, ca. 1941 edition Wise-Parslow, blue cloth-over-board cover, oversize, color illustrations by Kay. $25.00

Helping the Weatherman, 1920 Volland, hardcover, illustrated endpapers, color illustrations by Kay. $65.00
Jolly Old Shadow Man, 1920 Volland Sunny Book, small, illustrated paper-over-board cover, illustrated endpapers, color illustrations throughout by author. $65.00
Peter, Patter and Pixie, 1931 McBride, hardcover, oversize, illustrations by the author. ($50.00 with dust jacket) $25.00
Us Kids and the Circus, 1927 Volland first edition, color illustrated paper-over-board cover, illustrated endpapers, color illustrations throughout. (Original box doubles value.) $55.00

KEELER, Charles
Elfin Songs of Sunland, 1920 Live Oak, blue cloth-over-board cover, oversize, 115 pages, decorations by Louise Keller. $20.00

KELLAND, Clarence Budington
Catty Atkins, Riverman, 1921 Harper, print illustrated cover, 4 b/w plates. $15.00
Mark Tidd in Sicily, 1928 Harper, print illustrated cover, 4 b/w plates. $15.00

KELLY, Eric
Christmas Nightingale, Christmas Stories of Poland, 1939 Macmillan, hardcover, illustrated by Marguerite de Angeli. $20.00
Golden Star of Halich, 1931 Macmillan, hardcover, 3 color plates plus b/w illustrations by Angela Pruszynska. ($15.00 with dust jacket) $10.00
Hand in the Picture, 1947 Lippincott, hardcover, 243 pages. $15.00

KELSEY, Vera
Maria Rosa, 1942 Doubleday, first edition, oversize picture book, color illustrations by Candido Portinari. ($60.00 with dust jacket) $40.00

KENDALL, Oswald
Voyage of the Martin Connor, (1916) 1931 edition Houghton Riverside Bookshelf, color paste-on-pictorial cover, illustrated endpapers, 5 color plates by Donald Teague. $20.00

KENNEDY, Howard
Red Man's Wonder Book, 1931 Dutton, blue cloth-over-board cover, illustrations by George Cumine. $20.00

KENT, Karlene
Little Black Eyes, 1927 Macmillan, color frontispiece, b/w illustrations by Carroll Snell. $20.00

KETO, E.
Little Tee-Hee's Big Day, 1936 Grosset & Dunlap, paper-over-board cover, illustrated by author. $20.00
Pronto and Tonto, 1937 Grosset, small picture book, color illustrated paper-on-board cover, color endpapers, color illustrations by author. $20.00
Ting-Ling and Mee-Too, 1937 Grosset, small picture book, color illustrated paper-on-board cover, color endpapers, color illustrations by author. $20.00

KEYES, Mary Willard
Toplofty, 1931 Longmans, cloth-over-board cover, 270 pages, b/w illustrations by Pelagie Doane. $20.00
Toplofty, undated edition Grosset, orange cloth-over-board cover, 270 pages, b/w illustrations by Pelagie Doane. $10.00

KIEFFER, Harry
Recollections of a Drummer-Boy, ca. 1888 Houghton, green cloth-over-board cover, b/w illustrations throughout. $20.00

KING, C. F. Jr.
Boy's Vacation Abroad, 1906 Clark, red cloth-over-board cover with gilt, b/w photo illustrations. $15.00

KING, Edna Knowles
Doll's Family Album, 1937 Whitman, cloth-over-board cover, b/w photo illustrations. $25.00

KING, Marian
Kees, (1930) 1937 edition Whitman, oversize picture book, 79 pages, color paper-on-board cover, color endpapers, color illustrations by Elizabeth Enright. $35.00
Kees and Kleintje, (1934) 1938 edition Whitman, oversize picture book, 80 pages, color paper-on-board cover, color endpapers, color illustrations by Elizabeth Enright. $35.00

KINGMAN, Lee
Pierre Pidgeon, 1943 Houghton first edition, brown cloth-over-board cover, oversize, 48 pages, lithograph illustrations by Arnold Edwin Bare. $45.00

KINGSLEY, Charles
Madam How and Lady Why, 1893 Macmillan, cloth-over-board cover with gilt illustration, small, 321 pages, b/w illustrations throughout. $30.00

KINGSLEY, Florence
Those Brewster Children, 1910 Dodd Mead, first edition, illustrated tan cloth-over-board cover, small, 214 pages, b/w illustrations by E. H. Chamberlain. $20.00

KINGSTON, William
Mark Seaworth, undated Dutton ca.1880s, green cloth-over-board cover with gilt decoration, small, 384 pages, b/w illustrations by J. Absolon. $20.00
Peter the Whaler, ca. 1930 edition Juvenile Productions, blue cloth-over-board cover, small, color frontispiece. $25.00

KIPLING, Rudyard
Brushwood Boy, 1907 edition Doubleday, small, 73 pages, 12 color illustrations by F. H. Townsend. $40.00
Elephant's Child, 1942 edition Garden City, oversize picture book, illustrations by Rojankovsky. $40.00.
Incarnation of Krishna Mulvaney, 1899 edition Doubleday, hardcover, small, 95 pages. $30.00
Kipling's Stories for Boys, 1931 Cupples Leon, orange cloth-over-board cover, 499 pages, b/w illustrations by H. Hastings. ($20.00 with dust jacket.) $15.00
Land and Sea Tales for Boys and Girls, 1923 edition Doubleday, hardcover, 322 pages. $30.00

Second Jungle Book, 1895 edition Century Co., reddish orange cloth-over-board cover, titled in gilt with decorations on spine & vignette on both covers, textual illustrations by John Lockwood Kipling. First American edition. $65.00

Thy Servant a Dog: Told by Boots, 1931 edition McMillan, cloth-over-board cover. $25.00

KIRBY, Mary and **Elizabeth**

Aunt Martha's Corner Cupboard, (1928) 1936 Whitman edition, small, 125 pages, color paste-on-pictorial cover, color illustrated endpapers, color illustrations by Matilda Breuer. $25.00

KIRK, Ellen Olney

Dorothy Deane, 1898 Houghton, impressed and gilt cover, 325 pages, 4 b/w plate illustrations. $10.00

Dorothy and Her Friends, 1899 Houghton, 6 b/w plate illustrations. $10.00

KIRKMAN, Winifred

Boy Editor, 1913 Houghton, impressed cover, 231 pages, b/w frontispiece by H. J. Cue. $10.00

KIRKWOOD, Edith Brown

Animal Children, 1913 Volland, color illustrated paper-over-board cover, narrow, illustrated endpapers, color illustrations throughout by M. T. Ross. $50.00

Animal Children, undated edition Wise, cloth-over-board cover, illustrated endpapers, color illustrations throughout by M. T. Ross. $25.00

KNIGHT, Clayton

Quest of the Golden Condor, 1946 Knopf, 346 pages, printed illustration on cover, b/w/brown illustrations by author. $20.00

Secret of the Buried Tomb, 1948 Knopf, hardcover, illustrations by author. ($20.00 with dust jacket) $10.00

KNIGHT, Marjorie

Alexander's Birthday, 1940 Dutton, cloth-over-board cover, illustrated endpapers, b/w and color illustrations by Howard Simon. ($70.00 with dust jacket) $40.00

Alexander's Christmas Eve, 1938 Dutton, cloth-over-board cover, small, 93 pages, color endpapers, b/w and color illustrations by Howard Simon. $35.00

Doll House at World's End, 1936 Dutton, lst edition, hardcover, illustrated by Clinton Knight. ($40.00 with dust jacket) $20.00

KNOBEL, Elizabeth

When Little Thoughts Go Rhyming, 1916 Rand

McNally, rose cloth-over-board cover with paste-on-pictorial, 96 pages, poetry, color and b/w illustrations by Maginel Enright. $30.00

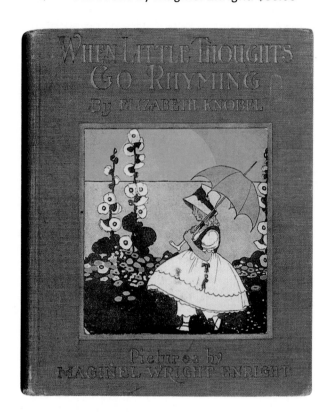

KNOX, Esther Melbourne

Swift Flies the Falcon, 1939 edition Hale, b/w illustrations by Ruth King. $10.00

KNOX, Kathleen

Queen Dora, undated ca. 1890 James Pott, print and gilt illustration on cover, b/w engraving illustrations by C. Paterson $15.00

KOEHLER-BROMAN, Mela, artist

When Grandma Was a Little Girl, text by Ingrid Smith, undated ca. 1930s, Duell, Sloan and Pearce, oversize picture book, color illustrated paper-over-board cover, full-page color illustrations. $45.00

KORDA, Alexander

Alexander Korda's Story of the Thief of Bagdad, 1940 Saalfield, oversize, color illustrated thin cardboard cover, 64 pages with b/w line drawing illustrations based on the movie. $20.00

KOS (Baroness Dombrowski)

Abdallah and the Donkey, 1928 Macmillan, green cloth-over-board cover, 155 pages, color plates by the author. $50.00

KRAKEMSIDES, Baron
Careless Chicken, ca.1924 undated Warne, small, paper-over-board cover with paste-on-pictorial, illustrated endpapers, 48 pages, 16 color plates by Harry Neilson. ($70.00 with dust jacket) $40.00

KRAUSS, Ruth
Backward Day, 1950 Harper, small picture book, color illustrated cover and three-color illustrations by Marc Simont. $15.00
Big World, 1949 Schuman, picture book, color illustrated paper-on-board cover, illustrated endpapers, color illustrations by Marc Simont. $20.00
Carrot Seed, 1945 Harper, small picture book, color illustrated cover, brown/yellow illustrations by Crockett Johnson. $30.00
Growing Story, 1947 Harper, oversize picture book, color illustrated cover, three-color illustrations by Phyllis Rowland. $20.00
Happy Day, 1949 Harper, oversize picture book, illustrated paper-on-board cover, b/w illustrations by Marc Simont. $20.00

KRISTOFFERSEN, Eva M.
Bee in Her Bonnet, 1944 Crowell first edition, hardcover, illustrations by Helen Sewell. ($35.00 with dust jacket) $20.00
Cyclone Goes A-Viking, 1939 Whitman, oversize, 94 pages, color illustrated paper-on-board cover, color endpapers, color illustrations by Hedvig Collin. $25.00
Hans Christian of Elsinore, 1937 Jr. Literary Guild, illustrated cloth-over-board cover, oversize, 80 pages, color illustrations by Hedvig Collin. $25.00
Merry Matchmakers, 1940 Whitman, oversize, 95 pages, color illustrated paper-on-board cover, color endpapers, color illustrations by Hedvig Collin. $25.00

KUNHARDT, Dorothy
Lucky Mrs. Ticklefeather, 1935 Harcourt, oversize oblong picture book, illustrated paper-on-board cover, b/w/blue illustrations by author. $25.00
Now Open the Box, 1934 Harcourt, oversize oblong picture book, illustrated paper-on-board cover, b/red/yellow illustrations by author. $25.00
Once There Was a Little Boy, 1946 Viking, hardcover, illustrations by Helen Sewell. $25.00
Pat the Bunny, undated ca.1940 Whitman, small spiral-bound "touch" picture book, illustrated by author. $35.00

KUTZER, Ernst
Tallie, Tillie, and Tag, 1932 Whitman, small oblong picture book, color paste-on-pictorial cover, color illustrations by author. $35.00

KYLE, Elizabeth
Gilbert the Page, 1923 Oxford, small, 95 pages, color paste-on-illustration on cover, illustrated endpapers, color frontispiece, b/w line drawings. $20.00

———— *⤙* **L** *⤚* ————

LABORDE, E. D.
Tales of the Wind King, 1929 Oxford, map endpapers, 8 color plates by Marjorie Whittington, also photo illustrations. $20.00

LAFLESCHE, Francis
Middle Five, (1900) 1914 edition Small Maynard, small, 227 pages, illustrated cover, frontispiece by Angel de Cora. $15.00

LAMB, Charles
Dream Children and Child Angel, 1929 Dent, chap-book edition with pictorial paper self-wrapper, small, 28 pages, b/w illustrations by Waudby. $15.00

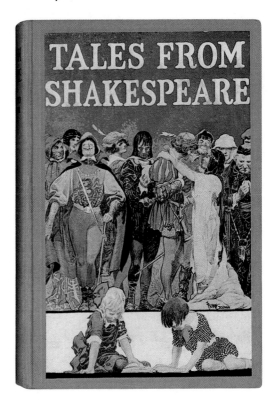

Ca. 1925 edition

LAMB, Charles and Mary
Tales from Shakespeare, 1909 Dutton first trade edition, blue hardcover with gilt-stamped lettering and illustration, 12 color plates by Arthur Rackham. $120.00

Tales from Shakespeare, (1807) undated ca. 1915 edition Scribner, gilt decorated cover, 324 pages, 20 color plates by Norman M. Price. $35.00

Tales from Shakespeare, ca. 1925 edition Winston, orange hardcover with paste-on-pictorial, illustrated endpapers, 4 color plates and 8 b/w plates by Frank Godwin. $25.00

LAMBERT, Janet, see Series section, PENNY PARRISH

LAMPREY, L.
Children of Ancient Rome, 1930 edition Little Brown, illustrated cover, 262 pages, b/w drawings by Edna Hart-Hubon. $10.00

In the Days of the Guild, 1918 Stokes, 291 pages, color paste-on-illustration and gilt lettering on cover, 4 color plates by Florence Gardiner, b/w drawings by Mabel Hart. $25.00

LANG, Andrew
Animal Story Book, 1896 Longmans, blue cloth-over-board cover with gilt illustration, gilt edged, 400 pages, illustrations by H. J. Ford. $110.00

Blue Poetry Book, poetry collection of other poets, edited by Lang, 1891 Longmans Green, London, limited edition of 150, oversize, 350 pages, illustrations by H. J. Ford and Lancelot Speed. $600.00

Blue Poetry Book, 1891 Longmans Green, London, trade edition, illustrations by H. J. Ford and Lancelot Speed. $100.00

Magic Ring and Other Stories from the Fairy Books, 1911 edition Longmans, hardcover, color frontispiece, b/w illustrations by Henry Ford. $35.00

Tartan Tales from Andrew Lang, edited, 1928 Longmans, impressed design on cloth-over-board cover, b/w/yellow plates by Mahlon Blaine. $35.00.

True Story Book, 1893 Longmans first edition, small, 337 pages, cloth-over-board cover with gilt, b/w illustrations by H. J. Ford. $120.00

LANG, Don
Strawberry Roan, 1946 Grosset, hardcover, b/w illustrations by Gertrude Howe. $20.00

Tramp, the Sheep Dog, 1943 Grosset, color illustrated hardcover, color illustrations by Kurt Wiese. $20.00

LANGSTAFF, John Brett
From Now to Adam, 1928 Harper, hardcover, oversize, 190 pages, color plates by Luxor Price. $25.00

LARNED, Trowbridge
Reynard the Fox & Other Fables, 1925 Volland, 9

inches tall, color paper-over-board cover, illustrated endpapers, color illustrations throughout by John Rae. $50.00

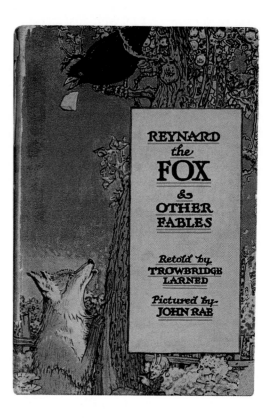

LATHROP, Dorothy
Made-to-Order Stories, 1925 Harcourt, decorated cloth-over-board cover, 263 pages, color frontispiece, b/w illustrations by Dorothy Canfield. $35.00

Presents for Lupe, 1934 Macmillan, oversize, cloth-over-board cover with paste-on-illustration, color illustrations by author. $60.00

LAUGHLIN, Clara
Where It All Comes True in France, 1929 Houghton, cloth-over-board cover, color frontispiece, b/w illustrations by Decie Merwin. $30.00

LAVER, James
Tommy Apple, 1935 Jonathan Cape, London, cloth-over-board cover, 95 pages, tinted photo illustrations by Henry Rox. $25.00

LAVERTY, Maura
Gold of Glenaree, 1941 Longmans first edition, cloth-over-board cover, 192 pages, illustrated endpapers, b/w illustrations by Betty Morgan Bowen. ($25.00 with dust jacket) $12.00

Never No More, 1942 Templegate, cloth-over-board cover, 284 pages. ($15.00 with dust jacket) $10.00

LAWRENCE, Isabelle
Gift of the Golden Cup, 1946 Bobbs Merrill first edition, cloth-over-board cover with gilt, 288 pages, b/w illustrations by Charles John. ($15.00 with dust jacket) $10.00

LAWRENCE, Josephine, see Series section, TWO LITTLE FELLOWS
Rosemary, 1922 Cupples Leon, 310 pages, oval color paste-on-illustration and gilt lettering on cover, 4 b/w plate illustrations by Thelma Gooch. $15.00

LAWSON, Marie
Sea is Blue, 1946 Viking first edition, hardcover, 126 pages, plates and drawings by author. $55.00

LAWSON, Robert, 1892-1957
At That Time, 1947 Viking first edition, oversize, 126 pages, illustrations by author. ($60.00 with dust jacket) $40.00
Fabulous Flight, 1949 Little Brown first edition, cloth-over-board cover, illustrations by author. ($70.00 with dust jacket) $50.00
I Discover Columbus, 1941 Little Brown first edition, cloth-over-board cover, illustrations by author. ($50.00 with dust jacket) $30.00
Mr. Twigg's Mistake, 1947 Little Brown, hardcover, illustrated endpapers, b/w illustrations by author. $40.00

LEAF, Munro
Aesop's Fables, 1941 Heritage Press first edition, oversize, cloth-over-board cover with gilt lettering, illustrated by Robert Lawson. ($100.00 with dust jacket) $50.00
Arithmetic Can be Fun, 1949 Lippincott first edition, oversize, 64 pages, Leaf cartoon illustrations throughout. $30.00
Boy Who Used to be Scared of the Dark, 1948 Random House first edition, hardcover, Illustrated by Frances Hunter. $45.00
Fair Play, 1939 Stokes, oversize, blue cloth-over-board cover, 94 pages, red/b/w illustrations by author. $45.00
History Can be Fun, 1950 Lippincott, Leaf cartoon illustrations throughout. $20.00
Let's Do Better, 1945 Lippincott, oversize, hardcover, illustrations by author. ($25.00 with dust jacket) $15.00
Noodle, 1937 Stokes first edition, illustrated tan cloth-over-board cover, oversize oblong, b/w/brown illustrations by Ludwig Bemelmans. $35.00
Robert Francis Weatherbee, 1935 Stokes, small, blue cloth-over-board cover. $60.00

Safety Can be Fun, 1938 Stokes first edition, oversize, illustrated endpapers, Leaf cartoon illustrations throughout. $30.00
Story of Simpson and Sampson, 1941 Viking first edition, oversize, illustrations by Robert Lawson. $45.00
War-Time Handbook for Young Americans, 1942 Stokes first edition, hardcover, illustrated. $35.00

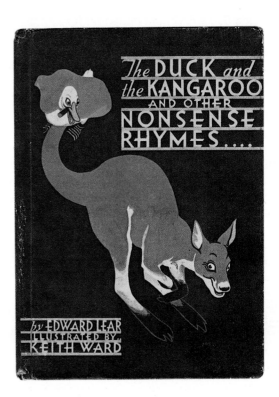

LEAR, Edward
Duck and the Kangaroo and Other Nonsense Rhymes, 1932 edition Whitman, small, color illustrated paper-over-board cover, color illustrations throughout by Keith Ward. $35.00
Nonsense ABCs, (1918) 1936 edition McNally, Bye-Lo series, small, illustrated paper-over-board cover, color illustrations by M. L. and W. C. Wheeler. $30.00

LEAVITT, Ann H.
Three Little Indians, 1937 Rand McNally, small picture book, color illustrated paper-over-board cover, b/w and color illustrations by H. C. and Lucille Holling. $35.00

LECKY, Walter
Mr. Billy Buttons, 1896 Benziger Bros., 2nd edition, illustrated cloth-over-board cover, 274 pages. $10.00

LEE, Mrs. Frank
Boy and His Box, 1909 David Cook, Elgin, gilt lettering on cover, 93 pages, full-page b/w illustrations. $15.00

LEE, Tina
Fun With Paper Dolls, 1949 Doubleday, color illustrated paper-over-board cover, foldout endpaper with nativity scene to cut out, 64 pages, color illustrations by Manning Lee. With endpaper intact, $30.00 Without endpaper foldout, $15.00
What to Do Now, 1946 Doubleday, color illustrated paper-over-board cover, illustrations and plans for cut-out projects, color illustrations by Manning Lee. $15.00

LEET, Frank, see PEAT, Fern
Animal Caravan, 1930 Saalfield, oversize, color illustrations by Fern Bisel Peat. $60.00
Hop, Skip and Jump, Three Little Kittens, 1936 oversize, color illustrated paper-over-board cover, color illustrations throughout by Fern Bisel Peat. ($95.00 with design-matched dust jacket) $60.00
Purr and Miew, 1931 Saalfield, oversize picture book, paper-over-board cover, 60 pages, color plates by Fern Bisel Peat. $55.00

LEFEVRE, Felicite
Cock, the Mouse and the Little Red Hen, 1907 Jacobs, small hardcover picture book, 24 color plates by Tony Sarg. $75.00

Cock, the Mouse and the Little Red Hen, undated ca. 1920 edition MacRae, small picture book, 103 pages, 24 color plates by Tony Sarg. $35.00
Cock, the Mouse and the Little Red Hen, 1931 edition Saalfield, oversize picture book, 38 pages, color illustrations by Fern Bisel Peat. $50.00
Soldier Boy, 1926 Greenberg, small, color and b/w illustrations by Tony Sarg. ($75.00 with dust jacket) $50.00
Soldier Boy, undated Whitman edition, small, color and b/w illustrations by Tony Sarg. $40.00

LeGRAND, Henderson
Augustus Saves a Ship, ca. 1945 edition Grosset, oversize, hardcover, 128 pages, illustrations by author. $20.00
Cats for Kansas, 1948 Abingdon, orange cloth-over-board cover, illustrations by author. $20.00

LEIGHTON, John Jay
Robert Royalton and His Covered Wagon, 1928 Rochester, red cloth-over-board cover with gilt, small, b/w illustrations. $15.00

LEMON, Mark
Legends of Number Nip, 1864 Macmillan, cloth-over-board cover with gilt, small, 140 pages, 6 b/w illustrations. $35.00

LENSKI, Lois, see Series section, LOIS LENSKI LITTLE SERIES
A-Going' Westward, 1937 Stokes first edition, brown cloth-over-board cover. ($100.00 with dust jacket) $55.00
Benny and the Penny, 1931 Alfred Knopf, oblong picture book, color illustrations throughout by author. $50.00
Blueberry Corners, 1940 Lippincott, cloth-over-board cover, illustrated endpapers, illustrations throughout by Lenski. $50.00
Blue Ridge Billy, 1946 Lippincott, cloth-over-board cover, illustrations throughout by Lenski. ($60.00 with dust jacket) $35.00
Boom Town Boy, 1948 Lippincott, cloth-over-board cover, illustrations throughout by Lenski. $35.00
Indian Captive, 1941 Stokes first edition, cloth-over-board cover, illustrations throughout by Lenski. $45.00
Judy's Journey, 1947 Lippincott, oversize, cloth-over-board cover, illustrations throughout by Lenski. ($65.00 with dust jacket) $30.00
Little Auto, 1934 Walck, (see Series section for other editions) small easy-read picture book, b/w/red illustrations throughout by author. $45.00
Little Engine that Could, Watty Piper, ca. 1930 Platt Munk, Never Grow Old Stories series, small, color

illustrated paper-over-board cover with cloth spine, illustrated endpapers, color and b/w illustrations throughout by Lois Lenski. $45.00

Little Fire Engine, 1946 Walck. $25.00

Little Girl of Nineteen Hundred, 1928 Stokes first edition, red cover with paste-on-illustration, illustrations by author. $95.00

My Friend the Cow, 1946 National Dairy Council, paper cover, promotional advertising story. $20.00

Phoebe Fairchild, 1936 Stokes, oversize, illustrations throughout by Lenski. $55.00

Puritan Adventure, 1944 Lippincott, cloth-over-board cover, illustrated endpapers, illustrations throughout by Lenski. $45.00

Read to Me Story Book, 1947 Crowell, orange cloth-over-board cover, b/w illustrations throughout by Lenski. $30.00

Strawberry Girl, 1945 Lippincott, cloth-over-board cover, illustrations throughout by Lenski. $35.00

Texas Tomboy, 1950 Lippincott first edition, oversize, tan cloth-over-board cover, illustrations throughout by Lenski. $50.00

LESTER, Pauline, see Series section, MARJORIE DEAN

LEVINGER, Elma Ehrlich
New Land, (1920) 1927 edition Bloch, small, printed illustration on cover, 175 pages. $20.00

Playmates in Egypt, 1920 Jewish Publication Society, small, impressed cover design, 130 pages. $25.00

LEWIS, Charles D.
Waterboys and Their Cousins, 1918 Lippincott, brown cloth-over-board cover, small, b/w illustrations by Suydam. $15.00

LEWIS, Elizabeth Foreman
Ho-Ming, Girl of New China, 1934 Winston, b/w illustrated endpapers, color frontispiece, b/w illustrations by Kurt Wiese. $10.00

LIDE, Alice Alison
Aztec Drums, 1938 Longmans first edition, small, 142 pages, illustrated endpapers, b/w illustrations by Carlos Sanchez. $30.00

Princess Yucatan, 1939 Longmans first edition, small, 187 pages, illustrated endpapers, b/w illustrations by Carlos Sanchez. $30.00

Yinka-Tu the Yak, 1938 Viking, oversize picture book, color illustrated paper-over-board cover, color end papers, color illustrations throughout by Kurt Wiese. $35.00

LIDE, Alice Alison and **ALISON, Annie H.**
Tambalo, 1930 Beckley-Cardy, Chicago, small, 160 pages, color frontispiece by Kathryn Roller, photo illustrations throughout. $20.00

LIDE, Alice Alison and **JOHANSEN, Margaret Alison**
Ood-Le-Uk the Wanderer, 1930 Little Brown, 265 pages, color frontispiece, b/w full-page illustrations by Raymond Lufkin. $20.00

Thord Firetooth, 1937 Lothrop, 226 pages, color endpapers, b/w illustrations by Henry Pitz. $20.00

LILJENCRANTZ, Ottilie J.
Thrall of Leif the Lucky, 1902 McClurg, impressed illustration on cover, 354 pages, color frontispiece, b/w designs by Troy and Margaret West Kinney. $20.00

LINDMAN, Maj, see Series section, SNIPP SNAPP SNURR
Fire Eye, 1950 Whitman, illustrated paper-over-board cover, 32 pages, color illustrations by author. $35.00

Snowboot, Son of Fire Eye, 1950 Whitman, first printing. $35.00

LINDSAY, Maud
Jock Barefoot, 1939 Lothrop, color illustrated cover, 177 pages, b/w illustrations by Jean Linton. $20.00

Mother Stories and More Mother Stories, 1944 edition Platt Munk, orange cloth-over-board cover, color frontispiece, b/w illustrations. $35.00

LIPMAN, Michael
Chatterlings in Wordland, (Volland) 1935 Wise-Parslow revised edition, 96 pages, orange cover, full color Golden Hour Rainbow edition endpapers, color illustrations by author. $45.00

LIPS, Julius E.
Tents in the Wilderness, 1942 Stokes first edition, 297 pages, b/w illustrated endpapers, b/w illustrations by Kurt Wiese. $20.00

LITTEN, Frederic Nelson
Air Trails North, 1939 Dodd, hardcover. $15.00
Pilot of the High Sierras, 1937 Dodd, hardcover. $20.00
Pilot of the North Country, 1940 Dodd, hardcover. $15.00
Transatlantic Pilot, 1940 Dodd, hardcover. $15.00

LITTLE, Frances
House of the Misty Star, 1915 Century, impressed illustrated cover w/gilt lettering, 270 pages, b/w full-page illustrations by Arthur Becker. $20.00

LIVINGSTONE, W. P.
Hero of the Lake, 1933 Hodder & Stoughton, blue cloth-over-board cover with paste-on-pictorial, small, 222 pages, photos and b/w illustrations. $15.00

LLOYD, Hugh, see Series section, HAL KEEN

LLOYD, John
Red Head, 1903 Dodd Mead, first edition, decorated green cloth-over-board cover, decorated text pages, b/w illustrations by Reginald Birch. $35.00

LOCKLIN, Anne Littlefield
Tidewater Tales, 1942 Viking, hardcover, color illustrated endpapers, b/w illustrations by Rafaello Busoni. $15.00

LOCKWOOD, Myna
Delecta Ann, 1941 Dutton, hardcover, 335 pages, illustrated endpapers, b/w illustrations by author. $15.00
Free River, 1942 Dutton, hardcover, 255 pages, illustrated endpapers, b/w illustrations by author. $15.00

LOMEN, Helen and **FLACK, Marjorie**
Taktuk an Arctic Boy, 1928 Doubleday, hardcover, small, 139 pages, map endpapers, color frontispiece, b/w illustrations by Flack. $20.00

LONDON, Jack
Burning Daylight, 1910 Macmillan, green cloth-over-board cover, frontispiece. $80.00
Cruise of the Dazzler, 1902 Century, St. Nicholas Books edition, small, 250 pages, impressed color illustrated cover, 6 b/w plates signed Burns. $20.00
Dutch Courage and Other Stories , 1922 Macmillan, cloth-over-board cover, hard-to-find. $65.00

LORING, Jules
West We Go, 1946 Putnam, hardcover, small, 198 pages. ($25.00 with dust jacket) $15.00

LOVELACE, Maud Hart, see Series section, BETSY-TACY

LOVELAND, Seymour
Illustrated Bible Story Book, 1923 Rand McNally, oversize, cloth-over-board cover, illustrations by Milo Winter. $65.00

LOVELL, Josephine, see Series section, EIGHT LITTLE INDIANS
Eight Little Indians, 1936 Platt & Munk, red cloth-over-board cover, collection of stories original-

ly printed as series with original illustrations, illustrated endpapers, b/w and color illustrations by Roger Vernam. $30.00

LOVETT, Eva
Billy Stories, 1901 Taylor, green cloth-over-board cover, 218 pages, small, b/w illustrations by Farnsworth Drew. $20.00

LOWE, Edith
Let's Play Fireman, 1939 Whitman, small, color illustrations by Ruth Newton. $25.00
Let's Play Postman, 1939 Whitman, small, color illustrations by Ruth Newton. $25.00
Let's Play Store, 1939 Whitman, small, color illustrations by Ruth Newton. $25.00

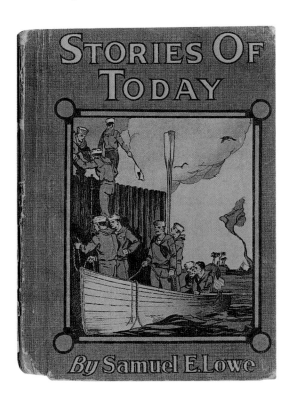

LOWE, Samuel E.
Stories of Today, (1920) undated edition ca. 1930s Whitman, small, 53+ pages, illustrated paper-over-board cover, 3 color plates by Neil O'Keeffe. $15.00

LOWNSBERY, Eloise
Boy Knight of Reims, 1927 Houghton, blue cloth-over-board cover with gilt, b/w illustrations by Elizabeth Wolcott. $30.00
Marta, the Doll, 1945 Longmans first edition, hardcover, small, 118 pages, b/w/red illustrations by Marya Werten. $15.00
Out of the Flame, 1931 Longmans first edition, gilt cover design, 352 pages, illustrated endpa-

pers, b/w illustrations by Elizabeth Tyler Wolcott. $15.00

LOWREY, Janette Sebring
Annunciata and the Shepherds, 1938 Harper, small, 3-color wood engraving illustrations by Willard Clark. $20.00
Rings on the Fingers, 1941 Harper first edition, 192 pages, b/w and color illustrations by Janice Holland. $20.00
Tap-A-Tan!, 1942 Harper first edition, small, green cloth-over-board cover, 98 pages, illustrated endpapers, b/w and color illustrations by Masha. $25.00

LUCAS, Jannette May
First the Flower, Then the Fruit, 1943 Lippincott, oversize, color illustrated paper-over-board cover, 69 pages, color illustrated endpapers, color and b/w illustrations by Helene Carter. ($25.00 with same-as-cover dust jacket) $20.00
Fruits of the Earth, 1942 Lippincott, oversize, color illustrated paper-over-board cover, 68 pages, color illustrated endpapers, color and b/w illustrations by Helene Carter. ($25.00 with same-as-cover dust jacket) $20.00
Where Did Your Garden Grow?, 1939 Lippincott, oversize, color illustrated paper-over-board cover, 64 pages, color illustrated endpapers, color and b/w illustrations by Helene Carter. ($25.00 with same-as-cover dust jacket) $20.00

LUCAS, Marie Seymour
Granny's Story Box, undated Dutton ca. 1890s, color illustrated paper-over-board cover, 15 color plates, 100 b/w illustrations. $85.00

LUCIA, Rosa, see Series section, PETER AND POLLY

LYNCH, Maude Dutton
Magic Clothes Pins, 1926 Houghton, cloth-over-board cover, illustrated by Benjamin. $30.00

LYNCH, Patricia
Donkey Goes Visiting, 1936 Dutton first edition, orange cloth-over-board cover, small, color plates and b/w illustrations by George Altendorf. ($40.00 with dust jacket) $25.00

—————— →→ **M** ←← ——————

MacDONALD, George
Princess and Curdie, 1908 Lippincott, red hardcover with printed illustration and gilt letter-

ing, 12 color plates by Maria Kirk, 305 pages. $50.00

MacDONALD, Zillah, see NEWTON, Ruth

MacINTYRE, Elisabeth
Ambrose Kangaroo, 1942 Scribner, oblong picture book, color illustrated paper-over-board cover, color illustrations throughout by author. $35.00

MACK, Robert Ellice
When All is Young, undated (inscription date 1888) Dutton-Lister, color paper-on-board cover, 16 chromolithograph illustrations by Harriet Bennett. $120.00

MacKAYE, Arthur
Viking Prince, 1928 Page, green cloth-over-board cover, b/w illustrations by A. Thieme. ($30.00 with dust jacket) $15.00

MacKINSTRY, Elizabeth
Fairy Alphabet as Used by Merlin, 1933 Viking, illustrated cloth-over-board cover, picture book, b/w illustrations by author. $30.00

MacNEIL, Marion Gill
Monty Marine, 1943 Oxford, small picture book, illustrated cloth-over-board cover, color illustrations by Frank Dobias. $25.00

Sailor Jack, 1942 Oxford, small picture book, two-color illustrations by Robert MacNeil. $30.00

MADDEN, Eva
Stephen, a Story of the Little Crusaders, 1901 Crowell, paste-on-pictorial cloth-over-board cover, 162 pages, small, b/w frontispiece by Copeland. $20.00

MALCOLMSON, Anne
Song of Robin Hood, 1947 Houghton, oversize, hardcover, 128 pages, illustrations by Virginia Burton. $75.00
Yankee Doodle's Cousins, 1941 Houghton, cloth-over-board cover, 267 pages, illustrated by Robert McCloskey. $45.00

MALKUS, Alida Sims
Dragonfly of Zuni, 1928 Harcourt, print illustrated cloth-over-board cover, 213 pages, illustrated endpapers, b/w illustrations by Erick Berry. ($20.00 with dust jacket) $15.00
Eastward Sweeps the Current, 1937 Winston, cloth-over-board cover, illustrated endpapers with map, 387 pages, b/w illustrations by Dan Sweeney. $15.00
Silver Lama, 1939 Winston, oversize, silver cloth-over-board cover, 108 pages, color illustrated endpapers, color and b/w illustrations by author. $20.00

MALOT, Hector
Little Sister, 1928 Cupples, first edition, blue cloth-over-board cover with paste-on-illustration, 303 pages, illustrations by Thelma Gooch. $35.00
Nobody's Girl, (1922) 1929 edition Cupples Leon, 301 pages, color plate illustrations by Thelma Gooch. $20.00

MALOY, Lois
Swift Thunder of the Prairie, 1942 Scribner, 74 pages, b/w and color illustrations throughout by author. $20.00
Toby's House, 1946 Grosset, small, illustrated by author. $20.00

MALVERN, Corrine
Tiny Tots, Simple Objects, 1948 Whitman, hardcover, oversize, 12 pages, color illustrations. $20.00

MANN, E. B.
Comanche Kid, 1940 Blakiston, cloth-over-board cover, 278 pages. ($20.00 with dust jacket) $12.00

MANSBRIDGE, Arthur
Ali Baba and the Forty Thieves, undated ca. 1920s

edition Renwick of Otley, London, color illustrated paper-over-boards cover, contains three short stories, two written and illustrated by Mansbridge, the third an easy-read uncredited story. $15.00

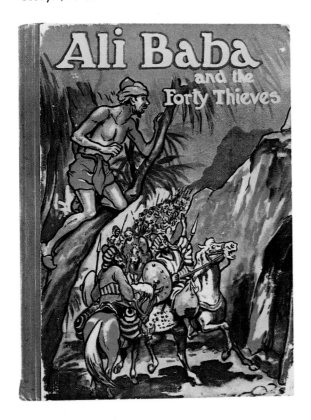

MARGE (Marjorie Henderson Buell)
Little Lulu and Her Pals, 1939 McKay, oversize, illustrated hardcover, color illustrations. ($75.00 in dust jacket) $55.00
Oh, Little Lulu!, 1943 McKay, oversize, illustrated hardcover, color illustrations. ($75.00 in dust jacket) $55.00

MARIANA (Foster)
Miss Flora McFlimsey's Christmas Eve, 1949 Lothrop, small, easy reader picture book, 40 pages, color illustrated hardcover, color and b/w illustrations by author. $15.00

MARIE, Queen of Romania
Magic Doll of Romania, 1929 Stokes, 319 pages, cloth-over-board cover with paste-on-illustration, 10 color plates by Maud and Miska Petersham. $50.00

MARKS, Edward N.
Our Vegetable Food, 1867 Nelson, oversize, 22 pages, gilt decorated cover, woodblock color prints. $250.00

MARRIOTT, Alice
Winter-Telling Stories, 1947 Sloane first edition, color illustrated paper-over-board cover, oversize, 84 pages, illustrated by Ronald Whitehorse. $35.00

MARRIOTTI, Jean
Tales of Poindi, 1938 Domino, oversize, cloth-over-board cover, 64 pages, b/w illustrations by F. Rojankovsky. $20.00

MARRYATT, Captain
Masterman Ready, 1928 Harper, paste-on-pictorial, b/w illustrations and color plates by John Rae. $40.00

MARSHALL, Emma
Edith Prescott, 1864 Williams, Boston, small cloth-over-board cover with gilt, 251 pages, b/w frontispiece. $35.00
Katie's Work, (1865) 1887 Merrill, small cloth-over-board cover with gilt, 168 pages, b/w frontispiece. $25.00

MARTIN, Eugene, see Series section, SKY FLYERS

MARTIN, Fran
Knuckles Down, 1942 Harper, cloth-over-board cover, 230 pages, illustrated endpapers, b/w illustrations by Dorothy McEntee. $15.00
No School Friday, 1945 Harper, cloth-over-board cover, 135 pages, illustrated endpapers, b/w illustrations by Dorothy McEntee. $15.00

MARTIN, John
Fairy Tales, 1944 John Martin's House, pictorial boards, oversize, full-color illustrations by John Nielsen. $60.00

MASEFIELD, John
Jim Davis, ca. 1945 edition Darton, cloth-over-board cover, 242 pages. $15.00
Martin Hyde, the Duke's Messenger, (1909) 1927 edition Little Brown, paste-on-illustration, cloth-over-board cover, 289 pages, 8 two-color plates by T. C. Dugdale. $30.00
Midnight Folk, 1927 Macmillan, cloth-over-board cover with gilt, 269 pages. $20.00
South and East, 1929 Macmillan first American edition, oversize, green cloth-over-board cover with gilt lettering, 29 pages, color plates by Jacynth Parsons. $25.00

MASON, Arthur
Cook and the Captain Bold, 1924 Atlantic Monthly Press, cloth-over-board cover with gilt, b/w frontispiece. $20.00

From the Horn of the Moon, (1930) 1937 edition Garden City, blue cloth-over-board cover with paste-on-pictorial, illustrated endpapers, b/w illustrations by Robert Lawson. $40.00

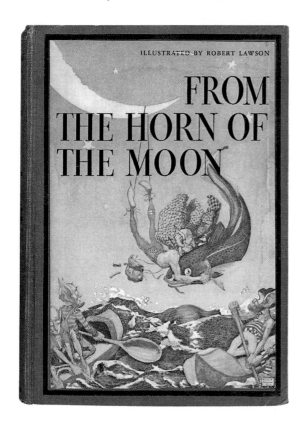

MASON, Frank W.
Pilots, Man Your Planes, 1944 Lippincott, color frontispiece, b/w illustrations by Frank Beaudouin. $35.00

Q-Boat, 1943 Lippincott, color frontispiece, b/w illustrations by Frank Beaudouin. $35.00

MASON, Miriam
Gray Nosed Kitten, 1950 edition Hale school binding, illustrations by Marie Nichols. $10.00

Herman the Brave Pig, 1949 Macmillan, hardcover, illustrations by George and Doris Hauman. $15.00

Hominy and the Blunt-Nosed Arrow, 1950 Macmillan, hardcover, illustrations by George and Doris Hauman. $15.00

Little Jonathan, 1945 Macmillan, hardcover, illustrations by George and Doris Hauman. $15.00

Matilda and Her Family, 1942 Macmillan, green cloth-over-board cover, 144 pages, b/w illustrations Meg Wohlberg. $15.00

Middle Sister, 1947 Macmillan, hardcover, illustrations by Grace Paull. ($35.00 with dust jacket) $20.00

Timothy Has Ideas, 1944 Macmillan, blue cloth-over-board cover, illustrations by Berta and Elmer Hader. $15.00

Young Audubon, Boy Nauralist, 1943 Bobbs Merrill first edition, hardcover, illustrations by Will Forrest. $15.00

MATES, Rudolph
Cock and the Hen, 1925 Harper, illustrated paper-over-board cover, illustrated endpapers, oblong picture book, color throughout by author. $35.00

MATHEWS, Joanna
Belle's Pink Boots, 1881 Dutton, oversize, brown cloth-over-board cover with gilt, 16 chromolith plates plus b/w illustrations by Ida Waugh. $85.00

MATTHEWSON, Christy
Catcher Craig, 1915 Dodd, hardcover, 347 pages, 4 b/w plates by Charles Relyea. $20.00

Pitcher Pollock, 1914 Dodd, hardcover, 335 pages, 4 b/w plates by Charles Relyea. $20.00

MAULE, Mary K.
Little Knight of the X Bar B, 1910 Lothrop, illustrated cloth-over-board cover, b/w illustrations by Maynard Dixon. $20.00

MAUROIS, Andre
Fatapoufs and Thinifers, translated by R. Benet, 1940 Holt, oversize picture book, illustrated endpapers and color illustrations throughout by Jean Bruller. ($65.00 with dust jacket) $40.00

MAXWELL, Violet and HILL, Helen
Charlie and His Kitten, (1922) 1926 Macmillan, small hardcover, 90 pages, 8 color plates by authors. $25.00

MAXWELL, William
Heavenly Tenants, 1946 Harper first edition, hardcover, oversize, 57 pages, artwork by Ilonka Karasz. $50.00

MAY, Carrie L.
Ruth Lovell, or Holidays at Home, 1881 Sumner, Chicago, cloth-over-board cover with gilt, 304 pages, b/w frontispiece. $20.00

MAYER, Albert
Falconer's Son, 1941 Westminster, impressed cloth-over-board cover, 241 pages, illustrated endpapers, 2-color illustrations by Sheilah Beckett. $20.00

MAYOL, Lurline
Story of a Happy Doll, 1928 Saalfield, illustrated paper-over-board cover, 142 pages, b/w illustrations by Fern Bisel Peat. $25.00

MAZER, Sonia
Masha, a Little Russian Girl, 1932 Doubleday, 285 pages, color frontispiece, b/w illustrations by author. $20.00

McCANDLISH, Edward
Little Miss Ducky-Daddles, 1926 Stoll and Edwards, illustrated paper-over-board cover, small easy-reader with full-page color illustrations by author. $25.00

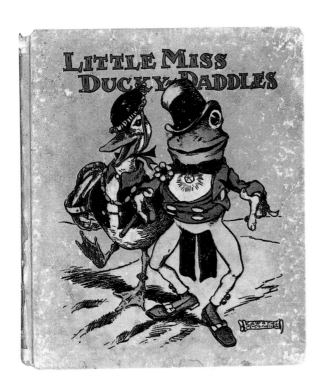

McCANN, Rebecca
Complete Cheerful Cherub, 1932 Covici Friede Inc., hardcover, poems and line drawing illustrations by author. ($35.00 with dust jacket) $20.00

McCAULEY, Anne M.
Jack O'Lantern Twins, 1941 Lyons, small, easy reader, 30 pages, color illustrations by Vera Stone Norman. $20.00

McCULLOUGH, John G.
At Our House, 1943 Wm. R. Scott, oversize, color illustrated paper-over-board cover, illustrated endpapers, b/w illustrations by Roger Duvoisin. $20.00

McDONALD, Lucile Saunders
Dick and the Spice Cupboard, 1936 Crowell, 205 pages, map endpapers, b/w illustrations by Helen Hawkes Battey. $20.00

McELRAVEY, May F.
Tortilla Girl, 1946 Whitman, color illustrated hardcover, color illustrations by Laura Bannon. $10.00

McFEE, Inez
Boy Heroes in Fiction, 1920 Crowell, impressed color illustration on cover, b/w illustrations. $20.00
Girl Heroines in Fiction, 1920 Crowell, impressed cloth-over-board cover, 312 pages, 4 b/w illustrations $25.00
Story of Idles of the King, 1912 Stokes, color illustrated hardcover. $30.00

McGEORGE, Alice Sutton
Kamaiwea, the Coeur d'Alene, 1939 Burton, Kansas City, cloth-over-board cover, 320 pages. $15.00

McINTYRE, John T.
Blowing Weather, (1923) 1928 edition Stokes, 6 color plates by George Mabie. $20.00

McKAY, Herbert
Noah and the Rabbit, 1932 Dutton, small, 87 pages, color illustrated paper-over-board cover, 20 b/w illustrations by Grace Lodge. $30.00

McKENNA, Dolores
Adventures of a Wee Mouse, 1921 Stokes, small, cloth-over-board cover with paste-on-pictorial, illustrated endpapers, 6 color plates by Ruth Bennett. $30.00
Adventures of Squirrel Fluffytail, 1921 Stokes, small, cloth-over-board cover with paste-on-pictorial, illustrated endpapers, color plates and b/w illustrations by Ruth Bennett. $30.00
Hootie the Owl, 1921 Saalfield, small, hardcover with paste-on-illustration, 6 color illustrations by Ruth Bennett. $20.00
Mr. Widdle Waddle Brings the Family, 1922 Penn first edition, hardcover with pictorial-paste-on, 82 pages, color plates by Ruth Bennett. $35.00

McKOWN, Gretchen, and GLEESON, Florence
All the Days Were Antonia's, 1939 Jr. Literary Guild, Viking, cloth-over-board cover, 268 pages, illustrated endpapers, b/w illustrations by Zhenda Gay. $20.00

McNEELY, Marian Hurd
Jumping-Off Place, 1929 Longmans first edition,

illustrated endpapers, b/w illustrations by William Siegel. $20.00

Way to Glory, 1932 Longmans first edition, impressed cloth-over-board cover, 240 pages, illustrated endpapers, b/w illustrations by Joan Esley. $25.00

McNEER, May

Golden Flash, 1947 Viking, illustrated endpapers, 8 color plates by Lynd Ward. ($40.00 in dust jacket) $30.00

Story of the Southwest, 1948 Harper, oversize, color illustrated paper-over-board cover, illustrated endpapers with map, lithograph color and b/w illustrations throughout by C. H. DeWitt, about 30 pages. ($35.00 in dust jacket) $25.00

Story of the Great Plains, 1943 Harper, oversize, color illustrated paper-over-board cover, illustrated endpapers with map, lithograph color and b/w illustrations throughout by C. H. DeWitt, about 30 pages. $25.00

Waif Maid, 1930 Macmillan, 212 pages, color frontispiece, b/w woodcut illustrations by Lynd Ward. $20.00

McNEIL, Everett

Shores of Adventure, 1929 Dutton, 371 pages, color frontispiece. $10.00

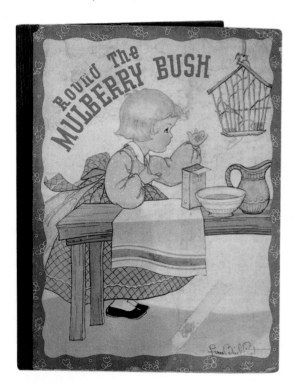

McNEIL, Marion

Little Green Cart, 1931 Saalfield, pictorial boards, oversize, color illustrations throughout by Francoise. $25.00

Round the Mulberry Bush, 1933 Saalfield first edition, oversize picture book, 36 pages, illustrated paper-over-board cover, 8 full-page color illustrations by Fern Bisel Peat. $75.00

McSWIGAN, Marie

Five on a Merry-go-Round, 1943 Dutton, 183 pages, illustrations by Mary Reardon. $15.00

Weather House People, 1940 Lippincott, blue cloth-over-board cover, illustrated endpapers, color and b/w illustrations by Dorothy Bayley. $15.00

MEADE, Julian R.

Peter by the Sea, 1940 Doubleday, first edition, illustrated cloth-over-board cover, small, 146 pages, b/w illustrations by Grace Paull. $35.00

Teeny and the Tall Man, 1936 Doubleday, illustrated cloth-over-board cover, 155 pages, b/w illustrations by Grace Paull. $35.00

MEADER, Stephen

Buckboard Stranger, (1939) 1945 edition Harcourt, cloth-over-board cover, b/w illustrations Paul Calle. $15.00

Cedar's Boy, 1949 Harcourt, cloth-over-board cover, b/w illustrations by Lee Townsend. ($20.00 with dust jacket) $15.00

MEADOWCROFT, Enid

Adventures of Peter Whiffen, 1936 Crowell, illustrated cloth-over-board cover, illustrated endpapers, b/w illustrations by Beatrice Bennetts. $20.00

Along the Erie Towpath, 1940 Crowell, hardcover, illustrations by Ninon McKnight. $20.00

By Wagon and Flatboat, 1938 Crowell, illustrated cloth-over-board cover, 170 pages, illustrated endpapers, two-color illustrations and b/w illustrations by Ninon McKnight. $20.00

Secret Railway, Crowell, cloth-over-board cover, b/w illustrations by Henry Pitz. $20.00

MEADOWCROFT, William

Boy's Life of Edison, 1949 Harper, pictorial hardcover, b/w photo illustrations. ($20.00 with dust jacket.) $10.00

MEANS, Florence

Moved Outers, 1945 Houghton, hardcover, small, 154 pages, illustrated endpapers, two-color illustrations by Helen Blair. $25.00

Ranch and Ring, 1932 Houghton, hardcover, b/w illustrations by Henry Peck. $20.00

MEDARY, Marjorie

College in Crinoline, 1939 Longmans, hardcover,

403 pages, illustrated endpapers and b/w illustrations by William Berger. $20.00

Edra of the Islands, 1940 Longmans first edition, hardcover, 280 pages, b/w illustrations by Dorothy Bayley. $20.00

Joan and the Three Deer, 1939 Random House, cloth-over-board cover, illustrations by Kurt Wiese. $20.00

Orange Winter, 1931 Longmans, impressed cloth-over-board cover, b/w illustrations by Harold Sichel. $20.00

Prairie Anchorage, 1933 Longmans, hardcover, 278 pages, b/w illustrations by John Gincano. $20.00

MENDEL, Marcella, and BERLA, Freda
Singing Around the Clock, 1936 Whitman, song book, color illustrated cover, b/w illustrations by Janet Laura Scott. $25.00

Singing Around the Seasons, 1936 Whitman, song book, color illustrated cover, b/w illustrations by Janet Laura Scott. $25.00

MENEFRE, Maud
Child Stories from the Masters, (1899) 1901 Rand McNally, impressed cloth-over-board cover, small, 104 pages, 2-color illustrations. $20.00

MERRILL, Anna, see Series section, MARY LEE

METCALFE, Francis
Side Show Studies, 1906 Outing Co., impressed color illustration on cover, b/w illustrations by Oliver Herford. $25.00

MEYER, Lucy Rider
Real Fairy Folks, 1887 Lothrop, cloth-over-board cover with gilt, small, 389 pages, b/w illustrations. $25.00

MILLER, Elizabeth
Pran of Albania, 1929 Doubleday first edition, hardcover, illustrations by Maud and Miska Petersham. ($80.00 with dust jacket) $50.00

MILLER, Jean Dupont
Miss Navy Junior, 1946 Dodd, hardcover, small, 211 pages. ($20.00 with dust jacket) $15.00

Shipmates in White, 1944 Dodd, hardcover, small, 210 pages. $15.00

MILLER, Olive Beaupre, editor
Engines and Brass Bands, 1933 Book House, brown cloth-over-board cover, 376 pages, b/w illustrations. $25.00

MILLS, Enos A.
Wild Animal Homesteads, 1923 Doubleday, cloth-over-board cover with gilt, b/w illustrations and photos by Will James. $20.00

MILLS, G. R. and NELSON, Zaida
Talking Dolls, 1930 Greenberg, oversize, hardcover, color illustrations throughout by Tony Sarg. ($90.00 in dust jacket) $45.00

MILLS, Winifred and Dunn, Louise M.
Story of Old Dolls and How to Make New Ones, 1940 Doubleday first edition, blue cloth-over-board cover with gilt, illustrated endpapers, 227 pages, photo and b/w illustrations. $20.00

MILMAN, Helen
Little Ladies, 1892 Lippincott, blue cloth-over-board cover, decorated endpapers, 192 pages, b/w illustrations by E. F. Harding. $25.00

MITCHELL, Edith
Otherside Book, 1915 Reilly Britton, oversize, paper-over-board cover, color illustrations throughout by author. $45.00

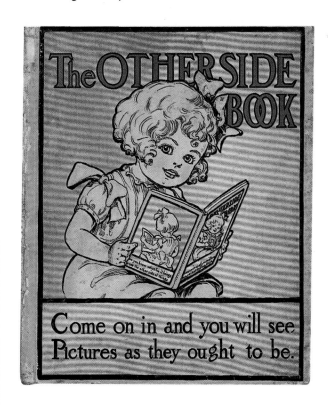

MITCHELL, J. A.
Romance of the Moon, 1886 Holt, cloth-over-board cover with gilt impressed illustration, small oblong picture book, green ink line drawings. $45.00

MOESCHLIN, Elsa
Little Boy with the Big Apples, 1932 edition

McCann, color illustrations and paper-over-board cover, oversize picture book, color illustrations by author. $45.00

Red Horse, 1929 edition McCann, color illustrations and paper-over-board cover, oversize picture book, color illustrations by author. $50.00

MOLESWORTH, Mrs.

Carrots, Just a Little Boy, 1925 edition Macmillan, red cloth-over-board cover, illustrations by Walter Crane. $25.00

Children of the Castle, 1890 Macmillan, illustrated orange cloth-over-board cover, plates by Walter Crane. $50.00

Christmas Posy, 1888 Macmillan, illustrated orange cloth-over-board cover, 8 plates by Walter Crane. $50.00

Cuckoo Clock, 1901 edition Burt, illustrated hardcover, illustrations by Walter Crane. $35.00

Cuckoo Clock, 1905 edition Macmillan, blue cloth-over-board cover, illustrations by Walter Crane. $35.00

Cuckoo Clock, 1931 edition Macmillan, illustrated cloth-over-board cover, square, 196 pages, color illustrated endpapers, b/w illustrations by C. E. Brock. $20.00

Mrs. Mouse and her Boys, 1897 Macmillan, orange cloth-over-board cover, 198 pages, 6 plates by L. Leslie Brooke. $35.00

Rectory Children, 1889 Macmillan, cloth-over-board cover with gilt, small, 212 pages, b/w illustrations by Walter Crane. $50.00

MOLLOY, Anne

Lucy's Christmas, 1950 Houghton, cloth-over-board cover, 46 pages, color illustrated endpapers, color and b/w illustrations by John Cosgrave. $25.00

Shooting Star Farm, 1946 Houghton, cloth-over-board cover, 231 pages, b/w illustrations by Barbara Cooney. $15.00

MOLNAR, Ferenc

Blue-Eyed Lady, 1942 Viking, cloth-over-board cover, 46 pages, color illustrations by Helen Sewell. $25.00

MONGIARDINI-REMBADI

Pinocchio Under the Sea, translated by C. M. Della Chiesa, 1913 Macmillan, cloth-over-board cover with gilt illustration and lettering, 201 pages, b/w illustrations throughout by Florence Wilde. $25.00

MONSELL, Helen A.

Paddy's Christmas, (1924) 1942 edition Knopf, oblong picture book, paper-over-board cover with color illustration, b/w/blue/yellow illustrations throughout by Kurt Wiese. $25.00

MONTGOMERY, Rutherford

Carcajou, 1936 Caxton library edition, orange cloth-over-board cover. $10.00

Ghost Town Adventure, 1942 Holt, cloth-over-board cover, 252 pages, double-page b/w illustrations by Russell Sherman. $20.00

Hurricane Yank, 1942 McKay, cloth-over-board cover, 250 pages, b/w illustrations by James Shimer. $15.00

Iceblink, 1941 Holt, illustrated cloth-over-board cover, 250 pages, illustrated endpapers, map and b/w illustrations by Rudolf Freund. $20.00

Rough Riders Ho!, 1946 McKay, cloth-over-board cover, 228 pages, b/w illustrations by E. F. Wittmack. $15.00

Yellow Eyes, 1937 Caxton library edition, illustrated cloth-over-board cover, illustrated endpapers, b/w illustrations by L. D. Cram. $10.00

MOON, Carl

Flamingo Arrow, (1927), 1935 edition Stokes, cloth-over-board cover with paste-on-illustration, 259 pages, illustrated endpapers, color frontispiece, illustrations by author. $20.00

Painted Moccasin, 1931 Stokes, cloth-over-board cover with gilt lettering, 318 pages, illustrated endpapers, color frontispiece by author. $35.00

MOON, Grace

Chi-Wee of the Desert, (1926) 1942 edition Doubleday, hardcover, color frontispiece, b/w illustrations by Carl Moon. $15.00

Daughter of Thunder, 1942 Macmillan, cloth-over-board cover, 184 pages, color frontispiece by Carl Moon. $20.00

Singing Sands, 1936 Doubleday, cloth-over-board cover, 245 pages, illustrated endpapers, color frontispiece, sepia plate illustrations by Carl Moon. $25.00

Tita of Mexico, 1934 Stokes, cloth-over-board cover, illustrated endpapers, b/w illustrations by Carl Moon. $20.00

MOON, Grace and Carl

Book of Nah-Wee, 1932 Doubleday, oversize easy-read picture book, cloth-over-board cover, 59 pages, color illustrations throughout by Carl Moon. $35.00

Lost Indian Magic, 1918 Stokes, cloth-over-board cover with paste-on-illustration, 301 pages, color frontispiece, color plates by Carl Moon. $30.00

MOORE, Anne Carroll

Century of Kate Greenaway, 1946 Warne first edition, paper cover, oversize, color plates. $30.00

Nicholas, 1924 Putnam, cloth-over-board cover with gilt, 331 pages, map endpapers, color frontispiece, b/w illustrations by Jay Van Everen. $30.00

Nicholas and the Golden Goose, 1932 Putnam first edition, cloth-over-board cover, illustrated endpapers, color frontispiece, b/w illustrations by J. V. Everen. $25.00

MOORE, Clement
Night Before Christmas, see Newton, Ruth

MOORE, David William
End of Black Dog, 1949 Crowell, 198 pages, cloth-over-board cover, illustrated endpapers, b/w illustrations by Henry Pitz. $20.00

MOORE, Ida Cecil
Lucky Orphan, 1947 Scribner, cloth-over-board cover, 122 pages, illustrated endpapers, b/w illustrations by Primrose. $15.00

MORGENSTERN, Elizabeth
Little Gardeners, retold by L. Encking, 1935 edition Whitman, cloth-over-board cover with paste-on pictorial, easy-read picture book, color illustrations by Marigold Bantzer. $35.00

MORLEY, Christopher
Where the Blue Begins, 1922 edition Lippincott, blue cloth-over-board cover, oversize, color and b/w illustrations by Arthur Rackham. $45.00

MORRISON, Mary Whitney
Stories True and Fancies New, 1898 Dana Estes, poetry, hardcover with wraparound printed illustration, 208 pages, color frontispiece, b/w illustrations by L. J. Bridgman. $35.00

MORRISON, Harry Steele
Adventures of a Boy Reporter, (1900 Page), undated edition World, b/w frontispiece. $10.00

MORROW, Elizabeth
Rabbit's Nest, 1914 Macmillan, pictorial boards, illustrated endpapers, small, 43 pages, b/w illustrations. ($25.00 with matching dust jacket) $20.00

Painted Pig, 1930 Knopf, oversize picture book, illustrated endpapers, color frontispiece and color illustrations throughout by Rene D'Harnoncourt. $50.00

Pint of Judgment, 1939 Knopf first edition, small, color illustrated paper-over-board cover, illustrated endpapers, brown/white illustrations by Susanne Suba. $25.00

Shannon, 1941 Macmillan first edition, small, 69 pages, b/w illustrations by Helen Torrey. $25.00

MORROW, Honore 1880-1940
On to Oregon, 1926 Morrow, cloth-over-board cover, 247 pages, b/w plates. $15.00

Ship's Monkey, 1933 Morrow, cloth-over-board cover, 188 pages, color and b/w illustrations by Gordon Grant. $35.00

MOSES, Montrose, editor
Treasury of Plays for Children, 1921 Little Brown, brown cloth-over-board cover, color frontispiece, b/w illustrations by Tony Sarg. $65.00

MOULTON, Louise
New Bed-Time Stories, 1880 Roberts, red cloth-over-board cover with gilt, small, 230 pages, b/w illustrations by Addie Ledyard. $30.00

MUKERJI, Dhan Gopal
Hindu Fables for Little Children, 1929 Dutton, cloth-over-board cover with gilt, 113 pages, illustrated endpapers, b/w illustrations by Kurt Wiese. $20.00

MUNCHAUSEN, Baron von (born in Hanover 1720)
Baron Munchausen's Narrative of His Marvelous Travels and Campaigns in Russia, 1928 edition Ginn, small, illustrated cloth-over-board cover, 134 pages, b/w illustrations by Leon D'Emo. $30.00

MUNN, Charles Clark
Uncle Terry, 1901 Lee & Shepard, cloth-over-board

cover with paste-on-illustration, 365 pages, b/w plates by Helena Higginbotham. $20.00

MUNRO, Neil
Bud, 1907 Harper, cloth-over-board cover with gilt lettering, 315 pages, b/w frontispiece. $20.00

MUNROE, Kirk
Canoemates, 1893 Harper, cloth-over-board cover with gilt design and lettering, b/w plates. $25.00
Flamingo Feather, (1887) 1923 edition Harper, oversize, cloth-over-board cover, 222 pages, 10 color plate illustrations by Frank Schoonover. $50.00
Fur-Seal's Tooth, 1894 Harper, cloth-over-board cover, 267 pages, illustrations. $15.00
Outcast Warrior, 1905 Appleton, cloth-over-board cover, 279 pages, 4 color illustrations by Hutchison. $25.00
Raftmates, (1893) 1900 edition Harper, green cloth-over-board cover with gilt, 341 pages. $25.00

MURRAY, Gretchen Ostrander
Shoes for Sandy, 1936 Grosset, oversize picture book, illustrated paper-over-board cover, illustrated endpapers, full-page color and b/w illustrations by author. $45.00

MURRAY, Martin
Two Boys in Eskimo Land, undated ca. 1930 Nelson "Seeing the World" series, small, cloth-over-board cover, color frontispiece, b/w illustrations. $15.00

MURRAY-AARON, Dr. Eugene
Butterfly Hunters, 1894 Scribner, 269 pages, b/w plate illustrations. $25.00

MUSSET, Paul de
Mr. Wind and Madame Rain, undated ca. 1905 Putnam, cloth-over-board cover, 151 pages, b/w illustrations by Charles Bennett. $35.00

MYERS, Jane Pentzer
Stories of Enchantment, 1901 McClurg, impressed design on cloth-over-board cover, 215 pages, b/w illustrations by Harriet Roosevelt Richards. $20.00

MYERS, Marcelline Flora
Story of Pioneers, 1937 Bobbs Merrill, cloth-over-board cover, 180 pages, b/w illustrations by Clothilde Funk. $20.00

MYHRE, Ethelyn
Hawaiian Yesterdays, 1942 Knopf first edition, oblong easy-read picture book, brown/white illustrations by author. $20.00

⤐ N ⤐

NASH, Harriet
Polly's Secret, (1902) 1939 edition Little Brown, Beacon Hill Bookshelf, cloth-over-board cover with paste-on pictorial, 292 pages, 4 color plates by Hattie Longstreet Price. $30.00

NATHAN, Robert
Portrait of Jennie, 1940 Knopf first edition, cloth-over-board cover, 212 pages. $35.00

NAY, Carol
Timmy Rides the China Clipper, 1941 Whitman, oversize, cloth-over-board cover with paste-on pictorial, 96 pages, map endpapers, color illustrations by author. $25.00

NEAL, Bigelow
Last of the Thundering Herd, 1933 Jr. Literary Guild, cloth-over-board cover, 287 pages, b/w illustrations by Charles Fox. $15.00

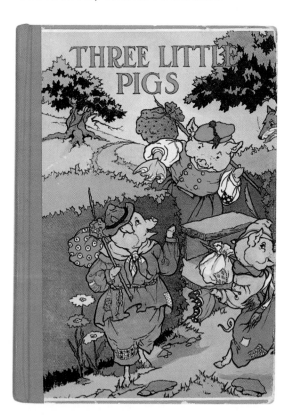

NEILL, John Rea
Three Little Pigs, undated ca. 1940 edition McKay, small, illustrated paper-over-board cover, full color full-page illustrations by Neill. $30.00

NEILSON, Frances Fullerton
Donkey from Dorking, 1943 Dutton, 85 pages,

b/w illustrations by Lidia Vitale and Janet Hopkins. $15.00

Giant Mountain, 1946 Dutton first edition, 120 pages, b/w illustrations by Mary Reardon. $15.00

NELSON, Faith

Randolph, the Bear Who Said No, (1940) 1946 edition Wonder Books, small, color illustrated paper-over-board cover, color illustrations by Nedda Walker. $20.00

NELSON, Mary Jarman

Fun With Music, 1941 Whitman, cloth-over-board cover with paste-on-pictorial, color illustrations by Grace and Olive Barnett. $25.00

NELSON, Rhoda

High Timber, 1941 Crowell, cloth-over-board cover, 280 pages, b/w illustrations by Mildred Boyle. $15.00

This is Freedom, 1940 Dodd, cloth-over-board cover, illustrated endpapers, b/w illustrations by author. $15.00

Wagon Train West, 1939 Crowell, cloth-over-board cover, 224 pages, illustrated endpapers, color and b/w illustrations by Elinore Blaisdell. $20.00

NESBIT, E. (Edith Bland)

Bastable Children, 1929 edition Jr. Literary Guild, cloth-over-board cover, 293 pages, color frontispiece, b/w illustrations. $30.00

Children's Shakespeare, undated ca. 1900 Altemus, illustrated and decorated cloth-over-board cover, full-page illustrations. $40.00

Daphne in Fitzroy Street, 1909 Doubleday, cloth-over-board cover with paste-on-pictorial, color frontispiece by F. G. Coates. $85.00

Enchanted Castle, (1906) 1933 edition Coward McCann, cloth-over-board cover, 297 pages, b/w illustrations by H. R. Millar. $25.00

Harding's Luck, (1923) 1930 edition Ernest Benn, cloth-over-board cover, color frontispiece, b/w illustrations by H. R. Millar. $25.00

Oswald Bastable and Others, 1905 Wells Gardner, red cloth-over-board cover with gilt, illustrations by Brock and H. Millar. $70.00

Story of the Amulet, ca. 1907 Dutton, first American edition, cloth-over-board cover, 374 pages, b/w illustrations by H. R. Millar. $150.00

Story of Five Rebellious Dolls, ca. 1890s Nister, London and Dutton, NY, oversize oblong, 20 pages, illustrated cover and endpapers, 8 color chromolithographs plus illustrations throughout by E. Stuart Hardy. $500.00

NEUMANN, Daisy

Sperli the Clockman, 1932 Macmillan, cloth-over-board cover, 117 pages, color frontispiece, b/w illustrations by Edward Thompson. $15.00

NEUMANN, Dorothy

Come Meet the Clowns, 1941 Macmillan, easy-read picture book, color illustrations by Lydia Furbush. $20.00

NEVIN, Evelyn C.

Lost Children of the Shoes, 1946 Westminster, cloth-over-board cover, 123 pages, illustrated endpapers, b/w/brown illustrations by Manning de V. Lee. $15.00

Sign of the Anchor, 1947 Westminster, cloth-over-board cover, 157 pages, illustrated endpapers, b/w illustrations by Manning de V. Lee. $15.00

NEWBERRY, Clare Turlay

Babette, 1937 Harper, oversize, 30 pages, illustrations by author. $40.00

Herbert the Lion, 1939 Harper, oblong picture book, color illustrated paper-over-board cover, color illustrations by author. $40.00

Pandora, 1944 Harper, oversize, illustrations by author. $40.00

T-Bone the Baby-Sitter, 1950 Harper, oblong picture book, color illustrated paper-over-board cover, b/w/red illustrations by author. $30.00

NEWBERRY, Fannie E.

Bubbles, 1897 Burt, color illustrated cloth-over-board cover, 304 pages, b/w illustrations. $20.00

NEWBERRY, Perry

Castaway Island, 1917 Penn, cloth-over-board cover, 320 pages, color frontispiece, b/w illustrations by F. A. Anderson. $20.00

NEWCOMB, Covelle

Red Hat, 1942 Longmans, cloth-over-board cover, b/w illustrations by Addison Burbank. $15.00

Silver Saddles, 1943 Longmans, cloth-over-board cover, illustrated endpapers, b/w illustrations by Addison Burbank. $15.00

Vagabond in Velvet, 1942 Longmans, cloth-over-board cover, illustrated endpapers, b/w illustrations by Addison Burbank. $15.00

NEWELL, Hope

Little Old Woman Carries On, 1947 Nelson, hardcover, illustrations by A. M. Peck. $20.00

Little Old Woman Who Used Her Head, (1935) 1940 edition Nelson, 63 pages, illustrated endpapers, b/w illustrations by Margaret Ruse. $20.00

NEWKIRK, Newton
Stork Book, 1907 Caldwell, decorated gray cloth-over-board cover, illustrated endpapers, small, 123 pages, b/w illustrations by Goldsmith. $20.00

NEWMAN, Gertrude
Delicia and Adolphus, 1938 Rand McNally, small picture book, color illustrated paper-over-board cover, b/w photo illustrations by Russell Benson. $35.00
Story of Delicia, 1935 Rand McNally, small picture book, color illustrated paper-over-board cover, b/w photo illustrations by Russell Benson. $40.00

NEWMAN, Isadora
Fairy Flowers, undated ca. 1926 Humphry Milford, London, tan cloth-over-board cover with gilt and color decorated boards, oversize, 160 pages, color plates by Willy Pogany. $110.00

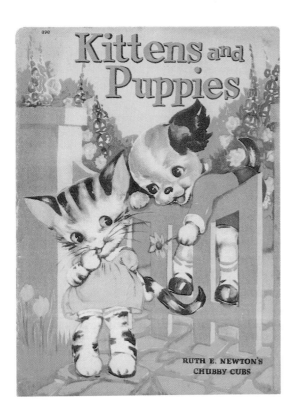

NEWTON, Ruth E.
Animal Mother Goose, 1942 Whitman, oversize softcover, linen-texture paper, color illustrations throughout. $25.00
Baby Animals, 1945 Whitman, oversize softcover, color illustrations throughout. $30.00
Kittens and Puppies, 1940 Whitman, Linen Like line, softcover, oversize picture book, 12 pages, color illustrations throughout by Newton. $45.00

Little Firemen, 1936 Whitman, oversize, 28 pages, color illustrations by Newton. $55.00
Little Postman, Kathryn Heisenfelt, 1936 Whitman, oversize, color illustrations by Newton. $55.00
Little Storekeepers, Helen Beeson, 1936 Whitman, oversize, 28 pages, color illustrations. $55.00
Little Travelers, Zillah MacDonald, 1937 Whitman, oversize, 28 pages, color illustrations. $55.00
Mother Goose, 1934 Whitman, linen-like paper cover, oversize, 28 pages, color and b/w illustrations, Newton and Mabel Horn. $45.00
Mother Goose, 1943 edition Whitman, Giant Tell-A-Tale, color illustrated paper-over-board cover, oversize, color illustrations. $45.00
Night Before Christmas, Clement Moore, 1937 Whitman, oversize, wraparound color illustration on paper-over-board cover, 33 pages, illustrated endpapers, color illustrations throughout by Newton. $55.00
Peter Rabbit, 1938 Whitman, oversize, linen-like softcover, 16 pages, color illustrations throughout. $20.00
Peter Rabbit, Ruth Newton's Chubby Cubs, 1940 Whitman, Giant Tell-A-Tale, color illustrated paper-over-board cover, oversize, color illustrations throughout by Newton. $45.00
Puppy Dogs and Pussy Cats, Helen Beeson, 1936 Whitman, oversize, 32 pages, color illustrations. $55.00
Soap and Bubbles, Mary Windsor, 1935 Whitman, oversize, illustrated cover, 14 pages, color illustrations throughout by Ruth Newton. $45.00

NICHOLS, Laura
Up Hill and Down Dale, 1886 Lothrop, blue cloth-over-board cover with decoration, 202 pages, b/w illustrations. $20.00

NICHOLS, Ruth Alexander
Nancy, 1933 Macmillan, small hardcover with photo illustrations by Nichols. $30.00

NICHOLS, W. T.
Making Good, 1915 Appleton, cloth-over-board cover with paste-on-illustration and gilt, color illustrations by George Varian. $20.00

NICHOLSON, Meredith
Little Brown Jug, 1908 Bobbs Merrill, illustrated by James Montgomery Flagg. $25.00

NIDA, William Lewis
AB, the Cave Man, (1911) 1918 edition Grosset, cloth-over-board cover, small, 166 pages, illustrated endpapers, b/w illustrations F. Stearns. $20.00

Dan-Hur and the First Farmer, 1931 Laidlaw, hardcover. $20.00

Little White Chief, (1923) 1927 edition Flanagan, 128 pages, b/w/red illustrations by Dorothy Dulin. $15.00

Tree Boys, 1929 Laidlaw, hardcover. $20.00

NIELSEN, Martin

Brownie Numbers Combine Work and Fun, (1934) 1935 edition Farwest, oversize picture book, illustrated cloth-over-board cover, b/w illustrations by Philip Sauve. $40.00

NOLEN, Barbara

Luck and Pluck, 1942 Heath, green cloth-over-board cover, 373 pages, b/w illustrations by Decie Merwin. $20.00

NORLING, Jo and **Ernest,** see Series section, POGO

NORTH, Grace May, see Series section, VIRGINIA DAVIS

NORTON, Charles, see Series section, FIGHTING FOR THE FLAG

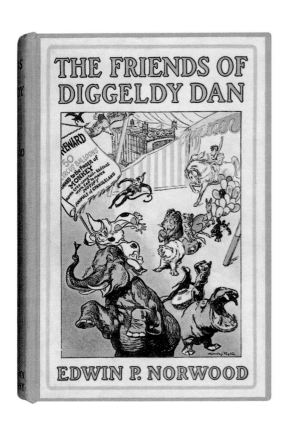

NORWOOD, Edwin

Adventures of Diggeldy Dan, 1922 Little Brown, color paste-on-pictorial cover, 240 pages, 8 color plate illustrations by A. Conway Peyton. $45.00

Circus Menagerie, 1929 Doubleday first edition, yellow cloth-over-board cover, photo illustrations. $30.00

Friends of Diggeldy Dan, 1924 Little Brown, color paste-on-pictorial cover, 240 pages, 8 color plate illustrations by A. Conway Peyton. $35.00

In the Land of Diggeldy Dan, 1923 Little Brown, color paste-on-pictorial cover, 240 pages, 8 color plate illustrations by A. Conway Peyton. $35.00

Other Side of the Circus, 1930 Doubleday first edition, cloth-over-board cover, photo illustrations. $25.00

—————— ⊷ **O** ⊶ ——————

O'BRIEN, Jack

Corporal Corey of the Royal Canadian Mounted, 1936 Winston, cloth-over-board cover with gilt, illustrated endpapers, color frontispiece, b/w illustrations by Kurt Wiese. $20.00

Rip Darcy, Adventurer, 1938 Winston, cloth-over-board cover, illustrated endpapers, color frontispiece, b/w illustrations by Bunty Witten. $15.00

O'DONNELL, T. C.

Ladder of Rickety Rungs, 1923 Volland, color illustrated paper-over-board cover, color illustrations by Janet Scott. $60.00

OGDEN, Ruth

Little Pierre and Big Peter, 1915 Stokes, cloth-over-board cover with paste-on-illustration, illustrated endpapers, color plates by Maria Kirk. $35.00

Little Queen of Hearts, 1893 Stokes first edition, green cloth-over-board cover with gilt, 232 pages, b/w illustrations by H. A. Ogden. $55.00

Loyal Hearts and True, ca. 1899 Stokes, brown cloth-over-board cover, illustrations by H. A. Ogden. $35.00

Loyal Little Red-Coat, 1890 Stokes, cloth-over-board cover with gilt, b/w illustrations by H. A. Ogden. $35.00

OLCOTT, Frances Jenkins

Book of Elves and Fairies, 1918 Houghton, hardcover, color illustrations by Milo Winter. $35.00

Go, Champions of Light, 1933 Revell, hardcover. $20.00

Good Stories for Great Holidays, 1914 Houghton, decorated hardcover, 248 pages, 4 color plates. $30.00

Grimm's Fairy Tales, 1922 Hampton Publishing, cloth-over-board cover with paste-on-illustration, color plates by R. Cramer. $45.00

Jolly Book for Boys and Girls, 1915 Houghton Ist edition, red cloth-over-board cover, illustrated by Amy Sacker. $25.00

More Tales of the Arabian Nights, 1915 Holt first edition, red cloth-over-board cover with gilt, 274 pages, 12 color plate by Willy Pogany. $85.00

Story-Telling Ballads, 1920 Houghton, collection, green cloth-over-board cover with paste-on-illustration, 4 color plates by Milo Winter. $40.00

Wonder Garden, 1919 Houghton first edition, cloth-over-board cover with paste-on-illustration, color plates by Milo Winter. $35.00

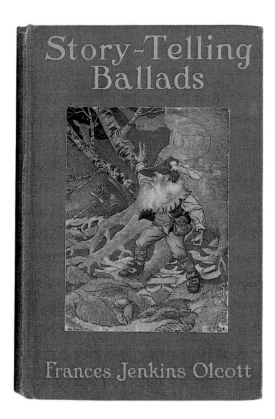

OLCOTT, Virginia

Adventures of Haroun Er Raschid and Other Tales from the Arabian Nights, 1923 Holt, red cloth-over-board cover with gilt, 363 pages, color frontispiece, b/w illustrations by Willy Pogany. $65.00

OLFERS, Sibylle

Little Princess in the Wood, 1931 Stokes, oversize picture book, cloth-over-board cover with paste-on-illustration, illustrated endpapers, color frontispiece, color illustrated by author. $85.00

When the Root Children Wake Up, 1941 Stokes, oversize picture book, cloth-over-board cover with paste-on-illustration, illustrated endpapers, color frontispiece, color illustrated by author. $85.00

When the Root Children Wake Up, ca. 1940s Lippincott reprinting of Stokes edition, oversize picture book, cloth-over-board cover with paste-on-illustration, illustrated endpapers, color frontispiece, color illustrated by author. ($100.00 with dust jacket) $55.00

OLLIVANT

Bob Son of Battle, (1898) 1917 Doubleday, cloth-over-board cover with paste-on-illustration, 4 photo plate illustrations. $20.00

O'MALLEY, Patricia

War Wings for Carol, 1943 Dodd, cloth-over-board cover. $15.00

Wider Wings, 1942 Jr. Literary Guild, b/w illustrations. $15.00

Wings for Carol, 1941 Dodd, cloth-over-board cover. $20.00

OPTIC, Oliver (William Adams), see Series section, OLIVER OPTIC

Under the pseudonym of Oliver Optic, Adams wrote dozens of juveniles, some as separate titles, some as series, and in later editions, some titles were mixed and matched to make up a new series or extend a series to a particular length for marketing purposes, so that there can be a confusing crossover of titles.

All Aboard, undated Homewood, illustrated tan cloth-over-board cover. $15.00

Boat Club, ca. 1908 edition Donohue, cloth-over-board cover with impressed illustration, b/w frontispiece. $15.00

Breaking Away, or, *Fortunes of a Student,* 1867 Lee and Shepard, brown cloth-over-board cover. $15.00

Fanny Grant Among the Indians, 1911 edition New York Book, hardcover. $10.00

Four Young Explorers, Vol. 3, 1896 Lee Shepard, pictorial hardcover, 357 pages, b/w illustrations by Burnham Shuta. $25.00

Now or Never, Adventures of Bobby Bright, ca. 1900 edition Donohue, illustrated tan cloth-over-board cover, 186 pages. $10.00

Oliver Optic's New Story Book, 1902 Hurst, pictorial boards, illustrated. $40.00

OSBORNE, Nancy Cabot
Good Wind and Good Water, 1934 Viking, cloth-over-board cover, 248 pages, map endpapers, b/w illustrations by Kurt Wiese. $20.00

OUIDA (Louise De la Ramee)
Editions vary, and sometimes her pseudonym is used, sometimes her name, on the same stories.

Bimbi, Stories for Children, 1910 edition Lippincott, red cloth-over-board cover, color illustrated by Maria Kirk. ($30.00 with dust jacket) $15.00

Dog of Flanders, 1890 edition Caldwell, small, cloth-over-board cover with impressed gilt design, 170 pages, b/w illustrations. $25.00

Dog of Flanders, 1909 edition Lippincott, red cover, illustrations by Maria Kirk. $30.00

Dog of Flanders, 1926 edition Saalfield, illustrated paper-over-board cover, illustrations by Frances Brundage. $15.00

Moufflou and Other Stories, 1892 Lippincott, green cloth-over-board cover with silhouette illustration. $20.00

Moufflou and Other Stories, 1910 edition Lippincott, small, 3 color plate illustrations by Maria Kirk, 3 b/w illustrations by Garrett. $25.00

Nurnberg Stove, 1901 edition Page, Cozy Corner Series, blue cloth-over-board cover, b/w illustrations. $20.00

Nurnberg Stove, 1916 edition Lippincott, small, 96 pages, color plates by Maria Kirk. $25.00

Nurnberg Stove, 1928 edition Macmillan, small, 138 pages, illustrated endpapers, color frontispiece, b/w illustrations by Frank Boyd. $15.00

OVINGTON, Mary White
Zeke, (1931) 1941 edition Harcourt, cloth-over-board cover, b/w illustrations by Natalie Davis. $20.00

OXLEY, J. MacDonald
Fife and Drum at Louisbourg, 1899 Little Brown, color illustration on cloth-over-board cover, 5 b/w plates by Clyde De Land. $20.00

PACKARD, Winthrop
Young Ice Whalers, 1903 Houghton, cloth-over-board cover w/ gilt, 16 photo illustrations. $25.00

PAGE, Thomas Nelson
Captured Santa Claus, (1891) 1902 edition Scribner, illustrated cloth-over-board cover, 81 pages, 4 color plates by Jacobs. $25.00

Page Story Book, 1906 edition Scribner, small, 125 pages, illustrated cloth-over-board cover, b/w illustrations. $20.00

Santa Claus's Partner, 1899 Scribner, cloth-over-board cover with gilt, small, 177 pages, 8 b/w/red plates by W. Glackens. $25.00

Tommy Trot's Visit to Santa Claus, and Captured Santa Claus, 1918 edition Scribner, small, 4 color plates. $30.00

Two Little Confederates, (1888) 1911 edition Scribner, illustrated cloth-over-board cover, 156 pages, b/w illustrations. $20.00

Two Little Confederates, 1932 edition Scribner, cloth-over-board cover with paste-on-illustration and gilt, 190 pages, color frontispiece and b/w illustrations by John Thomason. $20.00

PAINE, Albert Bigelow
Arkansaw Bear Complete, 1929 edition Altemus, includes *Arkansaw Bear* and *Arkansaw Bear and Elsie,* red cloth-over-board cover with impressed decoration with gilt, illustrated endpapers, 297 pages, ten color plates plus b/w illustrations throughout by Frank Ver Beck. $45.00

How Mr. Dog Got Even, 1900 Harper, cloth-over-board cover with paste-on-pictorial, small, 121 pages, b/w illustrations by J. M. Conde. $30.00

Making Up With Mr. Dog, 1900 Harper, cloth-over-board cover with paste-on-pictorial, small, 122 pages, b/w illustrations by J. M. Conde. $30.00

Mr. Rabbit's Big Dinner, 1915 Harper, cloth-over-board cover with paste-on-pictorial, small, 117 pages, b/w illustrations by J. M. Conde. $30.00

PAINE, Ralph D.
Blackbeard Buccaneer, 1922 Penn, illustrated cloth-over-board cover, color frontispiece and b/w illustrations by Frank Schoonover. $20.00

Comrades of the Rolling Ocean, 1923 Houghton, b/w frontispiece. $15.00

Fugitive Freshman, 1910 Scribner, illustrated cloth-over-board cover, 304 pages, 6 b/w illustrations by E. E. Stevens. $15.00

Head Coach, 1910 Scribner, cloth-over-board cover, 6 b/w illustrations by George Wright. $20.00

Privateers of '76, 1923 Penn, cloth-over-board cover with paste-on-illustration, color illustrated by Frank Schoonover. $30.00

Ships Across the Sea, 1920 edition Houghton, 4 b/w illustrations by S. Rogers. $10.00

Wrecking Master, 1918 edition Scribner, illustrated cloth-over-board cover, 8 b/w illustrations by Varian. $15.00

PALM, Amy
Wanda and Greta at Broby Farm, 1930 edition Longmans, cloth-over-board cover, 198 pages, illustrated endpapers, 6 color plates by Frank McIntosh. $20.00

PALMER, Elizabeth
Give Me a River, 1939 Scribner, cloth-over-board cover, 152 pages, color and b/w illustrations by Richard Holberg. $20.00

Nightingale House, 1937 Scribner, cloth-over-board cover, color and b/w illustrations by Marjorie Peters. $25.00

Up the River to Danger, 1940 Scribner, b/w illustrations. $15.00

PALTENGHI, Madalena
Honey on a Raft, 1941 Garden City, illustrations by C. W. Anderson. ($50.00 with dust jacket) $35.00

Honey the City Bear, 1937 Grosset, oversize, 31 pages, illustrated paper-over-board cover, illustrations by C. W. Anderson. $50.00

PALTOCK, Robert
Life and Adventures of Peter Wilkins, (1751) 1928 edition Dent, London, oversize, 342 pages, blue cloth-over-board cover with gilt, illustrations by Edward Bawden. $50.00

PANSY (Isabell Alden)
Sidney Martin's Christmas, ca. 1890 Ward Lock, illustrated cloth-over-board cover, 314 pages. $20.00

PANTER-DOWNES, Mollie
Watling Green, 1943 Scribner, 78 pages, b/w illustrations by Mildred Cloete. $20.00

PARK, George Frederick
Dick Judson, Boy Scout Ranger, 1916 McBride, cloth-over-board cover with gilt, color frontispiece by George Hood. $20.00

PARRY, Judge
Butter-Scotia, or a Cheap Trip to Fairy Land, (1896) 1927 edition Heinemann, green pictorial boards, 169 pages, b/w illustrations by Archie MacGregor +folding map. $25.00

Don Quixote of the Mancha, retold by Parry, 1925 edition Dodd Mead, color plates and b/w illustrations by Walter Crane. $50.00

PARTRIDGE, Edward Bellamy
Cousins, 1925 Grosset, cloth-over-board cover, b/w frontispiece. $15.00

Sube Cane, 1917 Penn, cloth-over-board cover, 356 pages, b/w/yellow plates by Widney. $25.00

PATCH, Kate Whiting
Prince Yellowtop, 1903 Page, small, illustrated cloth-over-board cover, 95 pages, b/w illustrations. $20.00

PATCHEN, Frank, see Series section, PONY RIDER BOYS

PATTESON, Madge
Marco, the Gypsy Elf, 1918 Hine Bros., red cloth-over-board cover with gilt lettering, small, 96 pages, b/w illustrations. $20.00

PAULL, Grace
Gloomy the Camel, 1938 Viking first edition, pictorial hardcover, illustrated endpapers, color illustrations. $25.00

Pancakes for Breakfast, 1946 Doubleday first edition, oblong, color and b/w illustrations by author. $25.00

Raspberry Patch, 1941 Doubleday, color illustrations paper-over-board cover, color illustrated endpapers, color and b/w illustrations by author. $30.00

Squash for the Fair, 1943 Doubleday first edition, color illustrations paper-over-board cover, color illustrated endpapers, color and b/w illustrations by author. ($30.00 with dust jacket) $20.00

PAYNE, Emmy
Katy No-Pocket, 1944 Houghton Weekly Reader Book Club edition, pictorial hardcover, color illustrations by H. A. Rey. $15.00

PAYSON, Lt. Howard, see Series section, MOTOR-CYCLE CHUMS

PEARY, Josephine D.
Snow Baby, 1901 Stokes, oversize, impressed design and lettering on cloth-over-board cover with paste-on-pictorial photo, 84 pages, photo illustrations throughout. $95.00

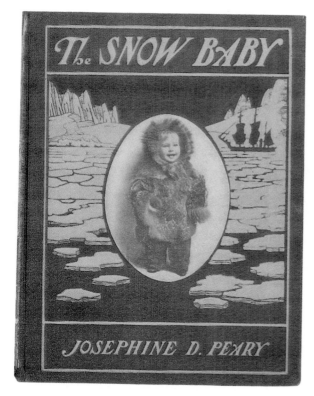

PEARY, Marie Ahnighito (daughter of Josephine Peary)

Little Tooktoo, the Story of Santa Claus' Youngest Reindeer, (1930) 1940 edition Morrow, red cloth-over-board cover, 62 pages, illustrations by Kurt Wiese. $65.00

Ootah and His Puppy, 1942 Heath, cloth-over-board cover with paste-on-illustration, small, 64 pages, map endpapers, color and b/w illustrations by Kurt Wiese. $25.00

Red Caboose, 1932 Morrow first edition, cloth-over-board cover, red/b/w illustrations by Horvath. $55.00

Snow Baby's Own Story, 1934 Stokes, cloth-over-board cover. ($50.00 with dust jacket) $30.00

PEASE, Howard, see Series section, TOD MORAN

PEAT, Fern Bisel, artist, b. 1893

Bird Book, written by F. Shankland, 1931 edition Saalfield, cloth spine, paper-over-board cover, color illustrations by Peat. ($100.00 in dust jacket) $65.00

Calico Pets, 1931 Saalfield, oversize picture book, linen-like paper cover, full-page color illustrations throughout. $45.00

Child's Garden of Verses, by Robert Louis Stevenson, 1940 Saalfield color-throughout, oversize picture book, 89 pages. ($120.00 in dust jacket) $60.00

Child's Garden of Verses, by Robert Louis Stevenson, 1943 edition Saalfield, illustrated soft cover, color-throughout. $40.00

Christmas Carols, by Frank Leet, 1937 Saalfield, oversize, 70 pages, illustrated. ($100.00 in dust jacket) $50.00

Cinderella, by Katharine Gibson, 1932 Harper, hardcover, 48 pages, color plate illustrations. $55.00

Cock, the Mouse, and the Little Red Hen, ca. 1931 Saalfield, color illustrated cover, color and b/w illustrations. $40.00

Forest Friends, by Marceline Dauzet, 1940 Saalfield, 16 pages, color and b/w illustrations. $40.00

Four Stories that Never Grow Old, 1943 Sandusky, oversize, 60 pages, color and b/w illustrations. $55.00

Friends of the Forest, written by F. Shankland, 1932 Saalfield, pictorial paper-over-board cover, 12 color plates. $60.00

Gingerbread Man, 1941 edition Whitman, oversize, 16 pages, color illustrations throughout. $50.00

Little Black Sambo, by Bannerman, ca. 1932 Saalfield, color and b/w illustrations. $150.00

Little Goody Two Shoes, adaptation of Oliver Goldsmith story, 1930 Saalfield, pictorial boards, two-color illustrations by Peat. $25.00

Long Eared Bat, by Horace Barnaby, 1929 edition Saalfield, 60 pages, color plates. $65.00

Mother Goose, 1929 Saalfield, hardcover, oversize, 60 pages, color illustrated. $65.00

Purr and Miew, by Frank Leet, 1931 Saalfield, oversize picture book, paper-over-board cover, 60 pages, color plates. $55.00

Rag-Doll Jane, Her Story, by Frank Leet, 1930 Saalfield, oversize picture book, 59 pages, color plates. $55.00

Round the Mulberry Bush, text by Marion McNeil, 1933 Saalfield first edition, oversize picture book, 36 pages, illustrated paper-over-board cover, color illustrations. $75.00

Stories Children Like, 1933 Saalfield, oversize, color illustrated cover, color illustrations throughout. $65.00

Sugar Plum Tree, Eugene Field poem, 1930 edition Saalfield, oversize picture book, color illustrated paper-over-board cover, b/w illustrations and full-page color illustrations by Peat. $75.00

Three Little Pigs, 1932 Saalfield, 20 pages, color and b/w illustrations. $50.00

Tommy and Jane and the Birds, by Daisy Semple, 1929 Saalfield, oversize, 94 pages, color and b/w illustrations. ($65.00 with dust jacket) $50.00

Treasure Book of Best Stories, by Alta Taylor, 1939 Saalfield, oversize, color plate illustrations. $60.00

Ugly Duckling, adaptation of H. Anderson story, 1932 Saalfield, color illustrated paper-over-board cover, illustrations by Peat. $35.00

When Toys Could Talk, text by Jane Randall, 1939
Saalfield, hardcover, full-page color illustrations. ($80.00 in dust jacket) $45.00

Wynken, Blynken and Nod, by Eugene Field, 1930
edition Saalfield, oversize, color plates. $65.00

PEATTIE, Donald Culross
Story of Ancient Civilization, Story of Middle
Ages, Story of Modern Age, 3-volume set, 1937
edition Grosset, illustrated paper-over-board
cover, litho illustrations. Set $60.00

PECK, Anne Merriman
Manoel and the Morning Star, 1943 Harper, oversize, 31 pages, color illustrated paper-over-
board cover, illustrated endpapers, color plates
and b/w illustrations by author. $30.00

PECKHAM, Betty
Other People's Children, 1943 Nelson, cloth-over-
board cover, 198 pages, b/w illustrations by
Howard Imhoff. $20.00

PEET, Creighton
Dude Ranch, 1939 Whitman, cloth-over-board
cover, photo illustration on every page. $20.00

PENDLETON, Louis
In Assyrian Tents, 1904 Jewish Publications, cloth-
over-board cover, 248 pages. $15.00

King Tom and the Runaways, 1911 Appleton, cloth-
over-board cover, 273 pages, 6 b/w plates. $20.00

Lost Prince Albon, 1898 Jewish Publications, cloth-
over-board cover with gilt, 218 pages, 4 b/w
plates. $20.00

PENNOYER, Sara
Polly Tucker, Merchant, 1937 Dodd, cloth-over-
board cover, 297 pages, b/w illustrations by
Jean Spadea. $15.00

PERKINS, Wilma Lord
Fannie Farmer Junior Cook Book, 1942 Little Brown
first edition, green cloth-over-board cover, illustrated endpapers, 198 pages, b/w/red illustrations by
Martha Setchell. ($25.00 with dust jacket) $15.00

PERRAULT
Cinderella, 1860s edition Seitz, Hamburg, shape book
cut to outline of illustrated character on cover, narrow, 16 pages, color illustrations. $250.00

PERRY, Nora
Another Flock of Girls, 1890 Houghton, cloth-over-
board cover, 8 b/w plates by Reginald Birch and
Charles Copeland. $25.00

Flock of Girls, 1887 Houghton, cloth-over-board
cover with gilt illustration, 8 b/w plates. $30.00

Flock of Girls and Boys, 1895 Little Brown, gray
cloth-over-board cover with gilt, 323 pages,
small, b/w illustrations C. Parker. $25.00

Three Little Daughters of the Revolution, 1896
Houghton, small, cloth-over-board cover, 3 b/w
plates by F. T. Merrill. $20.00

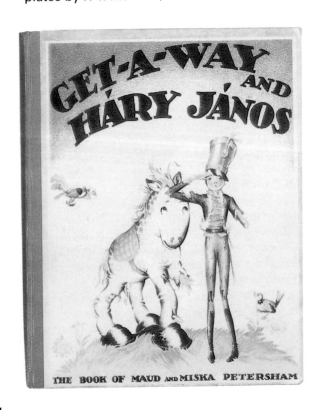

PETERSHAM, Maud and **Miska,** see Series section, PETERSHAM SERIES

Auntie and Celia Jane and Mike, 1932 edition Hale library weight cover, gray cloth-over-board cover, illustrations by authors. $25.00

Box with Red Wheels, 1949 Macmillan, illustrated paper-over-board cover, oversize picture book, color illustrations by authors. $35.00

Circus Baby, 1950 Macmillan first edition, color illustrated paper-over-board cover, oversize picture book, 28 pages, color illustrations by authors. ($60.00 with dust jacket) $40.00

Get-A-Way and Háry János, 1933 Viking, illustrated paper-over-board cover, oversize picture book, color illustrations by authors. ($125.00 with dust jacket) $85.00

PETERSON, Alice F.

Jolita of the Jungle, 1929 Beckley-Cardy, small, 193 pages, b/w illustrations by author. $20.00

PETROFF, Boris

Son of the Danube, 1940 Viking, cloth-over-board cover, 277 pages, illustrated endpapers, b/w woodcuts by H. A. Mueller. $15.00

PHELPS, Elizabeth Stuart

Gypsy's Sowing and Reaping, (1866) 1896 edition Dodd Mead, small, cloth-over-board cover, 286 pages, b/w illustrations. $20.00

Supply at Saint Agatha's, 1899 edition Houghton, green cloth-over-board cover with gilt, b/w plates by E. Boyd Smith and Marcia Woodbury. $50.00

PHELPS, Frances Brown

Nikita, a Story of Russia, (1932) 1937 edition Harcourt, cloth-over-board cover, 263 pages, illustrated endpapers, b/w illustrations by Maitland de Gogorza. $15.00

PHILLIPS, Ethel Calvert

Brian's Victory, 1942 Houghton, oversize, 87 pages, cloth-over-board cover, illustrated endpapers, b/w illustrations by Decie Merwin. $15.00

Calico, 1937 Houghton, hardcover, color illustrated frontispiece, b/w illustrations Maginel Wright Barney. $15.00

Little Rag Doll, 1930 Houghton, cloth-over-board cover with paste-on-pictorial, 174 pages, illustrated endpapers, 4 color plates by Lois Lenski. $40.00

Little Sally Waters, 1929 Houghton, hardcover. $25.00

Lively Adventures of Johnny Ping Wing, 1929 Houghton, hardcover, illustrations by Jack Perkins. $15.00

Name for Obid, 1941 Houghton, cloth-over-board cover, oversize, illustrated endpapers, b/w/blue illustrations by Lois Lenski. $30.00

Peter Peppercorn, 1939 Houghton, cloth-over-board cover, oversize, 148 pages, illustrated endpapers, b/w/orange illustrations by Ilse Bischoff. $20.00

Santa Claus Brownies, 1928 Houghton, hardcover. $30.00

Saucy Betsy, 1936 Houghton, cloth-over-board cover, illustrated endpapers, 122 pages, b/w/green illustrations by Maitland de Gogorza. $15.00

Story of Nancy Hanks, 1923 Houghton, blue cloth-over-board cover, small, 125 pages, b/w illustrations by Kleber Hall. $15.00

Wee Ann, a Story for Little Girls, 1919 Houghton, blue cloth-over-board cover, small, illustrated endpapers, 4 color illustrations by Edith Butler. $25.00

PHILLIPS, Henry W.

Pets, 1906 McClure, tan cloth-over-board cover, small, 47 pages, cream/black illustrations by A. F. Frost. $25.00

PIER, Arthur, see Series section, ST. TIMOTHY'S

PIERSON, Clara, see Series section, MILLERS

Among the Pond People, 1901 Dutton, small, decorated cover with gilt, b/w illustrations by F. C. Gordon. $25.00

PIPER, Watty, editor

Brimful Book, (1927) 1929 edition, oversize picture book, paste-on-pictorial cover, color illustrated endpapers, color illustrations throughout by Eulalie, C. M. Burd, W. Gurney. $55.00

Fairy Tales that Never Grow Old, 1927 Platt, oversize, cloth-over-board cover with paste-on-pictorial, color and b/w illustrations by Eulalie, Lenski, Colborne. $65.00

Famous Fairy Tales, 1923 Platt, oversize, brown cloth-over-board cover with gilt lettering and paste-on-illustration, color illustrations throughout signed Eulalie. $70.00

Little Engine that Could, ca. 1930 Platt Munk, Never Grow Old Stories series, small, color illustrated paper-over-board cover with cloth spine, illustrated endpapers, color and b/w illustrations throughout by Lois Lenski. $45.00

Little Folks of Other Lands, (1929) 1943 edition, oversize, blue cloth-over-board cover with paste-on illustration, No. 2002 Deluxe Edition, color map endpapers, b/w and full-page color illustrations by Lucille W. and H. C. Holling. $55.00

Nursery Tales Children Love, (1925) 1933 edition Platt, No. 100 C, oversize picture book, paste-on-pictorial cover, color illustrations throughout by Eulalie and others. $55.00

PLYMPTON, A. G.
Robin's Recruit, 1893 Roberts, gray cloth-over-board cover with illustration, 179 pages, small. $20.00

POGANY, Nandor
Magyar Fairy Tales, 1930 Dutton, green cloth-over-board cover with gilt, 268 pages, illustrations by Willy Pogany. $75.00

POLITI, Leo
Boat for People, 1950 Scribners, cloth-over-board cover, color illustrations by author. ($75.00 with dust jacket) $40.00

Juanita, 1948 Scribners, cloth-over-board cover, color illustrations by author. ($75.00 with dust jacket) $40.00

Pedro, the Angel of Olvera Street, 1946 Scribners, cloth-over-board cover, color illustrations by author. ($80.00 with dust jacket) $40.00

Song of the Swallows, 1948 Scribners, oversize picture book, cloth-over-board cover, color illustrations by author. ($75.00 with dust jacket) $40.00

POLLOCK, Katherine
Sly Mongoose, 1943 Scribner, cloth-over-board cover, illustrated endpapers, 78 pages, b/w/brown illustrations by Kurt Wiese. $25.00

POOL, Maria Louise
Roweny in Boston, (1892) 1901 Harper, cloth-over-board cover with gilt, 348 pages. $15.00

POSTON, Martha Lee
Ching-Li, 1941 Nelson, cloth-over-board cover, square, b/w/blue illustrations by Weda Yap. $15.00

Girl Without a Country, 1944 Nelson, hardcover, map and b/w illustrations by Margaret Ayer. $15.00

POTTER, Beatrix
Tale of Benjamin Bunny, 1932 edition Warne, hardcover, small, green pictorial boards, illustrated endpapers, illustrations by Potter. $60.00

Tale of Little Pig Robinson, 1939 edition Warne, paste-on-pictorial on cover, small, 111 pages, 6 color plates by author. $200.00

Tale of Peter Rabbit, 1916 edition Saalfield, small, color illustrated paper-over-board cover, color and blue/white illustrations by Virginia Albert. $35.00

Tale of Squirrel Nutkin, 1903 Warne, 1st edition, small square, small paste-on-pictorial on cover, 86 pages, 27 color plate illustrations by author. $800.00

Tale of Two Bad Mice, 1932 edition Warne, hardcover, small, green pictorial boards, illustrated endpapers, color illustrations by Potter. $20.00

POTTER, Edna
Land from the Sea, 1939 Longmans first edition, oversize, color illustrated paper-over-board cover, illustrated endpapers, b/w illustrations by author. $20.00

Story of Switzerland, 1937 Grosset, small, 47 pages, b/w illustrations by author. $20.00

POTTER, Miriam, see Series section, MRS. GOOSE

POULSSON, Emilie, see ZWILGMEYER, D.
In the Child's World, 1919 edition Milton Bradley, blue cloth-over-board cover with gilt lettering, illustrated by L. J. Bridgman. $20.00

Songs of A Little Child's Day, 1910 Milton Bradley, oversize, illustrated cover, 117 pages, color plates by Ruth E. Newton. $40.00

POWELL, A. VanBuren, see Series section, MYSTERY BOYS

POWERS, Tom
Scotch Circus, the Story of Tammas who Rode the Dragon, 1934 Houghton, 94 pages, frontispiece and 3 double-page color illustrations by Lois Lenski. $45.00

PRATT, Anna
Friends from My Garden, 1890 Stokes, square, white enameled cover decorated with gilt and colors, 12 color plates by Laura Hill. Hard-to-find. $150.00

PRATT, Ella Farman
Happy Children, 1896 Crowell, green and yellow design on gray cloth-over-board cover, oversize, 64 pages, b/w illustrations. $25.00
Play Lady, a Story for Other Girls, 1900 Crowell, half-cloth cover with color illustration, b/w frontispiece, 132 pages. $30.00

PRESTON, Helen Bradley
Blue Nets and Red Sails, 1936 Longmans first edition, 38 pages, frontispiece, color and b/w illustrations by Margaret Braley. $25.00

PRICE, Edith Ballinger
Enchanted Admiral, 1931 Century first edition, cloth-over-board cover with gilt, b/w illustrations by author. $25.00
Fork in the Road, 1930 Century first edition, cloth-over-board cover, b/w illustrations by author. $25.00
Fortune of the Indies, 1922 Century, cloth-over-board cover, b/w illustrations by author. $25.00
Garth, Able Seaman, 1923 Century, cloth-over-board cover, b/w illustrations by author. $25.00
Happy Venture, 1921 Century, cloth-over-board cover, b/w illustrations by author. $25.00
Lubber's Luck, 1935 Little Boston, cloth-over-board cover, b/w illustrations by author. $25.00
Ship of Dreams, 1927 Century, cloth-over-board cover, b/w illustrations by author. $25.00
Silver Shoal Light, 1920 Century, cloth-over-board cover, b/w illustrations by author. $25.00

PRICE, Margaret Evans
Child's Book of Myths, 1924 McNally, cloth-over-board cover with paste-on-pictorial, 111 pages, color illustrations by author. $40.00
Legends of the Seven Seas, 1929 Harper first edition, hardcover, color frontispiece, b/w illustrations. ($50.00 with dust jacket) $30.00
Monkey-Do, 1934 Harper, hardcover, b/w illustrations. ($40.00 with dust jacket) $25.00
Mota and the Monkey Tree, 1935 Harper first edition, hardcover, 146 pages, b/w illustrations by author. $35.00

PROCTOR, Beth
Little Sally Dutcher, (1924) 1940 edition Whitman, cloth-over-board cover with color paste-on-pictorial, color illustrated endpapers, color illustrations throughout by Fay Turpin. $40.00

PROVINES, Mary Virginia
Liz'beth Ann's Goat, 1947 Viking, oversize picture book, 40 pages, color illustrated paper-over-board cover, color illustrated by Grace Paull. $35.00

PUGH, Mabel
Little Carolina Blue Bonnet, (1933) 1937 edition Crowell, color frontispiece, b/w illustrations by author. $30.00

PUMPHREY, Margaret B.
Stories of the Pilgrims, 1912 McNally, green cloth-over-board cover, small, 4 color plates plus b/w illustrations by L. F. Perkins. $30.00
Under Three Flags, (1939) 3rd printing 1949 Caxton, cloth-over-board cover, color frontispiece, b/w illustrations by Hilda Preibisius. $20.00

PUNER, Helen Walker
Sitter Who Didn't Sit, 1949 Lothrop, oversize picture book, illustrated paper-over-board cover, illustrated endpapers, color illustrated by Roger Duvoisin. $25.00

PURDON, Eric
Valley of the Larks, 1939 Ferrar, cloth-over-board cover, 184 pages, drawings by Graham Peck. $20.00

PUTNAM, Nina and **JACOBSEN, Norman**
Adventures in the Open, 1938 Wise Parslow, navy cloth-over-board cover, illustrated endpapers, 112 pages, color illustrations by Katharine Dodge. $45.00

PYLE, Howard
Book of Pirates, 1921 edition Harper, cloth-over-board cover with paste-on-illustration, illustrations by author. $45.00
Men of Iron, 1919 Harpers, cloth-over-board cover, illustrations by author. $45.00
Story of Sir Launcelot and His Companions, 1907 Scribner first edition, decorated brown cloth-over-board cover, illustrations by author. $220.00
Within the Capes, 1899 Scribners, cloth-over-board cover, 226 pages, illustrations by author. $55.00

PYLE, Katharine, author-illustrator
Black-Eyed Puppy, (1923) 1931 edition Dutton, green cloth-over-board cover with gilt lettering and paste-on-pictorial, 89 pages, 12 color plates by author. $30.00
Counterpane Fairy, (1898) 1937 edition Dutton, small, 190 pages, b/w illustrations by author. $100.00

Fairy Tales from India, 1926 Lippincott, cloth-over-board cover, 12 color plates by author. $125.00

Nancy Rutledge, 1906 Little Brown, printed illustration on cloth-over-board cover, 206 pages, 6 b/w plates by author. $50.00

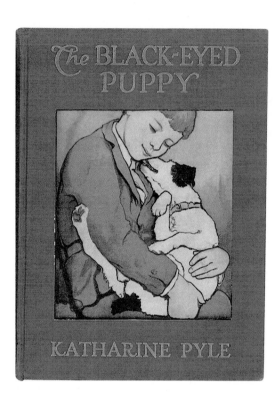

PYRNELLE, Louise Clarke

Diddie, Dumps, and Tot, (1882) 1916 edition Harper, printed illustration on cloth-over-board cover, b/w illustrations. $20.00

Diddie, Dumps, and Tot, 1930 edition Harper, cloth-over-board cover, 2 color plates plus b/w illustrations by Gertrude Kay. $30.00

⤙⧫⤚ **Q** ⤙⧫⤚

QUIGG, Jane

Betsy Goes A-Visiting, 1940 Oxford, color and b/w illustrations by Decie Merwin. ($45.00 with dust jacket) $20.00

Hickory Lane, 1938 Nelson, gray cloth-over-board cover, illustrated endpapers, illustrations by Ninon MacKnight. ($45.00 with dust jacket) $20.00

Polly Peters, 1942 Oxford, b/w illustrations by Pelagie Doane. $20.00

QUIRK, Leslie W.

Boy Scouts of Black Eagle Patrol, undated Grosset ca. 1930s, green illustrated boards. $20.00

Freshman Dorn, Pitcher, 1911 Century, print illustration on cloth-over-board cover, 12 b/w plates by Henry Watson. $25.00

⤙⧫⤚ **R** ⤙⧫⤚

RAABE, Martha

Little Lost Sioux, 1942 Whitman, cloth-over-board cover with paste-on-pictorial, illustrated endpapers, color throughout by Oscar Howe. $25.00

RAE, John

Granny Goose, 1926 Volland, oversize, pictorial boards, pictorial endpapers, and color illustrations throughout. $95.00

RANDALL, Jane, see PEAT, Fern Bisel

RAPHAEL, Arthur M.

Great Jug, 1936 Reilly Lee, cloth-over-board cover with impressed illustration, 136 pages, color frontispiece, b/w illustrations by Clifford Benton. $45.00

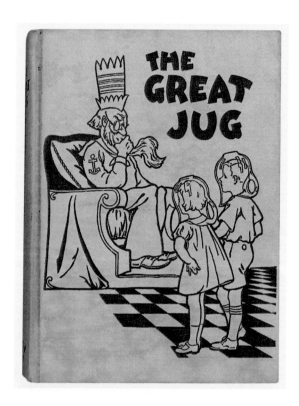

RASMUSSEN, Margrete

East O' the Sun and West O' the Moon, 1924 edition Whitman, cloth-over-board cover with paste-on-illustration, 192 pages, illustrated endpapers, b/w/red illustrations throughout by Violet Moore Higgins. $35.00

RAYMOND, R. W.
Children's Week, 1871 Ford, cloth-over-board cover with gilt, b/w illustrations. $20.00

REY, Margaret and **H. A.**
Billy's Picture, 1948 Harper, hardcover, illustrated by authors. $20.00
Pretzel, 1944 Harper lst edition, red cloth-over-board cover. ($125.00 with dust jacket) $40.00
Spotty, 1945 Harper, hardcover, illustrated by H. A. Rey. ($25.00 with dust jacket) $15.00

REYHER, Becky
My Mother is the Most Beautiful Woman in the World, 1945 Lothrop, cloth-over-board cover, small square, illustrated endpapers, color and b/w illustrations by Ruth Gannett. $20.00

RHOADES, Nina
Children on the Top Floor, 1904 Lothrop, decorated brown cloth-over-board cover, 219 pages, illustrated by Bertha Davidson. $15.00

RICE, Alice Hegan
Captain June, 1907 Century, cloth-over-board cover, 120 pages, b/w illustrations by C. D. Weldon. $20.00

RICHARDS, Laura, see Series section, LAURA RICHARDS LIBRARY
Captain January, (1890) 1924 Page, Baby Peggy edition, hardcover with paste-on-illustration and gilt lettering, illustrated with photos from the film. $45.00
Golden Windows, 1903, cloth-over-board cover with gilt, 123 pages, b/w illustrations by Arthur Becher. $25.00
Hildegarde's Home, 1892 Estes, red cloth-over-board cover. $45.00
Isla Heron, 1896 Estes, beige cloth-over-board cover with decorations, 109 pages, 4 b/w illustrations by Frank Merrill. $25.00
Jim of Hellas, 1895 Estes, gray cloth-over-board cover. $20.00
Mrs. Tree, 1902 Estes, decorated gray cloth-over-board cover with gilt, small 282 pages, b/w illustrations by Frank Merrill. $25.00
Narcissa, or Road to Rome, 1894 Estes, green cloth-over-board cover with silver decoration, 80 pages, small. $20.00
Piccolo, 1906 Estes, cloth-over-board cover with illustration, illustrated endpapers, two-color illustrations throughout by Josephine Bruce and others. $45.00
Queen Hildegarde, 1889 Estes, red cloth-over-board cover. $30.00

Silver Crown, 1906, cloth-over-board cover with decoration by Jessie Wilcox Smith. 105 pages. $30.00

RICHARDSON, Frederick, illustrator
Book for Children, 1938 Donohue, oversize oblong, cloth-over-board cover with paste-on-pictorial, 107 pages, illustrated endpapers, full-page color illustrations by author. $150.00
Mother Goose, (edited by Eulalie Osgood Grover) 1917 Volland, illustrated cloth-over-board cover with printed illustration and gilt lettering, oversize, 108 color plates by Richardson. $250.00
Mother Goose, 1921 Volland Popular Edition, oversize, cloth-over-board cover with paste-on-pictorial, color illustrations by Frederick Richardson. $100.00
Mother Goose, ca. 1937 edition Donohue, illustrated cloth-over-board cover, oversize, 128 pages, with full-page full color illustrations throughout by Richardson. $150.00
Old Old Tales Retold, ca. 1936 Donohue, oversize oblong, cloth-over-board cover with paste-on-pictorial, 108 pages, full-page full color illustrations by author. $150.00

RICHMOND, Grace S.
On Christmas Day in the Morning, (1905) 1909 edition Doubleday, small, cardboard cover, 40 pages, 4 color plate illustrations by Charles Relyea. $15.00
Red Pepper's Patients, 1917 edition Burt, cloth-over-board cover. $15.00

RICHMOND, Henry
Adventures of Cub Bear, 1917 Saalfield, color illustrated hardcover, b/w illustrations by Will Fitzgerald. $15.00

RIGGS, Ida Berry
Little Champion, 1944 Macmillan, hardcover, 144

pages, illustrations by Decie Merwin. ($20.00 with dust jacket) $10.00

RILEY, James Whitcomb
Defective Santa Claus, 1904 Bobbs Merrill, cloth-over-board cover with gilt and decoration, 78 pages, b/w illustrations by Relyea and W. Vawter. $30.00
Riley Fairy Tales, 1923 edition Bobbs Merrill, blue cloth-over-board cover with paste-on-illustration, oversize, 96 pages, color illustrated by Will Vawter. $25.00

RION, Hanna
Smiling Road, ca. 1910 Clode, green cloth-over-board cover, illustrated endpapers, small, 191 pages, 10 b/w illustrations by Frank Ver Beck. $15.00

ROBINSON, Tom
Buttons, 1938 Viking first edition, oversize, 64 pages, illustrations by Peggy Bacon. $55.00
Greylock and the Robins, 1946 Viking, first edition, oversize, 31 pages, color illustrations by Robert Lawson. ($65.00 with dust jacket) $50.00
Greylock and the Robins, Viking, later editions. $20.00
In and Out, 1943 Viking, poetry, cloth-over-board cover, illustrations by Marguerite de Angeli. $30.00
Trigger John's Son, (1934) 1949 edition Viking, illustrations by Robert McCloskey. ($35.00 with dust jacket) $20.00

ROBINSON, W. W.
Elephants, 1935 Harper first edition, color illustrated paper-over-board cover, oversize, 43 pages, b/w illustrations by Irene Robinson. $40.00

ROCKWOOD, Roy, see Series section, DAVE DASHAWAY

ROLLESTON, C. W.
Parsifal, undated ca. 1912 Crowell, oversize art book, 194 pages, suede cover with gilt design, 16 tipped in color plates plus full pages lithos and text illustrations by Willy Pogany. $275.00

ROOT, Harvey W.
Tommy with the Big Tents, 1924 Harper, cloth-over-board cover, 202 pages, b/w illustrations by T. Skinner. $20.00

ROSMAN, Alice Grant
Jock the Scot, 1930 Minton Balch, blue cloth-over-board cover with paste-on-pictorial, 204 pages, color plates by Joan Esley. $30.00

ROSTRON, Richard
Sorcerer's Apprentice, 1941 Morrow, oversize, cloth-over-board cover, illustrated endpapers, color and b/w illustrations by Frank Lieberman. $20.00

ROY, Lillian Elizabeth, see Series section, BLUE BIRDS, FIVE LITTLE STARRS, LITTLE WASHINGTON
Alice in Beeland, 1919 Cupples & Leon, color paste-on-illustration cover with gilt lettering, 4 full-page b/w illustrations by Julia Greene. $15.00

RUSKIN, John
Dame Wiggins of Lee and her Seven Wonderful Cats, 1925 edition Macmillan, small, cloth-over-board cover, illustrated endpapers, 76 pages, color illustrations throughout by Roy Meldrum. $35.00

SAGE, Agnes Carr
Two Girls of Old New Jersey, 1912 Stokes, brown cloth-over-board cover with illustration, b/w plates by Douglas Connah. $20.00

SAINSBURY, Noel, see Series section, BILL BOLTON

SAMUELS, Adelaide
Father Gander's Melodies for Mother Goose's Grandchildren, 1894 Roberts, green cloth-over-board cover with gilt lettering and illustration, 121 pages, illustrated. $60.00

SANFORD, Mrs. D. P.
Pussy Tip-Toes' Family, 1874 Dutton, color illustrated boards, large, b/w illustrations throughout. $25.00

SARG, Tony
Savings Book, a Trip to Golden City, 1946 World, first edition, oblong, hardcover, spiral binding, color illustrations, bank envelope attached to inside cover. ($90.00 with dust jacket and bank envelope in tact) $45.00
Tony Sarg's Book for Children, 1924 Greenberg first edition, oversize, paper-over-board cover with cut-out theatre, lifting curtain and turning wheel mounted on inside of front cover to show scenes from Red Riding Hood. Color illustrated endpapers, color illustrations throughout. $90.00
Tony Sarg's Book of Marionette Plays, 1927 Greenberg first edition, hardcover, title page and chapter heading illustrations. ($120.00 with dust jacket) $60.00

Tony Sarg's Magic Movie Book, 1943 B. F. Jay, oversize, cloth-over-board cover, complete with magic lenses. $200.00

Tony Sarg's Surprise Book, 1941 Jay, oversize, color pictorial boards, spiral binding, color illustrations, moveable and textured parts. ($100.00 with box) $80.00

Who's Who in Tony Sarg's Zoo, 1937 McLoughlin, oversize, color plates and centerfold illustration. ($120.00 with dust jacket) $50.00

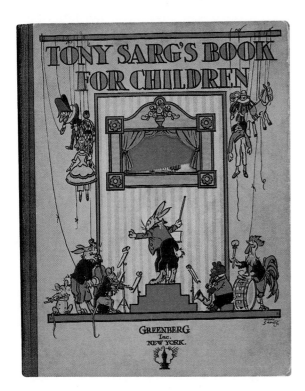

SARI
Coat for Klentje, 1939 Grosset, pictorial boards, illustrations by author. $20.00

Jeanne-Marie Goes to Market, 1938 Grosset, oversize, color illustrated paper-over-board cover, color illustrations by author. $25.00

SAUNDERS, Marshall
Bonnie Prince Fetlar, 1920 Doran, tan cloth-over-board cover with paste-on-illustration, 349 pages. $30.00

Charles and His Lamb, 1895 Banes, cloth-over-board cover, b/w illustrations. ($250.00 with hard-to-find dust jacket) $50.00

SAWYER, Ruth
Christmas Anna Angel, 1944 Viking, small, 48 pages, double page color illustrations by Kate Seredy. ($55.00 with dust jacket) $30.00

Least One, 1941 Viking, cloth-over-board cover, illustrations by Leo Politi. ($50.00 with dust jacket) $30.00

Roller Skates, 1936 Viking, first edition, Newbery Medal winner, illustrations by Sawyer. $65.00 Later editions, $25.00

This Way to Christmas, 1916 Harper, cloth-over-board cover with gilt, Norman Rockwell b/w frontispiece. $75.00

SAYERS, Frances Clarke
Bluebonnets for Lucinda, 1934 Viking first edition, hardcover, illustrations by Helen Sewell. $25.00

Tag-Along Tooloo, 1947 Viking, hardcover, illustrations by Helen Sewell. $25.00

SCANNELL, Florence and Edith
Dulce's Promise, undated ca. 1894, floral boards, small, 32 pages, red/white illustrations. $20.00

SCHMIDT, Earl
Our Friendly Animals and Whence They Came, 1938 Donohue, oversize picture book, color illustrated paper-over-board cover, illustrated endpapers, full-page color illustrations by Walter Weber. $40.00

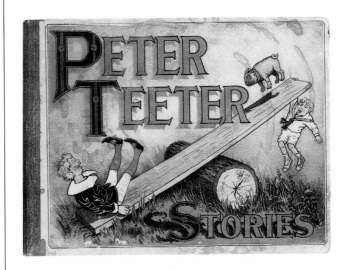

SCHWETZKY, Prof. Otto H. L.
Peter Teeter Stories, 1904 Thompson, oversize oblong, illustrated paper-over-board cover, illustrated endpapers, color illustrations throughout by Raymond H. Garman. $75.00

SCOTT, Morgan, see Series section, OAKDALE ACADEMY

SEMPLE, Daisy, see PEAT, Fern

SEWELL, Helen
Birthdays for Robin, 1947 edition Hale, illustrated paper-over-board cover, illustrated. $25.00

Blue Barns, 1933 Macmillan, b/w illustrations by author. $30.00

Jimmy and Jemima, 1940 Macmillan lst edition, cloth-over-board cover with paste-on-illustration, illustrated. $40.00

Peggy and the Pony, 1936 Oxford, blue cloth-over-board cover, color illustrations. $25.00

Three Tall Tales, 1947 Macmillan, oversize, illustrated boards, color illustrations. ($40.00 with dust jacket) $25.00

SHAKESPEARE, William

Midsummer-Night's Dream, 1908 edition William Heinemann, London, tan cloth-over-board cover with gilt, first Rackham edition, decorated title page, 40 color plates plus b/w illustrations by Arthur Rackham. $400.00

SHANKLAND, F., see PEAT, Fern

SHANNON, Monica

California Fairy Tales, 1943 Doran, cloth-over-board cover with print illustration, 298 pages, b/w illustrations by C. E. Millard. $15.00

Dobry, 1934 Viking, 176 pages, illustrations by A. Katchamakoff. $20.00

SKEAT, Walter

Tiger's Mistake, 1929 Macmillan, cloth-over-board cover, small, 93 pages, b/w illustrations by F. H. Townsend. $25.00

SKINNER, Ada M. and Eleanor M.

Child's Book of Modern Stories, 1920 Duffield, lst edition, dark blue cloth-over-board cover with paste-on-illustration and gilt, 341 pages, 8 color plates by Jessie Willcox Smith. $100.00

SMITH, E. Boyd, b. Canada, 1860–1943, illustrator-author

Aesop's Fables, 1911 Century, hardcover, b/w illustrations by author. $85.00

Early Life of Mr. Man, 1914 Houghton, hardcover, illustrated. $90.00

Farm Book: Bob and Betty Visit Uncle John, 1910 Houghton, oblong oversize, pictorial boards, illustrated endpapers, 12 color plates. $65.00

Lions 'n' Elephants 'n' Everything, 1929 Putnam, oblong oversize, hardcover, 12 color plates. $65.00

My Village, 1896 Scribner, hardcover, vignettes throughout text by author. $80.00

Railroad Book, Bob and Betty's Summer on the Railroad, 1913 Houghton, oblong oversize, pictorial boards, illustrated endpapers, 12 color plates. $65.00

Seashore Book: Bob and Betty's Summer with Captain Hawes, 1912 Houghton, oblong oversize, pictorial boards, illustrated endpapers, 12 color plates. $65.00

So Long Ago, 1944 edition Houghton, oversize, blue cloth-over-board, color plates by author. $70.00

Story of Noah's Ark, 1905 Houghton, hardcover, color plates by author. $65.00

SMITH, Jessie Willcox

Child's Book of Old Verses, 1910 Dutton, navy cloth-over-board cover with gilt lettering and paste-on-illustration with gilt background, color plates by author. $125.00

SMITH, Laura Rountree

Circus Animals in Funland, 1928 Whitman, illustrated cover, illustrations by Scannell, Lofts and Enslow. $20.00

Circus Book, ca. 1923 Grosset, cloth-over-board cover, small, 132 pages, illustrated. $20.00

Circus Stories, 1922 Whitman, illustrated cover, illustrations by Lofts and Enslow. $25.00

Fairy Babies, ca. 1924 Grosset, hardcover, illustrations by Dorothy Dolin. $20.00

Happy Mannikin in Manners Town, 1925 Whitman, small, hardcover, color and b/w illustrations by Mildred Lyon. ($35.00 with dust jacket) $25.00

Little Folks from Etiquette Town, ca. 1927 Whitman, dark green cloth-over-board cover with paste-on-pictorial, illustrated. $20.00

Party Twins and their Forty Parties, Plays and Games, 1924 Whitman, paste-on-illustration, small, 128 pages, illustrations by Helen Lyon. $25.00

Singing Twins, 1924 Whitman, lst edition, illustrated cloth-over-board cover, color. ($45.00 with dust jacket) $25.00

Tiddly Winks Primer, 1926 Whitman, small, black hardcover with paste-on-illustration, easy reader, illustrated. ($40.00 with dust jacket) $20.00

Treasure Twins, ca. 1920s Whitman, Just Right Books series, hardcover with paste-on-pictorial, easy-read print, two-color and b/w illustrations throughout by Marguerite Jones. $20.00

SMITH, Nora A.
Kate Douglas Wiggin as her Sister Knew Her, 1925 Houghton, yellow cloth-over-board cover, 283 pages, 16 b/w photo illustrations. $15.00

SMOCK, Nell Stolp
White Tail, 1938 Platt Munk, oversize, cloth-over-board cover with paste-on-pictorial, illustrated endpapers, b/w/orange illustrations by author. $20.00

SNELL, LeRoy, see Series section, NORTHWEST STORIES

SOWERBY, J. G.
Afternoon Tea, Rhymes for Children, 1881 Rhodes and Washburn, decorated hardcover, 64 pages, illustrated. $80.00

SOWERS, Phyllis Ayer
Dhan of the Pearl Country, 1939 Whitman, hardcover with paste-on-pictorial, color illustrations by Margaret Ayer. $25.00

Let's Go Round the World with Bob and Betty, 1934 Grosset, oversize, illustrated by Robert Von Neuman. ($30.00 in dust jacket) $20.00

Lin Foo and Lin Ching, 1932 Crowell, hardcover, illustrations by Margaret Ayer. $20.00

Swords and Sails in the Philippines, 1944 Whitman, cloth-over-board cover, 128 pages, b/w illustrations by Margaret Ayer. $20.00

Yasu-Bo and Ishi-Ko, a Boy and Girl of Japan, 1934 Crowell, 143 pages, illustrated endpapers, b/w/orange illustrations by Margaret Ayer. $20.00

SPAETH, Sigmund
Maxims to Music, 1939 McBride, oversize, hardcover, color illustrations by Tony Sarg. ($100.00 with dust jacket) $50.00

SPEED, Nell, see Series section, TUCKER TWINS

SPRAGUE, Besse Toulouse see Series section, TRAVEL-TOT-TALES

SQUIRE, Charles
Wonderful World of Being, the Story of the Travels and Perils of Four Brother Knights of Sicily who Adventured to the North and to the South and to the East and to the West, 1906 Ballantyne, decorated cloth-over-board cover. $35.00

STANDISH, Burt, see Series section, BIG LEAGUE

STANDISH, Winn, see Series section, JACK LORIMER

STEARNS, David and **Sharon**
Spunk the Donkey, 1945 Wilcox & Follett, hardcover. $15.00

STEPHENS, Dan
Cottonwood Yarns, 1935 Hammond & Stephens, cloth-over-board cover, 109 pages, photos and b/w illustrations by Ellsworth. $15.00

STEPHENS, Ruth
Mary and Sue, 1947 Saalfield, oversize easy-read, printed color illustration on cover, color and b/w illustrations by Eleanor Eadie. $15.00

STEPHENSON, T. W.
Songs for Little Children, undated ca. 1920 Milford, London, tan paper-over-board cover with illustration, oversize, 42 pages, full pages of b/w illustrations by L. Govey. $65.00

STERLING, Helen
Horse That Takes the Milk Around, 1946 Watts, oblong picture book, color illustrated paper-over-board cover, illustrated endpapers, color illustrated throughout by Marjorie Hartwell. $35.00

Little Moo and the Circus, 1945 Watts, hardcover, color illustrations by Harry Lees. $35.00

STERNE, Emma Gelders
All About Little Boy Blue, 1924 Cupples, small, hardcover, illustrations by Thelma Gooch. $25.00

Miranda is a Princess, 1937 Dodd, cloth-over-board cover, illustrated endpapers, 221 pages, b/w illustrations by Robert Lawson. $40.00

STEVENSON, Robert Louis
Child's Garden of Verses, undated ca. 1910 McKay,

illustrated tan cloth-over-board cover, small, 125 pages, color plates and b/w plates by Millicent Sowerby. $20.00

Child's Garden of Verses, 1930 edition Saalfield, oversize, black cloth-over-board cover with paste-on-pictorial and gilt trim, flowered endpapers, 60 pages, 13 color plate illustrations by Clara Burd. $85.00

Child's Garden of Verses, 1942 edition John Martin's House, oversize hardcover with illustrated endpapers and color illustrations by Pelagie Doane. $35.00

Also see PEAT, Fern Bisel for another version of this title.

STEWART, Anna Bird
Builder of Bridges, 1929 McBride first edition, cloth-over-board cover. ($30.00 with dust jacket) $15.00

Candy Box, 1929 McBride, hardcover, 57 pages. $15.00

Two Young Corsicans, 1944 edition Lippincott, cloth-over-board cover, illustrated by Catherine Richter. ($15.00 with dust jacket) $10.00

STEWART, Grace Bliss
Good Fairy, 1930 Reilly Lee, green cloth-over-board cover with gilt illustration, 128 pages, color and b/w illustrations by P. B. Adams. $35.00

STIGAND, Capt. Chauncey H.
Black Tales for White Children, translated from

Swahili, 1914 Constable first edition, illustrated cover, b/w illustrations by John Hargrove. $200.00

STOCKTON, Frank
Captain's Toll-Gate, 1903 Appleton, cloth-over-board cover, 359 pages. $25.00

Casting Away of Mrs. Lecks and Mrs. Aleshine, (1886) 1933 Appleton, hardcover, 290 pages, illustrations by George Richards. $20.00

Clocks of Rondaine, 1892 Scribner, cloth-over-board cover, 171 pages, b/w illustrations. $25.00

Round-About Rambles, 1872 Scribner, purple cloth-over-board cover with gilt, b/w illustrations. $30.00

STOKES, Katherine, see Series section, MOTOR MAIDS

STOKES, Vernon, and **HARNETT, Cynthia**
To Be a Farmer's Boy, 1940 Blackie, 160 pages, blue cloth-over-board cover, charcoal drawings by authors. $35.00

STONE, Amy Wentworth
P-Penny and His Little Red Cart, 1934 Lothrop, oversize, illustrated cloth-over-board cover, 165 pages, illustrated endpapers, color frontispiece, b/w illustrations by Hildegarde Woodward. $25.00

STONE, David, see Series section, YANK BROWN

STONG, Phil
Farm Boy, 1934 Doubleday, cloth-over-board cover, illustrated by Kurt Wiese. $25.00

No-Sitch, the Hound, 1936 Dodd, oversize, illustrated by Kurt Wiese. $20.00

STOW, Edith
Nancy the Joyous, 1914 Reilly Britton, decorated cloth-over-board cover, 253 pages, illustrated. $40.00

STRACK, Lilian Holmes
Swords and Iris, 1937 Harper, cloth-over-board cover, 125 pages, illustrated endpapers, color frontispiece on rice paper, b/w illustrations by Bunji Tagawa. $35.00

STRATEMEYER, Edward, see Series section, LAKEPORT, OLD GLORY, PUTNAM HALL

STRATTON, Clarence
Swords and Statues, 1937 Literary Guild, orange cloth-over-board cover, color frontispiece, b/w illustrations by Robert Lawson. ($45.00 with dust jacket) $25.00

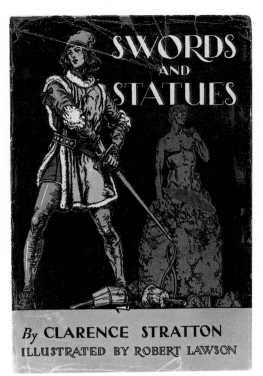

By CLARENCE STRATTON
ILLUSTRATED BY ROBERT LAWSON

STUART, Ruth McEnery
Napoleon Jackson, 1902 Century, cloth-over-board cover with gilt, small, 132 pages, b/w illustrations by Edward Potthast. $40.00

SUGIMOTO, Chiyono
Picture Tales from the Japanese, 1928 Stokes, small oblong, cloth-over-board cover with paste-on-pictorial, 124 pages, b/w illustrations. $25.00

SWEET, Frank H.
Stories of the Blue and Gray, 1907 McLoughlin, 188 pages, olive cloth-over-board cover. $20.00
Story of Puss and Boots, undated McLoughlin picture book. $30.00

— T —

TAGGART, Marion Ames
Beth's Wonder-Winter, a Story, 1914 Wilde, decorated cloth-over-board cover, 349 pages, illustrated by William Stecher. $10.00
Bottle Imp, 1921 Doran, cloth-over-board cover, illustrated by Ann Peck. ($15.00 with dust jacket) $10.00
Little Aunt, 1913 Donohue, illustrated green cloth-over-board cover, illustrated by Ruth Bingham. $10.00

TARRY, Ellen
Janie Belle, 1940 Garden City first edition, over-

size, cloth spine, paper-over-board cover, 32 pages, illustrations by Myrtle Sheldon. $45.00

TARSHIS, Elizabeth Kent
Village that Learned to Read, 1941 Houghton, oversize, illustrated. $20.00

TAYLOR, Alta, see PEAT, Fern

TAYLOR, Cathryn, illustrator
Sleepy Time Picture Book, 1946 Whitman, Weather-Bird Shoes promo, oversize, color illustrated paper cover, 12 pages, color illustrations throughout by Cathryn Taylor. $20.00

TENGGREN, Gustaf, illustrator
New Illustrated Book of Favorite Hymns, 1941 Garden City, pictorial boards, color illustrations throughout. $30.00
Tenggren Tell-It-Again Book, 1942 Little, Brown, oversize, 199 pages, illustrations by Tenggren. $50.00

THOMPSON, Blanche Jennings
Golden Trumpets, 1927 Macmillan, small, 163 pages, cloth-over-board cover with gilt, orange/b/w illustrations by Helen Torrey. $30.00

THOMPSON, Mary Wolfe
Blue Horizon, 1940 Longmans, cloth-over-board cover, b/w illustrations by Janice Holland. $15.00

Blueberry Muffin, 1942 Longmans, hardcover, illustrated endpapers, b/w illustrations by Erick Berry. $15.00

Highway Past Her Door, 1938 Longmans, hardcover, illustrated endpapers, b/w illustrations by Vera Neville. $15.00

Pattern for Penelope, 1943 Longmans, hardcover, illustrated endpapers, b/w illustrations by Vera Neville. $15.00

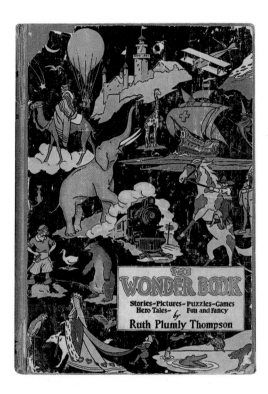

THOMPSON, Ruth Plumly
Perhappsy Chaps, 1918 Volland, color illustrated paper-over-board cover, color illustrations by Arthur Henderson. $200.00

Princess of Cozytown, 1922 Volland, color illustrated paper-over-board cover, color illustrations by Janet Laura Scott. $100.00

Wonder Book, 1929 Reilly Lee, brown cloth-over-board cover with paste-on-pictorial, color plate illustrations by William Donahey, b/w illustrations by other artists. $300.00

THOMPSON, William
Wigwam Wonder Tales, 1919 Scribner, cloth-over-board cover with decoration, small, 156 pages, b/w illustrations by Carle Michel Boog. $40.00

THORNE, Diana
Chips, 1944 Winston, picture book, illustrations by Connie Moran. $20.00

THORNE-THOMSEN, Gudrun
Birch and the Star, 1915 Row Peterson, cloth-over-board cover with paste-on-illustration, illustrated endpapers, small, 129 pages, 6 color plates by Frederick Poole. $30.00

East o' the Sun and West o' the Moon, 1912 Peterson, tan cloth-over-board cover, color plates by Frederick Richardson. $35.00

Sky Bed, a Norwegian Christmas, 1944 edition Scribner, illustrated paper-over-board cover, small, 25 pages, color illustrated by Nedda Walker. $25.00

THORPE, Rose H.
Year's Best Days for Boys and Girls, 1889 Shepard, cloth-over-board cover with gilt, small, 202 pages, b/w illustrations. $20.00

TINSLEY, Henry
Little Tommy Stuffin, 1904 Shultz, first edition, cloth-over-board cover with paste-on-illustration, small. $15.00

TIPPETT, James
Picnic, 1938 Grosset, small square, illustrated, easy reader. $20.00

Singing Farmer, (1927) 1940 edition Grosset, paper-over-board cover, illustrated endpapers, b/w/orange illustrations by Elizabeth Tyler Wolcott. $15.00

Toys and Toy Makers, 1931 Harper, small, 144 pages, red and gold cloth-over-board cover, color and b/w illustrations by Elizabeth Enright. $20.00

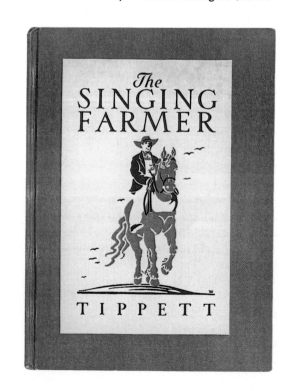

TITCHENELL, Elsa, see GRUELLE, Justin

TOUSEY, Sanford
Dick and the Canal Boat, 1943 Doubleday, illustrated paper-over-board cover, illustrated endpapers, color and b/w illustrations by author. $20.00
Jerry and the Pony Express, 1936 Doubleday, oblong, illustrated paper-over-board cover, illustrated endpapers, color illustrated throughout by author. $35.00
Stagecoach Sam, (1940) 1943 Doubleday, illustrated paper-over-board cover, illustrated endpapers, color and b/w illustrations by author. $25.00
Steamboat Billy, 1935 Doubleday, oblong, illustrated paper-over-board cover, illustrated endpapers, color illustrated throughout by author. $35.00

TRAVERS, P. L.
I Go by Sea, I Go by Land, 1941 Harper, cloth-over-board cover, illustrations by Gertrude Hermes. $30.00

TREGARTHEN, Enys
Doll who Came Alive, 1942 John Day, illustrated hardcover, illustrations by Nora Unwin. $30.00
Piskey Folk, 1940 John Day, photo illustrations by Wm. McGreal. $20.00
White Ring, 1949 Harcourt, hardcover, illustrations by Nora Unwin. $15.00

TUCKER, Anna B.
Simple Songs for Little Singers, 1931 Honolulu Star-Bulletin, oversize, cloth-over-board cover, 144 pages, b/w illustrations by J. May Fraser. $15.00

TUCKER, Charlotte
Backward Swing, ca. 1870s Nelson, small, 64 pages, cloth-over-board cover with color paste-on-illustration, b/w frontispiece. $40.00

TUDOR, Tasha
Linsey Woolsey, 1946 Oxford, hardcover, first edition, color illustrations by Tudor. ($220.00 with dust jacket) $125.00
Mother Goose, 1944 library edition, marked ex-library, color illustrations by Tudor. ($85.00 with dust jacket) $45.00
Snow Before Christmas, 1941 Oxford, first edition. ($295.00 with dust jacket) $180.00

TURNER, Ethel
Family at Misrule, undated Ward Lock edition ca. 1916, cloth-over-board cover, 256 pages, illustrations by A. Johnson. $30.00
In the Mist of the Mountains, 1906 London, hardcover, frontispiece. $20.00

Miss Bobbie, 1897 London, illustrated cloth-over-board cover, b/w plates. $35.00
Mother's Little Girl, 1904 London, hardcover, 255 pages, illustrated. $15.00
Raft in the Bush, 1910 London, hardcover, 16 plates by Sandy and Souter. $35.00
Three Little Maids, undated London, cloth-over-board cover with gilt, plate and text illustrations. $45.00

TURNER, Nancy Byrd
Magpie Lane, 1927 Harcourt, cloth-over-board cover, silhouette illustrations by Decie Merwin. $30.00

TWAIN, Mark (Clemens)
Prince and the Pauper, 1882 Osgood, Boston, first American edition, square, 411 pages, gilt decorated cover, 192 illustrations. $800.00

TYTLER, M. Fraser
Little Fanny's Journal, 1851 Kennedy, Edinburgh, small, cloth-over-board cover with gilt, 132 pages, b/w illustrations. $20.00

U

UNDSET, Sigrid
Sigurd and His Brave Companions, 1943 Knopf, cloth-over-board cover, illustrated endpapers, color and b/w illustrations by G. B. Teilman. $15.00

UPDEGRAFF, Florence Maule
Blue Dowry, 1948 Harcourt, cloth-over-board cover, 271 pages, b/w illustrations by R. Doremus. $15.00
Coat for a Soldier, 1941 Harcourt, cloth-over-board cover, 294 pages, b/w illustrations by Eva Watson. $15.00
Traveler's Candle, 1942 Harcourt, cloth-over-board cover, 237 pages, b/w illustrations by Eva Watson. $15.00

UPJOHN, Anna Milo
Friends in Strange Garments, 1927 Houghton, cloth-over-board cover, 148 pages, 4 color plates plus b/w illustrations by author. $20.00

UPTON, Bertha
Golliwog's Bicycle Club, 1903 edition Longmans, hardcover, color illustrations by Florence Upton. $130.00
Golliwog's Polar Adventures, 1900 Longmans, hardcover, color illustrations by Florence Upton. $200.00

Golliwog in War, 1903 Longmans, hardcover, color illustrations by Florence Upton. $200.00

UTTLEY, Alison
Adventures of Tim Rabbit, 1945 Faber, green cloth-over-board cover, 171 pages, illustrations by A. E. Kennedy. $15.00
Country Hoard, 1943 Faber, hardcover, illustrations by Tunnicliffe. $15.00
Little Grey Rabbit and the Weasels, 1947 edition Collins, pictorial cover. $15.00
Little Grey Rabbit's Party, 1935 Collins, small, illustrated hardcover, color illustrations by Margaret Tempest. ($30.00 with dust jacket) $15.00
Sam Pig at the Circus, 1943 Faber first edition, yellow cloth-over-board cover with illustration, 187 pages, illustrations by A. E. Kennedy. $15.00

V

VANCE, Marguerite
Marta, 1937 Harper, half-bound with illustrated boards, small, 56 pages, color and b/w illustrations by Mildred Boyle. $25.00
Paula, 1939 Dodd Mead, cloth-over-board cover, 220 pages, b/w illustrations by Valenti Angelo. $15.00
Paula Goes Away to School, Dodd Mead, 276 pages, b/w illustrations by Maginel Wright Barney. $15.00
Star for Hansi, 1936 Harper first edition, small, 30 pages, illustrated paper-over-board cover, illustrated endpapers, two-color illustrations by Grace Paull. $25.00

VanDOREN, Mark
Dick and Tom in Town, (1932) 1940 printing Macmillan, cloth-over-board cover, small square, illustrated endpapers, color frontispiece, b/w illustrations by George Richards. $25.00
Transplanted Tree, 1940 Holt, paper-over-board cover, illustrated endpapers, two-color illustrations by Margaret Van Doren. $25.00

VanEPPS, Margaret, see Series section, NANCY PEMBROKE

VanNORSTRAND, Frances, editor
Blossoms by the Wayside, poetry, 1888 Standard, Chicago, red cloth-over-board cover, illustrated endpapers, color bordered pages and b/w illustrations. $35.00

VanSTOCKUM, Hilda
Andries, 1942 Viking first edition, gray cloth-over-board cover, 192 pages, illustrations by author. $30.00

Day on Skates, 1934 Harper, cloth-over-board cover, illustrated endpapers, oversize oblong, 8 color plates by author. $35.00
Gerrit and the Organ, 1943 Viking first edition, gray cloth-over-board cover, 178 pages, illustrated by author. $20.00
Kersti and Saint Nicholas, 1940 Viking Junior Literary Guild, hardcover, 70 pages, color and b/w illustrations by author. $30.00

VAUGHN, Agnes Carr
Lucian Goes A-Voyaging, 1930 Knopf, cloth-over-board cover, 139 pages, illustrated endpapers, b/w illustrations by Harrie Woods. $20.00

VIMAR, A.
Curly Haired Hen, 1914 Fitzgerald first edition, oversize picture book, 95 pages, paste-on-pictorial cover, b/w illustrations by Nora Hills. $45.00

W

WADSWORTH, Wallace
Modern Story Book, (1931) 1941 edition Rand McNally, oversize picture book, paper-over-board cover with paste-on-pictorial, 112 pages, illustrated endpapers, color illustrations throughout by Ruth Eger. $40.00

WALKER, Margaret Coulson
Tales Come True, 1910 Baker Taylor, 146 pages, color paste-on-illustration on cover, b/w and color illustrations of vegetable characters by Louise Orwig. $45.00

WALSH, George Ethelbert, see Series section, TWILIGHT ANIMAL SERIES

WALTON, Frank, see Series section, FLYING MACHINE BOYS

WARD, Marion B.
Boat Children of Canton, 1944 McKay first edition, tan cloth-over-board cover, illustrated endpapers, color and b/w illustrations by Helen Sewell. ($60.00 with dust jacket) $35.00

WARNER, Anne
Susan Clegg and a Man in the House, 1907 Little Brown, decorated gray cloth-over-board cover, small, 279 pages, b/w illustrations by Alice Stephens. $15.00

WARNER, Frances Lester
Ragamuffin Marionettes, 1932 Houghton, cloth-

over-board cover, 145 pages, b/w illustrations by Margaret Freeman. $20.00

WARNER, Frank, see Series section, BOBBY BLAKE

WARNER, Gertrude
Star Stories, 1947 Pilgrim first edition, paper-over-board cover, illustrated by Winifred Bromhall. $15.00
World in a Barn, 1927 Friendship Press, illustrated hardcover, illustrated endpapers, illustrations by Florence Liley Young. $20.00

WARNER, Lucy
Five Little Finger Stories, 1893 Lothrop, oversize, cloth-over-board cover with gilt, 126 pages, b/w illustrations by Carida. $45.00

WASHBURNE, Heluiz, see Series section, LITTLE ELEPHANT
Letters to Channy, 1932 Rand McNally, oversize, cloth-over-board cover, 190 pages, b/w illustrations by Electra Papadopoulos. $15.00

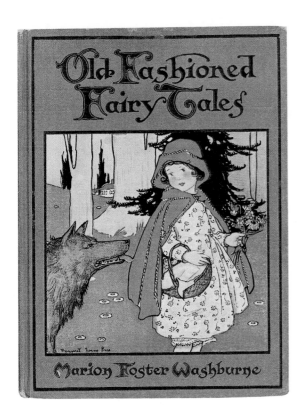

WASHBURNE, Marion Foster
Old Fashioned Fairy Tales, (1909) 1928 edition Rand McNally, green hardcover with paste-on-illustration, illustrated endpapers, 104 pages, two-color illustrations by Margaret Ely Webb. $60.00

WATKINS, Shirley
Georgina Finds Herself, 1922 Goldsmith, cloth-over-board cover. ($15.00 with dust jacket) $8.00
Jane Lends a Hand, 1923 Goldsmith, red cloth-over-board cover. ($15.00 with dust jacket) $8.00
Nancy of Paradise Cottage, 1921 Goldsmith, red cloth-over-board cover. ($15.00 with dust jacket) $8.00

WATKINS-PITCHFORD, Denys
Down the Bright Stream, 1948 Eyre, London, 16 color plates plus b/w illustrations by author. $35.00
Wild Lone, 1938 Eyre, London, first edition, hardcover, b/w illustrations by author. ($80.00 with dust jacket) $40.00

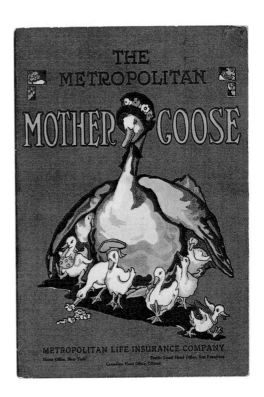

WATSON, Elizabeth C.
Metropolitan Mother Goose, ca. 1930 Metropolitan Life Insurance Co., small, illustrated paper cover, 11 pages, color illustrations throughout by Emma Clark. $20.00
Story of Milk, ca. 1927 Harper, orange spine, tan cloth-over-board cover, map endpapers, color plates by James Daugherty. ($20.00 with dust jacket) $10.00

WEATHERLY, Fred E.
Holly Boughs, undated ca. 1885 Dutton, cloth spine, pictorial boards, 8 chromolithograph plates. $45.00
Needles and Pins, ca. 1880 Hildesheimer, oversize, 29 pages, paper-over-board cover with color

and gilt illustration, chromos and brown/white illustrations by Helena Maguire. $55.00

WEHR, Julian, see Play Books section, WEHR

WELLS, Carolyn, see Series section, PATTY SERIES, DICK AND DOLLY, TWO LITTLE WOMEN
Folly for the Wise, 1904 Bobbs Merrill, small, 170 pages, cloth-over-board cover with gilt, b/w illustrations by Cory, Herford, Shinn, Verbeek. $45.00
Merry-Go-Round, 1901 Russell, cloth-over-board cover with Newell design and gilt, small, 152 pages, b/w illustrations by Peter Newell. $60.00
Such Nonsense, 1918 edition Doran, poetry, decorated cloth-over-board cover, 249 pages, b/w illustrations. $20.00

WELLS, Carveth
Jungle Man and His Animals, 1925 McBride, oversize, full color paper-over-board cover, 68 pages, 12 color plates plus b/w illustrations by Tony Sarg. $200.00

WELLS, Helen, see Series section, VICKI BARR

WESSELHOEFT, Lily
Madam Mary of the Zoo, 1899, small, cloth-over-board cover with gilt, b/w illustrations by Lowell and Verbeek. $25.00
Old Rough the Miser, 1907 Little Brown, hardcover. $30.00

WEST, Marvin, see Series section, MOTOR RANGERS

WEYMAN, Stanley J.
Castle Inn, 1898 Smith Elder, London, first edition, blue cloth-over-board cover with gilt, frontispiece by Arthur Rackham. $200.00

WHEELER, Marguerite and **Willard**
Dotty Dolly's Tea Party, 1914 Rand McNally, cloth-over-board cover with paste-on-pictorial, full color illustrations by author. $40.00

WHEELER, Opal
Handel at the Court of Kings, 1943 Dutton, cloth-over-board cover, 135 pages, b/w illustrations by Mary Greenwalt. $20.00
H. M. S. Pinafore, adaptation of Gilbert and Sullivan musical, 1946 Dutton, hardcover, full-page color illustrations by Fritz Kredel. ($25.00 with dust jacket) $20.00
Sing for America, 1944 Dutton, oversize, 127 pages, illustrated by Gustaf Tenggren. $30.00

WHEELER, Ruthe S.
Helen in the Editor's Chair, 1932 Goldsmith, Every Girl's Series edition, green cloth-over-board cover, 245 pages. Dust jacket illustration by Marie Schubert. ($20.00 with dust jacket) $7.00

WHITE, Billy and **Betty**
Land of Whatsit, 1935 Macaulay, cloth-over-board cover, 333 pages, cartoon illustrations by Joe Banks. $30.00

WHITE, Eliza Orne
Where is Adelaide?, 1933 Houghton first edition, orange cloth-over-board cover, 155 pages, b/w illustrations by Helen Sewell. ($70.00 in dust jacket) $35.00

WHITE, Ramy Allison, see Series section, SUNNY BOY

WHITE, Roma
Brownies and Rose-Leaves, 1892 Innes, cloth-over-board cover, small, 200 pages, b/w illustrations by L. L. Brooke. $45.00

WHITE, William Allen
Court of Boyville, 1908 McClure, green cloth-over-board cover with gilt, small, 358 pages, b/w illustrations by Lowell, Verbeek, and Gustav. $15.00

WHITEHILL, Dorothy, see Series section, POLLY, TWINS

WHITING, Helen Adele
Negro Folk Tales, 1938 Associated Publishers, cloth-over-board cover, b/w illustrations by Lois M. Jones. $30.00

WIEDERSEIM, Grace, see DRAYTON, Grace

WIGGIN, Kate Douglas
Diary of a Goose Girl, 1902 Houghton, small, 117 pages, cloth-over-board cover, b/w illustrations C. A. Shepperson. $35.00
Romance of a Christmas, 1913 Houghton, blue cloth-over-board cover with paste-on-illustration and gilt. $35.00
Story of Waitstill Baker, 1913 Houghton, green cloth-over-board cover, 373 pages, 4 color plates by Brett. $25.00
Summer in a Canyon: a California Story, ca. 1889 Houghton, cloth-over-board cover with scenic illustration. $40.00

WILKINS, Harold T.
Pirate Treasure, 1937 Dutton, cloth-over-board cover, 409 pages, frontispiece photo from a Douglas Fairbanks pirate movie, b/w charts and maps by author. $20.00

WILKINS, Mary E.
In Colonial Times, 1899 Lothrop, small, printed color illustration on cover, b/w illustrations. $25.00
Pot of Gold, 1892 Lothrop, small, collection of short stories, b/w illustrations. $20.00

WILLIAMSON, Hamilton
Little Elephant, 1930 Doubleday, small picture book, cloth-over-board cover, color and b/w illustrations by Berta and Elmer Hader. $30.00

WILLSON, Dixie
Favorite Stories of Famous Children, 1938 Holt, hardcover, illustrated with photos. $25.00
Where the World Folds Up at Night, 1932 Appleton first edition, red cloth-over-board cover with gilt lettering, 209 pages, photo illustrations. $50.00

WILSON, Eleanore
About Ricco, 1937 Whitman, oversize, 123 pages, map endpapers, color illustrations by author. $30.00
Within the Gates of Oxford, 1930 Dutton first edition, cloth-over-board cover, 177 pages, b/w illustrations. ($20.00 with dust jacket) $10.00

WINDSOR, Mary
About Things, 1935 Grosset, color illustrated boards, oversize, color and b/w illustrations by Charlotte Stone. $35.00

Merry Go Round, undated ca. 1950 Samuel Lowe, oversize, illustrated hardcover, 22 pages, color illustrations throughout by Elsie. $20.00
Soap and Bubbles, 1935 Whitman, oversize, illustrated cover, 14 pages, color illustrations throughout by Ruth Newton. $45.00

WINTER, Alice
Prize to the Hardy, 1905 Bobbs Merrill, illustrated cloth-over-board cover. $15.00

WINTER, Milo
Wonderful ABC Book, 1946 Reuben Lilja Co., Chicago, oversize picture book, paper cover, 12 pages, verses and color illustrations by Winter. $35.00
Wonder Garden, with Frances Olcott, 1919 Houghton, illustrated paste-on-pictorial, color illustrated by Winter. $35.00

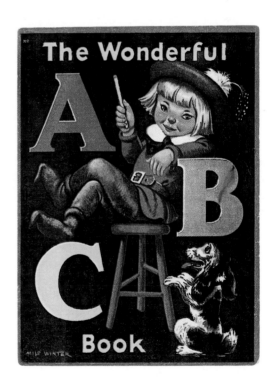

WIRT, Mildred, see Series section, DOT AND DASH, PENNY PARKER SERIES
Ghost Gables, 1939 Cupples Leon, hardcover. ($20.00 with dust jacket) $10.00
Mystery of the Laughing Mask, 1940 Cupples Leon, hardcover, frontispiece. ($20.00 with dust jacket) $10.00
Painted Shield, 1939 World, cloth-over-board cover, illustrations by Phillip Marini. $15.00
Sky Racers, 1946 Green Books, hardcover. ($25.00 with dust jacket) $15.00
Whispering Walls, 1946 Cupples Leon, hardcover. ($20.00 with dust jacket) $10.00

WISTER, A. L.
Journey in Search of Christmas, 1904 Harper, decorated cloth-over-board cover, 93 pages, illustrations by Frederic Remington. $60.00
Seaside and Fireside Fairies, 1864 Ashmead, cloth-over-board cover with gilt, small, 292 pages, b/w illustrations. $40.00

WISTER, Owen
New Swiss Family Robinson, 1922 edition Duffield, oversize, pictorial boards. ($60.00 with dust jacket) $20.00

WOODWARD, Hildegarde
Time Was, 1941 Scribner, oversize, color illustrations by author. $25.00

WPA, Federal Writers' Project
Who's Who in the Zoo, 1938 Whitman, first edition, oversize, cloth-over-board cover, illustrated endpapers, 204 pages, b/w illustrations, maps, photos. $60.00, later editions $20.00

WRIGHT, Henrietta Christian
Children's Stories in American History, 1887 Scribner, hardcover. $20.00
Children's Stories in American Literature, 1914 edition Scribner, hardcover. $15.00
Children's Stories of the Great Scientists, 1889 Scribner, brown cloth-over-board cover. $15.00
Little Folk in Green, 1883 White & Stokes, small, 92 pages, cloth-over-board cover with gilt decoration, color illustrations by Lydia Emmet. $45.00

WRIGHT, Mabel Osgood
Dream Fox Story Book, 1900 Macmillan, decorated cloth-over-board cover. $30.00
Gray Lady and the Birds, 1907 Macmillan, hardcover, illustrated. $30.00
Tommy-Anne and the Three Hearts, 1900 printing Macmillan, small, 322 pages, cloth-over-board cover with gilt, b/w illustrations by Blashfield. $25.00
Wabeno the Magician, 1899 Macmillan, green cloth-over-board cover with gilt decoration, small, 346 pages, b/w illustrations by Joseph Gleeson. $30.00

WYMAN, Levi P. see Series section, GOLDEN BOYS, LAKEWOOD BOYS
Battalion Captain, 1936 Burt, illustrated endpapers and b/w frontispiece. $10.00
Golden Boys Rescued by Radio, 1923 Burt, cloth-over-board cover, 244 pages, frontispiece. ($20.00 with dust jacket) $10.00

YALE, Catharine Brooks
Nim and Cum, and the Wonderhead Stories, 1895 Way & Williams, small, 126 pages, cloth-over-board cover with gilt, b/w chapter headings. $35.00

YAP, Weda
Abigail's Private Reason, 1932 Macmillan, cloth-over-board cover, small, 70 pages, color frontispiece, b/w illustrations by author. $25.00

YATES, Elizabeth
Haven for the Brave, 1941 Knopf first edition, cloth-over-board cover, 262 pages. $15.00
Mountain Born, 1943 Coward McCann, cloth-over-board cover, 118 pages, illustrated endpapers, b/w illustrations by Nora Unwin. $20.00
Nearby, 1947 Coward McCann, cloth-over-board cover, 276 pages. ($20.00 with dust jacket) $15.00
Once in the Year, 1947 Coward McCann, cloth-over-board cover, printed in red ink, page borders and line illustrations by Nora Unwin. $25.00
Patterns on the Wall, 1943 Knopf first, cloth-over-board cover with impressed design, 242 pages, b/w decorations by Warren Chappel. ($25.00 with dust jacket) $15.00
Quest in the North-land, 1940 Knopf first edition, 212 pages. $15.00
Under the Little Fir, 1942 Coward McCann, cloth-over-board cover, illustrated endpapers, two-color illustrations by Nora Unwin. ($35.00 with dust jacket) $20.00

YONGE, Charlotte
Chaplet of Pearls, 1903 edition Macmillan, blue cloth-over-board cover with gilt, 364 pages, illustrated by W. J. Hennessey. $15.00
Dove in the Eagle's Nest, 1926 edition Macmillan, impressed design on cloth-over-board cover, illustrated endpapers, 3 color plates and b/w illustrations by Marguerite de Angeli. $45.00
Heartsease, or the Brother's Wife, 1882 edition Macmillan, cloth-over-board cover with gilt, 548 pages, illustrations by Kate Greenaway. $30.00
Lances of Lynwood, 1931 edition Macmillan, impressed design on cloth-over-board cover, illustrated endpapers, color frontispiece, b/w illustrations by Marguerite de Angeli. $30.00
Little Duke, (1854) 1923 edition Duffield, impressed design on cloth-over-board cover, 4 color plates by Beatrice Stevens. $30.00

Prince and the Page, 1881 edition Lothrop, cloth-over-board cover with printed design, b/w illustrations. $25.00

Two Penniless Princesses, 1931 edition Macmillan, cloth-over-board cover with impressed illustration, illustrated endpapers, 3 color plates and b/w illustrations by Stafford Good. $25.00

Unknown to History, 1905 edition Macmillan, cloth-over-board cover with gilt. $15.00

YOUNG, Egerton R.
Children of the Forest, 1904 Fleming Revell, cloth-over-board cover with impressed design, 282 pages, 16 b/w plates by J. E. Laughlin. $20.00

Three Boys in the Wild North Land, 1896 Eaton Mains, 260 pages, impressed design with gilt on cover, b/w illustrations. $15.00

YOUNG, Ella
Unicorn with Silver Shoes, 1932 Longmans first edition, cloth-over-board cover with impressed silver illustration, illustrated endpapers, b/w illustrations by Robert Lawson. $65.00

YOUNG, Evelyn
Chinese Babies, 1933 Tientsin Press, oversize, rhymes, watercolor illustrations. $50.00

Tale of Tai, 1940 Oxford, small, cloth-over-board cover, illustrated endpapers, easy read, color illustrations throughout by author. $30.00

Wu and Lu and Lee, 1939 Oxford, small, cloth-over-board cover, illustrated endpapers, easy read, color illustrations throughout by author. $30.00

YOUNG, Martha
When We Were Wee, 1912 edition Macmillan, cloth-over-board cover with impressed illustration, Everychild's Series, small, b/w photos plus drawings by Sophie Schneider. $35.00

YOUNG, Stanley
Young Hickory, 1940 Farrar, cloth-over-board cover, illustrated endpapers, red/black illustrations by Robert Fawcett. ($25.00 with dust jacket) $15.00

YOUNG, W. Edward and HAYES, Will
Norman and the Nursery School, 1949 Platt Munk, cloth-over-board cover with paste-on pictorial, oversize picture book, color illustrations by Janet Robson Kennedy. $35.00

YULE, Emma Sarepta
In Kimono Land, (1927) 1929 edition Rand McNally, small, cloth-over-board cover with impressed illustration, easy read, 119 pages, color photo illustrations. $25.00

Z

ZOLLINGER, Gulielma
Maggie McLaneham, 1901 McClurg, cloth-over-board cover with impressed illustration, 5 b/w illustrations. $15.00

Rout of the Foreigner, 1910 McClurg, cloth-over-board cover with paste-on-pictorial, 10 b/w illustrations. $20.00

ZOLOTOW, Charlotte
Park Book, 1944 Harper, oblong picture book, color illustrations cloth-over-board cover, easy-read, color illustrations by H. A. Rey. $40.00

ZWILGMEYER, Dikken, translations by Emilie Poulsson
Four Cousins, 1923 edition Lothrop, 6 orange/b/w plates by Astri Welham Heiberg. $30.00

Inger Johanne's Lively Doings, 1926 edition Lothrop, cloth-over-board cover with printed illustration, 8 brown/b/w plates by Florence Liley Young. $40.00

Johnny Blossom, 1940 edition Lothrop, cloth-over-board cover with paste-on-illustration, 4 yellow/b/w plates by Florence Liley Young. $20.00

What Happened to Inger Johanne, 1919 edition Lothrop, 12 orange/b/w plates by Florence Liley Young. $40.00

Prices are for each book in good condition but without dust jacket, except when noted.

A

ADVENTURES IN THE UNKNOWN SERIES, Carl H. Claudy, Grosset, cloth-over-board cover, illustrated endpapers, frontispiece illustration by A. C. Valentine. ($55.00 with dust jacket) $30.00
Land of No Shadow, 1933
Mystery Men of Mars, 1933
Thousand Years a Minute, 1933
Blue Grotto Terror, 1934

AIRSHIP BOYS SERIES, H. L. Sayler, ca. 1910 Reilly Britton, cloth-over-board hardcover with impressed illustration, 300+ pages, b/w frontispiece by Riesenberg. $20.00
Airship Boys
Airship Boys Adrift
Airship Boys Due North
Airship Boys in the Barren Lands
Airship Boys in Finance
Airship Boys' Ocean Flyer

ALGONQUIN HAPPY BOOKS SERIES, ca. 1930 Algonquin Publishing, NY, small square picture books with linen-like paper covers, 12 pages, full color illustrations, these are inexpensive adaptations of earlier Volland books. $25.00
My Book of Pets, Carmen Browne
Piggy-Wiggy, Ruby Hart

ALGONQUIN SUNNY BOOKS SERIES, reprints of the Volland Sunny Books, ca. late 1920s-30s Algonquin, small, color illustrated paper-on-board covers, color endpapers and color illustrations. $25.00
Billy Bunny's Fortune
Dinky Ducklings
Little Slam Bang
Merry Murphy
Honey Bear
Grasshopper Green
Dinky Ducklings
Sunny Bunny

ALTEMUS FAIRY TALES SERIES, ca. 1906 Altemus, small, 94 pages, several edited by Hartwell James and with b/w/red illustrations by John Neill. $25.00
Magic Bed
Cat and the Mouse
Jeweled Sea
Magic Jaw Bone
Man Elephant
Enchanted Castle

ALTEMUS MOTHER GOOSE SERIES, undated ca. 1900 Altemus, cloth-over-board cover, gilt and color illustration, color frontispiece, 60 pages. Plain tan paper dust wrapper, title and series name in black lettering. ($25.00 with dust wrapper) $20.00
Aladdin
Our Animal Friends
Mother Goose
Beauty and the Beast

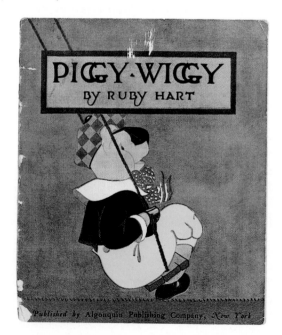

Bedtime Story-Books. 1933 Little Brown, 1946 Little Brown, 1947 Grosset.

Bird Stories
Cinderella
House that Jack Built
Jack and the Beanstalk
Jack the Giant Killer
Little Red Riding Hood
Puss in Boots
Sleeping Beauty
Who Killed Cock Robin?

AMELIARANNE SERIES, originated by Constance Heward and illustrator Susan Pearce, 1920 – 40 McKay, London and U. S., small hardcover, color illustrations. ($85.00 with dust jacket) $30.00

AMERICAN BOYS SPORTS SERIES, Mark Overton, ca. 1919 Donohue, cloth-over-board cover, b/w illustrations. $15.00
Jack Winters' Baseball Team
Jack Winters' Campmates
Jack Winters' Gridiron Chums
Jack Winters' Iceboat Wonder

ANDY BLAKE SERIES, by Leo Edwards, ca. 1930s Grosset & Dunlap. ($25.00 with dust jacket) $10.00
Andy Blake
Andy Blake's Comet Coaster
Andy Blake's Secret Service
Andy Blake and the Pot of Gold

ANNAPOLIS SERIES, see DAVE DARRIN.

ANN BARTLETT SERIES, by Martha Johnson, ca. 1940s Crowell. $15.00
Ann Bartlett: Navy Nurse

Ann Bartlett at Bataan
Ann Bartlett in the South Pacific
Ann Bartlett Returns to the Philippines

AVIATOR SERIES, Captain Frank Cobb, ca. 1920s Saalfield, impressed illustration on cloth-over-board cover, frontispiece illustration. ($20.00 with dust jacket) $10.00
Battling the Clouds, or, For the Comrade's Honor
Aviator's Luck, or, The Camp Knox Pilot
Dangerous Deeds, or, Flight in the Dirigible

B

BANBURY CROSS SERIES, ca. 1905 Altemus, illustrated cloth-over-board cover. $20.00
Ali Baba and the Forty Thieves.

BATTLESHIP BOYS SERIES, Frank Patchin, ca. 1911 Saalfield, silver cloth-over-board cover, b/w illustrations. $15.00
Books from this series have also been seen with gray, blue, green, purple, and brown covers. Sometimes the title is spelled correctly, sometimes not. Color cloth-over-board cover, b/w illustrations. ($15.00 with dust jacket) $5.00
Battleship Boys at Sea
Battleship Boys in Foreign Service
Battleship Boys' First Step Upward
Battleship Boys on the Sky Patrol

BEDTIME STORY-BOOKS SERIES, Thornton Burgess, originally published ca. 1917, this series has seen several reprints. The following editions all use the Harrison Cady illustrations, but in the following formats:

1933 edition Little Brown, (lists 20 books in series) small, gray cloth-over-board cover with red and black printed illustration on cover, about 120 pages, 6 b/w plates. ($20.00 with white dust jacket) $10.00

1946 edition Little Brown, (lists 8 books only) slightly oversize, yellow edged color illustrated paper-over-board cover, illustrated endpapers, about 94 pages, 8 full-page full color illustrations. ($25.00 with same-as-cover dust jacket) $20.00

1947 edition Grosset, (lists 20 books in series) cloth-over-board cover with black printed illustration, about 190 pages, illustrated endpapers, b/w illustrations. ($20.00 with brown dust jacket) $10.00

BERTRAM BOOKS, by Paul Gilbert, Rand McNally, small books, color illustrated endpapers, each about 125 pages long, illustrated with b/w line drawings. ($45.00 with dust jacket) $25.00

Bertram and His Funny Animals, 1934, blue cloth-over-board cover, illustrations by Minnie Rousseff.

Bertram and His Fabulous Animals, 1937, illustrations by Minnie Rousseff.

With Bertram in Africa, 1939, green cloth-over-board cover, illustrations by Anne Stossel.

Bertram's Trip to the North Pole, 1940, illustrations by Anne Stossel.

BETSY SERIES, Carolyn Haywood, Harcourt Brace, cloth-over-board cover, illustrated endpapers, b/w illustrations by author. (Dust jacket doubles price.) $20.00

"B" is for Betsy, 1939
Betsy and Billy, 1941
Back to School with Betsy, 1943
Betsy and the Boys, 1945
Snowbound with Betsy
Merry Christmas from Betsy

BETSY-TACY SERIES, Maud Hart Lovelace, Crowell, cloth-over-board cover, b/w illustrations by Lois Lenski, becoming highly collectible, first editions ($100.00 with dust jacket) $40.00; later printings ($30.00 with dust jacket) $15.00.

Betsy-Tacy, 1941
Betsy-Tacy and Tib
Betsy and Tacy Go Over the Hill, 1942
Betsy and Tacy Go Down Town, 1943
Heaven to Betsy
Betsy in Spite of Herself, 1946

Betsy was a Junior, 1947
Betsy and Joe, 1948

BIG LEAGUE SERIES, Burt L. Standish, ca. 1920s Barse, cloth-over-board cover, b/w illustrations. ($40.00 with dust jacket) $15.00

Lefty o' the Bush
Lefty o' the Big League
Lefty o' the Blue Stockings
Lefty o' the Training Camp
Brick King, Backstop
Making of a Big Leaguer
Courtney of the Center Garden
Covering the Look-in Corner
Lefty Locke, Pitcher-Manager
Guarding the Keystone Sack
Man on First
Lego Lamb, Southpaw
Grip of the Game
Lefty Locke, Owner
Lefty Locke Wins Out

BILL BRUCE AVIATOR SERIES, Maj. Henry H. Arnold, ca. 1928 Burt, hardcover with print illustration. $15.00

Bill Bruce and the Pioneer Aviators
Bill Bruce, the Flying Cadet
Bill Bruce Becomes an Ace
Bill Bruce on Border Patrol
Bill Bruce in the Trans-Continental Race
Bill Bruce on Forest Patrol

BILL BOLTON SERIES, Noel Sainsbury, ca. 1933 Goldsmith, hardcover. ($20.00 with dust jacket) $10.00

Bill Bolton and Hidden Danger
Bill Bolton and the Flying Fish
Bill Bolton, Flying Midshipman
Bill Bolton and Winged Cartwheels

BLUE BIRDS SERIES, Lillian Elizabeth Roy, ca. 1930s Burt, blue pictorial hardcover, illustrated. $15.00

Blue Birds of Happy Time Nest
Blue Birds' Winter Nest
Blue Birds' Uncle Ben
Blue Birds at Happy Hills

BLUE DOMERS SERIES, Jean Finley, ca. 1920s Burt, pictorial boards, small, color illustrated endpapers, color illustrations. $30.00

Blue Domers
Blue Domers' Alphabet Zoo
Blue Domers in the Deep Woods
Blue Domers and the Wishing Tree
Blue Domers Under Winter Skies
Blue Domers and the Magic Flute

BLUE GRASS SEMINARY GIRLS SERIES, Carolyn J. Burnett, ca. 1916 Burt, pictorial tan cloth-over-board cover, about 250 pages. ($20.00 with dust jacket) $15.00
Blue Grass Seminary Girls' Vacation Adventures
Blue Grass Seminary Girls' Christmas Holidays
Blue Grass Seminary Girls in the Mountains
Blue Grass Seminary Girls on the Water

BOBBSEY TWINS SERIES, Laura Lee Hope, ca. 1934 reprint Grosset Dunlap, the series was created in 1904 by the Stratemeyer syndicate, became one its best sellers and has been reprinted numerous times. The paper doll dust jacket of the 1930s reprint is somewhat scarce, probably because owners cut out the dolls, so even though the illustration is the same on all titles in this series, this dust jacket in good condition adds $20.00 to the price. This front illustration also appears on a dust jacket without the paper dolls, and in that form, adds $10.00 or less to the price. Plain green hardcover without dust jacket: $15.00

BOBBY AND DOLLY SERIES, Grace Drayton, ca. 1910, written and illustrated by the artist who created the Campbell Soup Kids and Dolly Dingle, this series features Bobby Blake and Dolly Drake, and sales reports in 1911 claimed that over 200,000 copies of the Bobby and Dolly books had been sold. However, they are hard to find, with prices starting at $65.00.

BOBBY BLAKE SERIES, Frank Warner, ca. 1920s Barse, cloth-over-board cover, b/w illustrations. ($20.00 with dust jacket) $10.00
Bobby Blake at Rockledge School
Bobby Blake at Bass Cove
Bobby Blake on a Cruise
Bobby Blake and his Chums
Bobby Blake on a Ranch
Bobby Blake on an Auto Tour
Bobby Blake in the Frozen North

BOB FLAME SERIES, Dorr Yeager, Sears Books, cloth-over-board cover, photo plate illustrations. ($30.00 with dust jacket) $20.00
Bob Flame Ranger, 1934
Bob Flame Rocky Mountain Ranger, 1935
Bob Flame in Death Valley, 1937

BONNIE BOOKS SERIES, 1940s John Martin's House, Kenosha, WI, small, 28 page picture books with color illustrations (similar in appearance to Little Golden Books), numbered series. $20.00
Bobbie Had a Nickel
Traveling Musicians
Choo-Choo Train
Elephant's Dilemma
Favorite Nursery Rhymes
Slappy
Little Boy Who Ran Away
Peter Gets His Wish
A is for Apple

Farm Animals
Valiant Tailor
Dumpy
Giddappy
Old Man and the Turnip
Make Believe
Mother Goose
Little Town on the Hill
Hesperus
Perry Poppet
Boys and Girls and Puppy Dogs

BORDER BOYS SERIES, Fremont B. Deering, ca. 1911 A. L. Burt, tan pictorial cloth-over-board cover, also ca. 1911 Hurst, illustrated cloth-over-board cover, illustrated by Charles Wrenn. $20.00
Border Boys on the Trail
Border Boys across the Frontier
Border Boys with the Mexican Rangers
Border Boys with the Texas Rangers
Border Boys in the Canadian Rockies
Border Boys along the St. Lawrence River

BOY ALLIES WITH THE ARMY SERIES, Clair W. Hayes, ca. 1915–1919 A. L. Burt, illustrated cloth-over-board cover, frontispiece illustration. Advertised as, "In this series we follow the fortunes of two American lads unable to leave Europe after war is declared. They meet the soldiers of the Allies and decide to cast their lots with them. Their experiences and escapes are many, and furnish plenty of good, healthy action that every boy loves." ($35.00 with dust jacket) $15.00
Books 1 through 12:
Boy Allies at Liege
Boy Allies on the Firing Line
Boy Allies with the Cossacks
Boy Allies in the Trenches
Boy Allies in Great Peril
Boy Allies in the Balkan Campaign
Boy Allies on the Somme
Boy Allies at Verdun
Boy Allies under the Stars and Stripes
Boy Allies with Haig in Flanders
Boy Allies with Pershing in France
Boy Allies with Marshall Foch

BOY ALLIES WITH THE NAVY SERIES, Ensign Robert L. Drake, ca. 1915-1919 A. L. Burt. Advertised as "Frank Chadwick and Jack Templeton, young American lads, meet each other in an unusual way soon after the declaration of war. Circumstances place them on board the British cruiser The Sylph and from there on, they share adventures..." ($35.00 with dust jacket) $15.00
Titles 1 through 10:

Boy Allies with the North Sea Patrol
Boy Allies under Two Flags
Boy Allies with the Flying Squadron
Boy Allies with the Terror of the Sea
Boy Allies under the Sea
Boy Allies in the Baltic
Boy Allies at Jutland
Boy Allies with Uncle Sam's Cruisers
Boy Allies with the Submarine D-32
Boy Allies with the Victorious Fleets

BOY AVIATORS SERIES, Captain Wilbur Lawton, 1910 Hurst, green pictorial hardcover. $12.00
Boy Aviators in Nicaragua, or, Leagued With Insurgents
Boy Aviators on Secret Service, or, Working With Wireless
Boy Aviators in Africa, or, Aerial Ivory Trail
Boy Aviators in Record Flight, or, Rival Aeroplane
Boy Aviators on Polar Dash, or, Facing Death in the Antarctic

BOY CHUMS SERIES, Wilmer M. Ely, ca. 1909 Burt, cloth-over-board cover with paste-on-pictorial. $15.00
Boy Chums on the Indian River
Boy Chums on Haunted Island
Boy Chums in the Forest
Boy Chums' Perilous Cruise
Boy Chums in the Gulf Of Mexico
Boy Chums in Florida Waters
Boy Chums in the Florida Jungle
Boy Chums in Mystery Land

BOYS AND GIRLS BOOKS SERIES, undated ca. 1910-20 Goldsmith, books are packaged uniformly in hardcover, each has 256 pages, b/w illustrated endpapers, individually designed four-color dust jackets. Fifty-one titles are listed on the back cover of S.W.F Club. This collection of authors and unrelated titles is a publisher's put-together series for marketing purposes; many of the titles are books from other series. ($15.00 with dust jacket) $8.00
Titles include:
Bobbsey Twins
Captain of the Eleven
Circus Dan
Girls of Silverspur Ranch
Herb Kent, Fullback
Janet Hardy in Hollywood
Mimi at Camp
Helen in the Editor's Chair
Becky Bryan's Secret
Penny Nichols Finds a Clue
S.W.F. Club
Unseen Enemy

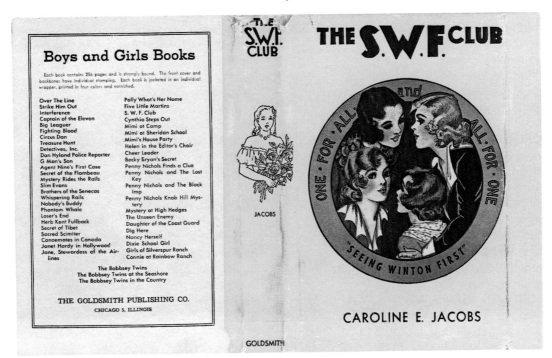

BOY SCOUT SERIES, by Maj. Robert Maitland, ca. 1910 Saalfield, small, impressed cover illustration, 150+ pages, illustrated endpapers, 20 or more volumes. $15.00

Boy Scout in Camp
Boy Scout to the Rescue
Boy Scout on the Trail
Boy Scout Fire-Fighters
Boy Scout Afloat
Boy Scout Pathfinders
Boy Scout Automobilists
Boy Scout Aviators
Boy Scouts with King George
Boy Scouts at Liege
Boy Scouts with the Cossacks
Boy Scouts Before Belgrade

BOY SCOUTS SERIES, by Maj. Archibald Lee Fletcher, Donohue, small, impressed illustration on cover, b/w frontispiece. $20.00

Boy Scout Pathfinders, 1913
Boy Scout Signal Senders, 1913
Boy Scouts in the Everglades

BOY SCOUTS SERIES, Herbert Carter, ca. 1913 Burt, mustard cloth-over-board cover with illustration, illustrations by J. Watson Davis. ($25.00 with dust jacket) $15.00

Boy Scouts' First Campfire
Boy Scouts in the Blue Ridge
Boy Scouts on the Trail
Boy Scouts in the Maine Woods
Boy Scouts through the Big Timber

Boy Scouts in the Rockies
Boy Scouts on Sturgeon Island
Boy Scouts Down In Dixie
Boy Scouts at the Battle of Saratoga
Boy Scouts Along the Susquehanna
Boy Scouts on War Trails in Belgium
Boy Scouts Afoot in France

BOYS' INDIAN SERIES, James Braden, ca. 1920–30 Saalfield, print illustrated cloth-over-board cover. ($20.00 with dust jacket) $10.00

Lone Indian
Far Past the Frontier

BOYS OF COLUMBIA HIGH, Graham B. Forbes, 1912–1920 Grosset, impressed illustration on cover, b/w illustrations, advertised as "never was there a cleaner, brighter, more manly boy than Frank Allan, the hero of this series of boys' tales, and never was there a better crowd of lads to associate with than students of the school." $10.00

Boys of Columbia High
Boys of Columbia High on the Diamond
Boys of Columbia High on the River
Boys of Columbia High on the Gridiron
Boys of Columbia High on the Ice
Boys of Columbia High in Track Athletics
Boys of Columbia High in Winter Sports

BOYS OF THE ROYAL MOUNTED POLICE, Milton Richards, ca. 1920s Burt, illustrated cloth-over-board cover, b/w illustration. $15.00

Dick Kent with the Mounted Police
Dick Kent in the Far North
Dick Kent with the Eskimos
Dick Kent, Fur Trader
Dick Kent and the Malemute Mail
Dick Kent on Special Duty

BOY TROOPERS SERIES, Clair W. Hayes, ca. 1920 A. L. Burt, cloth-over-board cover, frontispiece illustration, b/w illustrations, advertised as "adventures of two boys with the Pennsylvania State Police." ($40.00 with dust jacket) $15.00
Boy Troopers on the Trail
Boy Troopers in the Northwest
Boy Troopers on Strike Duty
Boy Troopers Among the Wild Mountaineers

BROWNIE SCOUTS SERIES, Mildred Wirt, ca. late 1940s Cupples Leon, cloth-over-board cover in bright colors. ($35.00 dust jacket) $15.00
Brownie Scouts at Snow Valley, 1949
Brownie Scouts in the Circus, 1949
Brownie Scouts in the Cherry Festival, 1950
Brownie Scouts and Their Tree House
Brownie Scouts at Silver Beach
Brownie Scouts at Windmill Farm

BUBBLE BOOK SERIES, "Books that Sing," ca. 1918 Harper, small, color illustrated paper-over-board cover, two-color illustrations, book contains three 78rpm one-sided records in envelope shaped pages, records include songs to augment the stories and games in the book. $100.00 with all records in good condition, $45.00 without records.
Bubble Book
Second Bubble Book

Third Bubble Book
Animal Bubble Book
Pie Party Bubble Book
Pet Bubble Book
Funny Froggy Bubble Book
Happy-Go-Lucky Bubble Book
Merry Midget Bubble Book
Little Mischief Bubble Book
Tippy-Toe Bubble Book
Gay Games Bubble Book

BUD BRIGHT SERIES, A. Van Buren Powell, ca. 1930 Penn, cloth-over-board cover, 200+ pages, b/w illustration. $15.00
Bud Bright, Boy Detective
Bud Bright and the Bank Robbers
Bud Bright and the Counterfeiters
Bud Bright and the Drug Ring

BUDDY SERIES, Howard Garis, ca. 1930s Cupples & Leon, small, approximately 210 pages, impressed illustration on red cloth-over-board cover, b/w illustrated endpapers, b/w illustrated frontispiece, advertised as "a really fascinating character-study of an up-to-date young lad…" ($20.00 with single-illustration-for-series dust jacket designed by Russell Tandy) $15.00
Books 6 through 13:
Buddy and His Flying Balloon
Buddy on Mystery Mountain
Buddy on Floating Island
Buddy and the Secret Cave
Buddy and His Cowboy Pal
Buddy and the Indian Chief
Buddy and the Arrow Club

⇒ C ⇐

CAMP FIRE AND TRAIL SERIES, Lawrence J. Leslie, ca. 1910–15 New York Book Co., small, about 185 pages, color paste-on-pictorial on cover, b/w frontispiece. $15.00
In Camp on the Big Sunflower
Rivals of the Trail
Strange Cabin on Catamount Island
Lost in the Great Dismal Swamp
With Trapper Jim in the North Woods
Caught in a Forest Fire

CAMP FIRE BOYS SERIES, Oliver Clifton, ca. 1920s Barse, cloth-over-board cover, b/w illustrations. ($20.00 with dust jacket) $10.00
Camp Fire Boys at Log Cabin Bend
Camp Fire Boys in Muskrat Swamp
Camp Fire Boys at Silver Fox Farm
Camp Fire Boys' Canoe Cruise
Camp Fire Boys' Tracking Squad

CASTLEMON SERIES, Harry Castlemon (C. A. Fosdick) This prolific writer turned out numerous adventure stories for boys, and his popular works were reprinted regularly, with the same title sometimes turning up under another series heading.
Boy Trapper, 1879 – Porter Coates, terra cotta cloth-over-board cover with gilt. First editions $30.00, later editions $15.00
Mail Carrier
Forest and Stream, ca. 1880s Porter Coates, small, impressed cover design, b/w frontispiece. $20.00
Joe Wayring at Home
Frank and Archie, ca. 1892, Winston reprints, gold pictorial cover. $15.00
Young Naturalist
Frank in the Woods
Frank on the Prairie
Frank Nelson, ca. 1904 Winston, tan decorated cloth-over-board cover. $10.00
Snowed Up
Gunboat, Winston reprint, cloth-over-board cover. $10.00
Frank on a Gunboat
Frank on the Lower Mississippi 1868
Lucky Tom, ca. 1895 Coates, illustrated blue cloth-over-board cover, frontispiece illustration. $10.00
Missing Pocket Book
Rocky Mountain, ca. 1869 Porter Coates, and Winston reprints. $15.00, 20th century reprints, Hurst or Burt. $10.00
Frank before Vicksburg
Frank at Carlos Ranch
Frank Among the Rancheros

Roughing It, ca. 1880s Porter Coates, small, impressed cover design, b/w frontispiece. $20.00
George at the Wheel
George in Camp
George at the Fort
Sportsman's Club, ca. 1880s Porter Coates, small, impressed and gilt cover design, b/w frontispiece and 3 additional plates. $35.00, later editions, $15.00
Sportsman's Club in the Saddle
Sportsman's Club Afloat 1874
Sportsman's Club Among the Trappers
War, ca. 1880s Coates, cloth-over-board cover, illustrations by George White. $25.00, later editions, $10.00
Rodney the Partisan
Marcy the Refugee
Harris the Runaway
Rodney the Overseer

CHARLIE SERIES, Helen Hill and Violet Maxwell, 1920s Macmillan, illustrated cloth-over-board cover, small, illustrated endpapers, illustrations by authors. ($65.00 with dust jacket) $30.00
Charlie and His Kitten Topsy
Charlie and His Coast Guards, 1925
Charlie and His Surprise House, 1926
Charlie and His Friends, 1927
Charlie and His Puppy Bingo, 1929

CHUMMY BOOK SERIES, undated ca. 1915–20 Sully and Kleinteich, NY, oversize, color illustrated paper-over-board cover, 300+ pages, annual, collected stories, poems, large print, 12 color plates plus b/w illustrations. $45.00 each

CIRCUS BOYS SERIES, Edgar B. P. Darlington, ca. 1910 Altemus, print illustration on cloth-over-board cover, about 250 pages, b/w illustrations. ($25.00 with dust jacket) $15.00
Circus Boys on the Flying Rings
Circus Boys Across the Continent
Circus Boys in Dixie Land
Circus Boys on the Mississippi
Circus Boys on the Plains

CLASSICS NEW AND OLD SERIES, see RAND MCNALLY CLASSICS OLD AND NEW

COLLEGE LIFE SERIES, Gilbert Patten, ca. 1920s Barse, cloth-over-board cover, b/w illustrations. ($20.00 with dust jacket) $10.00
Boltwood of Yale
College Rebel
On College Battlefields

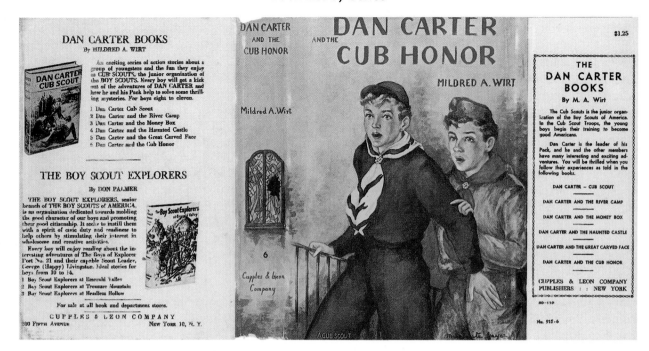

Call of the Varsity
Sons of Old Eli
Ben Oakman, Stroke

CONNIE BLAIR MYSTERY STORIES, Betsy Allen, ca. 1940s Grosset, cloth-over-board cover, advertised as "Connie is a career girl with a job in an advertising agency … you can identify A Connie Blair Mystery at a glance because a color is always in the title." ($25.00 with dust jacket) $15.00
Clue in Blue
Riddle in Red
Puzzle in Purple
Secret of Black Cat Gulch
Green Island Mystery
Ghost Wore White
Yellow Warning
Gray Menace
Brown Satchel Mystery
Peril in Pink

CORNER HOUSE GIRLS SERIES, Grace Brooks Hill, Barse, illustrated cloth-over-board cover, illustrated endpapers, 4 b/w illustrations by Emmett Owen. $20.00, Undated Grosset reprints, b/w illustration by Hastings. $15.00
Corner House Girls at School, 1915
Corner House Girls Under Canvas, 1915
Corner House Girls in a Play, 1916
Corner House Girls Growing Up, 1918
Corner House Girls Facing the World, 1926

COSY CORNER SERIES, collection of re-prints by Annie Fellows Johnson, ca. 1900 Page, small,

impressed illustration on cover, b/w illustrations. $20.00
Two Little Knights of Kentucky
Big Brother
Old Mammy's Torrent
Aunt Liza's Hero

— D —

DAN CARTER SERIES, Mildred Wirt, Cupples and Leon, 200+ pages, red cloth-over-board cover, b/w frontispiece. Individually illustrated dust jackets. ($20.00 with dust jacket) $10.00
Dan Carter, Cub Scout, and the River Camp, 1949
Dan Carter and the Money Box, 1950
Dan Carter and the Haunted Castle, 1951
Dan Carter and the Great Carved Face, 1952
Dan Carter and the Cub Honor, 1953

DAREWELL CHUMS SERIES, Allen Chapman, ca. 1908 Cupples and Leon, illustrated brown cloth-over-board cover, b/w illustrations by Boehm. $15.00
Darewell Chums
Darewell Chums in the Woods
Darewell Chums in a Winter Camp

DAVE DARRIN SERIES, Irving Hancock, ca. 1910 Altemus, hardcover, frontispiece illustration. Saalfield reprints about the same price. ($20.00 with dust jacket) $10.00
Dave Darrin's First Year at Annapolis
Dave Darrin's Second Year at Annapolis

Dave Darrin's Third Year at Annapolis
Dave Darrin's Fourth Year at Annapolis
Dave Darrin at Vera Cruz
Dave Darrin on Mediterranean Service
Dave Darrin's South American Cruise
Dave Darrin on the Asiatic Station
Dave Darrin and the German Submarines
Dave Darrin after the Mine Layers

DAVE DASHAWAY SERIES, Roy Rockwood, ca.
1915 Cupples Leon, hardcover, (Dust jacket
doubles price.) $12.00
Dave Dashaway, the Young Aviator
Dave Dashaway Around the World
Dave Dashaway and His Giant Airship
Dave Dashaway, Air Champion

DAVE DAWSON SERIES, Sidney Bowen, ca. 1940s
Saalfield, hardcover. (Dust jacket doubles
price.) $15.00
Dave Dawson with the Air Corps
Dave Dawson, Flight Lieutenant
Dave Dawson at Dunkirk
Dave Dawson with the R.A.F.
Dave Dawson with the Commandos
Dave Dawson with the Pacific Fleet
Dave Dawson on Convoy Patrol
Dave Dawson at Singapore
Dave Dawson in Libya
Dave Dawson with the Flying Tigers
Dave Dawson on Guadalcanal
Dave Dawson on the Russian Front

DICK AND DOLLY SERIES, Carolyn Wells, ca. 1909
Grosset and Dunlap, hardcover, illustrations by
Ada Budell. ($25.00 in dust jacket) $15.00
Dick and Dolly
Dick and Dolly's Adventures

DICK HAMILTON SERIES, Howard R. Garis, (1909 -
1914), circa 1925 Goldsmith reprints. $15.00
Fortune, or, *Stirring Doings of a Millionaire's Son*
Cadet Days, or, *Handicap of a Millionaire's Son*
Steam Yacht, or, *Young Millionaire and the Kidnappers*
Football Team, or, *Young Millionaire on the Gridiron*
Touring Car, or, *Young Millionaire's Race for a Fortune*
Airship, or, *Young Millionaire in The Clouds*

DICK KENT SERIES, see BOYS OF THE ROYAL
MOUNTED POLICE

DICK PRESCOTT SERIES, see WEST POINT
SERIES

DON STURDY SERIES, Victor Appleton, ca. 1925
Grosset Dunlap, small, cloth-over-board cover,

illustrated by Walter Rogers. ($25.00 with dust
jacket) $12.00
On the Desert of Mystery
With the Big Snake Hunters
In the Tombs of Gold
Across the North Pole
In the Land of Volcanoes
In the Port of Lost Ships
Among the Gorillas
Captured By Head Hunters
In Lion Land
In the Land of Giants
On the Ocean Bottom
In the Temples of Fear
Lost in Glacier Bay
Trapped in the Flaming Wilderness
With the Harpoon Hunters

DOT AND DASH SERIES, Mildred Wirt, Cupples
and Leon, hardback, $15.00
Dot and Dash at the Sugar Maple Camp, 1938
Dot and Dash at Happy Hollow, 1938
Dot and Dash in the North Woods, 1938
Dot and Dash at the Seashore, 1940

DRAWING BOOK SERIES, ca. 1930s England, no
publisher name, illustrated paper cover, 8
pages of line drawings and simple vocabulary
words to copy and color. $15.00
Tiny Tots' Drawing Book
Child's Day Drawing Book

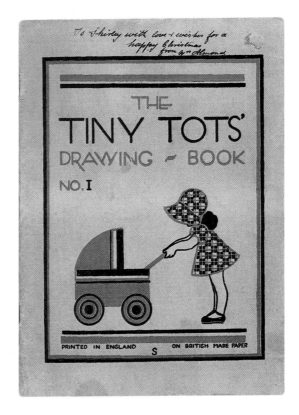

Noah's Ark Drawing Book
Our Trip to the Country Drawing Book

DREADNOUGHT BOYS, Capt. Wilbur Lawton, ca. 1910 Hurst, cloth-over-board cover. $15.00
Dreadnought Boys on Battle Practice
Dreadnought Boys Aboard A Destroyer
Dreadnought Boys in a Submarine
Dreadnought Boys on Aero Service

⊶ **E** ⊷

EIGHT LITTLE INDIANS SERIES, Josephine Lovell (see AUTHOR section for collected works), 1935 Platt Munk, small, illustrated paper cover, 12 pages, b/w and color illustrations by Roger Vernam, books numbered 3300 A thru H. $20.00
Antelope, a Navaho Boy
Gray Bird, a Little Plains Indian
Leaping Trout, a Little Iroquois Boy
Micco, a Seminole Indian Boy
Morning Star, a Little Pueblo Girl
Nigalek, a Little Eskimo Boy
Watlala, an Indian of the Northwest
Winona, a Little Indian of the Prairies

ELLERY QUEEN JR. SERIES, Grosset, cloth-over-board cover, illustrated endpapers with map, b/w illustrations. ($25.00 with dust jacket) $15.00
Black Dog Mystery, 1941, illustrations by William Sanderson
Golden Eagle

Green Turtle, 1944, illustrations by E. A. Watson
Red Chipmunk
Brown Fox

EVERY GIRL'S SERIES, ca. 1920s Goldsmith, a put-together (wannabe?) group of unrelated titles, in matching covers for marketing purposes, poor quality paper but colorful dust jackets. ($20.00 with dust jacket) $8.00
S.W.F. Club, Caroline E. Jacobs
Jane Lends A Hand, Shirley Watkins
Nancy Of Paradise College, Shirley Watkins
Georgina Finds Herself, Shirley Watkins
Helen In The Editor's Chair, Ruthe Wheeler

⊶ **F** ⊷

FAIRVIEW BOYS SERIES, Frederick Gordon (Stratemeyer Syndicate), ca. 1914 Graham and Matlock, hardcover, illustrated. $10.00
Fairview Boys at Camp Mystery

FAMOUS AMERICANS SERIES, collection of separate novels, ca. 1920s edition Barse, cloth-over-board cover, b/w illustrations. ($20.00 with dust jacket) $10.00
Story of George Washington, J. W. McSpadden
Story of John Paul Jones, C. C. Fraser
Story of Benjamin Franklin, C. T. Major
Story of David Crockett, J. Corby
Story of Thomas Jefferson, G. Stone
Story of Abraham Lincoln, J. W. McSpadden

Story of Robert Fulton, I. N. McFee
Story of Thomas A. Edison, I. N. McFee
Story of Harriet B. Stowe, R. B. MacArthur
Story of Mary Lyon, H. O. Stengel
Story of Theodore Roosevelt, J. W. McSpadden

FAMOUS DOG STORIES SERIES, ca. 1940s
Grosset Dunlap, plain tan cover. Collection of dog novels, mainly reprints, by various authors, b/w illustrations. Individually illustrated dust jackets. ($20.00 with dust jacket) $7.00

Lassie Come Home, Eric Knight
Silver Chief, Dog of the North, Jack O'Brien
Silver Chief to the Rescue, Jack O'Brien
Baree, Son of Kazan, James Oliver Curwood
Beautiful Joe, Marshall Saunders
Big Red, Jim Kjelgaard
Bob, Son of Battle, Alfred Ollivant
Boru: Story of an Irish Wolfhound, J. Allen Dunn
Call of the Wild, Jack London
Greyfriars Bobby, Eleanor Atkinson
Juneau, the Sleigh Dog, West Lathrop
Kazan, the Wolf Dog, James Oliver Curwood
White Fang, Jack London
Wild Dog of Edmonton, David Grew
Snow Dog, Jim Kjelgaard
Derry: Airdale of the Frontier, Hubert Evans

FAMOUS FIVE SERIES, Enid Blyton, 1942–1950
Hodder and Stoughton, this series continued into the 1970s and was reprinted regularly in paperback. Cloth-over-board cover, illustra-tions by Eileen Soper. Early editions ($65.00 with dust jacket) $30.00

Five on a Treasure Island
Five Go Adventuring Again
Five Run Away Together
Five Go to Smuggler's Top
Five Go Off in a Caravan
Five on Kirrin Island Again
Five Go Off to Camp
Five Get into Trouble
Five Fall into Adventure

FAMOUS HORSE STORIES SERIES, ca. 1940s
Grosset Dunlap, plain cloth-over-board cover. Collection of horse novels, mainly reprints, by various authors. Individually illustrated dust jackets. ($20.00 with dust jacket) $7.00

Mountain Pony and the Pinto Colt, Henry V. Larom
Cinchfoot, Thomas C. Hinkle
Frog: the Horse that Knew No Master, Col. S. P. Meek
Indian Paint, Glenn Balch
Kentucky Derby Winner, Isabel McMeekin
Magnificent Barb, Dana Faralla
Midnight, Rutherford Montgomery
Mountain Pony, Henry V. Larom
Sorrel Stallion, David Grew
Wild Palomino, Stephen Holt
Ticktock and Jim, Keith Robertson
Hoofbeats, John T. Foote
Mountain and the Rodeo Mystery, Henry Larom
Bluegress Champion, Dorothy Lyons
Strawberry Roan, Don Lang
Lost Horse, Glenn Balch

Beyond Rope and Fence, David Grew
Prairie Colt, Stephen Holt
Capture of the Golden Stallion, Rutherford Montgomery
Golden Stallion's Revenge, Rutherford Montgomery
Golden Stallion to the Rescue, Rutherford Montgomery
Mountain Pony and the Elkhorn Mystery, Henry Larom
Golden Stallion's Victory, Rutherford Montgomery
Phantom Roan, Stephen Holt

FAMOUS TRAMP SERIES, signed "A. No. 1" (Leon Ray Livingston), ca. 1910-20 A. No. 1 Publishing Co., Erie, Pa., black/red/orange illustrated paper cover, small, approximately 135 pages, b/w drawings, advertised as "books on tramp life" with the warning "To Restless Young Men and Boys who read this book, the author, who has led for over a quarter of a century the pitiful and dangerous life of a tramp, gives this well-meant advice: Do not jump on moving trains or street cars, even if only to ride to the next street crossing, because this might arouse the Wanderlust." $20.00

Life and Adventures of A. No. 1
Hobo Camp Fire Tales
Curse of Tramp Life
Trail of the Tramp
Adventures of a Female Tramp
Ways of the Hobo
Snare of the Road
From Coast to Coast with Jack London
Mother of the Hoboes
Wife I Won
Traveling with Tramps

FAULTLESS STARCH LIBRARY, ca. 1900 Faultless Starch Company, Kansas City, 3x5 inch, 15 page paper story books, advertising premiums, one-color printing line drawings on tan paper. Numerous titles, including popular fairy tales, such as Little Red Riding Hood and House that Jack Built. The following list includes some of the more unusual titles. $8.00 each

Trials of Mrs. Graycoat
Six Little Frogs
Trip to the Moon
Starch Ghosts
Upside Down Land
Reformed Pig
Lunch Party
Tuttles' Fourth of July

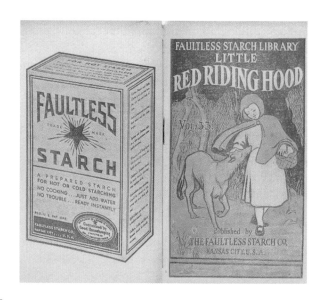

FIGHTING FOR THE FLAG SERIES, Charles Norton, 1890s Wilde, cloth-over-board cover with gilt design, b/w plate illustrations by George Gibbs. $20.00
Midshipman Jack
Jack Benson's Log
Medal of Honor Man

FIVE LITTLE STARRS SERIES, Lillian Elizabeth Roy, 1913 Platt & Peck, small, illustrated cloth-over-board cover, 190+ pages, b/w frontispiece. $10.00
Five Little Starrs
Five Little Starrs on a Canal Boat
Five Little Starrs on a Ranch

FLOWER FAIRIES SERIES, Cicely Mary Barker, undated Blackie, London, small, color illustrations throughout by author, first issued in the mid-1920s and apparently went through several printings through the 1930s. ($130.00 with dust jacket) $100.00. This series was re-issued in the 1970s by Blackie, again undated, and these later copies sell in the $20.00 range. A Warne re-issue was done in the 1990s.
Flower Fairies of the Garden
Flower Fairies of the Trees
Flower Fairies of the Spring
Flower Fairies of the Autumn
Flower Fairies of the Wayside
Flower Fairies of the Summer
Related song books by Barker, ($120.00 with dust jacket) $90.00
Autumn Songs with Music from "Flower Fairies of the Autumn", undated Blackie, oversize, music by Olive Linnell, tipped in color plates.
Spring Songs with Music from "Flower Fairies of the Spring", undated Blackie, oversize, music by Olive Linnell, tipped in color plates.
Summer Songs with Music from "Flower Fairies of the Summer", undated Blackie, oversize, music by Olive Linnell, tipped in color plates.

FLYING MACHINE BOYS SERIES, Frank Walton, ca. 1913 Burt, illustrated cloth-over-board cover, frontispiece illustration. ($45.00 with dust jacket) $20.00
Flying Machine Boys in Deadly Peril, or, *Lost in the Clouds*
Flying Machine Boys in Mexico, or, *Secret of the Crater*
Flying Machine Boys in the Wilds, or, *Mystery of the Andes*
Flying Machine Boys on Duty, or, *Clue Above the Clouds*
Flying Machine Boys on Secret Service, or, *Capture in the Air*

FRANK ALLEN SERIES, Graham Forbes (Stratemeyer Syndicate), ca. 1925 Garden City, cloth-over-board cover. $15.00

FRANK ARMSTRONG SERIES, Matthew Colton, 1911–1914 Hurst, illustrated green cloth-over-board cover, frontispiece illustration. $15.00
Frank Armstrong's Vacation
Frank Armstrong at Queens
Frank Armstrong's Second Term
Frank Armstrong, Drop Kicker
Frank Armstrong, Captain of the Nine
Frank Armstrong at College

FUZZY WUZZY BOOK SERIES, Whitman, oversize square, paper cover, 8 page picture book, short verses and color illustrations with flocking (velvet texturing) on one character, throughout book. $25.00 Later books, $20.00
Woofus the Woolly Dog, Jane Curry, 1944
Fuzzy Wuzzy Waddles, 1945
Fuzzy Wuzzy Kitten, No. 940, 1947
Patchy, Fuzzy Wuzzy Pony, Clarence Biers, 1946
Fuzzy Wuzzy Bear, 1947
Sir Gruff, Nan Gilbert, illustrations by Florence Winship, 1947
Santa Claus, 1947
Fuzzy Wuzzy Puppy, Clarence Biers, 1949

G

GIANT GOLDEN BOOKS, ca. 1940s Simon Schuster, 10¼ x 13 inches size, picture books with

 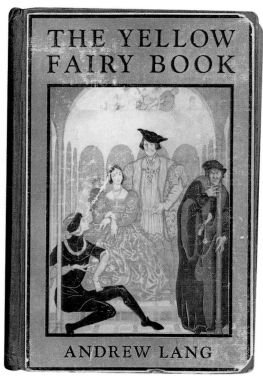

Golden Books Series

bright colored paper-over-board covers, full color illustrations. $35.00

Animal Stories, George Duplaix, illustrated by Feodor Rojankovsky

Farm Stories, Kathy and Byron Jackson, 1946, 76 pages, illustrations by Gustaf Tenggren

Tenggren's Cowboys and Indians, Kathryn and Byron Jackson, 1948, 96 pages, illustrations by Gustaf Tenggren

Golden Mother Goose, illustrated by Alice and Martin Provensen

Golden Dictionary, Ellen Walpole, illustrated by Gertrude Elliott

Golden Encyclopedia, Dorothy Bennett, illustrated by Cornelius DeWitt

Golden Bible, illustrated by Feodor Rojankovsky

Tenggren's Story Book, illustrations by Gustaf Tenggren

Walt Disney's Uncle Remus Stories

Walt Disney's Surprise Package

GINNY GORDON SERIES, Julie Campbell, 1948–50s Whitman, hardcover, illustrated end-papers, b/w illustrations by Margaret Jervis. ($15.00 with dust jacket) $10.00, later reprints in illustrated paper-over-board covers, $8.00

Ginny Gordon and the Disappearing Floor

Ginny Gordon and the Missing Heirloom

Ginny Gordon and the Disappearing Candlesticks

Ginny Gordon and the Mystery at the Old Barn

Ginny Gordon and the Broadcast Mystery

Ginny Gordon and the Lending Library

GIRLS' ELITE SERIES, ca. 1912 Donohue, small, impressed cover illustration, b/w frontispiece, collection of short novels. (Colorful dust jacket doubles price.) $10.00

Bee and the Butterfly, Lucy Foster Madison

Dixie School Girl, Gabrielle E. Jackson

Girls of Mount Morris, Amanda Douglas

Hope's Messenger, Gabrielle E. Jackson

Little Aunt, Marion Ames Taggart

Modern Cinderella, Amanda Douglas

GOLDEN BOOKS SERIES, undated ca. 1920 McKay, new editions of classics, cloth-over-board cover with paste-on-pictorial with gilt, series endpapers with series name, 250+ pages, four to six color plates by Jennie Harbour, Edna Cooke, and others. $30.00

GOLDEN BOYS SERIES, Levi P. Wyman, ca. 1920s Burt, impressed illustration on cover, b/w frontispiece. ($25.00 with dust jacket) $15.00

Golden Boys and their New Electric Cell

Golden Boys at the Fortress

Golden Boys in the Maine Woods

Golden Boys with the Lumber Jacks

Golden Boys on the River

Golden Boys Along the River Allagash

GOLDEN WEST BOYS SERIES, William S. Hart, ca. 1920 Houghton, illustrated cloth-over-board cover. $15.00
Injun and Whitey
Injun and Whitey to the Rescue
Injun and Whitey Strike Out for Themselves

GOLDEN YOUTH SERIES, series editions ca. 1928 P. F. Volland, color illustrations throughout.
Claws of the Thunderbird, written and illustrated by Holling C. Holling, gilt on cloth cover, color illustrated endpapers, listed on dust jacket as "Golden Youth" series, but opposite the title page listed as "Volland Adventure series." $35.00
Small Fry and the Winged Horse, Ruth Campbell, illustrated by Gustaf Tenggren. $45.00
Twins, Edgar Rice Burroughs, illustrated by Douglas Grant. $50.00
White Plume of Navarre, Carter. $40.00
Pirates' Treasure, written and illustrated by Edward Wilson. $35.00

GRACE MAY NORTH BOOKS FOR GIRLS, Grace May North, ca. 1920s Saalfield, green cloth-over-board cover. ($20.00 with dust jacket) $10.00
Meg of Mystery Mountain
Rilla of the Lighthouse
Nan of the Gypsies
Sisters

GRAMMAR SCHOOL BOYS SERIES, H. Irving Hancock, ca. 1910 Altemus, impressed cover design, b/w illustrations. $15.00
Grammar School Boys of Gridley
Grammar School Boys Snowbound
Grammar School Boys in the Woods
Grammar School Boys in Summer Athletics

GREEN FOREST SERIES, Thornton Burgess, ca. 1920s Little Brown, dark cloth-over-board cover with paste-on-pictorial, 200+ pages, 8 color plates by Harrison Cady. ($50.00 with dust jacket) $45.00
Lightfoot the Deer
Blacky the Crow
Whitefoot the Mouse
Buster Bear's Twins

HAL KEEN SERIES, Hugh Lloyd, 1931–34 Grosset, hardcover, illustrations by Bert Salg. ($20.00 with dust jacket) $10.00
Hermit of Gordon's Creek
Kidnapped in the Jungle
Copperhead Trail Mystery
Smuggler's Secret
Mysterious Arab
Lonesome Swamp Mystery
Clue at Skeleton Rocks

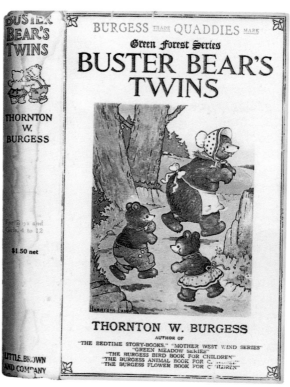

Doom of Stark House
Lost Mine of the Amazon
Mystery at Dark Star Ranch

HAPPY FAMILY SERIES, Cecil Aldin illustrator, ca. 1910, hardcover, illustrated endpapers, color plates by Aldin. $80.00
Hungry Peter, May Byron
Master Quack. No.5 in the Cecil Aldin Happy Family series

HAPPY HOME SERIES, Howard Garis, ca. 1925 Grosset Dunlap, small, about 160 pages, plain red covers with black lettering, color illustrated endpapers, b/w frontispiece by Lang Campbell. ($35.00 with dust jacket) $20.00
Adventures of the Galloping Gas Stove
Adventures of the Runaway Rocking Chair
Adventures of the Traveling Table
Adventures of the Sliding Foot Stool
Adventures of the Sailing Sofa
Adventures of the Prancing Piano

HAPPY HOUR BOOKS, ca. 1920s Macmillan, small, wraparound cover illustration, center panorama color illustration. $35.00
Bremen Band, Frank Dobias illustrations, 1927
Pied Piper, Frank Dobias illustrations
Little Black Sambo, Frank Dobias illustrations
Three Billy Goats Gruff, Frank Dobias illustrations
Ugly Ducking, Elmer and Berta Hader illustrations, 1927

Chicken Little, Elmer and Berta Hader illustrations
Wee Willie Winkie, Elmer and Berta Hader illustrations
Hansel and Gretel, Elmer and Berta Hader illustrations
Humpty Dumpty and Some Funny People, George Richards illustrations
Three Little Pigs, George Richards illustrations
Jack and the Beanstalk, George Richards illustrations
Steadfast Tin Soldier, George Richards illustrations
Golden Goose, Mary Lott Sieman illustrations, 1928
Three Little Kittens, Kurt Wiese illustrations, 1928

HEART OF OAK BOOKS SERIES, edited by Charles Eliot Norton, ca. 1895–1910 Heath, impressed cover design, b/w illustrations. $10.00

HERBERT STRANG'S ANNUAL, early 20th century, oversize volumes with paste-on-pictorial covers, 200+ pages, color endpapers and frontispiece, b/w and color illustrations. $25.00 each

HERB KENT SERIES, Graham Dean, ca. 1935 Goldsmith, hardcover. ($25.00 with dust jacket) $10.00
Herb Kent, West Point Cadet
Herb Kent, West Point Fullback

HIGH SCHOOL BOYS SERIES, by H. Irving Hancock, ca. 1910 Altemus, illustration impressed on cover, b/w illustrations. $15.00
High School Freshmen
High School Pitcher
High School Left End
High School Captain of the Team

HILDEGARDE-MARGARET SERIES, Laura Richards, (ca. 1889), ca. 1917 edition Grosset, cloth-over-board cover, about 275 pages, no illustrations. $15.00
Queen Hildegarde
Hildegarde's Holiday
Hildegarde's Home
Hildegarde's Harvest
Hildegarde's Neighbors
Three Margarets
Margaret Montfort
Peggy
Rita
Fernley House
Merryweathers

HILL TOP BOYS SERIES, Cyril Burleigh, ca. 1917 World, small, 122 pages, b/w illustrated end-papers. ($10.00 with dust jacket) $5.00
Hill Top Boys
Hill Top Boys in Camp
Hill Top Boys on Lost Island
Hill Top Boys on the River

IN WORDS OF ONE SYLLABLE, Mary Godolphin, written and published in the late 1800s, these are simplified re-writes of the classics and have been published in many editions. Following is a sampling of editions:

Aesop's Fables in Words of One Syllable, undated London, illustrated cloth-over-board cover, illustrations throughout. $45.00
Aesop's Fables in Words of One Syllable, undated Werner, hardcover. $40.00
Pilgrim's Progress in Words of One Syllable, 1884 McLoughlin Bros., hardcover, 6 full-page color illustrations. $65.00
Pilgrim's Progress in Words of One Syllable, undated ca. 1900 George Routledge, illustrated hardcover, small, 191 pages, b/w illustrations. $45.00
Pilgrim's Progress in Words of One Syllable, 1939 edition Lippincott, hardcover, b/w illustrations by Robert Lawson. $75.00
Robinson Crusoe in Words of One Syllable, 1882 McLoughlin, decorated hardcover, 6 full-page color illustrations. $55.00
Sanford and Merton in Words of One Syllable, undated ca. 1900, hardcover. $35.00
Swiss Family Robinson in Words of One Syllable, undated ca. 1913 edition McKay, 96 pages, brown cloth-over-board cover with illustration, illustrated with engravings. $35.00

ISABEL CARLETON BOOKS, Margaret Ashmun, ca. 1915 Macmillan, cloth-over-board cover, 3 b/w plates. $15.00
Isabel Carleton's Year
Heart of Isabel Carleton
Isabel Carleton's Friends
Isabel Carleton in the West
Isabel Carleton at Home

J

JACK HEATON SERIES, Archie Frederick Collins, Stokes, cloth-over-board cover, about 250 pages, b/w plate illustrations. $15.00
Jack Heaton, Wireless Operator, 1919
Jack Heaton, Oil Prospector, 1920
Jack Heaton, Gold Seeker, 1921

JACK LORIMER SERIES, Winn Standish, ca 1906 Page, pictorial cloth-over-board cover. $25.00 A. L. Burt reprints. $12.00
Jack Lorimer's Champions
Jack Lorimer's Holidays
Jack Lorimer's Substitute
Jack Lorimer, Freshman

JACK RALSTON SERIES, also listed as SKY DETECTIVE SERIES, Ambrose Newcomb, 1930 edition Goldsmith. ($15.00 with dust jacket) $8.00
Eagles of the Sky
Sky Detectives
Wings Over the Rockies
Sky Pilot's Great Chase
Trackers of the Fog Pack

JERRY TODD SERIES, Leo Edwards, 1923–38 Grosset, red hardcover, illustrated endpapers, illustrations by Bert Salg. First editions are priced to $65.00 with dust jacket. Later editions, ($35.00 with dust jacket) $15.00
Jerry Todd and the Whispering Mummy
Jerry Todd and the Rose-Colored Cat
Jerry Todd and the Oak Island Treasure
Jerry Todd and the Waltzing Hen
Jerry Todd and the Talking Frog
Jerry Todd and the Purring Egg
Jerry Todd and the Whispering Cave
Jerry Todd and the Pirate
Jerry Todd and the Bob-Tailed Elephant
Jerry Todd and the Editor-In-Grief
Jerry Todd and the Caveman
Jerry Todd and the Flying Flapdoodle
Jerry Todd and the Buffalo Bill Bathtub
Jerry Todd and the Up-The-Ladder Club
Jerry Todd and the Poodle Parlor
Jerry Todd and the Cuckoo Camp

JACK WINTERS SERIES, see AMERICAN BOYS SPORTS SERIES

JOHNSTON JEWEL STORIES, by Annie Fellows Johnston, 1920s Page, small, impressed and gilt illustration on cloth-over-board cover, color decorative text borders, b/w illustrations through-
out, including work by Winifred Bromhall. $20.00 Leather-bound editions $35.00
Road of the Loving Heart
Rescue of Princess Winsome
Keeping Tryst
In the Desert Waiting
Three Weavers
Legend of the Bleeding Heart
Jester's Sword

JOLLY JUMP-UPS, see Play Books section

JUNIOR CLASSICS SERIES, 1912 Collier, 10 volume set, brown leather spine with gilt lettering, cloth-covered boards, 500+ pages, illustrated endpapers, color frontispiece, sepia plates. ($100.00 for complete set) $8.00, later cloth-bound editions ($60.00 for complete set), $5.00
Fairy and Wonder Tales, Vol. 1
Folk Tales and Myths, Vol. 2
Tales from Greece and Rome, Vol. 3
Heroes and Heroines of Chivalry, Vol. 4
Stories That Never Grow Old, Vol. 5
Old Fashioned Tales, Vol. 6
Stories of Courage and Heroism, Vol. 7
Animal and Nature Stories, Vol. 8
Stories of Today, Vol. 9
Poems Old and New, Vol. 10

JUNIOR PROGRAMS BOOKS, ca. 1940 Garden City, color illustrated paper-over-board cover,

illustrated endpapers, color and b/w illustrations throughout. Simplified and illustrated retellings of theater scripts. ($25.00 with same-as-cover dust jacket) $15.00

JUST RIGHT BOOKS, ca. 1920 Whitman, cloth-over-board cover with paste-on-pictorial, illustrated endpapers, 120+ pages, two-color illustrations throughout, large print, includes classic and traditional stories and poems, and original stories by Edna Diehl, Laura Rountree Smith, and others, advertised as "Albert Whitman's Easy Reading Juvenile Library." $20.00

Tiddly Winks
Surprise Stories
Party Twins
Washington's Boyhood
Comical Circus Stories
Fifty Funny Animal Tales
In and Out-Door Playgames
Child's Garden of Verses
Treasure Twins
Open Air Stories
Gingerbread Boy
Doll Land Stories
Tale of Curly Tail
Reading Time Stories
Knowledge Primer Games
Jolly Polly and Curly Tail
Flower and Berry Babies
Little Boy France
Busy Fingers Drawing Primer
Happy Manikin in Manners Town
Vegetable and Fruit Children
Dinner that Was Always There
Six Tiddly Winks and the A to Zees

JUVENILE LIBRARY YOUNG FOLKS SERIES, ca. 1915 World, small, b/w illustrations. $10.00
Animal School and Other Stories, Lucy Calhoun
In Play Land, Lucy Calhoun
Jolly Jingle Book, Laura Chandler
Little Miss Muffet Abroad, Alice E. Ball

K

KINDERGARTEN CHILDREN'S HOUR SERIES, edited by Lucy Wheelock, 1920 Houghton Mifflin, 5 volumes, approximately 450 pages each, 5 or 6 color plate illustrations plus b/w illustrations, collected stories and poems. Complete set $90.00. $15.00 each.

KNOCKABOUT CLUB, ca. 1890s Estes, color illustrated paper-over-board cover, illustrated endpapers, b/w illustrations. $30.00

Knockabouts in the Woods, C. A. Stephens
Knockabouts Alongshore, Stephens
Knockabouts in the Tropics, Stephens
Knockabouts in the Everglades, F. A. Ober
Knockabouts in the Antilles, Ober

L

LAKEPORT SERIES, Edward Stratemeyer, ca. 1908 Lothrop Lee, cloth-over-board cover, frontispiece illustration, illustrations by John Goss. ($20.00 with dust jacket) $10.00
Boat Club Boys of Lakeport
Automobile Boys of Lakeport

LAKEWOOD BOYS SERIES, Levi Wyman, 1920s Burt, hardcover. ($20.00 with dust jacket) $10.00
Lakewood Boys on the Lazy S
Lakewood Boys and the Lost Mine
Lakewood Boys in the Frozen North
Lakewood Boys and the Polo Ponies
Lakewood Boys in the South Sea Islands
Lakewood Boys in Montana
Lakewood Boys in the African Jungle

LAURA RICHARDS LIBRARY FOR LITTLE PEOPLE, one of the CHILDREN'S FRIENDS SERIES packages, ca. 1900-1910, small, 40 to 55 pages, cloth-over-board cover with impressed illustration for specific title, some also had gilt lettering, b/w illustrations, originally sold for fifty cents each. $15.00 per book
Chop-Chin and the Golden Dragon
Golden Breasted Kootoo
Sundown Songs

LINDA LANE SERIES, Josephine Lawrence, ca. 1920s Barse, cloth-over-board cover, b/w illustrations. ($20.00 with dust jacket) $10.00
Linda Lane
Linda Lane Helps Out
Linda Lane's Plan
Linda Lane Experiments

LITTLE BEAR SERIES, Frances Margaret Fox, Rand McNally
Doings of Little Bear, 1915, cloth-over-board cover with paste-on-illustration, color illustrations by Warner Carr. ($60.00 with dust jacket) $45.00
Little Bear At Work and at Play, 1920, illustrated by Warner Carr. ($50.00 with dust jacket) $35.00
Little Bear's Playtime, 1922, paste-on-illustration on cover, illustrations by Frances Beem. $35.00

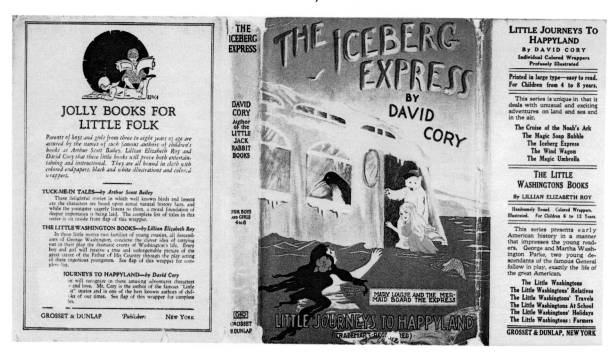

Little Bear's Adventures, 1923, illustrated cover, small, 64 pages, color illustrations by Frances Beem. $25.00

Little Bear's Laughing Times, 1924, red cover with illustration, illustrated by Frances Beem. $40.00.

Little Bear's Ups and Downs, 1925, color illustrations by Frances Beem. $25.00

LITTLE COLOR CLASSICS SERIES, ca. 1930s McLoughlin, easy read books, small, color illustrated paper-over-board cover, color illustrations. $30.00

LITTLE ELEPHANT SERIES, Heluiz Washburne, Whitman, large, color illustrations by Jean McConnell, 32 pages. $40.00

Little Elephant Catches a Cold, 1937
Little Elephant's Christmas Story, 1938
Little Elephant Visits the Farm, 1941
Little Elephant's Picnic, 1944

LITTLE INDIAN SERIES, David Cory, 1930s Grosset, color print illustration on cover, illustrated endpapers, b/w illustrations. ($25.00 with dust jacket) $20.00

Little Indian
White Otter
Red Feather
Star Maiden
Lone Star
Raven Wing

LITTLE JOURNEYS TO HAPPYLAND SERIES, David Cory, ca. 1922–27 Grosset, small, paste-on-pictorial covers, color illustrated endpapers, b/w illustrations by H. Barbour. ($30.00 with dust jacket) $20.00

Iceberg Express, 1922
Magic Soap Bubble, 1922
Magic Umbrella, 1923

LITTLE LULU BOOKS, Marge (Marjorie Henderson Buell), Little Lulu and her friends appeared in comic strips, comic books, individual magazine cartoons, and in numerous hardcover books, usually with brightly illustrated paper-over-board hardcovers.

Little Lulu, 1935 Curtis, collection of previously published b/w cartoons. $50.00

Little Lulu and Her Pals, 1939 McKay, oversize, illustrated hardcover, color illustrations. ($75.00 in dust jacket) $55.00

Little Lulu on Parade, 1941 David McKay, b/w/red cartoons. ($60.00 with same-as-cover dust jacket) $45.00

Oh, Little Lulu!, 1943 McKay, oversize, illustrated hardcover, color illustrations. ($75.00 in dust jacket) $55.00

LITTLE WASHINGTONS BOOKS, Lillian Elizabeth Roy, ca. 1920 Grosset, advertised as "This series presents early American history in a manner that impresses the young readers. George and Martha Washington Parke, two young descendants of the famous General, follow in play exactly the life of the great American." Color illustrated endpapers, b/w illustrations. $20.00

Little Washingtons
Little Washingtons' Relatives
Little Washingtons' Travels
Little Washingtons at School
Little Washingtons' Holidays
Little Washingtons: Farmers

LOIS LENSKI LITTLE SERIES, written and illustrated by Lenski, Oxford, illustrated cloth-over-board cover, square shape, b/w/contrasting color illustrations, illustrated endpapers, easy-readers. $45.00, With cloth-over-board cover plain covers. $20.00
Little Auto, 1934
Little Sail Boat, 1937
Little Airplane, 1938
Little Farm, 1942
Little Fire Engine, 1946

LORAINE SERIES, Elizabeth Gordon, ca. 1930s Rand McNally, small, color illustrated paper-over-cover, color and b/w illustrations by James McCracken. (4 books in this series) $35.00
Loraine
Loraine and the Little People of Summer

LOUISA M. ALCOTT LIBRARY FOR LITTLE PEOPLE, one of the Children's Friends Series packages, ca. 1900-1910, small, 40 to 55 pages, cloth-over-board cover with impressed illustration for specific title, some also had gilt lettering, b/w illustrations, originally sold for fifty cents each or five dollars for an eleven-book set, which included *Little Women*

Play and *Little Men Play.* (These were reprinted as new titles were added, and so set sizes vary.) $15.00 per book
Hole in the Wall
Marjorie's Three Gifts
May Flowers
Poppies and Wheat
Candy Country
Christmas Dream
Little Button Rose
Pansies and Water-Lilies
Doll's Journey
Little Women Play
Little Men Play
Mountain Laurel and Maiden Hair
Morning Glories and Queen Aster

LUCKY TERRELL SERIES, Canfield Cook, ca. 1943 Grosset, hardcover. ($20.00 with dust jacket) $10.00
Secret Mission
Lost Squadron
Springboard to Tokyo
Sky Attack

M

MARJORIE DEAN SERIES, Pauline Lester, ca. 1917 A. L. Burt, cloth-over-board cover with impressed illustration. ($25.00 with dust jacket) $15.00
Marjorie Dean, High School Freshman
Marjorie Dean, High School Sophomore

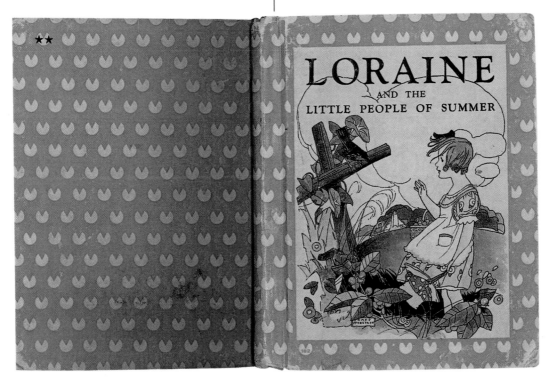

Marjorie Dean, High School Junior
Marjorie Dean, High School Senior
Marjorie Dean, College Freshman
Marjorie Dean, College Sophomore
Marjorie Dean, College Junior
Marjorie Dean, College Senior
Marjorie Dean, Post-Graduate
Marjorie Dean, Marvelous Manager
Marjorie Dean's Romance
Marjorie Dean Macy

MARS SERIES, Edgar Rice Burroughs. The following is a list of the titles, dates and publishers of the ten Mars books written by the creator of Tarzan.

First editions of the Mars books are scarce and prices for first editions with their original dust jackets often run into the thousands. The earlier books were reprinted often, and slight variations can help the collector identify exact printings. For collectors dealing in the RARE books price ranges, more detailed descriptions than can be given here will be required, and can be found in publications dedicated to Burroughs' work and to rare book collections.

The Mars books were written for adults, usually appearing as stories and serials in magazines such as *All-Story, Argosy, Blue Book,* and *Amazing Stories,* before appearing in hardbound novel form. Like the Tarzan books, their fast-paced, action-packed stories soon became favorites of young readers.

Princess of Mars, 1917 McClurg, brown cloth-over-board cover with red lettering, 5 sepia plates by Frank Schoonover. (RARE with dust jacket) $400.00

Princess of Mars, 1918 to 1940 Grosset editions, cloth-over-board cover, b/w plates by Frank Schoonover. Redesign of dust jacket by Schoonover, using original illustration but changing the placement of lettering. ($60.00 with dust jacket) $20.00

Princess of Mars, 1940 Grosset edition, blue cloth-over-board cover, no illustrations. ($50.00 with Schoonover dust jacket) $20.00

Princess of Mars, 1948 Edgar Rice Burroughs edition, tan cloth-over-board cover, frontispiece by Schoonover. ($75.00 with dust jacket) $30.00

Gods of Mars, 1918 McClurg, dark red cloth-over-board cover, black lettering, sepia frontispiece by Schoonover. (RARE with dust jacket) $150.00

Gods of Mars, 1919 McClurg reprint, dated 1919, dark red cloth-over-board cover, black lettering, frontispiece by Schoonover. $100.00

Gods of Mars, 1920s–30s Grosset editions, cloth-over-board cover, frontispiece by Schoonover. ($60.00 with dust jacket) $20.00

Gods of Mars, 1940 Grosset edition, green cloth-over-board cover, no frontispiece. Schoonover dust jacket. ($35.00 with dust jacket) $15.00

Gods of Mars, 1948 Edgar Rice Burroughs edition, tan cloth-over-board cover, frontispiece by Schoonover. ($50.00 with dust jacket) $30.00

Warlord of Mars, 1919 McClurg, red cloth-over-board cover with gold lettering, sepia frontispiece and dust jacket by J. Allen St. John. (RARE with dust jacket) $175.00

Warlord of Mars, 1920 Methuen UK, hardcover. $45.00

Warlord of Mars, 1920s-30s Grosset editions, cloth-over-board cover, frontispiece by J. Allen St. John. ($50.00 with dust jacket) $30.00

Warlord of Mars, 1940 Grosset edition, cloth-over-board cover, no frontispiece. ($35.00 with dust jacket) $15.00

Warlord of Mars, 1948 Edgar Rice Burroughs, tan cloth-over-board cover, frontispiece by J. Allen St. John. ($75.00 with dust jacket) $30.00

Thuvia, Maid of Mars, 1920 McClurg, yellow-green cloth-over-board cover with black lettering, ten sepia plates by J. Allen St. John. Dust jacket by P. J. Monahan. (RARE with dust jacket) $120.00

Thuvia, Maid of Mars, 1920s–30s Grosset editions, cloth-over-board cover, 4 b/w plates by J. Allen St. John. Variations of the Monahan dust jacket. ($50.00 with dust jacket) $20.00

Thuvia, Maid of Mars, 1940 Grosset edition, red cloth-over-board cover, no plates. ($35.00 with dust jacket) $15.00

Thuvia, Maid of Mars, 1948 Edgar Rice Burroughs, tan cloth-over-board cover, frontispiece by J. Allen St. John. ($100.00 with dust jacket) $45.00

Chessmen of Mars, 1922 McClurg, red cloth-over-board cover with black lettering, 8 sepia plates by J. Allen St. John. Dust jacket by J. Allen St. John. (RARE with dust jacket) $75.00

Chessmen of Mars, 1923 Methuen first UK edition, hardcover with St. John illustrations. ($1200.00 with dust jacket) $75.00

Chessmen of Mars, 1920s-30s Grosset editions, cloth-over-board cover, 4 b/w plates by J. Allen St. John. Dust jacket by J. Allen St. John. $55.00 with dust jacket) $30.00

Chessmen of Mars, 1940 Grosset edition, red cloth-over-board cover. Dust jacket by J. Allen St. John. ($35.00 with dust jacket) $15.00

Chessmen of Mars, 1948 Edgar Rice Burroughs, tan cloth-over-board cover, frontispiece by J. Allen St. John. ($75.00 with dust jacket) $40.00

Master Mind of Mars, 1928 McClurg, orange cloth-over-board cover with black lettering, b/w drawings on title page, 5 b/w illustrations with yellow background by J. Allen St. John. Dust jacket by St. John. (Robert Zeuschner states that only 5000 copies of this edition were printed.) (RARE with dust jacket) $250.00

Master Mind of Mars, 1920s–30s Grosset editions, cloth-over-board cover, 5 b/w illustrations by J. Allen St. John. ($65.00 with dust jacket) $25.00

Master Mind of Mars, 1948 Edgar Rice Burroughs, tan cloth-over-board cover, title page illustration by J. Allen St. John. ($75.00 with dust jacket) $40.00

Fighting Man of Mars, 1931 Metropolitan, textured red cloth-over-board cover with green lettering, b/w frontispiece by Hugh Hutton. Dust jacket by Hutton. Hard-to-find. $250.00

Fighting Man of Mars, 1932 John Lane, first UK edition, hardcover. $60.00

Fighting Man of Mars, 1932 Grosset edition, red cloth-over-board cover, frontispiece and dust jacket from first edition. ($60.00 with dust jacket) $20.00

Fighting Man of Mars, 1948 Edgar Rice Burroughs, tan cloth-over-board cover, frontispiece and dust jacket from first edition. ($75.00 with dust jacket) $30.00

Swords of Mars, 1936 Edgar Rice Burroughs, blue cloth with orange lettering, 5 b/w plates by J. Allen St. John. Wraparound dust jacket illustration by J. Allen St. John. (RARE with dust jacket) $60.00

Swords of Mars, 1937 Grosset edition, red cloth-over-board cover, 5 b/w plates by J. Allen St. John. Wraparound dust jacket illustration by J. Allen St. John. ($150.00 with dust jacket) $70.00

Swords of Mars, 1938 Grosset edition, red cloth-over-board cover, 2 illustrations by J. Allen St. John. Wraparound dust jacket illustration by J. Allen St. John. ($100.00 with dust jacket) $40.00

Swords of Mars, 1948 Edgar Rice Burroughs edition, tan cloth-over-board cover. Wraparound dust jacket illustration by J. Allen St. John with slight variation. ($85.00 with dust jacket) $30.00

Synthetic Men of Mars, 1940 Edgar Rice Burroughs, blue cloth-over-board cover with orange lettering, 5 b/w plates by John Coleman Burroughs. Dust jacket by J. C. Burroughs. ($600.00 with dust jacket) $60.00

Synthetic Men of Mars, 1948 Edgar Rice Burroughs edition, tan cloth-over-board cover, frontispiece by John Coleman Burroughs. Dust jacket by J. C. Burroughs. ($90.00 with dust jacket) $40.00

Llana of Gathol, 1948 Edgar Rice Burroughs, blue cloth-over-board cover with red lettering, 5 b/w plates by John Coleman Burroughs. Dust jacket by J. C. Burroughs. ($200.00 with dust jacket) $75.00

MARY FRANCES BOOKS, Jane Eayer Fryer, Winston, cloth-over-board cover with paste-on-pictorial, illustrated endpapers, color illustrations throughout. $165.00

Mary Frances Garden Book, or *Adventures Among the Garden People,* 1916, illustrations by William Zwirner.

Mary Frances Housekeeper Book, or, *Adventures Among the Doll People,* 250 pages. This is difficult to find and therefore priced in the $200.00 range.

Mary Frances Sewing Book, or, *Adventures Among the Thimble People,* 320 pages, illustrations by Jane Allen Boyer.

Mary Frances Cook Book, or, *Adventures Among the Kitchen People,* 170 pages, illustrations by Margaret Hayes and Jane Allen Boyer.

Mary Frances First Aid Book, hard to find therefore priced to $200.00.

Mary Frances Story Book, illustrations by Edwin Prittie.

MARY LEE SERIES, Anna Merrill, ca. 1920 Whitman, small, color illustration on cover, illustrated endpapers, b/w illustrations. $15.00

Mary Lee's Friend
Mary Lee at Washington
Mary Lee, the Red Cross Girl
Mary Lee, the Campfire Girl

MARY PERKS BOOKS, Perks Publishing, New York. The value usually depends on the illustrator for this line. The prices are for the Mary Perks books that were illustrated by less well-known artists. Exceptions would be books such as Helen Bannerman's *Little Black Sambo,* 1931, illustrated by Fern Bisel Peat, combining a highly collectible story with a highly collectible artist and usually priced in the $100.00 range.

Famous Books for the Nursery, ca. 1945, oversize, color illustrated cardboard cover, two-color illustrations, many by Mary and Wallace Stover. $35.00

Raggedy Ann in the Garden
Ranggedy Ann and the Laughing Brook
Raggedy Ann Helps Grandpa Hoppergrass
Raggedy Ann and the Hoppy Toad
Uncle Wiggily Goes Berrying
Uncle Wiggily Helps Jimmie
Ungle Wiggily and the Baker Cat
Uncle Wiggily and the Picture Book
Scare Crow and Tin Man
Story of Heidi
Little Folks Alphabet
Story of Peter Pan

Winnie the Pooh
Famous Bible Stories
Famous Rabbit Stories
Famous Chicken Stories
Famous Kitten Stories
Famous Dog Stories
Famous Mouse Stories
Pre-School Books,
Our Country Coloring Book
Animal and Birds Coloring Book
Fun With Crayons
Read, Draw and Color
Uncle Wiggily Stories, Howard Garis, ca. 1943, oversize, color illustrated cardboard cover, two-color illustrations by Mary and Wallace Stover. $35.00
Uncle Wiggily Starts Off
Uncle Wiggily and the Paper Boat
Uncle Wiggily and the Troublesome Boys
Uncle Wiggily and Granddaddy Longlegs
Uncle Wiggily and the Milkman
Uncle Wiggily and the Cowbird
Uncle Wiggily and the Starfish
Uncle Wiggily and the Red Monkey

MERRILL SERIES, ca. 1940 Merrill Publishing, Chicago, oversize picture books, linen-textured paper, paper cover, 12 pages, full color $30.00
Tale of Peter Rabbit, 1943, Book No. 4811
Three Bears, 1937, Book No. 3417, illustrated by Milo Winter

MILDRED SERIES, Martha Finley, ca. 1870-90 Routledge, also ca. 1915 Dodd Mead, also Burt reprints, illustrated cloth-over-board cover. $25.00
Mildred Keith
Mildred at Roselands
Mildred and Elsie
Mildred at Home
Mildred's Married Life
Mildred's Boys and Girls
Mildred's New Daughter

MILLERS SERIES, Clara Dillingham Pierson, ca. 1905 Dutton, illustrated cloth-over-board cover, b/w plates. $20.00
Millers at Pencroft
Three Little Millers
Millers and Their Playmates
Millers and Their New Home

MILLY-MOLLY-MANDY SERIES, Joyce L. Brisley, ca. late 1920s–30s London. McKay and Australian reprints $10.00
Milly-Molly-Mandy Stories, 1928 London. $65.00
More of Milly-Molly-Mandy, 1929 London. $60.00
Further Doings of Milly-Molly-Mandy, 1932 London. $50.00
Milly-Molly-Mandy Again, 1948 London. $20.00

MOTHER GOOSE RHYMES, Mary Royt illustrations, 1934 Whitman, series 514, miniature books 3 x 3½", cardboard cover, 39 pages, b/w illustrations by Royt. $20.00 each

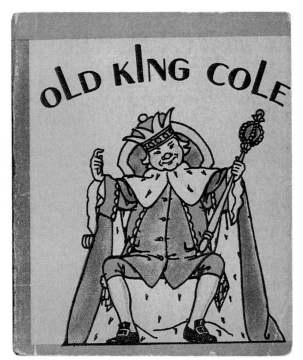

Little Tommy Tucker
Old King Cole

MOTOR CYCLE CHUMS SERIES, Lieut. Howard
Payson, 1912 Hurst, hardcover. $20.00
Motor Cycle Chums
Motor Cycle Chums Around the World
Motor Cycle Chums of the Northwest Patrol
Motor Cycle Chums in the Goldfields
Motor Cycle Chums Whirlwind Tour
Motor Cycle Chums South of the Equator
Motor Cycle Chums Through Historic America

MOTOR MAIDS SERIES, Katherine Stokes,
1911–12 Donohue, blue cloth-over-board cover.
($25.00 with dust jacket) $10.00. Hurst edition
with pictorial boards has same-design dust
jacket. ($20.00 with dust jacket) $15.00
School Days
By Palm and Pine
Across the Continent
By Rose, Shamrock and Heather

MOTOR RANGERS, Marvin West, 1911–14 Hurst,
illustrated cloth-over-board cover, illustrations
by Charles Wrenn. $20.00
Lost Mine
Through the Sierras
On Blue Water
Cloud Cruiser
Wireless Station
Touring for the Trophy

MOVING PICTURE BOYS, Victor Appleton, ca.
1913 Grosset. $15.00
Moving Picture Boys and the Flood
Moving Picture Boys at Panama
Moving Picture Boys Under the Sea
Moving Picture Boys on the War Front
Moving Picture Boys on French Battlefields
Moving Picture Boys' First Showhouse
Moving Picture Boys at Seaside Park
Moving Picture Boys on Broadway
Moving Picture Boys' Outdoor Exhibition
Moving Picture Boys' New Idea

MRS. GOOSE SERIES, Miriam Clark Potter,
1936–47 Lippincott, small, cloth-over-board
cover, b/w illustrations by author and Zenas
Potter. ($35.00 with dust jacket) $15.00
Mrs. Goose and Three-Ducks
Mrs. Goose of Animal Town
Our Friend Mrs. Goose
Hello, Mrs. Goose

MYSTERY BOYS SERIES, A. Van Buren Powell,
ca. 1930 Burt, and World Publishing, illustrat-
ed cover and illustrated endpapers, 280+
pages. ($20.00 with dust jacket) $15.00
Mystery Boys and the Inca Gold
Mystery Boys and Captain Kidd's Message
*Mystery Boys and the Secret of the Golden
  Sun*
Mystery Boys and the Chinese Jewels
Mystery Boys and the Hindu Treasure

NANCY PEMBROKE SERIES, Margaret Van Epps, 1930 World (also reprinted by Burt), hardcover, about 250 pages. ($15.00 with dust jacket) $10.00
Nancy Pembroke, College Maid
Nancy Pembroke's Vacation in Canada
Nancy Pembroke, Sophomore at Roxford
Nancy Pembroke in New Orleans
Nancy Pembroke, Junior

NAN SHERWOOD SERIES, Annie Rowe Carr, 1916–1937 Saalfield, (also in Goldsmith edition), hardcover, frontispiece illustration. ($15.00 with dust jacket) $10.00
Nan Sherwood at Pine Camp, 1916
Nan Sherwood at Lakeview Hall, 1917
Nan Sherwood's Winter Holidays, 1918
Nan Sherwood at Rose Ranch, 1919
Nan Sherwood at Palm Beach, 1921

NAT RIDLEY DETECTIVE SERIES, Nat Ridley Jr., (Stratemeyer), ca. 1926 Garden City, hardcover. $25.00
Daring Abduction,
Stolen Liberty Bonds, #11

NATURE STORIES SERIES, Thornton Burgess, 1946 Little Brown, cloth-over-board cover with silhouette illustration, about 184 pages, two-color and b/w illustrations by Harrison Cady. ($25.00 with cover) $15.00
Crooked Little Path
Dear Old Briar-Patch
At Paddy the Beaver's Pond
Along Laughing Brook

NEVER GROW OLD STORIES, ca. 1930 Platt Munk, small, color illustrated paper-over-board cover with cloth spine, illustrated endpapers, color and b/w illustrations throughout. $45.00
Little Engine That Could
Tale of Peter Rabbit
Little Black Sambo
Rooster, the Mouse, and the Little Red Hen
Gingerbread Boy
Little Red Hen and the Grain of Wheat
Three Little Pigs
First Circus

NORTHWEST STORIES SERIES, LeRoy W. Snell, ca. 1930s Cupples & Leon, cloth-on-board cover. $10.00
Lead Disk
Shadow Patrol
Wolf Cry
Spell of the North
Challenge of the Yukon
Phantom of the Rivers
Sergeant Dick
Carcajou

O

OAKDALE ACADEMY SERIES, Morgan Scott, 1911 – 1913 Hurst, embossed decoration and color printed illustration on hardcover. $25.00
Burt edition, hardcover. $15.00
Ben Stone At Oakdale
Boys Of Oakdale Academy
Rival Pitchers Of Oakdale
Oakdale Boys In Camp
Great Oakdale Mystery
New Boys At Oakdale

OLD GLORY SERIES, Edward Stratemeyer, ca. 1900 Lee & Shepard, illustrated tan or red cloth-over-board cover with gilt, b/w illustrations by A. B. Shute. $25.00
Campaign of the Jungle
Young Volunteer in Cuba
Fighting in Cuban Waters
Under Otis in the Philippines
On to Pekin

OLIVER OPTIC SERIES, (William T. Adams, 1822–1897), Adams was a prolific writer of adventure novels for young readers. His series dealing with Civil War themes is his most popular. Early editions with gilt-decorated or lettered covers generally sell in the $35.00 to $50.00 range, post-1900 editions, $15.00
Boat Club, or, *Bunkers of Rippleton,* 1855, may have been the first Optic title for children, printed as an individual title but in later editions, included in various series.
All-Over-the-World, $30.00
Millionaire at Sixteen, or, *Cruise of the Guardian-Mother,* 1892
Up and Down the Nile, or, *Young Adventurers in Africa,* 1894
Young Navigators, or, *Foreign Cruise of the Maud,* 1893
Pacific Shores, or, *Adventures in Eastern Seas,* 1898
American Boy, $30.00
Little by Little, or, *Cruise of the Flyaway*
Young Knight Errant, or, *Cruising in the West Indies*
Army and Navy, 1860s–1890s Lee and Shepard, brown cloth-over-board cover with gilt, Civil War novels. $30.00
Yankee Middy
Young Lieutenant, 1865
Blue and Gray, ca. 1880s Lee and Shepard, blue and gray cloth-over-board cover with gilt, small, b/w illustrations, Civil War novels. $35.00
At the Front
Fighting for the Right, 1892
Taken by the Enemy

On the Blockade, 1890
Within the Enemy's Lines, 1889
Lieutenant at Eighteen, 1895
An Undivided Union (last book in series, completed by Edward Stratemeyer, hard-to-find, double price), 1899
Goldwing Club, Lee & Shepard, pictorial hardcover, small, 340+ pages. $30.00
All Adrift, 1883
Great Western, ca. 1870s
Going South, or, *Yachting on the Atlantic Coast*
Lake Breezes, or, *Cruise of the Sylvania*
Going West, or *Perils of a Poor Boy,* 1875
Going South, or *Yachting on the Atlantic Coast,* 1879
Lake Shore, ca. 1870s Lee and Shepard, cloth-over-board cover, small, b/w illustrations. $30.00
Bear and Forbear
Brake Up, or, *Young Peacemakers*
Lightening Express, or, *Rival Academies*
Through by Daylight, or, *Young Engineer of the Lake Shore Railroad*
On Time, or, *Young Captain*
Sailor Boy, undated Donohue, color illustrated cloth-over-board cover. $15.00
Sailor Boy, or *Jack Somers in the Navy*
Soldier Boy, Donohue or A. L. Burt, decorated hardcover. $15.00
Fighting Joe, Soldier Boy
Fighting Joe, Fortunes of a Staff Officer
Tom Somers in the Army
Starry Flag, $35.00
Freaks of Fortune, or, *Half Round the World*
Make or Break, or, *Rich Man's Daughter*
Upward and Onward, ca. 1860s, $20.00
Field and Forest, or, *Fortunes of a Farmer*
Plane and Plank, or, *Mishaps of a Mechanic*
Poor and Proud, or, *Fortunes of Katy Redburn*
Yacht Club, ca. 1870s, blue cloth-over-board cover with gold lettering and sailing vessel decoration, small, b/w illustrations. $40.00
Little Bobtail
Young America Abroad, 1870s–1890s Lee and Shepard, cloth-over-board cover with gilt lettering and ship, frontispiece illustration, 300+ pages. $25.00
Dikes and Ditches, Young America in Holland and Belgium
Cross and Cresent, Young America in Turkey and Greece
Down the Rhine, Young America in Germany
Outward Bound, Young America Afloat
Palace or Cottage, Young America in France and Switzerland
Red Cross, or, *Young America in England and Wales*
Sunny Shores, Young America in Italy and Austria
Northern Lands, or, *Young America in Russia and Prussia*

ONCE-UPON-A-TIME SERIES, ca. 1920s Ginn, illustrated cloth-over-board cover, b/w illustrations. $40.00

Pinocchio, Adventures of a Marionette, Walter Cramp translation, 1904, illustrations by Charles Copeland.

Pinocchio in Africa, Angelo Patri, 1911, illustrations by Charles Copeland.

Pinocchio's First Visit to America, Angelo Patri, 1928, b/w illustrations by S. Gallagher.

OUR YOUNG AEROPLANE SCOUTS SERIES, Horace Porter, 1914–17 Burt, printed illustration on cloth-over-board cover. ($35.00 with dust jacket) $15.00

Our Young Aeroplane Scouts in England
Our Young Aeroplane Scouts in Italy
Our Young Aeroplane Scouts in France and Belgium
Our Young Aeroplane Scouts in Germany
Our Young Aeroplane Scouts in Russia
Our Young Aeroplane Scouts in Turkey
Our Young Aeroplane Scouts in the Balkans

OUTBOARD BOYS SERIES, Roger Garis, 1933–34, cloth-over-board cover. ($15.00 with dust jacket) $10.00

Outboard Boys
Outboard Boys at Mystery Island
Outboard Boys at Shadow Lake
Outboard Boys at Pirate Beach
Outboard Boys at Shark River

OUTDOOR CHUMS SERIES, Captain Quincy Allen, ca. 1911 Grosset, illustrated tan cloth-over-board cover. ($20.00 with dust jacket) $10.00. Goldsmith reprints ($15.00 in dust jacket) $7.00

Outdoor Chums
Outdoor Chums on the Lake
Outdoor Chums in the Forest
Outdoor Chums on the Gulf
Outdoor Chums after a Big Game
Outdoor Chums on a House Boat
Outdoor Chums in the Big Woods
Outdoor Chums at Cabin Point

P

PALMER COX PRIMERS, illustrated by Palmer Cox, 1897, small eight page pamphlets, done as a giveaway to insert in packages of Jersey Coffee. $25.00 each, $250.00 for a complete set of six.

Monkeys
Cock Robin
Birds' Wedding
Jolly Chinee
Merry Mice
First Trousers

PATTY SERIES, Carolyn Wells, (1901–19 Dodd) undated ca. 1930s editions Grosset, blue cloth-over-board cover. ($20.00 with dust jacket) $10.00

Patty Fairfield
Patty at Home
Patty in the City
Patty's Summer Days
Patty in Paris
Patty's Friends
Patty's Pleasure Trip
Patty's Success
Patty's Motor Car
Patty's Butterfly Days
Patty's Social Season
Patty's Suitors
Patty's Romance
Patty's Fortune
Patty Blossom
Patty Bride
Patty and Azalea

PENNY NICHOLS SERIES, Joan Clark (Mildred Wirt), Goldsmith, cloth-over-board cover. ($25.00 with dust jacket) $15.00

Penny Nichols Finds a Clue, 1936
Penny Nichols and the Black Imp, 1936
Penny Nichols and the Mystery of the Lost Key, 1936
Penny Nichols and the Knob Hill Mystery, 1939

PENNY PARKER MYSTERY STORIES SERIES, Mildred A. Wirt, 1940s Cupples Leon, cloth-over-board cover, frontispiece illustration, dust jacket illustrated by K. S. Woerner. ($30.00 with dust jacket) $15.00

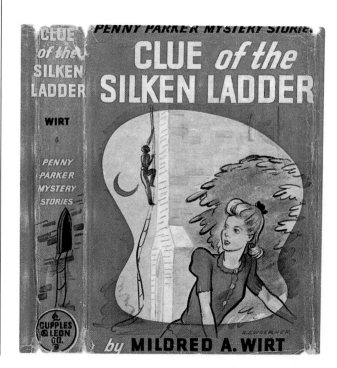

Tale of the Witch Doll
Vanishing Houseboat
Danger at the Drawbridge
Behind the Green Door
Clue of the Silken Ladder
Secret Pact
Clock Strikes Thirteen
Wishing Well
Saboteurs on the River
Ghost Beyond the Gate
Hoofbeats on the Turnpike
Voice from the Cave
Guilt of the Brass Thieves
Signal in the Dark
Whispering Walls
Swamp Island
Cry at Midnight

PENNY PARRISH SERIES, Janet Lambert, 1941–49
Grosset reprints. ($15.00 in dust jacket) $10.00
Star Spangled Summer
Dreams of Glory
Glory Be!
Just Jennifer
Up Goes the Curtain
Friday's Child
Miss Tippy
Little Miss Atlas

PETER AND POLLY, Rose Lucia, American Book
Co., ca. 1918, print illustrated cloth-over-board
cover, small, 175+ pages, two-color and b/w
illustrations. $20.00
Peter and Polly in Summer
Peter and Polly in Winter
Peter and Polly in Spring
Peter and Polly in Auturm

PETER RABBIT SERIES, undated ca. 1930-40
Donohue, small, b/w/orange cover with illus-
tration, 48 pages, 24 full color illustrations.
$35.00
Peter Rabbit
Little Black Sambo
Chicken Little
Cinderella
Little Red Riding Hood
Selfish Fox
Three Little Kittens
Three Bears
Little Small Red Hen
Three Little Pigs

PETERSHAM SERIES, Maud and Miska Petersham, mid-1930s Winston, square or oblong
cloth-over-board cover with paste-on-illustra-

tion, color illustrations throughout by authors.
($45.00 with dust jacket) $20.00
Story Book of Aircraft
Story Book of Clothes
Story Book of Coal
Story Book of Corn
Story Book of Cotton
Story Book of Food
Story Book of Gold
Story Book of Earth's Treasures
Story Book of Iron and Steel
Story Book of Oil
Story Book of Rayon
Story Book of Rice
Story Book of Sugar
Story Book of Things We Use
Story Book of Wheat

PHILIP KENT SERIES, T. Truxton Hare, ca. 1915 Penn,
color paste-on-illustration on cloth-on-board cover,
7 b/w plate illustrations by R. L. Boyer. $15.00
Philip Kent
Philip Kent in Lower School
Philip Kent in Upper School

PLATT & MUNK 3000 SERIES, ca. 1930s, paper
cover picture books with 12 pages, color illustrations, primarily by Eulalie. Linen-like paper
editions, back cover blank. $35.00. Smooth
paper editions of same books are trimmed ⅛"
shorter, have larger print, and an added poem
on the back cover. $10.00

Chicken Little
Cinderella
Dick Whittington
Gingerbread Boy
Jack and the Beanstalk
Puss in Boots
Three Bears
Tom Thumb

POGO SERIES, Jo and Ernest Norling, 1940s Holt, cloth-over-board cover, small educational picture books featuring a dog, illustrated endpapers, b/w illustrations by authors. ($25.00 with dust jacket) $10.00
Pogo's Fishing Trip
Pogo's Train
Pogo's Sky Ride
Pogo's House
Pogo's Mining Trip
Pogo's Letter
Pogo's Lamb
Pogo's Farm Adventure

POLLY SERIES, Dorothy Whitehill, ca. 1920s Barse, cloth-over-board cover, b/w illustrations. ($20.00 with dust jacket) $10.00
Polly's First Year at Boarding School
Polly's Summer Vacation
Polly's Senior Year at Boarding School
Polly Sees the World at War
Polly and Lois
Polly and Bob
Polly's Reunion
Polly's Polly
Polly at Pixies' Haunt
Polly's House Party

POLLY PAGE SERIES, Izola Forrester, ca. 1910 George Jacobs, b/w illustrations by Faith Avery. $10.00
Polly Page Yacht Club
Polly Page Ranch Club

PONY RIDER BOYS SERIES, Frank Patchen, 1920s Saalfield, illustrated cloth-over-board cover, b/w illustrations. Numerous titles including the following. $15.00
Pony Rider Boys in the Rockies
Pony Rider Boys in Texas
Pony Rider Boys in Montana
Pony Rider Boys in the Ozarks
Pony Rider Boys in New Mexico
Pony Rider Boys in the Grand Canyon
Pony Rider Boys with the Texas Rangers
Pony Rider Boys on the Blue Ridge
Pony Rider Boys in New England

Pony Rider Boys in Louisiana
Pony Rider Boys in Alaska

PRINCESS POLLY SERIES, Amy Brooks, (1914 Platt & Peck) undated A. L. Burt reprints, cloth-over-board cover with printed illustration, frontispiece. $15.00
Princess Polly
Princess Polly's Playmates
Princess Polly at School
Princess Polly by the Sea
Princess Polly at Play
Princess Polly's Gay Winter
Princess Polly at Cliffmore

PUTNAM HALL STORIES SERIES, Arthur M. Winfield (Edward Stratemeyer), Grosset, advertised as "Companion Stories to the famous Rover Boys Series." Putnam Hall was the military academy that the Rover Boys attended. These stories feature different characters. ($30.00 to $50.00 with pre-1920 dust jacket. Later editions, $20.00 with dust jacket) $15.00
Mystery of Putnam Hall
Camping Out Days at Putnam Hall
Rebellion at Putnam Hall
Champions of Putnam Hall
Cadets of Putnam Hall
Rivals of Putnam Hall

Q

QUEEN HILDEGARDE SERIES, see HILDEGARDE-MARGARET Series.

R

RADIO BOYS SERIES, Gerald Breckenridge, ca. 1920s A. L. Burt, hardcover with gilt lettering and stamped illustration. ($25.00 with dust jacket) $10.00
Radio Boys on the Mexican Border
Radio Boys on Secret Service Duty
Radio Boys with the Revenue Guards
Radio Boys Search for the Incas' Treasure
Radio Boys Rescue the Lost Alaska Expedition
Radio Boys in Darkest Africa
Radio Boys Seek the Lost Atlantis
Radio Boys with the Border Patrol
Radio Boys as Soldiers of Fortune

RAND MCNALLY CLASSICS NEW AND OLD SERIES, ca. 1916–24 Rand McNally, oversize, navy cloth-over-board cover with paste-on-pic-

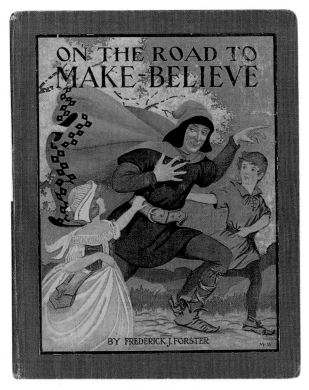 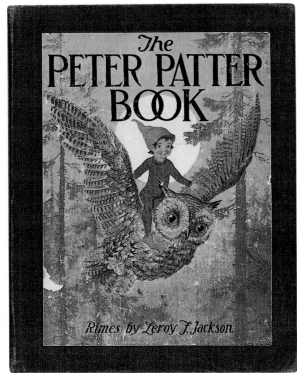

torial, illustrated endpapers, color and b/w illustrations. $65.00

Real Mother Goose, illustrations by Milo Winter and Blanche Fisher Wright.

Peter Patter Book, Leroy Jackson, 1918, illustrations by Milo Winter and Blanche Fisher Wright.

Aesop for Children, 1919, illustrations by Milo Winter.

Illustrated Bible Story Book, Seymour Loveland, 1923, illustrations by Milo Winter.

On the Road to Make-Believe, Frederick Forster, 1924, paste-on-pictorial by Milo Winter, illustrations by Uldenne Trippe.

RANDY STARR, see SKY FLYERS SERIES

RANGER BOYS SERIES, Claude H. La Belle, ca. 1920 Burt, illustrated cloth-over-board cover, frontispiece illustration. Advertised as "Adventures of three boys with the forest rangers in the State of Maine." ($15.00 with dust jacket) $10.00

Ranger Boys to the Rescue
Ranger Boys Find the Hermit
Ranger Boys and the Border Smugglers
Ranger Boys Outwit the Timber Thieves
Ranger Boys and Their Reward

RAPHAEL HOUSE LIBRARY OF GIFT BOOKS SERIES, undated ca. 1900–15 Raphael Tuck, London, and David McKay, Philadelphia, dark blue cloth-over-board cover with gilt lettering,

oversize, 10 to 12 color plates plus b/w illustrations. Thirty books.

Tales of the Alhambra, Irving, illustrated by H. M. Brock. $75.00

Animal Legends from Many Lands, Woolf, illustrated by Edwin Noble. $65.00

Tales of King Arthur and the Knights of the Round Table, Ashley, illustrated by A. A. Dixon. $65.00

My Book of Favourite Fairy Tales, Vredenburg, illustrated by Jennie Harbour. $150.00

Children's Stories from Old British Legends, Belgrave and Hart, illustrated by Harry Theaker. $65.00

Children's Stories from French Fairy Tales, Ashley, illustrated by Mabel Lucie Attwell. $150.00

Children's Stories from Italian Legends, Romano, illustrated by Howard Davie. $65.00

Children's Stories from Indian Legends, Belgrave and Hart, illustrated by Theaker. $65.00

Children's Stories from Japanese Fairy Tales, Kato, illustrated by Theaker. $65.00

Children's Stories from Roumanian Fairy Tales, Gaster, illustrated by C. E. Brock. $75.00

Children's Stories from Russian Fairy Tales, Pulman, illustrated by Dixon. $65.00

Children's Stories from the Northern Legends, Belgrave and Hart, illustrated by Theaker. $65.00

Children's Stories from Scott, Doris Ashley, illustrations by Harold Earnshaw. $65.00

Children's Stories from the Poets, Belgrave and Hart, illustrated by Frank Adams. $100.00

Children's Stories from English History, Nesbit, illustrations by Bacon, Davie, and others. $65.00

Children's Stories from the Arabian Nights, Woolf, illustrations by Theaker. $65.00

Children's Stories from Dickens, M. A. Dickens, illustrations by Harold Copping. $75.00

Children's Stories from Shakespeare, Nesbit, illustrations by Bacon, Davie, and Copping. $65.00

Children's Stories from Tennyson, Chesson, illustrations by Bacon, Dixon, Copping. $65.00

Children's Stories from Longfellow, Doris Ashley, illustrations by Dixon, Copping, and others. $65.00

Glorious Battles of English History, Wylly, illustrations by Harry Payne. $50.00

Water Babies, Kingsley, illustrations by Mabel Lucie Attwell. $150.00

Hans Andersen's Fairy Tales, illustrations by Mabel Lucie Attwell. $150.00

Grimm's Fairy Tales, edited by Eric Vredenburg, illustrations by Mabel Lucie Attwell. $150.00

Alice in Wonderland, illustrations by Mabel Lucie Attwell. $150.00

Mother Goose, illustrations by Mabel Lucie Attwell. $150.00

Aesop's Fables, illustrations by Edwin Noble. $65.00

Curly Heads and Long Legs, stories by editors, illustrations by Agnew Richardson. $75.00

Golden Locks and Pretty Frocks, stories by editors, illustrations by Agnew Richardson. $75.00

Tinker, Tailor, Vredenburg, illustrations by Louis Wain. $65.00

RED RANDALL SERIES, Sidney Bowen, ca. 1940s Grosset, hardcover. ($20.00 with dust jacket) $10.00

Red Randall on Active Duty
Red Randall over Tokyo
Red Randall on New Guinea
Red Randall in the Aleutians

ROCKSPUR SERIES, Gilbert Patten, ca. 1900 McKay, illustrated cloth-over-board cover, b/w plate illustrations. $20.00

Rockspur Nine
Rockspur Eleven
Rockspur Rivals

ROMANCE OF KNOWLEDGE SERIES, ca. 1920s Little Brown, hardcover with paste-on-illustration, about 300 pages, color plates plus b/w illustrations. $25.00

Young Folk's Book of the Heavens, Mary Proctor, 4 color plates

Young Folk's Book of Discovery, T. C. Bridges, 8 color plates

Young Folk's Book of Myths, Amy Cruse, 8 color plates

Young Folk's Book of Invention, T. C. Bridges, 4 color plates

Young Folk's Book of Other Lands, Dorothy Stuart, 4 color plates

Young Folk's Book of Epic Heroes, Amy Cruse, 8 color plates

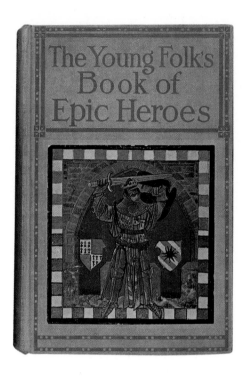

ROVER BOYS SERIES, Arthur M. Winfield (Edward Stratemeyer), 1899–1926 Stitt and Grosset, and Whitman reprints, cloth-over-board cover, b/w illustrations. Also, see PUTNAM HALL SERIES. ($30.00 to $50.00 with pre-1920 dust jacket. Later editions, $20.00 with dust jacket) $15.00

Rover Boys: First Series, ca. 1899–1910
Rover Boys at School
Rover Boys on the Ocean
Rover Boys in the Jungle
Rover Boys out West
Rover Boys on the Great Lakes
Rover Boys in the Mountains
Rover Boys in Camp
Rover Boys on Land and Sea
Rover Boys on the River
Rover Boys on the Plains
Rover Boys in Southern Waters
Rover Boys on the Farm
Rover Boys on Treasure Isle
Rover Boys at College
Rover Boys Down East
Rover Boys in the Air
Rover Boys in New York

Rover Boys in Alaska
Rover Boys in Business
Rover Boys on a Tour

Rover Boys: Second Series, ca. 1919, the main characters in the second series are the children of the first series' characters.
Rover Boys at Colby Hall
Rover Boys on Snowshoe Island
Rover Boys Under Canvas
Rover Boys on a Hunt
Rover Boys in the Land of Luck
Rover Boys at Big Horn Ranch
Rover Boys at Big Bear Lake
Rover Boys Shipwrecked
Rover Boys on Sunset Trail
Rover Boys Winning a Fortune

━━━ ⊷⇒ **S** ⇐⊷ ━━━

SAM GABRIEL PUBLISHERS SERIES, numbered books, small, paper cover, color illustrations on cover and throughout, numbered. $20.00
Dolly in Winter, No. 181, 1912

SCOTT BURTON SERIES, Edward Cheyney, Appleton, illustrated cloth-over-board cover. $15.00

Scott Burton, Forester, 1917
Scott Burton on the Range, 1920
Scott Burton and the Timber Thieves, 1922
Scott Burton, Logger, 1923
Scott Burton's Claim, 1926

SCOTT FOR BOYS AND GIRLS SERIES, ca. 1915 Jack Publishers, Edinburg-London, approximately 200 pages, color paste-on-pictorial covers, 8 color plates, includes classics by Scott, Dickens, and others. $20.00
Redgauntlet
Hereward the Wake
Last of the Barons
Tower of London
Forest Days
Days of Bruce
Crecy and Poictiers
Waverly
Ivanhoe
Kenilworth
Talisman
Peveril of the Peak
Fortunes of Nigel
Little Nell
David Copperfield
Dombey and Son
Oliver Twist
Nicholas Nickleby
Great Expectations

SHOES SERIES, Noel Streatfeild, Random House, hardcover, illustrated by Richard Floethe. ($35.00 with dust jacket) $15.00
Ballet Shoes, 1937
Circus Shoes, 1939
Theatre Shoes, 1945
Party Shoes, 1947
Movie Shoes, 1949, illustrated by Susanne Suba

SKY DETECTIVE SERIES, see JACK RALSTON SERIES

SKY FLYERS, RANDY STARR SERIES, Eugene Martin, ca. 1930s, Saalfield, cloth-over-board cover, 200+ pages, b/w illustrations. $10.00
Randy Starr After an Air Prize
Randy Starr Over Stormy Seas
Randy Starr Leading the Air Circus

SNIPP, SNAPP, SNURR SERIES, written and illustrated by Maj. Lindman, original oversize editions published in the 1930s. ($150.00 with dust jacket) $80.00. 8x10 reprints, ca. 1940 Whitman, cloth-over-board cover with paste-on-pictorial, color illustrations throughout. ($110.00 with

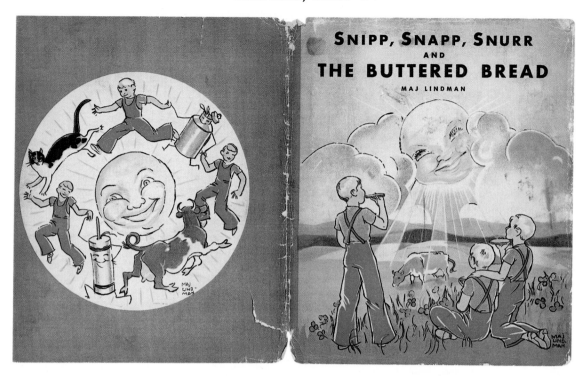

1940s edition

same-as-cover dust jacket) $50.00. Hale and ex-library editions, $25.00
Snipp, Snapp, Snurr and the Red Shoes
Snipp, Snapp, Snurr and the Gingerbread
Snipp, Snapp, Snurr and the Magic Horse
Snipp, Snapp, Snurr and the Buttered Bread
Snipp, Snapp, Snurr and the Big Surprise
Snipp, Snapp, Snurr and the Yellow Sled

STARS AND STRIPES SERIES, Captain Frank Cobb, ca. 1915 Saalfield, hardback. ($20.00 with dust jacket) $10.00
Potter Boys Hunting Down the Spy, 4
Potter Boys with the Tank

ST. TIMOTHY'S SERIES, Arthur Stanwood Pier, several editions and reprints include: ca. 1905-10 Houghton, cloth-over-board cover with gilt, 8 b/w plate illustrations, $25.00; ca. 1920 Houghton, cloth-over-board cover with impressed illustration, 4 b/w plates, $15.00; ca. 1920 Grosset Boy Scout edition, cloth-over-board cover, 4 b/w plates, $25.00.
Dormitory Days
Jester of St. Timothy's
Harding of St. Timothy's

"STORY BOOK OF" SERIES, see PETERSHAM SERIES

SUBMARINE BOYS SERIES, Victor Durham, ca.

1910 Altemus, and Saalfield, cloth-over-board cover, frontispiece illustration. $10.00
Submarine Boys' Trial Trip
Submarine Boys and the Middies
Submarine Boys and the Spies
Submarine Boys for the Flag
Submarine Boys' Lightning Cruise
Submarine Boys on Duty
Submarine Boys' Secret Mission

SUNNY BOY SERIES, Ramy Allison White, ca. 1920s Barse, cloth-over-board cover, b/w illustrations. ($20.00 with dust jacket) $10.00
Sunny Boy in the Country
Sunny Boy at the Seashore
Sunny Boy in the Big City
Sunny Boy in School and Out
Sunny Boy and His Playmates
Sunny Boy and His Games
Sunny Boy in the Far West
Sunny Boy on the Ocean
Sunny Boy with the Circus
Sunny Boy and His Dog

SUNNYBROOK SERIES, Elsie M. Alexander, ca. 1920s Burt, small, illustrated by Marie Schubert. ($25.00 in dust jacket) $15.00
Happy Family of Beechnut Grove (Peter Gray Squirrel and Family)
Buster Rabbit, the Explorer (Bunny Rabbit Family)
Adventure of Tudie (Field Mouse)

Tabitha Dingle (Famous Cat of Sunnybrook Meadow)
Roody and His Underground Palace (Mr. Wood-chuck In His Happy Home)
Buff and Duff (Adventures of Mrs. White Hen and Her Two Children)

SUSAN COOLIDGE LIBRARY FOR LITTLE PEOPLE,

one of the **CHILDREN'S FRIENDS SERIES** packages, ca. 1900-1910, small, 40 to 55 pages, cloth-over-board cover with impressed illustration for specific title, some also had gilt lettering, b/w illustrations, originally sold for fifty cents each or three dollars for a boxed six-volume set. $15.00 per book

Little Knight of Labor
Curly Locks
Two Girls
Little Tommy Tucker
Little Bo-Peep and Queen Blossom
Uncle and Aunt

TARZAN SERIES,

Edgar Rice Burroughs. Following is a list of the first printings of first editions. Later editions are listed at the end of this section. These first printings have become highly collectible, demand escalating prices, with wide variations due to availability. Later printings would have less value. The Zeuschner reference listed in the bibliography gives detailed descriptions of editions and printings.

Because the covers were not illustrated and the dust jackets were highly decorative, a mint dust jacket of a first edition Tarzan can increase the value about ten times. In this price range, it is wise to remember that dust jackets are easy to reproduce and should be examined carefully. Excellent quality reproduction jackets are being sold in the $10.00 range, jacket only.

Wide fluctuations in price are due to the wide variety of print runs, making some books far easier to find than others. McClurg printed over 75,000 copies total of *Jungle Tales of Tarzan,* but less than 8,000 copies total of their last book, *Tarzan, Lord of the Jungle.*

Tarzan titles in order of publication:

Tarzan of the Apes, 1914 McClurg, green cloth-over-board cover with gold lettering, 8 sepia plates by J. Allen St. John. $900.00

Return of Tarzan, 1915 McClurg, green cloth-over-board cover with gold lettering, b/w illustrations by J. Allen St. John ($4,500.00 with dust jacket. This jacket has N. C. Wyeth illustration). $600.00

Beasts of Tarzan, 1916 McClurg, olive cloth-over-board cover with gold lettering, b/w illustrations by J. Allen St. John. $350.00

Son of Tarzan, 1917 McClurg, green cloth-over-board cover with gold lettering, b/w illustrations by J. Allen St. John. $180.00

Tarzan and the Jewels of Opar, 1918 McClurg, dark green cloth-over-board cover with gold lettering, 8 sepia plates by J. Allen St. John. $225.00

Jungle Tales of Tarzan, 1919 McClurg, orange cloth-over-board cover, 5 sepia plates plus b/w drawings by J. Allen St. John. ($600.00 with dust jacket) $200.00

Tarzan the Untamed, 1920 McClurg, olive cloth-over-board cover, 9 sepia plates by J. Allen St. John. ($1,600.00 with dust jacket) $100.00

Tarzan the Terrible, 1921 McClurg, red cloth-over-board cover, 9 sepia plates by J. Allen St. John, plus a map and glossary by author. $125.00

Tarzan and the Golden Lion, 1923 McClurg, yellow-brown cloth-over-board cover, 8 sepia plates by J. Allen St. John. $125.00

Tarzan and the Ant Men, 1924 McClurg, brown cloth-over-board cover, b/w illustrations by J. Allen St. John. $225.00

Tarzan, Lord of the Jungle, 1928 McClurg, green cloth-over-board cover, 5 sepia plates by J. Allen St. John, plus a map by author. ($2,000 with dust jacket) $85.00

Tarzan and the Lost Empire, 1929 Metropolitan, orange cloth-over-board cover, b/w frontispiece by A. W. Sperry. ($500.00 with dust jacket) $120.00

Tarzan at the Earth's Core, 1930 Metropolitan, light green cloth-over-board cover, b/w frontispiece by J. Allen St. John. $120.00

Tarzan the Invincible, 1931 Edgar Rice Burroughs Inc., blue cloth-over-board cover, b/w frontispiece by Studley Burroughs. $85.00

Tarzan Triumphant, 1932 Edgar Rice Burroughs Inc., blue cloth-over-board cover, b/w frontispiece and 5 b/w plates by Studley Burroughs. ($300.00 with dust jacket) $85.00

Tarzan and the City of Gold, 1933 Edgar Rice Burroughs Inc., marked "1st edition," blue cloth-over-board cover, 5 b/w plates by J. Allen St. John. ($950.00 with dust jacket) $100.00

Tarzan and the Lion Man, 1934 Edgar Rice Burroughs Inc., gray cloth-over-board cover, 5 b/w plates by J. Allen St. John. ($600.00 with dust jacket) $75.00

Tarzan and the Leopard Men, 1935 Edgar Rice Burroughs Inc., marked "1st edition," blue cloth-over-board cover, 4 b/w plates by J. Allen St. John. ($600.00 with dust jacket) $75.00

Tarzan's Quest, 1936 Edgar Rice Burroughs Inc., marked "1st edition," blue cloth-over-board cover, 5 b/w plates by J. Allen St. John. ($600.00 with dust jacket) $75.00

Tarzan and the Forbidden City, 1938 Edgar Rice Burroughs Inc., blue cloth-over-board cover, color frontispiece and 4 b/w plates by John Burroughs. ($400.00 with dust jacket) $50.00

Tarzan the Magnificent, 1939 Edgar Rice Burroughs Inc., marked "1st edition," blue cloth-over-board cover, 5 b/w plates by John Burroughs. ($400.00 with dust jacket) $50.00

Tarzan and the Foreign Legion, 1947 Edgar Rice Burroughs Inc., marked "1st edition," blue cloth-over-board cover, 5 b/w plates by John Burroughs. ($150.00 with dust jacket) $50.00

Edgar Rice Burroughs Inc., Tarzana, reprints:
Reprints in the late 1940s, with dust jacket, are in the $100.00 range. Without dust jacket, $25.00

A. L. Burt reprints:
1915–28 A. L. Burt, plain hardback reprints of first five titles were published on poorer quality paper than the McClurg originals but used the original McClurg interior illustrations and dust jacket designs. As these are fragile books, condition causes a wide variation in price. (Early Burt printings with very good condition dust jacket $100.00, later Burt printings with dust jacket $65.00) $30.00

Grosset and Dunlap editions:
1920s editions Grosset and Dunlap, plain cloth-over-board cover, about 400 pages, 4 b/w plate illustrations. G&D editions use earlier illustrations from both the McClurg and the Metropolitan books and also copied the original dust jackets, with the Grosset Dunlap mark added to the spine. Dating is unclear, listing the original McClurg or Metropolitan date rather than the date of the G&D printing. ($100.00 with dust jacket) $25.00

Tarzan and the Golden Lion, 1929 photoplay edition Grosset, 2nd printing, orange cloth-over-board cover. ($150.00 with dust jacket) $50.00

1940s editions Grosset, cloth-over-board cover, newsprint quality paper, no interior illustrations, easy to identify by the title page paragraph referring to war printing shortages. ($35.00 with dust jacket) $15.00

Other Grosset editions combined illustrations or came out with new illustrations or came out with new dust jacket designs. The books were constantly re-issued in various formats to appeal to the market at the time of publication. Usually, they show the original copyright date but not the publication date and are confusing to identify. Most of these later Grosset editions sell in the range of $40.00 with dust jacket to $15.00 without dust jacket.

TARZAN, other books based on the series:
Tarzan Twins, 1927 Volland, illustrated paper-over-board cover, 127 pages, illustrated endpapers, color and b/w illustrations by Douglas Grant. (First edition with dust jacket, $200.00) First edition $100.00. (Second edition in its original Volland box with cover illustration, $150.00.) Second edition, $65.00. Later editions, $45.00

Tarzan and the Tarzan Twins with Jad-Bal-Ja, the Golden Lion, 1936 Whitman, oversize, marked "Big Big Book," color illustrated paper-over-

board cover, coloring book drawings by Juanita Bennett. $100.00

The Tarzan books were reprinted in several other editions, including the highly collectible Big Little Books and Better Little Books, Whitman, and in condensed versions for younger readers. Non-Burroughs stories were also added. Prices vary on availability and can be found in price guides to these specific series.

TED SCOTT SERIES, Franklin Dixon, 1927–1943 Grosset Dunlap, red or tan hardcover, illustrations by Walter Rogers. ($25.00 with dust jacket) $20.00

Ted Scott, Lost at the South Pole
Ted Scott, Over the Ocean to Paris, 1927
Ted Scott, Rescued in the Clouds, 2, 1927
Ted Scott, Over the Jungle Trails, 10
Ted Scott Over the Pacific, or, *First Stop Honolulu,*
    4, 1927
Ted Scott, Over the Rockies with the Air Mail, 1927
Ted Scott, Search for the Lost Flyers, 1928
Ted Scott's Hop to Australia, or, *Across the Pacific,* 1928
Ted Scott Flying Against Time, 1929
Lone Eagle of the Border
Ted Scott's Search in Nugget Valley, or, *Through the Air to Alaska,* 1930
Ted Scott, Danger Trails of the Sky, 1931

TEEN-AGE LIBRARY SERIES, ca. 1948 Grosset, hardcover, about 250 pages, b/w illustrations throughout, each book is a collection of short stories on the title subject. ($15.00 with dust jacket) $5.00

Teen-Age Adventure Stories
Teen-Age Aviation Stories
Teen-Age Baseball Stories
Teen-Age Boy Scout Stories
Teen-Age Companion Stories
Teen-Age Football Stories
Teen-Age Historical Stories
Teen-Age Mystery Stories
Teen-Age Outdoor Stories
Teen-Age Sea Stories
Teen-Age Sports Stories
Teen-Age Stories of Action
Teen-Age Stories of the West
Teen-Age Treasure Chest of Sports Stories

TEENIE WEENIES SERIES, Wm. Donahey, (1920s) ca. 1940s Rand McNally Jr. Edition, color illustrated paper-over-board cover, small, color illustrations by author. $50.00

Adventures of the Teenie Weenies
Down the River with the Teenie Weenies
Teenie Weenies Under the Rosebush
Teenie Weenies in the Wildwood

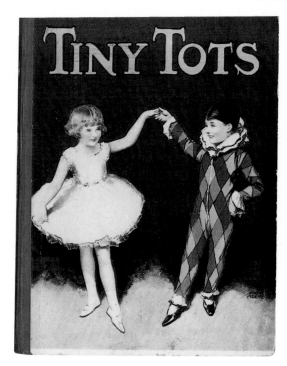

TINY TOTS ANNUAL, Amalgamated Press, London, color illustrated paper-over-board cover, oversize, about 134 pages, collection of stories, articles, poems, games, connected to *Little Folks* magazine, color and b/w illustrations throughout. $45.00

THRILLING NAVAL STORIES SERIES, T. T. Jeans, R. N., ca. 1920 Blackie and Son, impressed illustration on cover, b/w plate illustrations. $15.00
Naval Venture
Gunboat and Gun-runner
John Graham, Sub-Lieutenant, R. N.
On Foreign Service
Ford of H.M.S. Vigilant
Mr. Midshipman Glover

TOD MORAN SERIES, Howard Pease, Doubleday, hardcover. ($20.00 with dust jacket) $10.00
*Tod Moran: The Tattooed Man,*1926
Tod Moran: The Jinx Ship, 1927
Tod Moran: Shanghai Passage, 1929
Tod Moran: The Ship Without A Crew, 1934
*Tod Moran: Wind in the Rigging,*1935
Tod Moran: Hurricane Weather, 1936
Tod Moran: Foghorns, 1937
Tod Moran: Highroad to Adventure, 1939
Tod Moran: The Black Tanker, 1941
Tod Moran: Night Boat, 1942
Tod Moran: Heart of Danger, 1946

TOM STRONG SERIES, Alfred Mason, ca. 1915, Grosset, cloth-over-board cover, b/w illustrations. $15.00
Tom Strong, Washington's Scout ($25.00 in Boy Scout edition with logo)

Tom Strong, Boy-Captain
Tom Strong, Junior

TRAVEL-TOT-TALES SERIES, 1920s Reilly Lee, oversize picture books with color illustrated paper-on-board covers, blue/white illustrations by Bess Devine Jewell. $30.00
Gretchen of Holland, Besse Toulouse Sprague

TRIGGER BERG SERIES, Leo Edwards, ca. 1930s Grosset & Dunlap, b/w illustrations ($20.00 with dust jacket) $10.00
Trigger Berg and the Treasure Tree
Trigger Berg and his 700 Mouse Traps
Trigger Berg and the Sacred Pig

TUCKER TWINS SERIES, Nell Speed, ca. 1915 Hurst, illustrated cloth-over-board cover, illustrated by Arthur Scott. Dust jackets all have same wraparound illustration. ($20.00 with dust jacket) $10.00
At Boarding School with the Tucker Twins
Vacation with the Tucker Twins
Back at School with the Tucker Twins
Tripping with the Tucker Twins
House Party with the Tucker Twins
In New York with the Tucker Twins

TUFFY BEAN SERIES, Leo Edwards, ca. 1931 Grosset & Dunlap, about 210 pages, 18 b/w line drawings by Bert Salg, advertised as "Some-

thing else to howl about...." ($30.00 with dust jacket) $15.00
Tuffy Bean's Puppy Days
Tuffy Bean's One-Ring Circus
Tuffy Bean at Funny-Bone Farm
Tuffy Bean and the Lost Fortune

TWILIGHT ANIMAL SERIES, George Ethelbert Walsh, 1922 Winston, decorated cloth-over-board cover, small, about 130+ pages, color plates by E. J. Prittie. ($30.00 with wraparound pictorial dust jacket) $15.00
Bobby Gray Squirrel's Adventures
Bumper the White Rabbit and his Friends
White Tail the Deer

TWINKLE TALES, Laura Bancroft (L. Frank Baum) ca. 1906 Reilly Britton, small, illustrated cloth-over-board cover, approximately 62 pages, color illustrations throughout. $85.00
Mr. Woodchuck
Bandit Jim Crow, illustrated by Maginel Wright Enright
Prairie-Dog Town
Prince Mud-Turtle
Sugar-Loaf Mountain
Twinkle's Enchantment

TWINS SERIES, Dorothy Whitehill, ca. 1925 Barse Hopkins, gray cloth-over-board cover, b/w illustrations by Mary Ludlam. Same wraparound illustration on all dust jackets. ($15.00 with dust jacket) $10.00
Janet, a Twin
Phyllis, a Twin

Twins in the West
Twins in the South
Twins' Summer Vacation
Twins and Tommy Jr.
Twins at Home
Twins' Wedding
Twins Adventuring

TWO LITTLE FELLOWS SERIES, Josephine Lawrence, ca. 1920s Barse, cloth-over-board cover, b/w illustrations. ($20.00 with dust jacket) $10.00
Two Little Fellows
Two Little Fellows Start School
Two Little Fellows Go Visiting
Two Little Fellows Secret
Two Little Fellows in April

TWO LITTLE WOMEN SERIES, Carolyn Wells, ca. 1915 Grosset, cloth-over-board cover, illustrated endpapers, about 270 pages. ($20.00 with dust jacket) $10.00
Two Little Women
Two Little Women and Treasure House
Two Little Women on a Holiday

⇒ **U** ⇐

UMBRELLA BOOK SERIES, Macmillan, stories collected and edited by Literary Committee, cloth-over-board cover, illustrated. Numerous printings, so value depends heavily on condition. ($40.00 with dust jacket) $20.00
Told Under the Green Umbrella, 1930, color frontispiece, b/w illustrations by Grace Gilkison.

Told Under the Blue Umbrella, 1933, b/w/blue frontispiece, b/w illustrations by Marguerite Davis.

Sung Under the Silver Umbrella, 1935, illustrated by Dorothy Lathrop.

Told Under the Magic Umbrella, 1939, b/w/red frontispiece, b/w illustrations by Elizabeth Orton Jones.

Told Under the Stars and Stripes, 1945, b/w illustrations by Nedda Walker.

Told Under the Christmas Tree, 1948, illustrated by Maud and Miska Petersham.

─────── ≈ **V** ≈ ───────

VICKI BARR FLIGHT STEWARDESS SERIES, Helen Wells and Julie Tatham, 1940s Grosset. ($30.00 with dust jacket) $15.00

Silver Wings for Vicki
Vicki Finds the Answer
Hidden Valley Mystery
Secret of Magnolia Manor
Clue of the Broken Blossom
Behind the White Veil
Mystery at Hartwood House
Mystery of the Vanishing Lady
Ghost at the Water Fall

─────── ≈ **W** ≈ ───────

WASHINGTON SQUARE CLASSICS, ca. 1900 Geo. Jacobs Publishers, cloth-over-board cover with

paste-on-illustration, 400+ pages, 6 to 8 color plates (see illustration p. 11). ($20.00 with dust jacket.) Book without dust jacket, $15.00

Alice's Adventures in Wonderland
Andersen's Fairy Tales
Black Beauty
Grimm's Fairy Tales
Kidnapped
King Arthur and the Knights of the Round Table
Robinson Crusoe
Swiss Family Robinson
Treasure Island
Water Babies
Wonder Book and Tanglewood Tales

WEST POINT SERIES, Irving Hancock, ca. 1910 Altemus, tan illustrated cloth-over-board cover, frontispiece illustration. ($25.00 with dust jacket) $15.00

Dick Prescott's Second Year at West Point
Dick Prescott's Third Year at West Point

WESTY MARTIN, Percy Keese Fitzhugh, ca. 1920s Grosset, cloth-over-board cover. ($30.00 with dust jacket) $15.00

Westy Martin
Westy Martin in the Yellowstone
Westy Martin in the Rockies
Westy Martin on the Santa Fe Trail
Westy Martin on the Old Indian Trail
Westy Martin in the Land of the Purple Sage
Westy Martin on the Mississippi
Westy Martin in the Sierras

WHITMAN SERIES, oversize picture books, ca. 1930s Whitman Publishing, cardboard covers, 12 pages, full color illustrations, new editions of old stories with no author credits. $30.00

New Story of the Three Bears, 1932, illustrations by Charlotte Stone

Peter Rabbit, a New Story, 1932, illustrations by Charlotte Stone

WILDWOOD SERIES, Ben Field, ca 1928 A. L. Burt, small, color paste-on-pictorial cover, illustrated comic strip styled endpapers, b/w/brown illustrations by Eloise Burns. $25.00

Exciting Adventures of Mr. Tom Squirrel
Exciting Adventures of Mister Jim Crow
Exciting Adventures of Mister Gerald Fox
Exciting Adventures of Mister Robert Robin
Exciting Adventures of Mister Bob White

WOODRANGER TALES SERIES, G. Waldo Browne, (ca. 1900) ca. 1907 editions Wessels, N. Y., red cloth-over-board cover w/ impressed illustration on cover, b/w plate illustrations. $15.00

Hero of the Hills
With Rogers' Rangers
Woodranger
Young Gunbearer

YANK BROWN SERIES, David Stone, ca. 1920s Barse, cloth-over-board cover, b/w illustrations. ($20.00 with dust jacket) $10.00

Yank Brown, Halfback
Yank Brown, Forward
Yank Brown, Cross-Country Runner
Yank Brown, Miler
Yank Brown, Pitcher
Yank Brown, Honor Man

YOUNG ENGINEERS SERIES, Irving Hancock, ca. 1910–20 Saalfield, also Altemus, illustrated boards, frontispiece illustration. ($25.00 with dust jacket) $12.00

Young Engineers in Colorado
Young Engineers in Arizona
Young Engineers in Nevada
Young Engineers in Mexico
Young Engineers on the Gulf

YOUNG FOLK'S BOOK, see ROMANCE OF KNOWLEDGE SERIES

YOUNG FOLKS LIBRARY SERIES, ca. 1900 Hall & Locke, Boston, 20 volumes, collections of stories and short pieces, cloth-over-board cover with gilt, about 390 pages, 12 color plates plus b/w illustrations, artists not creditted. The fiction volumes are more popular, with little resale value for the science, history, and biography volumes alone, so that a complete set values at about $200.00. The more popular volumes sold individually are $20.00 each.

Story Teller
Merry Maker
Famous Fairy Tales
Tales of Fantasy
Myths and Legends
Animal Story Book
School and College Days
Book of Adventure
Famous Explorers
Brave Deeds
Wonders of Earth, Sea and Sky
Famous Travels
Sea Stories
Book of Natural History
Historic Scenes in Fiction
Famous Battles by Land and Sea
Men Who Have Risen
Book of Patriotism
Leaders of Men
Famous Poems

Z

ZIGZAG JOURNEYS SERIES, Hezekiah Butterworth, ca. 1880s Estes, Boston, travels of the fictional Zigzag Club, illustrated hardcovers, some with gilt, 300+ pages, map endpapers, numerous b/w illustrations. These were written originally for *Youth's Companion* periodical, then published in book format. The price range is extremely wide for these books. ($70.00 with dust jacket) $35.00

Zigzag Journeys in Classic Lands, 1882
Zigzag Journeys to Europe, 1882
Zigzag Journeys in the Occident, 1882
Zigzag Journeys in the Orient, Adriatic to Baltic, 1882
Zigzag Journeys in the Levant, 1885
Zigzag Journeys in Europe, 1885
Zigzag Journeys in Northern Lands, 1885
Zigzag Journeys in the Sunny South, 1886
Zigzag Journeys in the Antipodes, 1888
Zigzag Journeys in the Great Northwest, 1890
Zigzag Journeys on the Mississippi, 1892
Zigzag Journeys on the Mediterranean, 1893
Zigzag Journeys Around the World, 1895

Play books became highly popular during the late nineteenth century. There are numerous examples available for collectors. A few are in high demand by collectors of specific subjects, such as anything Disney or Oz or comic strip related, or books by specific artists, such as the animated books by Julian Wehr, but many play books can be found at low prices.

The following list is a small sampling of activity books, intended to give an idea of the types of activity books that are easily found. Because these books were designed to be used, they were quickly worn out and discarded. However, they were published on such a large scale and in such variety that there are still many in existence, and those found are apt to be "one-of-a-kind," because they are among the few copies that survived of a specific book. This is what makes activity books fun to collect. And if the collector doesn't mind crayon marks or cuts and pastings, the prices can be very low.

Prices shown here are for good condition books. If cuts or coloring have been made to activity books, even though the work is neat, this lowers the value of the book to less than half. Therefore, a $30.00 book with cuts or coloring would be worth less than $15.00.

Separate listings of **Animated Books by Julian Wehr** and of **Pop-Up Books** are at the end of this section.

ACTIVITY BOOKS: Books made to cut-and-paste, color, paint, write in, fold out, or use for a variety of entertainments. Also included are a few decorative music books.

A

ABC Picture Book, Pasting Without Paste, 1943 Saalfield, color stickers to put on b/w pages, oversize, color illustrated paper cover, 4 pages of stickers, 8 pages of shapes. $25.00

Animal Tracing and Drawing Book, illustrations by Corinne Bailey, undated Saalfield, oversize,

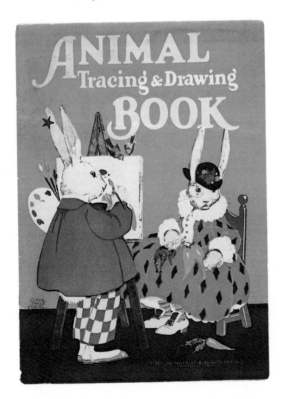

color illustrated cardboard cover, 16 pages with b/w line drawings, separated by tracing paper pages. $20.00

Animated Circus, Edward Ernest, 1943 Saalfield Animateons book. $50.00

B

Bright Wits, Prince of Mogadora and the Puzzles He Had to Solve, by Burren Loughlin and L. L. Floyd, 1909 Caldwell, 64 page puzzle book with color illustrations and 3 pages of to-cut-out game pieces. $35.00

Bunty "Magic Action" Book, 1935 Whitman, square shape, 25 pages with color fold-out pictures. $35.00

C

Circus Panorama, 1946 J. L. Schilling, oblong book, color illustrated cardboard cover, opens with foldout color illustrated circus scenario. $55.00

Circus Put-Together Book, Esther Merriam Ames, undated ca. 1930s Sam Gabriel Publishers, oversize, red cloth spine, 6 double-page full color circus scenes, stickers to add to scenes. Uncut with stickers unused, price is $100.00 If stickers have been used, price is $55.00

Colleen Moore's Doll House Cut-Outs, 1934 Ullman, oversize, 14 pages, cardboard cover with color photo illustration of the Colleen Moore doll castle, uncut $65.00

━━━ ⊷ **F** ⊶ ━━━

Fire House, 1949 World, a Rainbow Playbook, oversize with illustrated cover, 4 fold-out sets with punch-out figures, artwork by Leo Manso. $65.00

Follow the Dots, 5 books: ABC, Answer Riddles, Little Artist, Play Time, Story Book, boxed set, 1938 Saalfield, each book 20 pages, illustrated paper covers. Set in box $45.00

Follow the Dots Rhymes and Riddles, undated ca. 1930s Cupples, small size, color board covers, b/w illustrations. $20.00

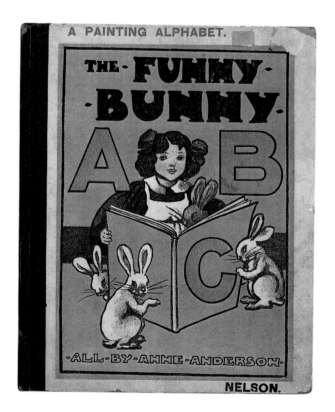

Funny Bunny ABC, Anne Anderson, undated ca. 1920 Nelson, oversize coloring book, color illustrated paper-over-board cover, 12 glossy color plates by Anderson of pictures, words, and letters, with facing plain paper pages with b/w outlines of color plate illustrations, to paint or color. $100.00

━━━ ⊷ **I** ⊶ ━━━

In and Out, Up and Down, Jo L. G. McMahon, 1922 John Martin, oversize picture book with windows to cut out in pages, b/w/orange illustrations by author. $35.00

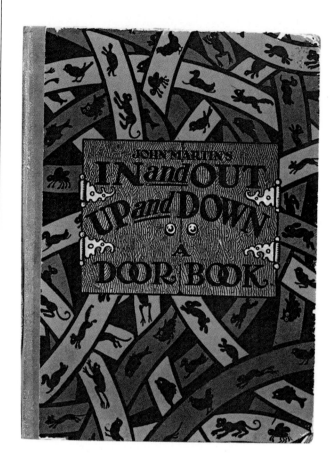

John Martin's Something-to-Do Book, ca. 1920 John Martin, a monthly publication in book form. Hard cover, illustrations, advertised as "Things to do in infinite variety, to cut out, draw, paste, and color with scissors, crayons, paste and brush contained in the portfolio cover." With all pieces, $75.00; book only $20.00

John Thompson's Easiest Piano Course, Part Two, 1940 Willis Music Company, oversize oblong, 47 pages, illustrated paper cover, piano lessons with b/w comic character illustrations and instructions by D. and H. Hauman. $15.00

Julian Wehr animated books, see end of this section.

Just So Song Book, Rudyard Kipling poems set to music by Edward German, green cloth-over-board cover, 62 pages, 1903 Doubleday. $30.00

General Tiger and Jester Bear
Attend the Queen at the Animal Fair.

←⊷ **K** ⊷→

Kellogg's Funny Jungleland, 1932 Kellogg Company, full color flip-strip "moving pictures" book, each page cut into three horizontal strips so that reader can match or mismatch heads with bodies with legs of picture animals. Cereal advertisement on back. $45.00

←⊷ **L** ⊷→

Little Oz Books with Jig Saw Oz Puzzles, 1932 Reilly Lee, each box contains two Little Wizard Series books and two jigsaw puzzles. Each good condition. Set: box, two complete jigsaws, two books is $500.00 complete. Individual piece prices: $40.00 for a good box, $20.00 for one complete puzzle, $50.00 for each book.
Set Number One: *Ozma and the Little Wizard, Scarecrow and the Tin Woodman.*
Set Number Two: *Tiktok and the Nome King, Jack Pumpkinhead and the Saw Horse.*

Little Postcard Painter, 1904 McLaughlin Bros, oversize coloring book with 16 postcards to color. $50.00

←⊷ **M** ⊷→

Mickey Mouse Waddle Book, 1934 Disney, w/cardboard punch-out figures. RARE with waddles. Without waddles: $150.00

Mother Goose, 1939 Whitman, punch-out stand-up book. $50.00

Mother Goose Melodies, 1908 McLoughlin, song book, illustrated cloth-over-board cover with gilt, color illustrations throughout by F. Schuyler Mathews. $95.00

←⊷ **O** ⊷→

Oz Toy Book, Cut-outs for Kiddies, 1915 Reilly Britton, color illustrations by John Neill, cardboard figures with stands. Uncut $500.00

←⊷ **P** ⊷→

Patchwork Poster Book of Mother Goose, illustrations by Helene Nyce, 1927 Saalfield, oversize, cardboard cover, 12 gray paper pages with line drawings and rhymes, 6 pages of color cut-outs to paste to line drawings. Uncut $25.00; cut and pasted $10.00

Peter on the Paddle-boat, George Zaffo, 1946 Saalfield, animated pictures. $25.00

Peter Puzzlemaker, ca. 1920 John Martin, cardboard cover, illustrations, advertised as containing "Fascinating brain twisters, never so hard as to discourage nor so easy as to fail to sustain interest." $20.00

Peter Rabbit the Magician, by Mel Richards, 1942 Jewel Tea premium, spiral bound book in box with magic tricks and wand, color illustrations. $95.00

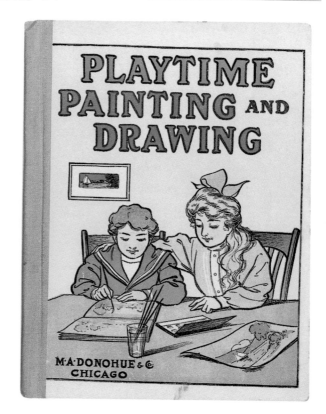

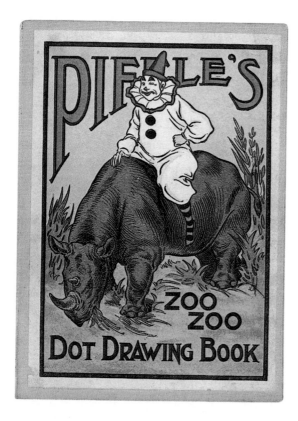

Piffle's Zoo Zoo Dot Drawing Book, 1920 Altemus, cloth-over-board cover with color paste-on-pictorial, page of instructions, 25 full-page b/w draw-between-numbered-dots animal illustrations with two line verse for each. If neatly drawn, $15.00. Unmarked, $35.00.

Play-It Book, Days of Games for Children, by Jean Hosford Fretwell, 1928 Macmillan, oversize, b/w/orange illustrations. $15.00

Playtime, fold-out book, undated ca.1930s Whitman, #2032, eight oversize boards, bound with cloth hinges to unfold to five foot long strip, color illustration and one sentence story on each side of each board. $30.00

Playtime Painting and Drawing, by F. I. Wetherby, undated ca. 1900 Donohue, 12 pages of color illustrations with 12 facing pages of same illustration in b/w to be painted or colored by reader. $35.00

Pop-Up books, see end of this section.

R

Raggedy Ann's Sunny Songs, author-illustrator Johnny Gruelle, music by Will Woodin, 1930 Miller Music, song book with 16 illustrated songs. $110.00

Raggedy Ann Cut-Out Paper Dolls, 1935 Whitman, color paper doll book with art work and poems by Johnny Gruelle, uncut. $125.00

Raggedy Ann's Joyful Songs, words and illustrations by Johnny Gruelle, music by Charles Miller, 1937 Miller Music Co., oblong song book with twenty illustrated songs. $85.00

S

Something to Do for Every Day, Louise Tessin, 1928 McLoughlin,oversize, 16 pages, color illustrated cardboard cover, color and b/w illustrations by Tessin, paint, cut, paste projects. $30.00

Something to Draw, undated ca. 1910-30 Hodder & Stoughton, paper-on-board cover plus paste-

page contains a poem explaining the loss of that toy, plus color illustration. Color printing and illustrations throughout. $95.00

W

Willy Pogany's Drawing Lessons, 1946 revised edition McKay, ring-bound oversize, color cover, b/w illustrations. $25.00

Wizard of Oz Waddle Book, 1934 Blue Ribbon Books, Denslow color plate illustrations, with 6 waddles (cardboard cut-out figures on pages at end of book). With waddles, RARE. Without waddles $75.00

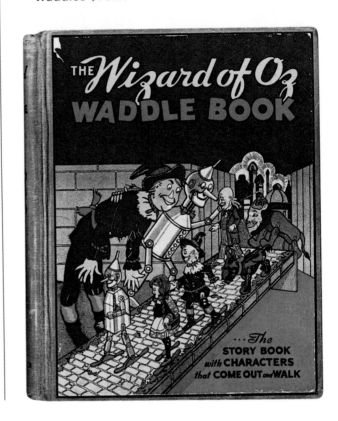

on-pictorial illustration, about 28 pages, b/w and color illustrations to copy. $15.00

Surprise! Rub A Pencil Book, 1946 Saalfield, small, color illustrated cardboard covers, inner pages include b/w line drawings to color and empty pages with instructions to "rub a pencil over the 'invisible' pages" to make pictures appear. $15.00

T

Tale of Ten Little Toys, Agnes Hucke, author-illustrator, ca. 1900 Gabriel, color illustrated paper-over-board cover, 10 heavy cardboard pages with cut top, so that as each flips, there is one less toy across the top margin of book. Each

---

ANIMATED BOOKS BY JULIAN WEHR

Animated Animals, 1943 Saalfield, oblong, illustrated paper-over-board cover with red spiral spine, color illustrated and animated by Julian Wehr. ($90.00 with dust jacket) $45.00

Animated Antics in Playland, 1946 Saalfield, illustrated paper-over-board cover with red spiral spine, color illustrated and animated by Julian Wehr. $45.00

Animated Picture Book of Alice in Wonderland, 1945 Grosset, oblong picture book, red plastic spiral-bound paper-over-board cover, color illustrations and animations by Julian Wehr. $35.00

Blanche Neige, "Snow White" in French by Lise Laurent, 1948 Barbe, hardcover, color illustrated and animated by Julian Wehr. (Dust jacket doubles price.) $45.00

Cock, the Mouse, and the Little Red Hen, 1946 Dutton, oblong, oversize, spiral binding. ($90.00 with dust jacket) $45.00

Gingerbread Boy, 1943 Dutton, illustrated paper-over-board cover with ring spine, color illustrated and animated by Julian Wehr. $45.00

Jack & The Beanstalk, 1944 Duenewald, animated by Julian Wehr, 20 pages, color illustrations. $55.00

Mother Goose, 1950 Duenewald, oblong, illustrated paper-over-board cover with red spiral spine, color illustrated and animated by Julian Wehr. ($65.00 with dust jacket) $40.00

Puss in Boots, 1944 Duenewald, oblong, illustrated paper-over-board cover with red spiral spine, color illustrated and animated by Julian Wehr. $65.00

Rip Van Winkle, Stephen Daye, 1945 Duenewald, illustrated paper-over-board cover with red spiral spine, color illustrated and animated by Wehr. $55.00

Raggedy Ann and Andy with Animated Illustrations, by Johnny Gruelle, 1944 Saalfield, color illustrated, animation by Julian Wehr . $60.00

Snow White, 1949 or 1950 Duenewald, illustrated paper-over-board cover with red spiral spine, color illustrated and animated by Wehr. $55.00

Toyland, stories by Martha Paulsen, 1944 Saalfield, red plastic spiral-bound paper-over-board cover, color illustrations and animations by Julian Wehr. $35.00

Wizard of Oz, adaptation of L. Frank Baum story, 1944 Saalfield, illustrated paper-over-board cover with red spiral spine, color illustrated and animated by Julian Wehr. $35.00

POP-UP BOOKS
Prices are for good condition books with pop-ups in working order and no missing pieces.

Animals' Merry Christmas, Kathryn Jackson, 1950 Golden Press, illustrated blue hardcover, color illustrations including a pop-up tree. $125.00

Buck Rogers, 1934 Pleasure Books, color illustrations. $600.00

Christmas Time in Action, pop-up, 1949 Newton, oblong, illustrated boards, plastic spiral bound, illustrated by Wm K. Tilley. $45.00

Christmas Treasure Book, 1950 Simon & Schuster, 38 pages, one pop-up of a large Santa in a chimney. $40.00

Cinderella, Disney pop-up,1950 Simon and Schuster Giant Golden Book, oversize, illustrated hardcover, pumpkin pop-up on inside cover, Disney color illustrations throughout. $55.00

Dick Tracy, Capture of Boris Arson, ca. 1934 Pleasure Books, three pop-ups. $350.00

Ducks Come to the Farm, a Pop-up Book, 1949 John Martin's House. $30.00

Funny Bunny, pop-up, by Rachel Learnard, 1950 Golden Book, oversize, color illustrated throughout, pop-up bunny and friends. $30.00

Jack the Giant Killer, Harold Lentz, 1932 Blue Ribbon, color illustrated paper-over-board cover, color illustrations, 3 pop-ups. $250.00

Jolly Jump-Ups ABC, Geraldine Clyne, ca. 1948 McLoughlin, oversize pop-up book with color illustrations. $75.00

Jolly Jump-Ups Child's Garden of Verse, Geraldine Clyne, 1946 McLoughlin, oversize pop-up book with color illustrations. $60.00

Jolly Jump-Ups and Their New House, Geraldine Clyne, 1939 McLoughlin, oversize, color pop-ups. $55.00

Jolly Jump -Ups Favorite Nursery Stories, Geraldine Clyne, ca. 1942 McLoughlin, oversize, color pop-ups. $55.00

Jolly Jump-Ups on Vacation Trip, Geraldine Clyne, 1942 McLoughlin, pop-up book, color illustrations. $60.00

Jolly Jump-Ups Number Book, 1950 McLoughlin, oversize pop-up book with color illustrations by Geraldine Clyne. $45.00

Jolly Jump-Ups See the Circus, ca. 1944 McLoughlin, oversize pop-up book with color illustrations. $65.00

Koko's Circus, 1942 Animated Book Co., pop-up and slide animated, by Hank Hart. $55.00

Let's Have a Farm, Victor, "A build-up book," 1945 Capitol, metal spiral bound pop-up book, 9 pages. $30.00

New Adventures of Tarzan, 1935 Pleasure Books, color illustrated with 3 pop-ups. $350.00

Pop-Up Cinderella, 1933 Blue Ribbon, oversize, color illustrations by Harold Lentz. $250.00

Pop-Up Goldilocks and the Three Bears, 1934 Blue Ribbon, oversize, color paper-over-board cover, 3 double-page pop-up color illustrations plus b/w illustrations throughout, art work by C. Carey Cloud and Harold B. Lentz. $125.00

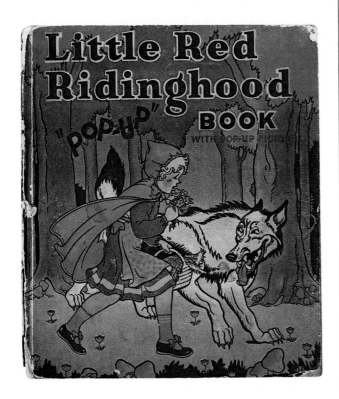

Pop-Up Little Red Ridinghood, 1934 Blue Ribbon, color paper-over-board cover, 3 double-page pop-up color illustrations plus b/w illustrations throughout, art work by C. Carey Cloud and Harold B. Lentz. $150.00

Pop-Up Little Orphan Annie and Jumbo the Circus Elephant, Harold Gray, 1935 Blue Ribbon Books, color illustrations. $225.00

Pop-Up Mickey Mouse, 1933 Walt Disney Studios, Blue Ribbon Books, illustrated paper-covered boards, 3 pop-ups, color illustrated. $400.00

Pop-Up Minnie Mouse, 1933 Walt Disney Studios, Blue Ribbon Books, illustrated paper-covered boards, 3 pop-ups, color illustrated. $700.00

Pop-Up Mother Goose, 1934 Blue Ribbon, art work by Harold Lentz. $125.00

Pop-Up Puss in Boots, 1934 Blue Ribbon Books, Carey Cloud and Harold B. Lentz. Color covers. Illustrated. $150.00

Rudolph the Red-Nosed Reindeer Pop-Up Book, Robert May, 1950 pop-up edition Maxton Publishing, oversize, cardboard cover, spiral bound, 5 pop-up illustrations plus color illustrations throughout by Marion Guild. $60.00

The value of a particular edition of a child's book often depends on the work of the illustrator. We began our search for information about these talented artists in Volume 1, and here are a few more names and facts to help the collector identify favorite illustrators.

Baker, Mary (b. 1897 England)

Mary Baker received her childhood education at home in Runcorn, attended the Chester Art School, and took a correspondence course in commercial illustration. She is best known for her winsome silhouettes, drawn to illustrate her sister Margaret Baker's books. Her work also included magazine illustrations and watercolor landscapes.

Burroughs, John Coleman (1913–1979)

The son of author Edgar Rice Burroughs, John Burroughs trained as an artist and illustrator in the 1930s. He took over the illustration of his father's books in 1937 (see also James Allen St. John) and also co-authored science fiction stories with his brother, Hulbert.

Bromhall, Winifred (b. England)

Bromhall studied art in England at Walsall Art School. After her move to New York in the 1920s, she worked in a bookstore, a pet store, the New York City Library, and the art department of a New York settlement, while building her career as an author and illustrator. Her works include *Wee Willow Whistle,* 1947, by Kay Avery, and *Star Stories,* 1947, by Gertrude Warner.

Clark, Mary Cowles (b. 1871 NY, d. 1950)

Clark was raised and educated in Syracuse, New York. Her early published art assignments included a cookbook for Scribners that featured fairyland creatures. Her best-known work in children's book illustration is L. Frank Baum's *The Life and Adventures of Santa Claus,* 1902.

Collin, Hedvig

Danish-born Hedvig Collin grew up on the Island of Zealand, Denmark. She studied art at the Royal Academy of Art in Copenhagen, then at the Ecole des Beaux Arts in Paris. Her work includes portraits, landscapes, and children's book illustrations. She has illustrated her own books and those of other writers, including Eva Kristoffersen's *Cyclone Goes A-Viking,* and *Merry Matchmakers.*

Wesley Dennis

154

Dennis, Wesley (1903–1966)

Dennis illustrated more than 80 books, primarily horse or animal stories, and is best-known for his illustrations for the books of Marguerite Henry. Dennis attended the New School of Art in Boston. After trying a variety of jobs, the young artist quickly decided that he just wanted to paint horses and other animals. For a short time, he traveled around race tracks, supporting himself by selling portraits of horses to their owners. Marguerite Henry called their long collaboration "a joint venture" where Dennis had as much say in the development of the book as herself. Dennis and Henry often traveled together to locations, where Henry would conduct interviews while Dennis did location sketches. She would cut the text to make Dennis' many pictures fit, just as he would crop the paintings to accommodate her writing. After Dennis' death, Henry quit writing for a year, reluctant to tackle another book without the help of her friend.

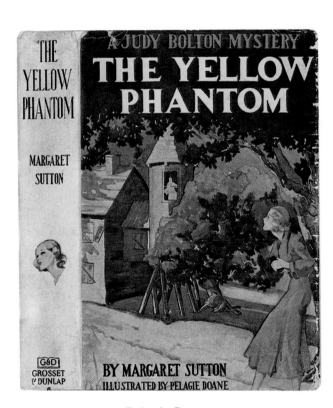

Pelagie Doane

Doane, Pelagie (b. New Jersey, 1906–1996)

Doane grew up in a creative family of artists and writers and received her art training at the School of Design, Philadelphia. She began her career in a greeting card company art department, but her stylistic versatility qualified her for a long career in book illustration. Her sweetly charming illustrations for *Child's Garden of Verses,* 1942, and *Mary Graham's Book of Christmas Carols,* 1938, are very different from the stylish, mysterious, and very collectible dust jackets created for the teen Judy Bolton mystery series.

SUGAR PLUMS FROM AUNTIE

Grace Drayton

Drayton, Grace Gebbie Wiederseim (b. Philadelphia 1877)

The creator of the famous round-eyed, chubby cheeked Campbell Soup kids, (ca. 1900), created the Dolly Dingle character in 1913. Dolly Dingle and her friends were featured in full-page color paperdoll spreads in *Pictorial Review* magazine for many years. Drayton also wrote and illustrated the Bobby and Dolly Series, a runaway best seller with over a quarter million volumes sold. Her career included book and magazine illustration, advertising illustration, paperdoll illustrations, and doll and toy designs for several manufacturers.

DuBois, William Pene (1916–1993)

DuBois received the 1948 Newbery Medal for his book *The Twenty-One Balloons.* His earliest picture books appeared in 1936 when he

Marjorie Flack

was only twenty. The son of French painter Guy Pene DuBois, he grew up in New York and France and later worked as the art director for the *Paris Review*. His illustrations often featured animals in human clothing and circus scenes.

Duvoisin, Roger (b. Switzerland, 1904–1980)
The son of an architect, Duvoisin's interest in art developed early, and he studied mural painting and set design at Ecole des Arts, Geneva. His career includes ceramic works, textile design, and in 1932 he wrote and illustrated his first children's book, *A Little Boy was Drawing*. He went on to illustrate his own books, including the popular Petunia stories, and the books of others, winning a Caldecott Medal in 1948.

Edwards, M. E. (Mary Ellen) (1839–1910)
Mary Ellen Edwards was a prolific magazine illustrator in Great Britain, contributing to such publications as *Aunt Judy's Magazine* and *Girl's Own Paper*. She used her maiden name until 1869, then the name of her first husband, Freer, until 1872, then her second husband's name, Staples, for later work, a detail which helps date her illustrations. Examples of her work are found in children's books by Adams-Acton and by Ellen Hale.

Fabres, Oscar (b. Chile 1900)
Fabres grew up in South America, then studied art at the Academie Julian in Paris. His fine art paintings have been exhibited worldwide. His work in commercial art includes magazine and book illustration His love of travel is reflected in his own children's book, *Choo-Choo Train.*

Flack, Marjorie (b. Long Island, 1897–1958)
Flack attended the Art Students League in New York. Although she trained as an artist, her career began with writing a children's book about Eskimos, then expanded as she pursued both writing and illustration. Best known as an author, she also produced excellent drawings for much of her own work, including *Taktuk an Arctic Boy*, 1928, written with Lomen, and for many of her books about children and pets, such as the Angus books, *Topsy*, and *William and His Lost Kitten.*

Floethe, Richard (1901–1992)
This Bauhaus-trained German artist immigrated to the United States in the early 1930s. From 1936 to 1939, Richard Floethe worked as the art director of the New York City Federal Art Project's art division. He is probably best-known as the illustrator of Noel Streatfeild's *Ballet Shoes* (1937) and its sequels.

Gutmann, Bessie Pease (b. Philadelphia, 1876–1960)
Bessie Pease grew up in Philadelphia and attended the Philadelphia School of Design for Women, then continued her art education at the New York School of Art, then the Art Students League of New York. A serious and talented artist, she had already begun her career when she married Gutmann, a printer. Combining her delightful portraits of their three babies with his printing skills, the Gutmanns built an extremely successful business. Her own book, *Our Baby's Early Days*, 1908 Best, is a collector's item, along with early Gutmann prints. Other children's books illustrated by Gutmann include *Child's Garden of Verses* and *Alice in Wonderland.*

Hader, Berta and Elmer

Berta Hoerner (1891–1976) was born in Mexico, educated in Mexico, Texas, and New York, studied art at the University of Washington, Seattle, and at the California School of Design. She began her career in magazine art. Elmer Hader (1889–1973) was born in California and also studied art at the California School of Design. After their marriage, they began a lifelong career collaboration on children's books, both writing and illustrating their own stories, as well as illustrating the works of other writers. Their stylistic illustrations show the influences of their California training, often featuring sunshine bright colors, and clear, simple forms that appeal to children.

*Holling Clancy Holling and
Lucille Webster Holling*

Berta and Elmer Hader

Holling, Holling Clancy

Holling, Holling Clancy (b. Holling Corners, Michigan, 1900–1973), and Lucille Webster Holling. Holling Clancy repeated his first name as his last name after he became a commercial artist. He graduated from the Chicago Art Institute, worked at the Field Museum in Chicago, worked briefly as an art instructor, and travelled around the United States with his artist wife, Lucille Webster Holling, scouting out story and illustration ideas for their children's books. The Hollings made their home in California.

Hudson, Gwynedd

Hudson studied at the Brighton School of Art, and worked as both a poster artist and a book illustrator in England. Her work appeared primarily in the 1920s and 1930s, and included a 1922 version of Carroll's *Alice in Wonderland* and a 1931 edition of Barrie's *Peter Pan and Wendy.*

Jones, Elizabeth Orton (b. Chicago, 1910)

Elizabeth Orton Jones was the granddaughter of a bookshop owner. Her love of books led to a long career in illustrating children's books, including Rachel Field's picture book, *Prayer For A Child,* 1944, for which Jones won the Caldecott Medal.

McCann, Rebecca (b. Quincy, Illinois, 1897–1927)

McCann began her art career as a freelance illustrator for Volland while still attending high school in Chicago, won a scholarship to the Chicago Academy of Fine Arts, then sold the Cheerful Cherub (a short verse and line drawing) to the *Chicago Evening Post*. Cherub was picked up by the Adams syndicate. Besides the daily Cherub illustrated verse for syndication, she illustrated books for other authors, including Mary Bonner, and wrote and illustrated *About Annabel.* Her Annabel stories first appeared in *John Mar-*

tin's Book Magazine. Her early death was from pneumonia.

Rebecca McCann

Merwin, Decie (b. Kentucky, 1894–1961)

Raised in Kentucky and Tennessee, Merwin attended private schools, then studied art in Boston. Her childhood ambition to be an illustrator started with her love of Reginald Birch illustrations. Her lively line drawings and silhouettes add charm to the books of Nancy Turner, Clara Laughlin, Barbara Nolen, Ethel Phillips, Ida Riggs, and others, as well as to the picture book series, *Dulcie*.

Moon, Carl (b. Ohio 1879)

From an Ohio childhood, Moon travelled to the Southwest to build his career as a chronicler of Indian culture. His photographs, paintings, and writings earned him a reputation as an expert on Indian lore, and in 1906 he was invited by President Theodore Roosevelt to exhibit his paintings at the White House. Moon illustrated and co-authored numerous children's books with his wife, Grace Moon.

Nichols, Ruth Alexander (1893–1970)

American photographer Ruth Nichols launched a series of picture books for young readers with *Nancy* (1933). Nichols won her first camera in a magazine contest at the age of nine. Her first magazine spread in 1925 featured snapshots of her two-year-old daughter. Nichols freelanced for a variety of magazines and advertisers. Most of her photographs featured children.

Ruth Alexander Nichols

Paull, Grace A. (1898–1990)

Starting out as a greeting card designer, this New York artist moved into book illustration in the 1930s. At one point, Paull shared a studio with Helen Sewell, another popular illustrator of the time. Early works include Margery Bianco's *A Street of Little Shops* (1932) and *Good Friends* (1934).

Richardson, Frederick (b. Chicago, 1862–1937)

Richardson attended the St. Louis School of Fine Arts and the Academie Julien in Paris. He taught at the Chicago Art Institute for a time as well as working for the *Chicago Daily News*. In 1903, he moved to New York. According to Baum historian Martin Gardner, Richardson's first children's book was probably *Queen Zixi of Ix* by popular Oz author, L. Frank Baum. The story first appeared as a serialization in the *St. Nicholas* magazine in 1904, and most of Richardson's pictures were reproduced in the book edition published in 1905 by the Century Company. Richardson's most famous work was done for Volland, a Chicago publisher who specialized in full-color picture books, usually listed under his name, included an elaborate *Mother Goose* first published in 1915 and kept in print for more than 60 years by the M. A. Donahue company. He also illustrated a series of elementary school textbooks called *The Winston Readers.*

Frederick Richardson

Rounds, Glenn (b. 1906 South Dakota)
Rounds was raised on a horse ranch, a childhood that shaped his career as an illustrator.

He studied art at the Art Institute in Kansas City and the Art Students League in New York. A born storyteller, he combined his tales of life in the West with his excellent drawings and colorful paintings of horses, ranch life, children, and any other subject that fired his imagination. His work includes his popular Whitey series.

Sarg, Tony (1880–1942)
Born in Guatemala and educated in Germany, Sarg moved to America in 1915 and worked in window display and magazine illustration. A favorite hobby and pastime of designing marionettes spread into the writing of plays as well as books about marionette theatre. His work is collected for his bold, stylized, colorful illustrations.

Seredy, Kate (b. Hungary, 1896–1975)
Seredy studied at the Academy of Art in Hungary, them moved to New York in 1922 where she began her art career as an illustrator of greeting cards. She also worked in fashion design illustration as well as magazine illustration, then gained recognition as an illustrator of children's books. Much of her work reflects her ethnic background, especially in her use of color.

Kate Seredy

Sewell, Helen M. (b. California, 1896–1957)

Sewell's childhood years included residence in New York and then in Guam, where her father served as a governor. She studied at Packer Institute, the Pratt Art School and Archipenko's Art School, and spent most of her adult years in New York state. She illustrated her own writing but is also widely known for the large volume of her work for other authors, including the first editions of the Laura Ingalls Wilder books. Her drawing style is highly distinctive and immediately recognizeable.

Slobodkin, Louis (1903–1975)

The son of immigrants from the Ukraine, New York-born Slobodkin brought much of that colorful background to his later art work. He studied at Beaux Arts Institute of Design in New York, and then built his career as a sculptor. In the forties, he was commissioned to illustrate *The Moffats* and began another phase of his art career. Four years later he won the Caldecott Medal for his illustrations for Thurber's *Many Moons*. His bright illustrations for a 1946 edition of McSpadden's *Robin Hood and His Merry Outlaws* are interesting examples of his color work.

Stahr, Paul (1883–1953)

Primarily a magazine illustrator in the 1920s and 1930s, Stahr did the original illustrations for the serialization of several Edgar Rice Burroughs stories including *Tarzan and the City of Gold* (1932). Sometimes his work was used to illustrate the book editions of these tales or a magazine cover painting might be adapted for dust jacket art.

St. John, James Allen (1872–1957)

American artist James Allen St. John decided to become a professional artist while still in his teens. After a stint as a Western artist and then as a New York society painter, St. John moved back to his native Chicago and worked as an illustrator for local publishers including A. C. McClurg Company. In 1916, St. John provided the illustrations for the first hardcover edition of *The Beasts of Tarzan.* From then until the 1930s, St. John provided the black-and-white illustrations, title lettering, and full-color dust jacket paintings for many Burroughs novels published by McClurg. He is considered the best of the Burroughs illustrators from the early years, and his original artworks command auction prices in the thousands of dollars in the science fiction market. When Burroughs took over the publishing of his own work in the 1930s, he decided that St. John's fees were too expensive and turned the illustration of his novels over to other artists, including his son (see John Coleman Burroughs). St. John continued to work in Chicago and taught at the Chicago Art Institute.

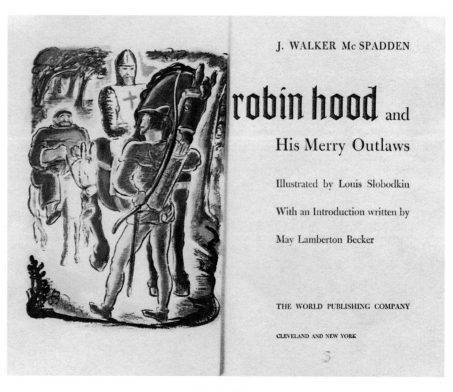

Louis Slobodkin

Arthur Szyk

Szyk, Arthur (1894–1951)

Polish-born Szyk studied art in Poland and Paris. He built his art reputation exhibiting his paintings in Europe and then in the United States, including a series of paintings titled "George Washington and His Times." He lived in England, then in the United States, and after most of his relatives in Poland were killed in the Second World War, Szyk and his wife remained in the States. He continued his career in fine art, magazine illustration, and children's books illustration. His fine art background is obvious in his brilliant and detailed illustrations for the 1945 edition of *Andersen's Fairy Tales.* In 1946 the Limited Edition Club published several books with gorgeous Szyk illustrations, including Mary Chase's *Book of Ruth* and *Chaucer's Canterbury Tales.*

Tandy, Russell H. (1893–1961)

Tandy was a New York commercial artist, already recognized for his work in catalog and fashion illustration, when he was hired to design a cover for the new Nancy Drew series in 1930. Tandy was a graduate of the Art Students League in New York City. Karen Plunkett-Powell, in her excellent *Nancy Drew Scrapbook,* explains that Tandy based Nancy's face on fashion model Grace Horton. As well as painting the dust jacket designs and interior illustrations for 25 Nancy Drew books, he hand-lettered the dust jacket titles. He also did covers for other series, including *Hardy Boys* and Howard Garis' *Buddy* series.

Tenggren, Gustaf (b. Sweden, 1896–1970)

Tenggren grew up in Sweden, studied at an art school in Gothenburg, and began his career illustrating Scandanavian fairy tales. When he was 24, he moved to the U. S. and built his career as an illustrator. His work includes a 1923 version of Spyri's *Heidi* and the illustrations for Opal Wheeler's *Sing for America.*

Van Stockum, Hilda (b. 1908 Holland)

An exceptionally charming example of Van Stockum's delicate color work is her own first book, *Day on Skates,* 1934 Harper. Van Stockum grew up in the Netherlands and later studied art in Dublin, Amsterdam, and at the Corcoran School of Art in Washington, D. C., after she moved to this country. She continued to write and illustrate stories based on her childhood travels, then expanded her career to include illustrations for other writers, including a 1946 edition of Dodge's *Hans Brinker.*

VerBeck, Frank (William Francis) (1858–1933)
This Ohio artist specialized in comic drawings, often featuring animals mimicking human behavior. Early books included *A New Wonderland,* 1900 (reprinted as *Magical Monarch* of Mo), by L. Frank Baum, as well as contributions to *Told by Uncle Remus* by Joel Chandler Harris. Baum told family members that he preferred VerBeck's illustrations to those of any of the other artists he had worked with, quite a compliment considering that Baum's earlier books had been illustrated by Maxfield Parrish and W. W. Denslow. One of the most popular VerBeck projects was Paine's *Arkansas Bear.*

Ward, Lynd (1905–1985)
Ward began his art career in 1929 when he produced a graphic novel, *God's Man,* illustrated with woodcuts. The son of a Methodist minister who worked in the Boston settlements, Ward identified with the problems of the working class. Ward illustrated two Newbery Medal winners, *The Cat Who Went to Heaven,* 1930, and *Johnny Tremaine,* 1944. From 1937 through 1938 Ward directed the graphic arts division of the Federal Writers Project in New York City. In 1953 he won a Caldecott Medal for his picture book, *The Biggest Bear.*

Weisgard, Leonard (b. 1916)
Weisgard trained at the Pratt Institute and worked in New York as a commercial artist and illustrator. Strongly influenced by the modern art of his time, such as the cubist paintings of Stuart Davis, Weisgard used modern design and form elements in his illustrations. He illustrated the Noisy Book series, 1939–1951, and numerous other children's books. He won the Caldecott Medal in 1947 for his illustrations for *Little Island* by Margaret Wise Brown.

Tony Sarg. See page 159.

GLOSSARY

Annuals: Books issued once a year that collected the works published in a magazine. Since many children's writers and illustrators of the nineteenth and early twentieth centuries also wrote for the children's magazines, annuals are a source of this additional material.

Antiquarian Booksellers Association of America: The trade association of American antiquarian booksellers, founded in 1949. The British equivalent is the Antiquarian Bookseller's Association (International) founded in 1906.

Board: Material used to form the cover of a hardbound book, usually paste-board. These boards were then covered with cloth or leather or paper.

Cloth Binding: The majority of hardbound children's books published in the nineteenth and twentieth centuries were "cloth bound." As opposed to leather bindings, cloth bindings were relatively inexpensive. The cloth was wrapped around a "board" (usually paste-board or another stiff base) and glued on the edges. Children's book publishers, such as Reilly & Britton, often used whatever cloth was available so the color of binding may vary even when books are all from the same edition.

Color plate: Colored picture printed on a paper that is different from the regular pages. Generally color plates were bound directly into the text (see also "tipped in"). A color plate might also be mounted on a stiffer paper.

Copyright: The date that the copyright was claimed for a work. This information is usually printed on the back of the title page. Publication date of a book can be any time after the copyright date.

Dust jacket or dust wrapper: A protective paper wrapped around a hardcover book.

Edition: A presentation of a book by a publisher, including text, layout, illustrations. Publishers who re-issue an old manuscript, such as Stevenson's *Child's Garden of Verses,* in a different format with new illustrations, create a new edition.

Endpapers: The double leaves (pages) added at the front and back during the binding process. The outer leaf is pasted down to the inner surface of the cover, while the inner leaves form the first or last page of the book. Endpapers can be plain or form a double page illustration related to the text. Sometimes they are called endleaves. See also flyleaf.

Errata: Errors made in the printing or binding of the book. Sometimes, the errata can be used to identify first editions and first printings because such mistakes are usually corrected by the publisher as soon as possible.

Ex-library: This term applies to a book that has been removed from the collection of a public library. Ex-library editions are usually priced far less than originals because they have been altered or marked by the library. They might be rebound by the library, have cards pasted over the endpapers, or be stamped with the library's name throughout the text.

First edition: A first edition is generally defined to be the first time that a book appeared in print. For collectors and dealers of illustrated books, a first edition may be the first time that the text and pictures have appeared together. For example, although the Maxfield Parrish illustrated copy of Nathaniel Hawthorne's *Wonder Book* was printed many years after Hawthorne's work first appeared, it would be the "first edition" that appeared with Parrish's pictures. For books that are first privately printed by author, such as Beatrix Potter, a "first" may be termed "first published edition" to designate the first edition published by a company, such as Warne. Collectors of first editions may also seek first state of books, a first edition that contains certain features (usually errors) that do not appear in other copies.

First printing/first state: The first edition, first printing, is the first print production of a book by the publisher. If sales are good, a second printing is scheduled, then a third, and so on, still using the same layout, illustrations, and so forth. However, in older children's books later printings, the color illustrations often lost quality of color and clarity, and so collectors pay more for earlier printings. And then there are collectors who only collect first edition first printings, regardless of quality, and are willing to pay a higher price, which is why first edition first printings of rare books demand such high prices.

Flyleaf: The blank leaf found in the front or back of the book is often described as the flyleaf. See also endpaper.

Folio: The largest size of a paper sheet used by printers to make a book. The term is also used by book dealers to designate books that are over 13 inches in height. See also size.

Foxed or foxing: A book is considered foxed when brown or rust-colored stains appear on the pages. The causes for foxing vary, ranging from iron gall based inks to the paper's reaction to temperature or humidity, or to the paper's acid content. Typically, heavy foxing is seen on older books, particularly 19th century works.

Frontispiece: The illustration that faces the title page of the book.

Furred: Worn edges of dust jackets that exposed the paper fiber. This can also occur on paper-over-board covers and cardboard covers.

Gilt edges: Many finer editions of books had their pages trimmed and gilded along the outer edges. Sometimes, to save money, the publisher gilded only the top of the pages.

Gilt lettering: When the letters are printed with metallic ink, the book has "gilt lettering." Gilt lettering usually appears on the cover. In some cases, it may appear in the interior text as chapter headings and as an addition to illustrations.

Half bound: A "half bound" book has a leather spine and paper or cloth covered boards.

Half cloth: A "half cloth" book has a cloth spine and paper covered boards.

Hand colored, hand tinted: Color or tint has been added by hand to pictures by anonymous professional artists, a common practice in the nineteenth century, where buyers could chose between colored or uncolored versions of children's books. This does not refer to coloring done after the sale of the book, often by small children with paint sets or crayons.

Illustrated boards: A book cover that has the illustration on the hardcover itself. This can refer to a printed illustration on either a cloth-over-board or a paper-over-board cover, but is most commonly used to refer to paper-over-board picture book covers.

Library binding: As books become worn by library patrons, they may be rebound. These library bindings replace the original binding and often required the page edges to be trimmed slightly from the original size. Library bindings are usually easy to spot as they are of a thicker, more durable material than regular book covers. They also considerably reduce the price of the book (see also ex-library).

Limited edition: A book issued in a stated number of copies. Around the turn of the century, fine illustrated books were often issued in a "limited edition" with leather bindings as well as a "trade edition" with regular cover.

Marbled paper: Marbled paper is generally used for endpapers or cover and has a colored pattern similar to marble. Marbled paper is made by lowering the sheet of paper into a bath of dye where the colors have been swirled into a pattern by a stick or comb. Marbled papers first appeared in Europe in the 1600s. Starting in the nineteenth century, some publishers experimented with using marbled cloth for covers.

Mounted illustrations: Engravings or color plate illustrations which have been attached to another type of paper by the printer. For fine illustrated books, the illustration may be mounted on a much stronger sheet of paper and further protected by a tissue overlay to prevent the ink from rubbing off on the opposing page.

Movables: Movables is a term most commonly used by British booksellers to describe pop-ups and other children's books that have illustrations that move.

No date: In this guide and most dealer catalogs, "no date" or "undated" means that the book has no date of publication printed on the copyright or title page.

Paper boards: The paper boards are the stiff material that forms the outer cover of a book. Generally, these are made from paste boards (layers of paper). When used by a dealer to describe a cover of a book, this generally means that the boards are plain and not covered by cloth, leather or marbled paper. See also half bound and half cloth.

Paper-over-board: Rigid boards covered with a hard finish paper suitable for printed color illustrations. This type of cover is most often used for children's books.

Picture book: In this text, a picture book is a book that relies mostly on pictures to convey the story to very young readers.

Plate, plates: Generally, this term is used by booksellers to designate illustrations printed on a different paper stock than the rest of the text. These can be either color plates or black-and-white plates. "Plate" may also refer to the actual printing plates used to produce the book.

Points: Points are differences in printing or paper between one edition or one state of a book and another, such as mis-spelled words or mis-prints.

Pop-ups: Three-dimensional pictures have been cut and glued so they "pop up" when the book is opened.

Provenance: The pedigree of a book's ownership presented by a dealer to justify a higher than normal price.

Re-backed: When the spine or backstrip of a book has been replaced, the book is called "re-backed."

Series: A set of books with an on-going theme, a continuation of stories about specific characters, or a label put on set of books by a publisher.

Set: Several books meant to be sold together, such as the My Bookhouse series which came in sets of six or twelve volumes.

Size: Some dealers use folio, quarto, octavo, and duodecimo to identify book height and width. These terms originally referred to the size of the paper sheet on which the book was printed and the number of times that sheet was folded to form the page size of a book. There is disagreement over the exact dimensions and proper use of these terms, so we have tried to stay with general terms such as "oversize" or "small." See also the Abbreviations at the end of this section.

Spine: The part of the book which is visible when the book is closed and placed on the shelf.

Tipped in: A separate piece of paper, usually a color plate, that has been inserted into the text of the book and lightly attached with gum on the inner edge.

Tissue overlay: A fine piece of tissue paper inserted between a full-page illustration and the text page to protect the illustration and prevent ink from rubbing off the text page onto the picture.

Volume: As used in this guide, a volume generally means one book in a set, such as a volume in a set of encyclopedias.

Wood-block, wood-cut: A wood-block illustration is created by carving a wooden block rather than making a metal engraving.

ABBREVIATIONS

Many dealers use abbreviations to describe books and their conditions in their catalogs and Internet listings. The abbreviations listed below seem to be the most commonly used, but usage can vary. When in doubt, query first, especially if this information makes a difference in the desirability of the book for you.

4to – Quarto, approximately 12" tall

8to – Octavo, approximately 9" tall

12mo – Twelvemo or duodecimo, approximately 7" tall

16mo – Sixteenmo, usually meaning about 5½" tall or less

(Note on sizes: librarians, bibliographical references, and many antiquarian booksellers use 4to, etc., to refer to the original size of the paper and the number of folds taken by the printer, rather than the height of the book.)

Anon. – Anonymous author.

Bndg. – Binding.

BW, b/w – Black-and-white, as in black-and-white illustrations.

C. – Copyright date (c. 1947) or circa (c. 1920s). This is an abbreviation that may need to be doublechecked.

Ca. – Circa, meaning "about" that time (ca. 1920s).

Cond. – Condition, as in "good cond." or "gd cond."

DJ, dw, dc – Dust jacket, dust wrapper, or dust cover.

Ex. lib., exlib, ex-lib – Ex-library.

Exc. – Excellent as in "exc. dj."

F. – Fine as in "f. cond."

Fly, fr. fly, r. fly – Flyleaf, front flyleaf, rear flyleaf.

Fxd., fxng. – Foxed, foxing.

Fr. – Front or frontispiece.

G, gd – Good as in "g. cond." but "g" may also mean gilt.

G.e. – Gilt edges.

Hf-bnd – Half-bound.

Ill., illus. – Illustrated or illustrations

Lg., lge. – Large

Lt. – Light as in "lt. marks on dj"

Ltd. – Limited as in "ltd. edition"

Med. – Medium

ND – No date

NDJ – No dust jacket

Obl. – Oblong, as in a book that is wider than it is tall.

O.P. – Out of print.

PC, p.c. – Price clipped.

Phots. – Photographs as in "illus. w/phots."

Pg., pgs. – Page, pages

Pl, pls – Plate or plates as in "12 color pls"

Pub. – Published as in "pub. 1947" or publisher as in "pub. Reilly & Lee."

Qto. – Quarto-sized

Rev. – Revised as in "rev. edition."

Rpt. – Reprint or reprinted as in "rpt. by IWOC" (reprint by International Wizard of Oz Club).

Sigd., sgd. – Signed as in "sigd. by author." May also use sig. for signature.

Sl. – Slightly as in "sl. fxd."

Sm. – Small

Sp. – Spine as in "dj sp torn"

T.e.g. – Top edge gilt

TP – Title page

Trans. – Translator or translated by.

V. – Very or volume

VG – Very good as in "vg dj"

VG/VG, G/VG, etc. – Refers to condition of book and dust jacket (very good edition, very good dust jacket).

Vol. – Volume as in "8 vol. set"

W/ or w/o – With or without as in "w/dj" or "w/o dj"

Resources

For collectors, there are a variety of resources to find antiquarian book dealers, chat with other collectors, research titles, and swap want lists. Below you'll find a few newsletters, magazines, fan clubs, and Internet newsgroups that we've enjoyed or that have been recommended to us by other collectors.

If you are connected to a commercial on-line service such as America Online, check the members' bulletin boards for areas of interest to book collectors.

If you have found another resource for children's book collectors, we would like to hear from you. You can reach us at lostlvs@aol.com or write to Rosemary Jones, 600 W. McGraw #2, Seattle, WA 98119.

Fan Clubs

Horatio Alger Society

The members of this society are Alger collectors and scholars, and many are interested in other juvenile series. This club has an annual convention. Their newsletter, *The Newsboy,* is published bi-monthly (six issues per year). Write to Horatio Alger Society, P.O. Box 70361, Richmond, VA 23255.

International Wizard of Oz Club

The IWOC has members around the world, and holds three national conventions each summer in the United States. Members are fans of the Wizard of Oz books and Oz-related materials. The club reprints some Oz titles, has a quarterly magazine, and a "trading post" newsletter for members. For more information, write to International Wizard of Oz Club, P. O. Box 266, Kalamazoo, MI 49004-0266. Web page: http://www.ozclub.org/~iwoc/

Magazines & Newsletters

Martha's KidLit Newsletter

This monthly newsletter covers a wide variety of topics concerning children's books including auction news, exhibitions, biographies of authors and illustrators, and tips for collectors. For current subscription rates, write to Martha's KidLit Newsletter, Box 1488, Ames, IA 50014.

Uncle Wiggily News

This newletter has ten issues a year and contains stories, games, and articles of biographical or historical information of interest to Garis fans. For subscription information write Uncle Wiggily News, PO Box 305, Lancaster, NY 14086.

Whispered Watchword

This is a ten-issues-a-year magazine put out by Phantom Friends, a group of girls' series book collectors. For subscription information, write to Kate Emburg, PO Box 1437, N. Highlands, CA 95660-1437.

Yellowback Library

This monthly magazine is devoted to juvenile series books such as the works of Horatio Alger. For current subscription rates, write to Yellowback Press, PO Box 36172, Des Moines, IA 50315.

Newsgroups

Children's Books
rec.arts.books.childrens

This Internet newsgroup discusses everything from new titles to collecting various series books. Members are extremely helpful in identifying books, and this is one of our favorite places to describe that book that we read as a child but can't remember the title or author. Like most Internet newsgroups, advertising is not welcome, and you should read a few messages before posting, or check the group's FAQ file. Since our last book came out, "For Sale" (FS) notices have been actively discouraged by many participants.

Marketplace
rec.arts.books.marketplace

The one place that any individual can post For Sale (FS) and Want To Buy (WTB) notices without any fear of flaming. Regard this newsgroup as an unregulated electronic flea market and take the usual precautions before sending money or credit card numbers.

Nancy Drew
alt.books.nancy-drew

Besides discussing everybody's favorite girl sleuth, members of this newsgroup are very knowledgable about series books such as Hardy Boys, and other topics of interest to fans of the Stratemeyer Syndicate.

Winnie-The-Pooh
alt.fan.pooh

Winnie-The-Pooh and the works of A.A. Milne are the major topics in this newsgroup.

Web Pages For Research

Antiquarian Booksellers Association
http://www.abaa-booknet.com

The homepage of the Antiquarian Booksellers Association of America serves as a great launching place for searching for antiquarian book dealers in your area. The ABAA site has links to their member booksellers with catalogs on the Web, information about book fairs throughout the country, a directory of member booksellers by region or specialty, and links to international organizations of booksellers.

Horatio Alger Society
http://www.ihot.com/~has

The Horatio Alger Society has its own web site. The e-mail address for the society is has@ihot.com.

Bowker's Out-of-Print Database
http://www.reedref.com/bowker/index.html

The official (U.S.) Books-Out-Of-Print database allows users to search by author, title, subject, series, or ISBN. Probably this database is most useful for fairly recent children's books. You will be given an user ID and password the first time that you sign on. No charge for this service at this time, but like all web resources, this may be subject to change. Read the conditions carefully before signing on.

Library of Congress
http://www.loc.gov/

The Library of Congress offers an on-line version of their catalog. This is a useful tool for searching for more information about books if you have part of the name of the author or only the title. Many collectors use it for finding other titles written by a favorite author.

Web Pages For Buying Books

Many collectors are now starting to buy books through the Internet, and these are the three most commonly used web sites.

The web sites listed are all professional services where dealers pay to list their catalogs. The customer makes arrangements directly with the bookseller, usually a store, for payment and shipping.

American Book Exchange
http://www.abebooks.com/

At ABE, you can search for out-of-print books by author, title, or other factors like illustrators through the on-line catalogs of more than 2,000 book dealers. Searches are free, and you can leave free want lists on the database for ABE to notify you if they find a book that you are looking for.

Bibliofind
http://www.bibliofind.com/

Like ABE, Bibliofind does not charge you to search through the on-line catalogs of their members and leave want lists.

Interloc
http://www.interloc.com/

This search service started out being available for book dealers only, but their web site is now open to the public. This service seems to have a wide mix of dealers, including many foreign dealers. Format may change in 1999.

Library Research

If you're doing research in a public or university library, ask if they subscribe to the CD-ROM called Children's Reference Plus. This CD is updated annually and contains information from several Bowker reference works including Fiction, Folklore, Fantasy and Poetry for Children 1876–1985; Children's Books In Print; and Books-Out-Of-Print (children's section).

Updates

Lost Loves Collector Guide's Links Page
http://members.aol.com/lostlvs/links.htm

This is the web site where the authors of this guide maintain links to the various web sites mentioned here. Check here for updates and new resources.

Bibliography

Bader, Barbara. *American Picturebooks from Noah's Ark to the Beast Within,* 1976, Macmillan, NY.

Billman, Carol. *Secret of the Stratemeyer Syndicate,* 1986, Ungar Publishing.

Darth, Captain Robert L., USNR/R. *G. A. Henty, a Bibliography,* 1971, Dar-Web Incorporated.

Doyle, Brian. *Who's Who of Children's Literature,* 1968 Schocken Books.

Feaver, William. *When We Were Young: Two Centuries of Children's Book Illustration,* 1977, Holt, Rinehart and Winston.

Gardner, Martin. "Introduction to Dover Edition," *The Magical Monarch of Mo* (Baum), 1968, Dover, NY, pg. vi - vii.

Gardner, Martin. "Introduction to Dover Edition," *Queen Zixi of Ix* (Baum), 1971, Dover, NY, pg. vi-xi.

Haviland, Virginia, editor. *Children's Literature,* 1966, Library of Congress.

Horne, Alan. *The Dictionary of 20th Century British Book Illustrators,* 1994, Antique Collector's Club, Woodbridge Suffolk, UK.

Houfe, Simon. *Dictionary of British Book Illustrators and Caricaturists 1800–1914,* 1981 (revised edition), Antique Collector's Club, Woodbridge Suffolk UK

Mahoney, Bertha, and Elinor Whitney. *Realms of Gold in Children's Books,* 1930, Doubleday.

Marcus, Leonard. *75 Years of Children's Book Week Posters,* 1994, Alfred A Knopf, New York.

McBride, Bill. *Pocket Guide to the Identification of First Editions,* 1995, McBride/Publisher, West Hartford.

Meyer, Susan E. *America's Great Illustrators,* 1978, H. N. Abrams, NY.

Miller, Betha E. Mahoney, editor. *Illustrators of Children's Books, 1744–1945,* 1947, Horn Book.

Pitz, Henry Clarence. *Treasury of American Book Illustration,* 1947, American Studio Books and Watson-Guptill Publications, Inc., New York, London.

Roy, John Flint. *Guide to Barsoom,* 1976, Ballantine.

Tillman, Albert. *Pop-Up! Pop-Up!,* 1997, Whalestooth Farm Publications.

Weinberg, Robert. *A Biographical Dictionary of Science Fiction and Fantasy Artists,* 1988, Greenwood Press, Westport, CT.

Whalley, Joyce Irene and Tessa Rose Chester. *History of Children's Book Illustration,* 1988, John Murray Ltd., London.

Yesterday's Authors of Books for Children, Vol. 1, 2, 1977–8, Gale Research.

Zeuschner, Robert B. *Edgar Rice Burroughs,* 1996, McFarland & Co., Inc.

ABBOTT, Jane
ADAMS, Eustace
ADAMS, Frank
ADAMS, Katherine
ADDINGTON, Sarah
ADE, George
AESOP
ALCOTT, Louisa May
ALDIS, Dorothy
ALDRICH, Thomas Bailey
ALGER, Horatio Jr
ALLEE, Marjorie Hill
ALLINGHAM, William
ALMOND, Linda
ALTSHELER, Joseph
AMES, Esther Merriam
ANDERSEN, Hans Christian
ANDERSON, Anne
ANDERSON, Clarence W
ANDERSON, Helen Foster
ANDREWS, Jane
ARASON, Steingrimur
ARDIZZONE, Edward
ARMER, Laura Adams
ARMOUR, R. C.
ARTZYBASHEFF, Boris
ASBJORNSEN and MOE
ASQUITH, Cynthia
ATKINSON, Eleanor
ATWATER, F.
ATWATER, Montgomery
AUNT FANNY
AUNT HATTIE
AVERILL, Esther H.
AWDRY, Rev. W.
BACON, Peggy
BAGNOLD, Enid
BAILEY, Alice Cooper
BAILEY, Arthur Scott
BAILEY, Carolyn
BAILEY, Margaret
BAIN, Edward U.
BAKER, Cornelia
BAKER, Margaret and Mary
BAKER, Nina Brown
BAKER, Rachel Mininberg
BALCH, Glenn

BALDWIN, Arthur J.
BALDWIN, James
BALL, Martha
BALLANTYNE, Robert Michael
BANCROFT, Alberta
BANCROFT, Edith
BANCROFT, Laura
BANNERMAN, Helen
BANNON, Laura
BARBOUR, Ralph Henry
BARNES, Annie M.
BARNETT, Grace and Olive
BARRIE, James
BARRINGER, Marie
BARROWS, Marjorie
BARTON, George
BARTON, May Hollis
BARTUSEK, Libushka
BARUCH, Dorothy
BATES, Katherine Lee
BAUM, L. Frank
BAYLOR, Frances Courtenay
BEAMAN, S. G. Hulme
BEATY, John Yocum
BECK, Ruth
BECKER, Edna
BEERS, Ethel Lynn
BEIM, Jerrold and Lorraine Levey
BELL, Lilian
BELL, Margaret
BELL, Thelma
BELLOC, Hillaire
BEMELMANS, Ludwig
BENET
BENNETT, Charles H.
BENNETT, John
BENNETT, Richard
BENSON, Sally
BERNARD, Florence
BERRY, Erick
BESKOW, Elsa
BETTS, Ethel
BETZ, Betty
BIANCO, Margery
BIANCO, Pamela
BIGHAM, Madge
BIRNEY, Hoffman

BISHOP, Claire Huchet
BLACK, Irma
BLAIR, Walter
BLAISDELL, Mary F.
BLAKE, William
BLANCHARD, Amy
BLOUGH, Glenn
BLUMBERG, Fannie
BLUNT, Betty
BLYTON, Enid
BOLTON, Ivy May
BONNER, Mary
BONTEMPS, Arna
BOSHER, Kate Langley
BOSSCHERE, Jean de
BOTHWELL, Jean
BOURGEOIS, Florence
BOUVET, Marguerite
BOWMAN, Anne
BOWMAN, James
BOYLAN, Grace
BRADLEY, Milton
BRANDEIS, Madeline
BRANN, Esther
BRAZIL, Angela
BRENDA
BRENT-DYER, Elinor
BRETT, Edna
BREWSTER, John
BRICE, Tony
BRILL, Ethel C.
BRINK, Carol
BROCK, Emma Lillian
BROCK, Henry
BROMHALL, Winifred
BRONSON, Wilfrid
BROOKE, L. Leslie
BROOKS, Amy
BROOKS, Gwendolyn
BROOKS, John
BROOKS, Walter R.
BROWN , Helen Dawes
BROWN, Abbie Farwell
BROWN, Margaret Wise
BROWN, Paul
BROWNE, Frances
BROWNING, Robert

BRUCE, Dorita
BRUCE, Mary Grant
BRYANT, Sara Cone
BUCK, Pearl
BUGBEE, Emma
BULLER, Marguerite
BUNNY
BUNYAN, John
BURGESS, Gelett
BURGESS, Thornton
BURLINGAME, Eugene Watson
BURNETT, Emma
BURNETT, Frances
BURNHAM, Clara Louise
BURROUGHS, Edgar Rice
BURTON, Virginia Lee
BUSH, Bertha E.
BUTLER, Ellis
CALDECOTT, Randolph
CALHOUN, Frances
CAMPBELL, Ruth
CANFIELD, Dorothy
CANIFF, Milton
CAPUANA, Luigi
CARPENTER, Frances
CARPENTER, Frank O.
CARR, Mary Jane
CARR, Warner
CARRIGHAR, Sally
CARROLL, Lewis
CARTER, Russell Gordon
CAUDILL, Rebecca
CAVANNA, Betty
CHAMBERLAIN, Ethel
CHAMBERS, Maria
CHAMBERS, Robert W.
CHAMOUD, Simone
CHAPIN, Anna Alice
CHAPIN, Frederic
CHAPMAN, Maristan
CHELEY, Frank Howard
CHENEY, Edna
CHIPMAN, Charles P.
CHISHOLM, Louey
CHRISMAN, Arthur
CHURCH, Alfred John
CLARK, Ann Nolan
CLARK, Margery
CLARKE, Covington

CLARKE, Sarah
CLAUDY, Carl
CLEARY, Beverly
COATSWORTH, Elizabeth
COE, Fanny
COLLIER, Virginia
COLLINGS, Ellsworth
COLLODI, Carlo
COLT, Terry Strickland
COLUM, Padraic
COOK, M. E.
COOKE, Donald E.
COOPER, James F.
COPELAND, Walter
CORE, Sue
CORYELL, Hubert V.
COTHRAN, Jean
COUSSENS, Penryhn
COX, Palmer
COX-McCORMACK, Nancy
CRANE, Alan
CRANE, Lucy
CRANE, Walter
CREEKMORE, Raymond
CRESSWELL, Beatrice
CREW, Helen
CROCKETT, Lucy
CROCKETT, S. R.
CROSBY, Percy
CROWLEY, Maude
CRUIKSHANK, George
CULBERTSON, Polly
CUNNINGHAM, Caroline
CURTIS, Alice
CURWOOD, James Oliver
CUTLER, Mary
D'AULAIRES
D'AULNEY, Mme.
DALGLIESH, Alice
DALLAS, Dorin
DALY, Maureen
DALZIEL
DANA, Charles
DANE, George
DANIEL, Hawthorne
DARBY, Ada
DARINGER, Helen
DARLING, Mary
DAUDET, Alphonse

DAUGHERTY, James
DAUGHERTY, Sonia
DAVENPORT, Emma
DAVIDSON, Edith
DAVIES, E. Chivers
DAVIS, Lavinia
DAVIS, Mary Gould
DAVIS, Richard
DAVIS, Robert
DAWSON, Lucy
DAWSON, Mitchell
DeANGELI, Marguerite
DeHUFF, Elizabeth
DeJONG, Meindert
DeLaMARE, Walter
DEAN, Graham
DEFOE, Daniel
DELAFIELD, Clelia
DENISON, Muriel
DENNIS, Morgan
DENSLOW, W. W
DETMOLD, E.
DIAZ, Abby
DICKENS, Charles
DILLINGHAM, Frances
DIONNE
DISNEY
DOANE, Pelagie
DODGE, Mary
DONAHEY, Mary
DONAHEY, William
DONNELL, Annie
DOOTSON, Lily Lee
DOUGLAS, Amanda
DOYLE, A. C.
DuBOIS, William
DULAC, Edmund
DUMAS, Alexandre
DUNCAN, Norman
DUNHAM, Curtis
DUNNE
DURSTON, George
DUVOISIN, Roger
E. V. B.
EAMES, Genevieve
EASTWICK, Ivy
EATON, Seymour
ECHOLS, William
EDMONDS, Walter

A, Apple Pie, GREENAWAY, Kate
A-Going Westward, LENSKI, Lois
Abbey Girls, OXENHAM, Elsie J.
ABC Book, FALLS, Charles
Abe Lincoln Grows Up, SANDBURG, Carl
Abraham Lincoln, D'AULAIRE, Ingri
Abraham Lincoln, DAUGHERTY, James
Adam of the Road, GRAY, Elizabeth
Adopted Jane, DARINGER, Helen
Adventure Rare and Magical, FENNER, Phyllis
Adventures in a Dishpan, GROTH, Eleanor
Adventures in Wallypug Land, FARROW, G. E.
Adventures of Andy, BIANCO, Margery
Adventures of Barbie and Wisp, UPTON, Bertha
Adventures of Chicchi, LOMBROSO-CARRARA, Paolo
Adventures of Herr Baby, MOLESWORTH, Mary Louisa
Adventures of Huckleberry Finn, TWAIN, Mark
Adventures of Jack Ninepins, AVERILL, Esther H.
Adventures of Odysseus and the Tale of Troy, COLUM, Padraic
Adventures of Pinocchio, COLLODI, Carlo
Adventures of Sonny Bear, FOX, Frances Margaret
Adventures of Tom Sawyer, TWAIN, Mark
Adventures of Two Dutch Dolls, UPTON, Bertha
Adventures of Ulysses, LAMB, Charles
Adventures of Uncle Lubin, ROBINSON, W. Heath
Adventures on a Dude Ranch, COLLINGS, Ellsworth
Aesop for Children, WINTER, Milo
Aesop's Fables, ARTZYBASHEFF, Boris
Aesop's Fables, DETMOLD, E.
Aesop's Fables, AESOP
Aesop's Fables, RACKHAM, Arthur
Airplane Andy, TOUSEY, Sanford
Aladdin and His Wonderful Lamp in Rhyme, RANSOME, Arthur
Alexander the Gander, TUDOR, Tasha
Alice and Thomas and Jane, BAGNOLD, Enid
Alice's Adventures in Wonderland, CARROLL, Lewis
Alice-Albert Elephant, HAYES, Marjorie
Alice-sit-by-fire, BARRIE, James
All the Mowgli Stories, KIPLING, Rudyard
All Around Town, FLACK, Marjorie
All Over Town, BRINK, Carol
All Round Our House, HOLLAND, Rupert
All-American, TUNIS, John R.
Allies' Fairy Book, RACKHAM, Arthur
Almanacks, GREENAWAY, Kate
Almost as Good as a Boy, DOUGLAS, Amanda
Along Comes Judy-Jo, HILL, Mabel Betsy
America Travels, DALGLIESH, Alice
American Alphabet, PETERSHAM, Maude and Miska
American Fairy Tales, BAUM, L. Frank

American Folk and Fairy Tales, FIELD, Rachel
American Patty, THOMPSON, Adele E.
Among the Tartar Tents, BOWMAN, Anne
An Ear for Uncle Emil, GAGGIN, Eva R.
And to Think that I Saw It on Mulberry Street, SEUSS, Dr.
Andersen's Fairy Tales, ANDERSEN, Hans Christian
Andy and the Lion, DAUGHERTY, James
Angel in the Woods, LATHROP, Dorothy
Angora Twinnies, PRICE, Margaret Evans
Angus and the Cat, FLACK, Marjorie
Angus and the Ducks, FLACK, Marjorie
Angus Lost, FLACK, Marjorie
Animal Stories, DE LA MARE, Walter
Animals of the Bible, LATHROP, Dorothy
Ann's Surprising Summer, ALLEE, Marjorie Hill
Anna Elizabeth, LONG, Lucile
Anna Elizabeth, LONG, Lucile
Annabel, METCALF, Susanne
Anne Anderson's Fairy Book, ANDERSON, Anne
Anne of Seacrest High, HORNIBROOKE, Isabel
Annie and the Wooden Skates, FRISKEY, Margaret
Another New Year, BRANN, Esther
Anton and Trini, OLCOTT, Virginia
Anything Can Happen on a River!, BRINK, Carol
Apache Gold, Guns of Bull Run, ALTSHELER, Joseph
Apple Pie Inn, DONAHEY, Mary
Apple Tree, BIANCO, Margery
Appleby John the Miller's Lad, HAWKINS, Sheila
April's Kittens, NEWBERRY, Clare Turlay
Aprilly, ABBOTT, Jane.
Arabella and Araminta, SMITH, Gertrude
Arabella and Her Aunts, LENSKI, Lois
Arabian Nights, WINTER, Milo
Araminta's Goat, EVANS, Eva
Araminta, EVANS, Eva
Arkansaw Bear, PAINE, Albert Bigelow
Around the World With Children, CARPENTER, Frank O.
Arthur Rackham Fairy Book, RACKHAM, Arthur
Ask Mr. Bear, FLACK, Marjorie
At the Back of the North Wind, MAC DONALD, George
At the Foot of the Rainbow, STRATTON-PORTER, Mrs. Gene
At the Gateways of Day, COLUM, Padraic
At the Sign of the Three Birches, BROOKS, Amy
Audacious Ann, MARSHALL, Archibald
Auno and Tauno, HENRY, Marguerite
Aunt Brown's Birthday, BESKOW, Elsa
Aunt Green, Aunt Brown and Aunt Lavendar, BESKOW, Elsa
Aunt Martha's Corner Cupboard, KIRBY, Mary
Awakening, GALSWORTHY, John

Away Goes Sally, COATSWORTH, Elizabeth
Away to Sea, MEADER, Stephen W.
Azor and the Blue Eyed Cow, CROWLEY, Maude
Azor and the Haddock, CROWLEY, Maude
Bab: a Sub-Deb, RINEHART, Mary Roberts
Babes and Blossoms, COPELAND, Walter
Babes in Birdland, BANCROFT, Laura
Babes in Toyland, CHAPIN, Anna Alice
Babes in Toyland, MAC DONOUGH, Glen
Babette, NEWBERRY, Clare Turlay
Baby Island, BRINK, Carol
Baby Whale, Sharp Eyes, BEATY, John Yocum
Baby's Own Aesop, CRANE, Walter
Baby's Red Letter Days, SMITH, Jessie Wilcox
Bad Child's Book of Beasts, BELLOC, Hillaire
Bad Penny, MORRIS, Rhoda
Ballad of Tangle Street, BACON, Peggy
Ballet Shoes, STREATFELD, Noel
Bam Bam Clock, MC EVOY, J. P.
Bambi's Children, SALTEN, Felix
Bambi, SALTEN, Felix
Banana Tree House, GARRARD, Phillis
Barkis, NEWBERRY, Clare Turlay
Barry and Daughter, CAUDILL, Rebecca
Bartholomew and the Oobleck, SEUSS, Dr.
Bat, MEADER, Stephen W.
Bay and Chestnut, ANDERSON, Clarence W
Beachcomber Bobbie, BOURGEOIS, Florence
Bear Facts, CULBERTSON, Polly
Bear Hunters, BOWMAN, Anne
Bear Twins, HOGAN, Inez
Bears, KRAUSS, Ruth
Beautiful Stories from Shakespeare, NESBIT, E.
Beaver Twins, TOMPKINS, Jane
Beck's Fortune, THOMPSON, Adele E.
Becky and Tatters, a Brownie Scout Story, THOMAS, Eleanor
Behind the Battlements, LINNELL, Gertrude
Bell Haven Nine, BARTON, George
Bells of the Harbor, DE JONG, Meindert
Beloved Belindy, GRUELLE, Johnny
Ben and Me, LAWSON, Robert
Bennett's Fables: From Aesop and Others, BENNETT, Charles H.
Beppo, BROCK, Emma Lillian
Beric the Briton, HENTY, G. A.
Bertha's Christmas Vision, ALGER, Horatio Jr.
Bertram and His Funny Animals, GILBERT, Paul
Best Stories to Tell Children, BRYANT, Sara Cone
Best Stories to Tell Children, BRYANT, Sara Cone
Betsy in Spite of Herself, LOVELACE, Maud Hart
Betsy-Tacy, LOVELACE, Maud Hart
Betty and Dolly, NICHOLS, Ruth Alexander
Betty Lou of Big Log Mountain, JUSTUS, May

Betty Seldon, Patriot, THOMPSON, Adele E.
Betty, Bobby and Bubbles, MITCHELL, Edith
Bevis, Story of a Boy, JEFFERIES, Richard
Bewitched Lamp, MOLESWORTH, Mary Louisa
Beyond the Clapping Mountains, GILLHAM, Charles
Beyond the Dog's Nose, SHERMAN, Harold
Big Snow, HADER, Berta
Big Tree of Bunlahy, COLUM, Padraic
Big, Little, Smaller and Least, HILL, Mabel Betsy
Bill the Minder, ROBINSON, W. Heath
Billabong novels, BRUCE, Mary Grant
Billy and Blaze, Black, ANDERSON, Clarence W
Billy Bounce, DENSLOW, W.
Billy Bunny's Fortune, GORDON, Elizabeth
Billy Butter, HADER, Berta
Billy-Boy, LONG, John Luthar
Biography of a Grizzly, SETON, Ernest Thompson
Bird Children, GORDON, Elizabeth
Birds' Christmas Carol, WIGGIN, Kate Douglas
Birthday of the Infanta, WILDE, Oscar
Biscuit Eater, STREETER, James
Black Beauty, SEWELL, Anna
Black Box, LIENTZ, Thelma
Black Buccaneer, MEADER, Stephen W.
Black Face, BELL, Thelma
Black Schooner, SNELL, Roy
Black Storm, HINKLE, Thomas C.
Black-Eyed Puppy, PYLE, Katherine
Blackfoot Lodge Tales, GRINNELL, George
Blackie and His Family, COOK, M. E.
Blacksmith of Vilno, KELLY, Eric
Blaze and the Forest Fire, ANDERSON, Clarence W
Blaze and the Gypsies, ANDERSON, Clarence W
Blind Colt, ROUNDS, Glen
Blowing Away of Mr. Bushy Tail, DAVIDSON, Edith
Blue Bird, MAETERLINCK, Maurice
Blue Bird for Children, Le BLANC, G.
Blue Hills, GOUDGE, Elizabeth
Blue Teapot, DALGLIESH, Alice
Blue Treasure, GIRVAN, Helen
Blue Willow, GATES, Doris
Blueberries for Sal, McCLOSKEY, Robert
Blueberry Mountain, MEADER, Stephen W.
Boats on the River, FLACK, Marjorie
Bobby and the Big Road, LINDSAY, Maud
Bobby in Search of a Birthday, MITCHELL, Lebbeus
Bold Dragoon, IRVING, Washington
Bomba the Merry Old King, COX, Palmer
Bomzoobo Book, STUDDY, G. E.
Bonny Bairns, WAUGH, Ida
Bonny's Wish, GAY, Romney
Book for Jennifer, DALGLIESH, Alice
Book of the Little Past, PEABODY, Josephine
Book of Americans, BENET

Book of Animal Tales, SOUTHWOLD, Stephen
Book of Cowboys, HOLLING, Holling
Book of Dragons, NESBIT, E.
Book of Elves and Fairies, OLCOTT, Frances
Book of Fairy Poetry, OWEN, Dora
Book of Fairy Tales, BROCK, Henry
Book of Friendly Giants, FULLER, Eunice
Book of Indian Braves, SWEETSER, Kate Dickinson
Book of Indians, HOLLING, Holling
Book of Joys, PERKINS, Lucy Fitch
Book of Nonsense, LEAR, Edward
Book of Pirates, MIKOVARO, E.
Book of Three Dragons, MORRIS, Kenneth
Bound Girl of Cobble Hill, LENSKI, Lois
Bow Bells, GIBSON, Katherine
Boy Hikers, FRASER, Chelsea
Boy Hunters in Demerara, HARTLEY, George Inness
Boy Jones, GORDON, Patricia
Boy Lives on Our Farm, RILEY, James
Boy of Poland, KING, Marian
Boy Pioneer or Strange Stories of the Great Valley, GROSVENOR, Johnston
Boy Riders of the Rockies, CHELEY, Frank Howard
Boy Scout and Other Stories, DAVIS, Richard
Boy Scout Yearbook of Fun and Fiction, MATTHEWS, Franklin
Boy Scouts to the Rescue, DURSTON, George
Boy Voyagers, BOWMAN, Anne
Boy With a Pack, MEADER, Stephen W.
Boy's King Arthur, LANIER, Sydney
Boy's Ride, ZOLLINGER, Gulielma
Boys and Girls at Work and Play, WHITE, Margaret
Boys and Girls from Eliot, SWEETSER, Kate Dickinson
Boys and Girls from Thackery, SWEETSER, Kate Dickinson
Boys and Girls of Bookland, SMITH, Nora Archibald
Boys' Book of Adventures, LOWE, V. R.
Boys' Book of Remarkable Machinery, HAWKS, Ellison
Boys' Book of Sea Fights, FRASER, Chelsea
Bred in the Bone, SINGMASTER, Elsie
Bridget and the Bees, WALL, Dorothy
Bright April, DeANGELI, Marguerite
Brothers and Sisters Holiday, LAWRENCE, Josephine
Brown Castle, RICE, Rebecca
Brownie Scouts at Snow Valley, WIRT, Mildred
Brownie Year Book, COX, Palmer
Brownies and Other Tales, EWING, Juliana
Brownies at Home, COX, Palmer
Brownies Round the World, COX, Palmer
Brownies: Their Book, COX, Palmer
Bruzzy Bear and the Cabin Boy, HAWKINS, Sheila
Buddy's Adventure in the Blueberry Patch, BESKOW, Elsa

Buffalo Bill, GARST, Shannon
Buffalo Roost, CHELEY, Frank Howard
Bunnikias Bunnies in Camp, DAVIDSON, Edith
Bunny Rabbit's Diary, BLAISDELL, Mary F.
Burgess Animal Book for Children, BURGESS, Thornton
Burgess Flower Book for Children, BURGESS, Thornton
Burgess Nonsense Book, BURGESS, Gelett
Burlap, DENNIS, Morgan
Burro that Had a Name, BEIM, Jerrold and Lorraine Levey
By Emberglow, CHELEY, Frank Howard
By the Gail Water, LEFROY, Ella
Cabin on Kettle Creek, JUSTUS, May
Caddie Woodlawn, BRINK, Carol
Calico Pets, PEAT, Fern Bisel
Calico, the Wonder Horse, Lee BURTON, Virginia
Call It Courage, SPERRY, Armstrong
Call of the Mountain, MEIGS, Cornelia
Camp and Trail, HORNIBROOKE, Isabel
Camp Fire Girls and Mount Greylock, HORNIBROOKE, Isabel
Camping Out on the St. Lawrence, TOMLINSON, Everett
Cap-O-Yellow, HERBERTSON, Agnes Grozier
Captain Boldheart, DICKENS, Charles
Captain January, RICHARDS, Laura E.
Captain of the Crew, BARBOUR, Ralph Henry
Captain Sylvia, TAGGART, Marion Ames
Captains Courageous, KIPLING, Rudyard
Carnival Time, HARRIS, May
Carolina Castle, WIRT, Mildred
Carolina's Toy Shop, RICE, Rebecca
Cast Away in the Land of Snow, MOORE, Fenworth
Castle Number Nine, BEMELMANS, Ludwig
Cat and the Captain, COATSWORTH, Elizabeth
Cat and the Kitten, HADER, Berta
Cat in Grandfather's House, GRABO, Carl
Cat That Jumped Out of the Story, HECHT, Ben
Cat Who Went to Heaven, COATSWORTH, Elizabeth
Cat Whose Whiskers Slipped, CAMPBELL, Ruth
Catcalls, BACON, Peggy
Cautionary Tales for Children, BELLOC, Hillaire
Cecily G. and the Nine Monkeys, REY, H. A. and Margret
Celtic Fairy Tales, JACOBS, Joseph
Checkered Love Affair, FORD, Paul
Cheery Scarecrow, GRUELLE, Johnny
Cherished and Shared of Old, GLASPELL, Susan
Chestery Oak, SEREDY, Kate
Child of the Tide, CHENEY, Edna
Child's Book of Old Verses, SMITH, Jessie Wilcox
Child's Book of Stories, COUSSENS, Penrhyn

Child's Garden of Verses, STEVENSON, Robert Louis
Child's History of England, DICKENS, Charles
Child's Play, E. V. B.
Child's Rip Van Winkle, IRVING, Washington
Children Come and Sing, LYDEN, Clara
Children of Holland, HEISENFELT, Kathryn
Children of Odin, COLUM, Padraic
Children of Other Lands, PIPER, Watty
Children of the Clouds, WILLIAMS, Herschel
Children of the Cold, SCHWATKA, Frederick
Children of the Handcrafts, BAILEY, Carolyn
Children of the Revolution, HUMPHREY, Maud
Children Who Followed the Piper, COLUM, Padraic
Children's Book, SCUDDER, Horace E.
Chimney Story Fairy Tales, HUTCHINSON, Veronica S.
Choo Choo, BURTON, Virginia Lee
Choosing Book, LINDSAY, Maud
Christmas Angel, PYLE, Katherine
Christmas Carol, DICKENS, Charles
Christmas Child, MOLESWORTH, Mary Louisa
Christmas Horse, BALCH, Glenn
Christmas on the Isthmus, CORE, Sue
Christmas Star, MOORE, Gertrude
Christmas Tree Scholar and Other Stories, DILLINGHAM, Frances
Christopher Robin Story Book, MILNE, A. A.
Christopher, FLACK, Marjorie
Cinderella, EVANS, C. S.
Cinderella, RACKHAM, Arthur
Circus Day at Catnip Center, FREES, Harry
Circus Shoes, STREATFELD, Noel
Citadel of a Hundred Stairways, MALKUS, Alida Sims
Clarabelle Cow, DISNEY
Clear Track Ahead, LENT, Henry
Clearing Weather, MEIGS, Cornelia
Clock Strikes Thirteen, WIRT, Mildred
Cocker Spaniel, BLACK, Irma
Cold Lands, SCOTT, J. M.
Colt from Moon Mountain, LATHROP, Dorothy
Come Hither, DE LA MARE, Walter
Complete Mother Goose, BETTS, Ethel
Conjuror's House, WHITE, Edward Stewart
Connecticut Yankee in King Arthur's Court, TWAIN, Mark
Conquerors of the Sea, WIECHERS, Jerome
Coot Club, RANSOME, Arthur
Cora and the Doctor, AUNT HATTIE
Coral Island, BALLANTYNE, Robert Michael
Country Bunny and the Little Gold Shoes, HEYWARD, DuBose
County Fair, TUDOR, Tasha
Cousin Toby, NEWBERRY, Clare Turlay

Cousins, ANDERSON, Helen Foster
Covered Bridge, MEIGS, Cornelia
Coward of Thermopylae, SNEDEKER, Caroline Dale
Coyotes, BRONSON, Wilfrid
Crazy Quilt, BROWN, Paul
Crazy Weather, McNICHOLS, Charles
Creepers Jeep, GRAMATKY, Hardie
Crimson Sweater, BARBOUR, Ralph Henry
Cross Currents, PORTER, Eleanor
Crossings: A Fairy Play, DE LA MARE, Walter
Cruise of Rickety Robin, GRUELLE, Johnny
Cruise of the Little Dipper, LANGER, Susanne
Cup of Tea, TUCKER, Elizabeth S.
Curious Chipmunk, LASKEY, Muriel
Curious George, REY, H. A. and Margret
Daddy Dander, HANKINS, Maude
Daddy Domino, MERRYMAN, Mildred Plew
Daddy Jake the Runaway, HARRIS, Joel Chandler
Daddy Long Legs, WEBSTER, Jean
Daddy's Bedtime Stories, BONNER, Mary
Daddy's Goodnight Stories, SMITH, George Henry
Dalziel's Arabian Nights, DALZIEL
Dancing Queen, FINST, Rudy
Dandelion Down and Small Flowerpot, DALLAS, Dorin
Danger on Old Baldy, BELL, Margaret
Daniel Boone, DAUGHERTY, James
Daniel Boone, DAUGHERTY, James
Danish Fairy Legends and Tales, ANDERSEN, Hans Christian
Dark Circle of Branches, ARMER, Laura Adams
Dark Frigate, HAWES, Charles
Davy Jones's Locker, FULTON, Reed
Day in A Child's Life, GREENAWAY, Kate
Day with Betsy Ann, BARUCH, Dorothy
Day With Our Gang, PACKER, Eleanor
Dealings with Fairies, MacDONALD, George
Dear Enemy, WEBSTER, Jean
Deering of Deal, GRISWALD, Lotta
Deerslayer, COOPER, James F.
Demons and Dervishes, FENNER, Phyllis
Denslow's Animal Fair, DENSLOW, W. W
Denslow's Mother Goose, DENSLOW, W. W
Dick Langdon's Career, HERBERT, Mrs. S. A. F.
Dickey Byrd, WOODRUFF, Elizabeth
Dimsie Goes Back, BRUCE, Dorita
Dimsie Moves Up Again, BRUCE, Dorita
Dimsie Moves Up, BRUCE, Dorita
Dionne Quintuplets Picture Album, DIONNE
Dirk's Dog Bello, DE JONG, Meindert
Docas, Indian Boy, SNEDDEN, Genevra
Dog Next Door, ROBERTSON, Keith
Dollie Stories, SMITH, George Henry
Don Coyote, PECK, Leigh

Donald and Dorothy, DODGE, Mary
Door in the Wall, DE ANGELI, Marguerite
Doris and the Trolls, ATWATER, F.
Dorkus Porkus, TUDOR, Tasha
Dorothy Dainty at Foam Ridge, BROOKS, Amy
Dorothy Stanhope, Virginian, DANIEL, Hawthorne
Dorothy's Dolls, GOLDSMITH, Milton
Dot and Tot of Merryland, BAUM, L. Frank
Double Trouble, BLUNT, Betty
Down a Down Derry, DeLaMARE, Walter
Down Along Apple Market Street, HILL, Mabel Betsy
Downright Dencey, SNEDEKER, Caroline Dale
Dr. Latimer, BURNHAM, Clara Louise
Dragon Fish, BUCK, Pearl
Dream Coach, PARRISH, Anne
Dream Days, GRAHAME, Kenneth
Duke Decides, TUNIS, John R.
Dumpies, and the Arkansas Bear, PAINE, Albert Bigelow
Dy-Dee Doll Days, VANDEGRIFF, Peggy
Early Moon, SANDBURG, Carl
East O' the Sun and West O' the Moon, ASBJORNSEN and MOE
East O the Sun, NIELSEN, Kay
East of the Sun and West of the Moon, D'AULAIRE, Ingri
Easter Rabbit's Parade, LENSKI, Lois
Eddie Elephant, GRUELLE, Johnny
Edmund Dulac's Fairy Book, DULAC, Edmund
Elizabite, REY, H. A. and Margret
Emmy Lou, MARTIN, George Madden
Enchanted Book, DALGLIESH, Alice
Enchanted Castle, MOORE, Colleen
Enchanted Garden, MOLESWORTH, Mary Louisa
Enchanted Island of Yew, BAUM, L. Frank
Enchanted Land, CHISHOLM, Louey
Enemies in Icy Strait, BELL, Margaret
Enemy to the King, STEPHENS, Robert Neilson
English Fairy Tales, STEEL, Flora A.
English Fairy Tales, JACOBS, Joseph
English Spelling Book, MAVOR, William
Eric's Book of Beasts, JORDAN, David Starr
Erik and Britta, OLCOTT, Virginia
Ernestine Takes Over, BROOKS, Walter R.
Eskimo Robinson Crusoe, SNELL, Roy
Everybody's Lonesome, LAUGHLIN, Clara
Everything and Anything, ALDIS, Dorothy
Fair American, COATSWORTH, Elizabeth
Fairies and Suchlike, EASTWICK, Ivy
Fairy Book: Fairy Tales of Allied Nations, DULAC, Edmund
Fairy Book: Fairy Tales of Allied Nations, DULAC, Edmund
Fairy Caravan, POTTER, Beatrix

Fairy Circus, LATHROP, Dorothy
Fairy Gifts, KNOX, Kathleen
Fairy Know a-bit, TUCKER, Charlotte Marie
Fairy Library, CRUIKSHANK, George
Fairy Shoemaker and Other Poems, ALLINGHAM, William
Fairy Tales from Brazil, EELLS, Elsie
Family from One End Street, GARNETT, Eve
Faraway Tree, STORM, John
Farm on the Hill, HORN, Madeline
Farmer Brown and the Birds, FOX, Frances Margaret
Farmer Giles of Ham, TOLKIEN, J. R. R.
Farmer in the Dell, HADER, Berta
Fast Sooner Hound, BONTEMPS, Arna
Father Goose: His Book, BAUM, L. Frank
Father Goosey Gander, HULE, Blanche
Favorite Nursery Songs, DOANE, Pelagie
Favorite Rhymes from Mother Goose, HUMPHREY, Maud
Favorite Rhymes of Mother Goose, KIRK, Maria
Felicity Dances, HADALL, Arnold
Felicity Way, GIRVAN, Helen
Fern's Hollow, STRETTON, Hesba
Fighting Seagull, MARSH, D. E.
Firebird, COOKE, Donald E.
Fireside Stories, HUTCHINSON, Veronica S.
First Book of Stories for the Story Teller, COE, Fanny
First Christmas Tree, VAN DYKE, Henry
First Woman Doctor, BAKER, Rachel Mininberg
Fish Hook Island Mystery, DAVIS, Lavinia
Fish Story, GAY, Zhenya
Five Bushel Farm, COATSWORTH, Elizabeth
Five Children and It, NESBIT, E.
Five Chinese Brothers, BISHOP, Claire Huchet
Five Hundred Hats of Bartholomew Cubbins, SEUSS, Dr.
Five Little Bears, NORTH, Sterling
Five Little Peppers and How They Grew, SIDNEY, Margaret
Five Mice in a Mouse Trap, RICHARDS, Laura E.
Flip and the Cows, DENNIS, Morgan
Flip, DENNIS, Morgan
Floating Island, PARRISH, Anne
Flora's Feast, a Masque of Flowers, CRANE, Walter
Flower Children, GORDON, Elizabeth
Flower Fables, ALCOTT, Louisa May
Fog Magic, SAUER, Julia
Folk Tales from the Far East, MEEKER, Charles H.
Forest Pool, Waterless Mountain, ARMER, Laura Adams
Forge in the Forest, COLUM, Padraic
Forgotten Daughter, SNEDEKER, Caroline Dale
Fort in the Forest, TOMLINSON, Everett

Fortunes of Phillippa, BRAZIL, Angela
Four and Lena, BARRINGER, Marie
Four Boys in the Yellowstone, TOMLINSON, Everett
Four Boys, ELLIS, Edward S
Four Corners, BLANCHARD, Amy
Four Girls at Chatauqua, PANSY
Four-Storey Mistake, ENRIGHT, Elizabeth
Freckles, STRATTON-PORTER, Mrs. Gene
Freddy Goes to Florida, BROOKS, Walter R.
Freddy the Detective, BROOKS, Walter R.
Friends of Jimmy, KAY, Gertrude Alice
Froggy's Little Brother, BRENDA
From Office Boy to Reporter, GARIS, Howard
Full-Back Foster, BARBOUR, Ralph Henry
Funny House, GUYOL, Louise
Funny Little Book, GRUELLE, Johnny
Funny Thing, GAG, Wanda
Funnybone Alley, KREYMBORG, Alfred
Gabby Gaffer, JUSTUS, May
Gallery of Children, MILNE, A. A.
Garden Behind the Moon, PYLE, Howard
Garden of the Little Lame Princess, JAMISON, Jane
Gateway to Storyland, PIPER, Watty
Gay Go Up, FYLEMAN, Rose
Gay-Neck, MUKERJI, Dhan Gopal
General Frankie: A Story for Little Folks, BEERS, Ethel Lynn
George Washington, D'AULAIRE, Ingri
Georgina of the Rainbows, JOHNSTON, Annie
Geraldine Belinda, HENRY, Marguerite
German Fairy Tales, DANA, Charles
German Popular Stories, GRIMM, The Brothers
Get-A-Way and Hary Janos, PETERSHAM, Maude and Miska
Ghond the Hunter, MUKERJI, Dhan Gopal
Giant Scissors, JOHNSTON, Annie
Giant-Killer, TUCKER, Charlotte Marie
Giles of the Star, RICE, Rebecca
Ginger and Pickles, POTTER, Beatrix
Gingerbread Man, LAWRENCE, Josephine
Giovanni and the Other, BURNETT, Frances
Giovanni and the Other, BURNETT, Frances
Girl and the Fawn, PHILLPOTTS, Eden
Girl of the Century, DARLING, Mary
Girl of the Limberlost, STRATTON-PORTER, Mrs. Gene
Girl Reporter, CLAUDY, Carl
Girl Warriors, WILLIAMS, Adene
Girl Who Kept Up, CUTLER, Mary
Girl Who Sat by the Ashes, COLUM, Padraic
Gladys, A Romance, DARLING, Mary
Glory Be!, LAMBERT, Janet
Glory of the Sea, HEWES, Agnes Danforth
Gloucester Joe, CRANE, Alan

Goal to Go, BARBOUR, Ralph Henry
Goat Afloat, FRISKEY, Margaret
Goblin Island, OXENHAM, Elsie J.
Goblin Market and Other Poems, ROSSETTI, Christina
Goblin Market, ROSSETTI, Christina
Goblins of Haubeck, BANCROFT, Alberta
Going on Sixteen, CAVANNA, Betty
Gold Laced Coat, ORTON, Helen F.
Gold, PETERSHAM, Maude and Miska
Golden Age, GRAHAME, Kenneth
Golden Bird, GIBSON, Katherine
Golden Egg Book, BROWN, Margaret Wise
Golden Feather, CAPUANA, Luigi
Golden Fleece and the Heroes Who Lived Before Achilles, COLUM, Padraic
Golden Goblin, DUNHAM, Curtis
Golden Goose Book, BROOKE, L. Leslie
Golden Horseshoe, COATSWORTH, Elizabeth
Golden Porch, HUTCHINSON, W. M. L.
Golden Tales from Faraway, FINGER, Charles
Golden Wedge, LOVELACE, Maud Hart
Golliwogg's Circus, UPTON, Bertha
Golliwogg's Desert Island, UPTON, Bertha
Gone is Gone, GAG, Wanda
Good Friends, BIANCO, Margery
Good King Wenceslas, NEALE, Dr.
Good Little Boy's Book, HALE, Sarah
Good Little Hearts, AUNT FANNY
Good Manners for Boys, BARBOUR, Ralph Henry
Good Old Chums, FRASER, Chelsea
Good Shepard, GUNNARSON, Gunnar
Good Stories for Great Holidays, OLCOTT, Frances
Goody-Naughty Book, RIPPEY, Sarah Cory
Goop Directory of Juvenile Offenders, BURGESS, Gelett
Goop Tales Alphabetically Told, BURGESS, Gelett
Goops and How to Be Them, BURGESS, Gelett
Gorilla Hunters, BALLANTYNE, Robert Michael
Government Hunter, ATWATER, Montgomery
Granny's Wonderful Chair, BROWNE, Frances
Grasshopper Green and the Meadow Mice, RAE, John
Grasshopper Green, RAE, John
Grateful Elephant, BURLINGAME, Eugene Watson
Greased Lightening, NORTH, Sterling
Great Adventure of Mrs. Santa Claus, ADDINGTON, Sarah
Great Small Cats and Others, SOUTHWORTH, May E.
Green Ginger Jar, JUDSON, Clara
Green Grass of Wyoming, O'HARA, Mary
Green Mansions, HUDSON, W. H.
Green Willow and Other Japanese Fairy Tales, JAMES, Grace

Gresha and His Clay Pig, GRISHINA, N. G.
Grimm's Fairy Tales, GRIMM, The Brothers
Grimm's Fairy Tales, GRIMM, The Brothers
Gulliver's Travels, SWIFT, Jonathan
Gutta Percha Willy, MAC DONALD, George
Gypsy Caravan, PEASE, Howard
Half-Back, BARBOUR, Ralph Henry
Hannah Marie, BENNETT, Richard
Hans Brinker, DODGE, Mary
Hansel and Gretel, NIELSEN, Kay
Hansi, BEMELMANS, Ludwig
Happy Harbor, HAUMAN, George and Doris
Happy Holidays, DAVENPORT, Emma
Happy Home Children, GORDON, Elizabeth
Happy Little Family, CAUDILL, Rebecca
Happy Prince, WILDE, Oscar
Happy Times in Czechoslovakia, BARTUSEK, Libushka
Hazel Hood's Strange Discovery, BARTON, May Hollis
He Wouldn't Be King, BAKER, Nina Brown
Heels of the Gale, GRANT, Capt. George
Heidi Grows Up, TRITTEN, Charles
Heidi, SHIRLEY TEMPLE BOOKS
Heidi, SPYRI, Johanna
Heir of Redclyffe, YONGE, Charlotte
Helen Ford, ALGER, Horatio Jr.
Helen Grant's School Days, DOUGLAS, Amanda
Helen's Babies, HABBERTON, John
Henner's Lydia, DE ANGELI, Marguerite
Henry Huggins, CLEARY, Beverly
Her Sixteenth Year, BROWN, Helen Dawes
Hercules, GRAMATKY, Hardie
Herdboy of Hungary, FINTA, Alexander
Heroes of Asgard, KEARY, A. and E.
Heroes, Greek Fairy Tales for My Children, KINGSLEY, Charles
Heroes, Outlaws, & Funny Fellows of American Popular Tales, MILLER, Olive Beaupre
Hickory Limb, FILLMORE, Parker
Hidden Village Mystery, BONNER, Mary
Hide and Go Seek, LATHROP, Dorothy
High Deeds of Finn, ROLLESTON, T. W.
Hike and the Aeroplane, GRAHAM, Tom
Hills of Gold, GREY, Katherine
Hitty, FIELD, Rachel
Hobby Horse, DAVIS, Lavinia
Hole Book, NEWELL, Peter
Holiday, DENNIS, Morgan
Hollyberries, DALGLIESH, Alice
Homer Price, McCLOSKEY, Robert
Homesteaders' Horses, BARNETT, Grace and Olive
Honey Bear, WILLSON, Dixie
Honey Jane, JUSTUS, May
Honey of the Nile, BERRY, Erick
Honk the Moose, STONG, Phil

Honor Bright, ROWSELL, Mary C.
Hoosier School Boy, EGGLESTON, Edward
Hoosier School-Master, EGGLESTON, Edward
Horse Who Lived Upstairs, McGINLEY, Phyllis
Horton Hatches the Egg, SEUSS, Dr.
House at Pooh Corner, MILNE, A. A.
House Between, PARTON, Ethel
House in No-End Hollow, JUSTUS, May
House on the Edge of Things, ELIOT, Ethel
House That Jack Built, CALDECOTT, Randolph
House that Ran Away, FRISKEY, Margaret
Houseboat Summer, COATSWORTH, Elizabeth
Household Stories, CRANE, Lucy
How Do You Get There?, REY, H. A. and Margret
How It Came About Stories, LINDERMAN, Frank
How Old Stormalong Captured Mocka Dick, SHAPIRO, Irwin
How Phoebe Found Herself, BROWN, Helen Dawes
How Sing Found the World is Round, REID, Sydney
How the Flying Fishes Came Into Being, REY, H. A. and Margret
Howard Pyle's Book of the American Spirit, PYLE, Howard
Howard Pyle's Book of Pirates, PYLE, Howard
Huldy's Whistle, MILLER, Anne Archibald
Humphrey, FLACK, Marjorie
Hundred Dresses, ESTES, Eleanor
Hungry Moon, ROSS, Patricia
Hunters of the Guns of Bull Run, ALTSHELER, Joseph
Hurdy Gurdy Holiday, GALE, Leah
Hurdy Gurdy Man, BIANCO, Margery
I Know a Secret, MORLEY, Christopher
In Fairy Land, ALLINGHAM, William
In Glory's Van, LOUNSBERRY, Lieut.
In My Mother's House, CLARK, Ann Nolan
In the Court of King Arthur, LOWE, Samuel E.
In the Day s of Giants, BROWN, Abbie Farwell
In the Morning Glow, GILSON, Roy
In the Navy, or, Father Against Son, GOSS, Warren
Indian Brother, CORYELL, Hubert V.
Indian Fairy Tales, JACOBS, Joseph
Indian Why Stories, LINDERMAN, Frank
Indoor Noisy Book, BROWN, Margaret Wise
Invincible Louisa, MEIGS, Cornelia
Iron Duke, TUNIS, John R.
Iron Heart, War Chief of the Iroquois, ELLIS, Edward
It's Perfectly True, ANDERSEN, Hans Christian
Italian Fairy Tales, CAPUANA, Luigi
Jack Allen, GOSS, Warren
Jack and the Beanstalk, PRICE, Margaret Evans
Jack Gregory, GOSS, Warren
Jack London, Magnet for Adventure, GARST, Shannon
Jackanapes, EWING, Juliana

Jackieboy in Rainbowland, HILL, William L.

Jade Necklace, GINTHER, Mrs. Pemberton

Jamba the Elephant, WALDECK, Theodore J.

Jane Allen of the Sub Team, BANCROFT, Edith

Japanese Fairy Tales, HEARN, Lafcadio

Japanese Fairy Tales, WILLISTON, Teresa

Jean and Fanchon, OLCOTT, Virginia

Jeanne-Marie Goes to Market, SARI

Jed the Poor-House Boy, ALGER, Horatio Jr

Jenny's First Party, AVERILL, Esther H.

Jeremy's Isle, LATTIMORE, Eleanor F.

Jerome Anthony, EVANS, Eva

Jerry and Jean Detectors, JUDSON, Clara

Jerry and the Pusa, LATTIMORE, Eleanor F.

Jessica's Last Prayer, STRETTON, Hesba

Jessie Wilcox Smith's Mother Goose, SMITH, Jessie Wilcox

Jewel's Story Book, BURNHAM, Clara Louise

Jewish Fairy Book, FRIEDLANDER, Gerald

Jibby Jones, BUTLER, Ellis

Jibby Jones, and the Alligator, BUTLER, Ellis

Jibby the Cat, SALTEN, Felix

Jimmy Makes the Varsity, BROOKS, John

Jinglebob, ROLLINS, Philip Ashton

Jinx Ship, PEASE, Howard

Jo Ann, Tomboy, BUTLER, Ellis

Jo of the Chalet School, BRENT-DYER, Elinor

Jo's Boys, ALCOTT, Louisa May

Jock of the Bushveld, FITZPATRICK, Sir Percy

Jock's Castle, GIBSON, Katherine

Johanna Arrives, BROMHALL, Winifred

John Boyd's Adventures, KNOX, Thomas

John Dough and the Cherub, BAUM, L. Frank

John Holmes at Annapolis, GODFREY, Vincent

Johnny Appleseed, ATKINSON, Eleanor

Johnny Crow's Garden, BROOKE, L. Leslie

Johnny Giraffe, BARROWS, Marjorie

Johnny Longbow, SNELL, Roy

Johnny Longfoot, BASTERMAN, Catherine

Johnny Mouse and the Wishing Stick, GRUELLE, Johnny

Johnny Tremain, FORBES, Esther

Jolly Chinee, COX, Palmer

Jolly Good Times at Hackmatack, SMITH, Mary P. W.

Jolly Jingle Picture Book, JACKSON, Leroy F.

Jolly Old Shadow Man, KAY, Gertrude Alice

Joy and the Christmas Angel, BIANCO, Pamela

Joyous Story of Toto, RICHARDS, Laura E.

Juan and Juanita, BAYLOR, Frances Courtenay

Juarez, Hero of Mexico, BAKER, Nina Brown

Jungle Book, KIPLING, Rudyard

Junior Miss, FIELDS, Joseph

Junior Miss, FIELDS, Joseph

Junior, LATTIMORE, Eleanor F.

Just for Fun, LAWSON, Robert

Just Patty, WEBSTER, Jean

Just So Stories for Little Children, KIPLING, Rudyard

Justin Morgan Had a Horse, HENRY, Marguerite

Kalak of the Ice, KJELGAARD, Jim

Kangaroo Hunters, BOWMAN, Anne

Kangaroo Twins, HOGAN, Inez

Kari the Elephant, MUKERJI, Dhan Gopal

Kate Greenaway's Alphabet, GREENAWAY, Kate

Kate Greenaway's Birthday Book for Children, GREENAWAY, Kate

Katrinka, HASKELL, Helen Eggleston

Katy and the Big Snow, BURTON, Virginia Lee

Katy Kruse Dolly Book, FYLEMAN, Rose

Keel to Kite, HORNIBROOKE, Isabel

Kensington Rhymes, MACKENZIE, Compton

Keturah Came Round the Horn, DARBY, Ada

Kewpies, Their Book, O'NEILL, Rose

Keystone Kids, TUNIS, John R.

Khyberie, ENRIQUEZ, Major C. M.

Kid Comes Back, TUNIS, John R.

Kid from Tomkinsville, TUNIS, John R.

Kidnapped, STEVENSON, Robert Louis

Kids of Many Colors, BOYLAN

Kim, KIPLING, Rudyard

King Arthur and his Knights of the Round Table, LANIER, Sydney

King Arthur and His Knights, FRITH, Henry

King Arthur and His Knights, MERCHANT, Elizabeth Lodor

King Kojo, THOMPSON, Ruth Plumly

King of the Golden River, RUSKIN, John

King of the Grizzlies, RICHARDSON, Alfred

King of the Wind, HENRY, Marguerite

King Philip the Indian Chief, AVERILL, Esther H.

King Solomon's Mines, HAGGARD, H. Rider

King's Stilts, SEUSS, Dr.

King, Story of a Sheep Dog, HINKLE, Thomas C.

Kintu, ENRIGHT, Elizabeth

Kit Carey's Protege, LOUNSBERRY, Lieut.

Klondike Gold, CORYELL, Hubert V.

Knave of Hearts, PARRISH, Maxfield

Knee-High to a Grasshopper, PARRISH, Anne

Knight of the Golden Spur, HOLLAND, Rupert

Knights of Charlamagne, ECHOLS, William

Knights, Goats and Battleships, COLT, Terry Strickland

Koos the Hottentot, MARAIS, Josef

La-La Man in Music Land, KILMER, Colleen Browne

Laboulaye's Fairy Book, LABOULAYE

Lad of Kent, HARRISON, Herbert

Laddie, STRATTON-PORTER, Mrs. Gene

Lance of Kanana, FRENCH, Harry W.

Land of Really True, OLMSTED, Millicent

Land That Never Was, OLMSTED, Millicent
Larry Dexter, the Young Reporter, GARIS, Howard
Lassie Come Home, KNIGHT, Eric
Last of the Mohicans, COOPER, James F.
Latest Larks of Foxy Grandpa, BUNNY
Laughable Lyrics, LEAR, Edward
Laughing Boy, LA FARGE, Oliver
Laughing Prince, FILLMORE, Parker
Laurel Token, BARNES, Annie M.
Legend of Sleephy Hollow, IRVING, Washington
Legends of the Evergreen Coast, GRIFFIN, George
Lentil, McCLOSKEY, Robert
Let's Pretend, MacHARG, William
Life & Adventures of Santa Claus, BAUM, L. Frank
Light Princess and Other Fairy Stories, MacDONALD, George
Lincoln Conscript, GREENE, Homer
Lincoln High School novels, GOLLUMB, Joseph
Linda and Dick of Colonial Williamsburg, JAMISON, Jane
Lion, the Witch and the Wardrobe, LEWIS, C. S.
Lion-Hearted Kitten, BACON, Peggy
Lions on the Hunt, WALDECK, Theodore J.
Listening, SEREDY, Kate
Little Eagle, a Navajo Boy, SPERRY, Armstrong
Little American Girl, ALLEE, Marjorie Hill
Little Angel, DALGLIESH, Alice
Little Ann and Other Poems, TAYLOR, Jane and Ann
Little Boat Boy, BOTHWELL, Jean
Little Book of Days, FIELD, Rachel
Little Book of Nonsense, JOHNSON, Burges
Little Boy Lost, HUDSON, W. H.
Little Britches, MOODY, Ralph
Little Brothers to the Scouts, HYDE, Elizabeth
Little Brown Bear, UPHAM, E.
Little Brown Bear, GRUELLE, Johnny
Little Brown Bruno, RADFORD, Alice E.
Little Brown Koko, HUNT, Blanche
Little Buffalo Robe, BECK, Ruth
Little Cat That Could Not Sleep, FOX, Frances Margaret
Little Child's Book of Stories, SKINNER, Cornelia Otis
Little Colonel's Good Time Book, JOHNSTON, Annie
Little Colonel, JOHNSTON, Annie
Little Dog Toby, FIELD, Rachel
Little Dorrit, DICKENS, Charles
Little Duke, YONGE, Charlotte
Little Dutch Tulip Girl, BRANDEIS, Madeline
Little Engine that Could, LENSKI, Lois
Little Fire Engine, LENSKI, Lois
Little Fu, CREEKMORE, Raymond
Little Grey Goose, LEFEVRE, Felicite
Little Grey Men, WATKINS-PITCHFORD, Denys

Little Hippo and his Red Bicycle, BRICE, Tony
Little House on the Prairie, WILDER, Laura
Little House, BURTON, Virginia Lee
Little Indian Weaver, BRANDEIS, Madeline
Little Jean, BROWN, Helen Dawes
Little King Davie, HELLIS, Nellie
Little King, SOGLOW, Otto
Little Lame Prince, MULUCK, Dinah Maria
Little Lame Prince and Adventures of a Brownie, MULUCK, Dinah Maria
Little Lame Prince and His Travelling Cloak, MULUCK, Dinah Maria
Little Lord Fauntleroy, BURNETT, Frances
Little Lord Fauntleroy, BURNETT, Frances
Little Lost Lammie, CARR, Warner
Little Lulu on Parade, MARGE
Little Lulu, MARGE
Little Maid in Toyland, SUTTON, Adah Louise
Little Maid of Quebec, CURTIS, Alice
Little Man With One Shoe, BAILEY, Margaret
Little Men, ALCOTT, Louisa May
Little Mermaid, ANDERSEN, Hans Christian
Little Miss Fret, AUNT HATTIE
Little Miss Peggy, Only A Nursery Story, MOLESWORTH, Mary Louisa
Little Miss Weezy, SHIRLEY, Penn
Little Missy, LINDSAY, Maud
Little Navajo Bluebird, CLARK, Ann Nolan
Little Nemo, McCAY, Winsor
Little Pear and His Friends, LATTIMORE, Eleanor F.
Little Pear, LATTIMORE, Eleanor F.
Little Pet Books, AUNT FANNY
Little Pink Pig, VAN DRESSER, Jasmine Stone
Little Prince, SAINT EXUPERY, Antoine de
Little Rabbit Who Wanted Red Wings, BAILEY, Carolyn
Little Red Balloon, HOFMAN, Caroline
Little Saint Sunshine, GOSS, Charles
Little Sallie Mandy Story Book, VAN DERVEER, Helen
Little Sisters to the Camp Fire Girls, HYDE, Elizabeth
Little Spanish Dancer, BRANDEIS, Madeline
Little Stone House, HADER, Berta
Little Sunny Stories, GRUELLE, Johnny
Little Susie Sunbonnet, UNCLE MILTON
Little Swiss Wood Carver, BRANDEIS, Madeline
Little Tim and the Brave Sea Captain, ARDIZZONE, Edward
Little Toot, GRAMATKY, Hardie
Little Train, GREENE, Graham
Little White Goat, LATHROP, Dorothy
Little White Horse, GOUDGE, Elizabeth
Little Women, ALCOTT, Louisa May

Little Wooden Doll, BIANCO, Margery
Loopy, GRAMATKY, Hardie
Lords of the Wild, ALTSHELER, Joseph
Loraine and the Little People, GORDON, Elizabeth
Lost Hole of Bingoola, HARRIS, Leila
Lost in the Fur Country, LANGE, Dietrich
Lost Merry-Go-Round, LATHROP, Dorothy
Lost Queen of Egypt, MORRISON, Lucile
Lovable Tales of Janey & Josey & Joe, SMITH, Gertrude
Loveliness, PHELPS, Elizabeth Stuart
Lovey Mary, RICE, Alice Hegan
Lucio and His Nuong, CROCKETT, Lucy
Lucretia Ann and the Sagebrush Plains, PLOWHEAD, Ruth Gipson
Lucy Brown and Mr. Grimes, ARDIZZONE, Edward
Lucy Dawson's Dogs, DAWSON, Lucy
Lullabye Land, FIELD, Eugene
Lulu, STEINER, Charlotte
Lumbercamp, ROUNDS, Glen
Lupe Goes to School, BRANN, Esther
Lure of the Black Hills, LANGE, Dietrich
Macaroni, an American Tune, LOCKWOOD, Myna
Madcap of the School, BRAZIL, Angela
Made-to-Order Stories, CANFIELD, Dorothy
Madeleine Takes Command, BRILL, Ethel C.
Madeline, BEMELMANS, Ludwig
Madge, a Girl in Earnest, SMITH, Jennie S.
Magic Aeroplane, NELSON, Emile
Magic Bedknob, NORTON, Mary
Magic Bells, COTHRAN, Jean
Magic City, NESBIT, E.
Magic Firecrackers, DAWSON, Mitchell
Magic Image from India, BAKER, Cornelia
Magic Squirrel, GRISHINA, N. G.
Magical Land of Noom, GRUELLE, Johnny
Magical Melons, BRINK, Carol
Magical Monarch of Mo, BAUM, L. Frank
Maid in Arcady, BARBOUR, Ralph Henry
Make Way for Ducklings, McCLOSKEY, Robert
Make-Believe Men and Women, HUMPHREY, Maud
Man Who Lost His Head, BISHOP, Claire Huchet
Man in the Moon Stories Told Over the Radio Phone, LAWRENCE, J.
Mansion, VAN DYKE, Henry
Manuela's Birthday, BANNON, Laura
Many Moons, THURBER, James
Marcos, LEE, Melicent Humason
Margaret Ellison, GRAYHAM, Mary
Marigold Garden, GREENAWAY, Kate
Marshmallow, NEWBERRY, Clare Turlay
Martin the Goose Boy, BARRINGER, Marie
Mary Cary, BOSHER, Kate Langley
Mary Frances Books, FRYER, Jane Eayer

Mary in California, JOHNSON, Constance
Mary in New Mexico, JOHNSON, Constance
Mary Mouse and the Doll's House, BLYTON, Enid
Mary Poppins Comes Back, TRAVERS, P. L.
Mary Poppins Opens the Door, TRAVERS, P. L.
Mary Poppins, TRAVERS, P. L.
Mason and His Rangers, GREGOR, Elmer
Master Key, BAUM, L. Frank
Master Monkey, MUKERJI, Dhan Gopal
Master Skylark, BENNETT, John
Matchlock Gun, EDMONDS, Walter
Maud Humphrey's Book of Fairy Tales, HUMPHREY, Maud
May Day Revels, GREEN, Elizabeth
Mazli, SPYRI, Johanna
McElligot's Pool, SEUSS, Dr.
Medicine Buffalo, GREGOR, Elmer
Mei Li, HANDFORTH, Thomas
Melindy's Medal, FAULKNER, Georgene
Menino, EDWARDS, Florence
Mercy and the Mouse, BACON, Peggy
Merry Adventures of Robin Hood, PYLE, Howard
Merry Christmas Book, BAILEY, Carolyn
Merry Five, CLARKE, Sarah
Merry Scout, BRETT, Edna
Middle Moffat, ESTES, Eleanor
Middle Sister, MASON, Miriam E.
Midnight and Jeremiah, NORTH, Sterling
Midnight Moon, LYONS, Dorothy
Midsummer Night's Dream, SHAKESPEARE, William
Midsummer, ADAMS, Katherine
Mighty Mikko, a Book of Finnish Fairy Tales, FILLMORE, Parker
Mike Mulligan and His Steam Shovel, BURTON, Virginia Lee
Mile High Cabin, PLOWHEAD, Ruth Gipson
Millions of Cats, GAG, Wanda
Minnie the Fish Who Lived in a Shoe, CHAMBERLAIN, Ethel
Mischief in Mayfield, BACON, Peggy
Miss Hickory, BAILEY, Carolyn
Miss Minerva and William Green Hill, CALHOUN, Frances
Missionary Twig, BURNETT, Emma
Mister Penny, ETS, Marie
Mistress Jennifer and Master Jeremiah, JAMISON, Jane
Misty of Chincoteague, HENRY, Marguerite
Mittens, NEWBERRY, Clare Turlay
Moffatts, ESTES, Eleanor
Molly and Michael, BOURGEOIS, Florence
Monkey with a Notion, BLOUGH, Glenn
Mopsa the Fairy, INGELOW, Jean
Moral Alphabet, BELLOC, Hillaire

More About the Roosevelt Bears, EATON, Seymour
More Beasts for Worse Children, BELLOC, Hillaire
More Celtic Fairy Tales, JACOBS, Joseph
More Goops and How Not to Be Them, BURGESS, Gelett
More Mother Stories, LINDSAY, Maud
More Silver Pennies, THOMPSON, Blanche Jennings
Mother Carey's Chickens, WIGGIN, Kate Douglas
Mother Goose Children, BLAISDELL, Mary F.
Mother Goose in Prose, BAUM, L. Frank
Mother Goose Stories, SMITH, Laura Rountree
Mother Goose, NEWTON, Ruth
Mother Goose, GREENAWAY, Kate
Mother Goose, PEAT, Fern Bisel
Mother Goose, DOANE, Pelagie
Mother Goose, Her Chimes, WARE, Buzz
Mother Goose, The Old Nursery Rhymes, RACKHAM, Arthur
Mother Makes Christmas, MEIGS, Cornelia
Mountain Boy, BELL, Thelma
Mountain Mystery, CHAPMAN, Maristan
Movie of Me, SHIRLEY TEMPLE BOOKS
Mr. Bunny, His Book, SUTTON, Adah Louise
Mr. Pink and the House on the Roof, HEAL, Edith
Mr. Popper's Penguins, ATWATER, F.
Mr. Stubbs's Brother, OTIS, James
Mr. Woodchuck, BANCROFT, Laura
Mrs. Cucumber Green, BONNER, Mary
Mrs. Eli and Policy Ann, OLMSTEAD, Florence
Mrs. Mallard's Ducklings, DELAFIELD, Clelia
Mrs. Piggle-Wiggle, MacDONALD, Betty
Mrs. Polly's Party, BROMHALL, Winifred
Mrs. Wiggs of the Cabbage Patch, RICE, Alice Hegan
Muffin Shop, GARNETT, Louie Ayers
Muggins Mouse, BARROWS, Marjorie
Munro Leaf's Fun Book, LEAF, Munro
Music of the Wild, STRATTON-PORTER, Mrs. Gene
Musical Box, LEIGHTON, Clare
Musical Tree, WEBER, Sarah Stilwell
Mutineers, HAWES, Charles
My Children's Picture Book, LONDON GOSPEL
My Father's Dragon, GANNETT, Ruth
My Friend Flicka, O'HARA, Mary
My Poetry Book, POGANY, Willy
My Travel Ship, MILLER, Olive Beaupre
Myself When Young, MIRZA, Youel B.
Mysterious Caboose, BONNER, Mary
Mysterious Island, VERNE, Jules
Mystery at the Black Cat, WADSWORTH, Leda
Mystery at the Old Place, ORTON, Helen F.
Mystery of Black Pearl Island, HADOTH, Gunby
Mystery Rides the Trail, LATHROP, Gilbert
Myths and Enchantments, PRICE, Margaret Evans
Myths of Northern Lands, GUERBER, Helene

Nanette and the Wooden Shoes, BRANN, Esther
Narcissus and de Chillun, GOVAN, Christine
National Nursery Rhymes, DALZIEL
National Velvet, BAGNOLD, Enid
Nautilus, RICHARDS, Laura E.
Neighbors Near and Far, WAHLERT, Jennie
Nellie West, GRAYHAM, Mary
Nelly's Silver Mines, JACKSON, Helen Hunt
New Child's Play, E. V. B.
New England Bean Pot, JAGENDORF, M.
New Forest, WISE, John R.
New Moon, MEIGS, Cornelia
New Story of Peter Rabbit, LOWE, Samuel E.
New Treasure Seekers, NESBIT, E.
Nibbles Poppelty Poppett, DAVIDSON, Edith
Nicanor, Teller of Tales, TAYLOR, Bryson C.
Nice Puppy!, PAULSEN, Martha
Night Before Christmas (Moore), DENSLOW, W. W
Night Before Christmas and Jingles, MOORE, Clement C.
Night Before Christmas, MOORE, Clement C.
Nine Hundred Buckets of Paint, BECKER, Edna
Nize Baby, GROSS, Milt
No Mistaking Corker, EDWARDS, Monica
No Trouble at All, BROWN, Paul
Nobody's Boy, MALOT, Hector
Nobody's Buddy, MOROSO, John
Nobody's Rose, THOMPSON, Adele E.
Noddy Goes to Toyland, BLYTON, Enid
Noddy in Toytown, BLYTON, Enid
Nonsense Songs, Stories, Botany and Alphabets, LEAR, Edward
North American Fairy Tales, ARMOUR, R. C.
Now It's Fall, LENSKI, Lois
Now We Are Six, MILNE, A. A.
Now-A-Days Fairy Book, CHAPIN, Anna Alice
Nura's Garden of Betty and Booth, NURA
Nursery Alice, CARROLL, Lewis
Nursery Rhyme, BROOKE, L. Leslie
Oak Tree House, GIBSON, Katherine
Odyssey for Boys and Girls, CHURCH, Alfred John
Off to Philadelphia, ALLEE, Marjorie Hill
Oh Skin-nay! The Days of Real Sport, NESBIT, Wilbur
Oh, Look Who's Here, SMITH, George Henry
Old Fashioned Girl, ALCOTT, Louisa May
Old Lollipop Shop, NOKES, Ethel
Old Peabody Pew, WIGGIN, Kate Douglas
Old Possum's Book of Practical Cats, ELIOT, T. S.
Old Raven's World, MAURY, Jean West
Olle's Ski Trip, BESKOW, Elsa
On the Railroad, HENRY, Robert S.
On the Trail of the Sioux, LANGE, Dietrich
Once on a Time, MILNE, A. A.

Once There Was and Was Not, DANE, George
Once Upon a Monday, WILLSON, Dixie
Once Upon a Time, BATES, Katherine Lee
One Day on Beetle Rock, CARRIGHAR, Sally
One Foot in Fairyland, FARJEON, Eleanor
One Thousand Poems for Children, BETTS, Ethel
Orphant Annie Story Book, GRUELLE, Johnny
Orpheus with his Lute, HUTCHINSON, W. M. L.
Orpheus, Myths of the World, COLUM, Padraic
Orpheus, Myths of the World, COLUM, Padraic
Other People's Houses, BIANCO, Margery
Otherside Book, MITCHELL, Edith
Otto of the Silver Hand, PYLE, Howard
Our Old Nursery Rhymes, Le MAIR, H. Willebeek
Over the Polar Ice, an Andy Lane Story, ADAMS, Eustace
Over the Rainbow Bridge, HAYNES, Louise Marshall
Overall Boys, GROVER, Eulalie
Paddle-to-the-Sea, HOLLING, Holling
Padre Porko, the Gentlemanly Pig, DAVIS, Robert
Page and the Prince, CHIPMAN, Charles P.
Painting Book, GREENAWAY, Kate
Palmer Cox's Queer People, COX, Palmer
Pancakes - Paris, BISHOP, Claire Huchet
Panchita, GOETZ, Delia
Paradise of Childhood, BRADLEY, Milton
Pat Rides the Trail, EAMES, Genevieve
Patsy Ann, Her Happy Times, KING, *Mona Reid*
Patsy for Keeps, AMES, Esther Merriam
Paul Bunyan Marches On, TURNEY, Ida Virginia
Paul Bunyan the Work Giant, TURNEY, Ida Virginia
Paul Bunyan's Bears, STEVENS, James
Paul Bunyan, SHEPARD, Esther
Pawnee Hero Stories, GRINNELL, George
Pawnee, BELL, Thelma
Pay Dirt, ROUNDS, Glen
Peace Pipes at Portage, DARBY, Ada
Peacock Eggs, BAKER, Margaret and Mary
Peacock Pie, DeLaMARE, Walter
Pearl and the Pumpkin, WEST, Paul
Pecos Bill and Lightning, PECK, Leigh
Pecos Bill, BOWMAN, James
Peeps, COX-McCORMACK, Nancy
Peggy and Paul and Laddy, CARR, Mary Jane
Peggy Goes Overseas, BUGBEE, Emma
Pelican Here, Pelican There, WEISGARD, Leonard
Pelle's N ew Suit, BESKOW, Elsa
Penelope's Progress, WIGGIN, Kate Douglas
Penguin Twins, TOMPKINS, Jane
Penny and Peter, LLOYD, Marion
Penny and the White Horse, BIANCO, Margery
Penrod & Sam, TARKINGTON, Booth
Penrod, TARKINGTON, Booth
People Who Work Near Our House, JUDSON, Clara

Pepper and Salt, PYLE, Howard
Pepper Moon, WOOD, Esther
Personally Conducted, STOCKTON, Frank
Pet Show, BARROWS, Marjorie
Peter and Gretchen of old Nuremberg, JONES, Viola M.
Peter and Prue, DONAHEY, Mary
Peter and the Princess, GRABO, Carl
Peter and Wendy, BARRIE, James
Peter Duck, RANSOME, Arthur
Peter Pan in Kensington Gardens, BARRIE, James
Peter Patter Book, JACKSON, Leroy F.
Peter Pea, GRISHINA, N. G.
Peter Pocket, JUSTUS, May
Peter Rabbit Story Book, WILL, Bess Goe
Peter Rabbit's Easter, ALMOND, Linda
Peter's Voyage, BESKOW, Elsa
Peter, Peter, Pumpkin Grower, BOURGEOIS, Florence
Peterkin Papers, HALE, Lucretia P.
Peterkin, POGANY, Willy
Petunia, DUVOISIN, Roger
Phantom on Skis, GIRVAN, Helen
Phoenix and the Carpet, NESBIT, E.
Pickett's Gap, GREENE, Homer
Picture Tales from the Chinese, METZGER, Bertha
Picture Tales from India, METZGER, Bertha
Picture Tales from Scandinavia, OWEN, Ruth Bryan
Picture Tales from the French, CHAMOUD, Simone
Picturesque Tales of Progress, MILLER, Olive Beaupre
Pie and the Patty Pan, POTTER, Beatrix
Pied Piper of Hamelin, BROWNING, Robert
Pierre Keeps Watch, GLEIT, Maria
Pigeon Post, RANSOME, Arthur
Pilgrim Kate, DARINGER, Helen
Pilgrim's Inn, GOUDGE, Elizabeth
Pilgrim's Progress, BUNYAN, John
Pinky and the Plumed Knight, CHAPIN, Frederic
Pinocchio, COLLODI, Carlo
Pinto Pony, BIRNEY, Hoffman
Pinto's Journey, BRONSON, Wilfrid
Piper's Pony, BROWN, Paul
Pirate's Treasure, WILSON, Edward A.
Pirates in the Deep Green Sea, LINKLATER, Eric
Plain Princess, McGINLEY, Phyllis
Playmates in Print, WHITEMAN, Edna
Playtime & Company, LUCAS, E. V.
Playtime in Cherry Street, BIANCO, Pamela
Poems of Childhood, FIELD, Eugene
Policeman Bluejay, BANCROFT, Laura
Polly Cologne, DIAZ, Abby
Polly of the Pines, THOMPSON, Adele E.
Polly Put the Kettle On, ABBOTT, Jane.

Pollyanna Grows Up, PORTER, Eleanor
Pollyanna, PORTER, Eleanor
Poo-Poo and the Dragons, FORESTER, C. S.
Poor Cecco, BIANCO, Margery
Poor Count's Christmas, STOCKTON, Frank
Poor Shaydullah, ARTZYBASHEFF, Boris
Pope's Mule, DAUDET, Alphonse
Poppy Seed Cakes, CLARK, Margery
Powder Dock Mystery, FULTON, Reed
Practically Perfect, LAMBERT, Janet
Prairie Rose, BUSH, Bertha E.
Prince Commands, NORTON, Andre
Prince and the Pauper, TWAIN, Mark
Prince Bantam and His Faithful Henchmen, McNEER, May
Prince Pimpernel, RIX, Herbert
Prince Prigio, LANG, Andrew
Prince Ricardo of Pantouflia, LANG, Andrew
Prince Tip-Top, BOUVET, Marguerite
Princess and Curdie, MacDONALD, George
Princess and the Goblin, MacDONALD, George
Princess Nobody, LANG, Andrew
Princess Pocahontas, WATSON, Virginia
Princess Rosette and Other Fairy Tales, SEGUR, Comtesse de
Princess September and the Nightingale, MAUGHAM, W. Somerset
Princesses and Peasant Boys, FENNER, Phyllis
Probable Sons, LE FEUVRE, Amy
Proud Little Baxter, DILLINGHAM, Frances
Proverb Stories, ALCOTT, Louisa May
Puck of Pook's Hill, KIPLING, Rudyard
Pumpkin Moonshine, TUDOR, Tasha
Pup Himself, DENNIS, Morgan
Pups and Pies, BUTLER, Ellis
Purple Pennant, BARBOUR, Ralph Henry
Purr and Miew, LEET, Frank R.
Quacky Doodles' and Danny Daddles' Book, HUBBELL, Rose
Queen of Hearts, CALDECOTT, Randolph
Queen of Pirate Isle, HARTE, Bret
Queen Tiny's Little People, WETMORE, Claude
Queen Zixi of Ix, BAUM, L. Frank
Queen's Story Book, GOMME, George
Queerie Queers with Hands, Wings and Claws, COX, Palmer
R. Caldecott's Picture Book No. 1, CALDECOTT, Randolph
Rabbit Hill, LAWSON, Robert
Rabelais for Boys and Girls, THAYER, Tiffany Ellsworth
Racketty-Packetty House, BURNETT, Frances
Rag Doll Susie, WURTH, A.
Raggedy Ann, GRUELLE, Johnny

Raggylug the Cottontail Rabbit, SETON, Ernest Thompson
Railway Series, AWDRY, Rev. W.
Railway Children, NESBIT, E.
Rain on the Roof, MEIGS, Cornelia
Rainbow Cat, FYLEMAN, Rose
Rainbow in the Sky, UNTERMEYER, Louis
Ralestone Luck, NORTON, Andre
Rambillicus Book, McDOUGALL, Walt
Rambles of a Rat, TUCKER, Charlotte Marie
Ranald Bannerman's Boyhood, MacDONALD, George
Read Another Story, PRATT, Marjorie
Real Mother Goose, WRIGHT, Blanche Fisher
Really So Stories, GORDON, Elizabeth
Rebecca Mary, DONNELL, Annie
Red Arrow, GREGOR, Elmer
Red Book of Heroes, LANG, Mrs. Andrew
Red Horse Hill, MEADER, Stephen W.
Red Roan Pony, LIPPINCOTT, Joseph Wharton
Red Robin, ABBOTT, Jane.
Reformed Pirate, STOCKTON, Frank
Relief's Rocker, DALGLIESH, Alice
Remarkable Tale of a Whale, WRIGHT, Isa
Rhyme? And Reason? CARROLL, Lewis
Rhymes for Kindly Children, SNYDER, Fairmont
Rhymes for the Young Folk, ALLINGHAM, William
Rhymes of Real Children, SAGE, Betty
Rico the Young Rancher, FLEMING, Patricia
Rifles for Washington, SINGMASTER, Elsie
Right Princess, BURNHAM, Clara Louise
Riley Child Verse, RILEY, James Whitcomb
Rimskittle Book, JACKSON, Leroy F.
Ring o' Roses, a Nursery Rhyme Picture Book, BROOKE, L. Leslie
Rip Van Winkle, IRVING, Washington
River-Land, A Story for Children, CHAMBERS, Robert W.
Road to Storyland, PIPER, Watty
Robbut, a Tale of Tails, LAWSON, Robert
Roberta Goes Adventuring, RAYMOND, Margaret Thomsen
Robin Hood and His Merry Outlaws, McSPADDEN, J. Walker
Robin Hood, WYETH, N. C.
Robin Redbreast and Other Verses, ALLINGHAM, William
Robinson Crusoe, DEFOE, Daniel
Roby Family, TUCKER, Charlotte Marie
Rocket Book, NEWELL, Peter
Roland the Warrior, COLLIER, Virginia
Rolling Wheels, GREY, Katherine
Roly-Poly Pudding, POTTER, Beatrix
Roosevelt Bears Abroad, EATON, Seymour

Roosevelt Bears, Their Travels and Adventures, EATON, Seymour

Rooster Crows, PETERSHAM, Maude and Miska

Rootabaga Pigeons, SANDBURG, Carl

Rootabaga Stories, SANDBURG, Carl

Rose and the Ring, THACKERAY, William Makepeace

Rose Fyleman Fairy Book, FYLEMAN, Rose

Rose in Bloom, ALCOTT, Louisa May

Rose O' the River, WIGGIN, Kate Douglas

Round and Round Horse, GURY, Jeremy

Round the Year in Pudding Lane, ADDINGTON, Sarah

Roundabout, DALGLIESH, Alice

Rowena Teena Tot and the Blackberries, BLUMBERG, Fannie

Rowena Teena Tot and the Runaway Turkey, BLUMBERG, Fannie

Royal Children of English History, NESBIT, E.

Royal Mimkin, GALL, Alice

Royal Progress of King Pepito, CRESSWELL, Beatrice

Rudolph the Red-Nosed Reindeer, MAY, Robert L.

Rufus M, ESTES, Eleanor

Run, Run!, GRANICK, Harry

Runaway Boy, RILEY, James Whitcomb

Runaway Bunny, BROWN, Margaret Wise

Runaway Equator, BELL, Lilian

Runaway Prentice, PARTON, Ethel

Running Fox, GREGOR, Elmer

Rupert's Ambition, ALGER, Horatio Jr.

Rusted Knight and Other Stories, VOLKMANN, Richard von

S-O-S Helicopter, BAIN, Edward U.

Sad-Faced Boy, BONTEMPS, Arna

Sajo and Her Beaver People, GREY OWL

Sally Does It, BARUCH, Dorothy

Sally Williams, the Mountain Girl, CHENEY, Edna

Sally's ABC Sewed in a Sampler, TATE, Sally Jane

Saltwater Boy, LEE, Melicent Humason

Sam Steele's Adventures on Land and Sea, FITZGERALD, Capt. Hugh

Sam Steele's Adventures in Panama, FITZGERALD, Capt. Hugh

Sampo, Wonder Tale of the Old North, BALDWIN, James

Sara Crewe, BURNETT, Frances

Sarah's Idea, GATES, Doris

Saturdays, ENRIGHT, Elizabeth

Sawdust in His Shoes, McGRAW, Eloise Jarvis

Scalp Hunters, CORYELL, Hubert V.

Scarlet Oak, MEIGS, Cornelia

Scottish Chiefs, PORTER, Kathryn

Scottish Fairy Book, GRIERSON, Elizabeth

Scrambled Eggs, MACKALL, Lawton

Sea Fairies, BAUM, L. Frank

Secret Cache, BRILL, Ethel C.

Secret Cargo, PEASE, Howard

Secret Cave, EVERSON, Florence

Secret Garden, BURNETT, Frances

Secret in the Rosewood Box, ORTON, Helen F.

Secret of the Circle, JOHANSEN, Margaret

Secret Stair, GINTHER, Mrs. Pemberton

Sensible Kate, GATES, Doris

Seven Bear Skins, BERRY, Erick

Seven Crowns, LATTIMORE, Eleanor F.

Seven Little Sisters Who Live on the Round Ball That Floats in the Air, ANDREWS, Jane

Seven Simeons, ARTZYBASHEFF, Boris

Seven Voyages of Sinbad the Sailor, BEAMAN, S. G. Hulme

Seventeenth Summer, DALY, Maureen

Seventy-Six!, KAUFFMAN, Reginald Wright

Shadow of the Crown, BOLTON, Ivy May

Shadow Show, NEWELL, Peter

Shag, HINKLE, Thomas C.

Shanghai Passage, PEASE, Howard

Shawneen and the Gander, BENNETT, Richard

Shen of the Sea, CHRISMAN, Arthur

Shirley Temple at Play, SHIRLEY TEMPLE BOOKS

Shirley Temple Story Book, SHIRLEY TEMPLE BOOKS

Shirley Temple's Book of Fairy Tales, SHIRLEY TEMPLE BOOKS

Shuttle and Sword, DANIEL, Hawthorne

Shuttle, BURNETT, Frances

Siegfried and Twilight of the Gods, WAGNER, Richard

Silk and Satin Lane, WOOD, Esther

Silver Casket, TUCKER, Charlotte Marie

Silver Chief, O'BRIEN, Jack

Silver Pennies, THOMPSON, Blanche Jennings

Silver Spurs for Cowboy Boots, GARST, Shannon

Silverfoot, LINDSAY, Maud

Sing for Your Supper, FARJEON, Eleanor

Sing-Song, A Nursery Rhyme Book, ROSSETTI, Christina

Singing Cave, LEIGHTON, Margaret

Skating Gander, BAILEY, Alice Cooper

Skazki: Tales and Legends of Old Russia, ZEITLIN, Ida

Skimmer and His Thrilling Adventures, SNELL, Roy

Skippack School, DE ANGELI, Marguerite

Skipping Along Alone, WELLES, Winifred

Skippy: A Novel, CROSBY, Percy

Sky Caravan, CLARKE, Covington

Sky Island, BAUM, L. Frank

Slant Book, NEWELL, Peter

Sleeping Beauty and Other Fairy Tales, QUILLER-COUCH, Sir Arthur

Sleeping Beauty, RACKHAM, Arthur
Slim Princess, ADE, George
Slovenly Peter, HOFFMANN, Heinrich
Small, GREENE, Kathleen
Smarter and Smoother, DALY, Maureen
Smiths and Rusty, DALGLIESH, Alice
Smoky Bay, ARASON, Steingrimur
Smoky House, GOUDGE, Elizabeth
Smoky the Cowhorse, JAMES, Will
Snow Before Christmas, TUDOR, Tasha
Snow Dog, KJELGAARD, Jim
Snow Queen, ANDERSEN, Hans Christian
Snow White, GRIMM, The Brothers
Snowbaby's Own Story, STAFFORD, Marie
Snuggle Tales, BAUM, L. Frank
Sod House Winter, JUDSON, Clara
Some of Aesop's Fables, CALDECOTT, Randolph
Songs of Innocence, BLAKE, William
Sonny's Father, STUART, Ruth McEnery
Sou'wester Goes North, BALDWIN, Arthur J.
Space Cadet, HEINLEIN, Robert
Spinning Wheel Stories, ALCOTT, Louisa May
Spotted Deer, GREGOR, Elmer
Springtide of Life Poems of Childhood, SWINBURNE, Algernon Charles
St. George and the Witches, DUNNE
Stars Through Magic Casements, WILLIAMSON, Julia
Stars To-night, TEASDALE, Sara
Steps to Nowhere, BOYLAN
Stories by Juliana Horatia Ewing, EWING, Juliana
Stories Children Like, PEAT, Fern Bisel
Stories for Boys, DAVIS, Richard
Stories from the Greek Tragedians, CHURCH, Alfred John
Stories from the Old Testament, PETERSHAM, Maude and Miska
Stories from Toytown, BEAMAN, S. G. Hulme
Stories of Little Brown Koko, HUNT, Blanche
Stories of Mother Goose Village, BIGHAM, Madge
Stories of the Gods and Heroes, BENSON, Sally
Stories to Shorten the Road, POWER, Effie
Stories to Tell to Children, BRYANT, Sara Cone
Stories True and Fancies New, MORRISON, Mary Whitney
Story about Ping, FLACK, Marjorie
Story Book of Clothes, PETERSHAM, Maude and Miska
Story Book of Knowledge, FRANKLIN, Laurence B.
Story Book of Ships, PETERSHAM, Maude and Miska
Story Book of Trains, PETERSHAM, Maude and Miska
Story Garden for Little Children, LINDSAY, Maud
Story of a Bad Boy, ALDRICH, Thomas Bailey

Story of a Needle, TUCKER, Charlotte Marie
Story of Appleby Capple, PARRISH, Anne
Story of Beowulf, RIGGS, Strafford
Story of Evangeline, LONGFELLOW, Henry Wadsworth
Story of Ferdinand, LEAF, Munro
Story of Grettir the Strong, FRENCH, Allen
Story of King Arthur and His Knights, PYLE, Howard
Story of Little Black Bobtail, BANNERMAN, Helen
Story of Little Black Mingo, BANNERMAN, Helen
Story of Little Black Quibba, BANNERMAN, Helen
Story of Little Black Sambo, BANNERMAN, Helen
Story of Mankind, VAN LOON, Hendrik
Story of My Life, SHIRLEY TEMPLE BOOKS
Story of Roland, BALDWIN, James
Story of Rolf, FRENCH, Allen
Story of Siegfried, BALDWIN, James
Story of the Golden Age, BALDWIN, James
Story of Woofin-Poofin, BULLER, Marguerite
Story-Teller, LINDSAY, Maud
Storyland, PEAT, Fern Bisel
Strange Adventures of Captain Marwhopple, FYLEMAN, Rose
Strange Stories of the Great River, GROSVENOR, Johnston
Street in Bronzeville, BROOKS, Gwendolyn
Street of Little Shops, BIANCO, Margery
String and the No-Tail Cat, GOVAN, Christine
Stuart Little, WHITE, E. B.
Sugar Loaf Mountain, BANCROFT, Laura
Sugar Plum Tree and Other Verses, FIELD, Eugene
Suitable Child, DUNCAN, Norman
Suki, WEISGARD, Leonard
Sunbonnet Babies Book, GROVER, Eulalie
Sunny Bunny, PUTNAM, Nina Wilcox
Sunny Rhymes for Happy Children, MILLER, Olive Beaupre
Sunny-Sulky Book, RIPPEY, Sarah Cory
Surprise for Judy-Jo, HILL, Mabel Betsy
Susan and the Little Lost Bird, MORRIS, Rhoda
Susanna and Sue, WIGGIN, Kate Douglas
Susannah at Boarding School, DENISON, Muriel
Susannah of the Mounties books, DENISON, Muriel
Swallowdale, RANSOME, Arthur
Swallows and Amazons, RANSOME, Arthur
Swamp Island, WIRT, Mildred
Sweet Possum Valley, GOVAN, Christine
Sweetheart Travelers, CROCKETT, S. R.
Swiss Family Robinson, WYSS, David
Sword in Sheath, NORTON, Andre
Sword in the Stone, WHITE, T. H.
Sword is Drawn, NORTON, Andre
Sword of Roland Arnot, HEWES, Agnes Danforth
Swords of Steel, SINGMASTER, Elsie

Swords on the Sea, HEWES, Agnes Danforth
Sylvie and Bruno Concluded, CARROLL, Lewis
Sylvie and Bruno, CARROLL, Lewis
'Twas the Night Before Christmas, MOORE, Clement C.
Tailor and the Crow, an Old Rhyme with New Drawings, BROOKE, L. Leslie
Tailor of Gloucester, POTTER, Beatrix
Tale of Cuffy Bear, BAILEY, Arthur Scott
Tale of Flopsy Bunnies, POTTER, Beatrix
Tale of Johnny Mouse, GORDON, Elizabeth
Tale of Lohengrin, ROLLESTON, T. W.
Tale of Mrs. Tiggy-Winkle, POTTER, Beatrix
Tale of Mrs. Tittlemouse, POTTER, Beatrix
Tale of Peter Rabbit, POTTER, Beatrix
Tale of Squirrel Nutkin, POTTER, Beatrix
Tale of the Wee Little Old Woman, BESKOW, Elsa
Tale of Tom Kitten, POTTER, Beatrix
Tale of Two Cities, DICKENS, Charles
Tales from Grimm, GRIMM, The Brothers
Tales from Shakespeare, LAMB, Charles
Tales from Silver Lands, FINGER, Charles
Tales from the Storyteller's House, BURGESS, Thornton
Tales from Washington Irving's Traveller, IRVING, Washington
Tales of a Russian Grandmother, CARPENTER, Frances
Tales of a Basque Grandmother, CARPENTER, Frances
Tales of a Chinese Grandmother, CARPENTER, Frances
Tales of Laughter, WIGGIN, Kate Douglas
Tales of Little Cats, JACOBS-BOND, Carrie
Tales of Little Dogs, JACOBS-BOND, Carrie
Tales of Momolu, GRAHAM, Lorenz
Tales of Mother Goose Village, BIGHAM, Madge
Tales of Passed Time, PERRAULT, Charles
Tales of Serbian Life, DAVIES, E. Chivers
Tales of the Punjab, STEEL, Flora A.
Tales of Toytown, BEAMAN, S. G. Hulme
Tales Told in Hawaii, METZGER, Bertha
Talk of Many Things, WILSON, Richard
Talking Stone, CUNNINGHAM, Caroline
Talking Totem Pole, MAYOL, Lurine
Tall Book of Fairy Tales, VANCE, Eleanor
Tall Tale America, BLAIR, Walter
Tanglewood Tales, HAWTHORNE, Nathaniel
Tapestry Room, MOLESWORTH, Mary Louisa
Tarzan Twins, BURROUGHS, Edgar Rice
Tattooed Man, PEASE, Howard
Tawny, HINKLE, Thomas C.
Tawnymore, SHANNON, Monica

Taytay's Tales, DE HUFF, Elizabeth
Tea Time Tales, FYLEMAN, Rose
Ted and Nina Have a Happy Rainy Day, DeANGELI, Marguerite
Teddy and Trots in Wonderland, HERBERTSON, Agnes Grozier
Teddy B and Teddy G, The Bear Detectives, EATON, Seymour
Teddy Bears, SUTTON, Adah Louise
Teddy, OTIS, James
Teen-Age Animal Stories, CARTER, Russell Gordon
Teen-Age Historical Stories, CARTER, Russell Gordon
Teenie Weenie Land, DONAHEY, William
Teenie Weenie Neighbors, DONAHEY, William
Teenie Weenie Town, DONAHEY, William
Tell Me a Story, MOLESWORTH, Mary Louisa
Tell Me Why stories, CLAUDY, Carl
Ten American Girls from History, SWEETSER, Kate Dickinson
Ten Boys from Dickens, SWEETSER, Kate Dickinson
Ten Boys from History, SWEETSER, Kate Dickinson
Ten Boys Who Lived on the Road from Long Ago to Now, ANDREWS, Jane
Ten Girls from Dickens, SWEETSER, Kate
Ten Girls from History, SWEETSER, Kate Dickinson
Ten Great Adventures, SWEETSER, Kate Dickinson
Ten Little Servants, SARI
Terrible Nuisense, BACON, Peggy
Terry and the Pirates, CANIFF, Milton
That Year at Lincoln High, GOLLUMB, Joseph
The Frog Who Would A-Wooing Go, ADAMS, Frank
The Hobbit, TOLKIEN, J. R. R.
The Magic Pudding, LINDSAY, Norman
The Runaway, HART, Elizabeth Anne
Theatre Shoes, STREATFELD, Noel
Thee, Hannah, DeANGELI, Marguerite
Then There Were Five, ENRIGHT, Elizabeth
Theras and His Town, SNEDEKER, Caroline Dale
There Was a Horse, FENNER, Phyllis
They Were Strong and Good, LAWSON, Robert
Thidwick, SEUSS, Dr.
Thimble Summer, ENRIGHT, Elizabeth
Thirteen Clocks, THURBER, James
Thirteenth Spoon, GINTHER, Mrs. Pemberton
This Singing World, UNTERMEYER, Louis
This Way to Christmas, SAWYER, Ruth
Thomas the Tank Engine, AWDRY, Rev. W.
Those Plummer Children, GOVAN, Christine
Thousand Years a Minute, CLAUDY, Carl
Three Christmas Trees, EWING, Juliana
Three Golden Oranges, DAVIS, Mary Gould
Three Little Pigs, DISNEY
Three Mulla-Mulgars, DeLaMARE, Walter

Three Musketeers, DUMAS, Alexandre
Through the Cloud Mountain, BERNARD, Florence
Through the Looking Glass, CARROLL, Lewis
Through Thick and Thin, FRANCIS, Laurence
Thunderhead, O'HARA, Mary
Ticktock and Jim, ROBERTSON, Keith
Ticktock and Jim, Deputy Sheriffs, ROBERTSON, Keith
Tide's Secret, FULTON, Reed
Tiger Roan, BALCH, Glenn
Tim and Lucy Go to Sea, ARDIZZONE, Edward
Tim Tadpole and the Great Bullfrog, FLACK, Marjorie
Tim, the Scissors Grinder, AUNT HATTIE
Timothy Crunchit, the Calico Bunny, BALL, Martha
Timothy Keeps a Secret, SEYMOUR, Alta Halverson
To Sweep the Spanish Main, EVANS, E.
Toad of Toad Hall, MILNE, A. A.
Toby Tyler, OTIS, James
Told Beneath the Northern Lights, SNELL, Roy
Told by the Campfire, CHELEY, Frank Howard
Tom Brown's School Days, by an Old Boy, HUGHES, Thomas
Tom Clifton, GOSS, Warren
Tom Cringle's Log, SCOTT, Michael
Tom Sawyer Abroad, TWAIN, Mark
Tom Whipple, EDMONDS, Walter
Tommy and the Telephone, MacGREGOR, Ellen
Tommy Grows Wise, GAY, Romney
Tommy Helps Too, REY, H. A. and Margret
Tomson's Halloween, BAKER, Margaret
Tony Sarg's Animal Book, SARG, Tony
Tony Sarg's Book for Children, SARG, Tony
Tony Sarg's Wonder Zoo, SARG, Tony
Toonerville Trolley and Other Cartoons, FOX, Fontaine
Topsy, FLACK, Marjorie
Topsys and Turvys, NEWELL, Peter
Towhead, McLEAN, Sally Pratt
Trail of the Buffalo, MONTGOMERY, Rutherford
Trail of the Sandhill Stag, SETON, Ernest Thompson
Travels of Timmy Toodles, GRUELLE, Johnny
Treasure Hunt of the S 18, DEAN, Graham
Treasure Hunter, PROUDFIT, Isabel
Treasure in the Little Trunk, ORTON, Helen F.
Treasure Island, STEVENSON, Robert Louis
Treasure Mountain, KELLY, Eric
Treasure of the Isle of Mist, TARN, W. W.
Treasure Ship, ASQUITH, Cynthia
Treasure Things, WYNNE, Annette
Treasures Long Hidden, CHRISMAN, Arthur
Tree for Peter, SEREDY, Kate
Tree in the Trail, HOLLING, Holling
Tree of Freedom, CAUDILL, Rebecca
Tribes on My Frontier, EHA

Trojan Boy, CREW, Helen
True Annals of Fairyland, RHYS, Ernest
True Bear Stories, MILLER, Joaquin
True Story of Humpty Dumpty, CHAPIN, Anna
Trumpeter of Krakow, KELLY, Eric
Tumbledown Town, NESBIT, Wilbur
Turn of the Tide, PORTER, Eleanor
Turned-Into's, GORDON, Elizabeth
Twelve Dancing Princesses, QUILLER-COUCH, Sir Arthur
Twenty-One Balloons, DU BOIS, William
Twilight Town, BLAISDELL, Mary F.
Twinkle and Chubbins, BANCROFT, Laura
Twinkle Tales, BANCROFT, Laura
Twinkle Town Tales, EMERY, Carlyle
Twins and Tabiffa, HEWARD, Constance
Two Boys and a Dog, CHIPMAN, Charles P.
Two in a Zoo, DUNHAM, Curtis
Two is a Team, BEIM, Jerrold and Lorraine Levey
Two Jungle Books, KIPLING, Rudyard
Two Little Girls, GARIS, Lilian
Uncle Tom's Cabin, STOWE, Harriet Beecher
Uncle Wiggily, GARIS, Howard
Uncrowned King, WRIGHT, Harold Bell
Under the Greenwood Tree, SHAKESPEARE, William
Under the Lilacs, ALCOTT, Louisa May
Under the Tent of the Sky, BREWSTER, John
Under the Tree, ROBERTS, Elizabeth Madox
Under the Window, GREENAWAY, Kate
Understood Betsy, CANFIELD, Dorothy
Unicorn with Silver Shoes, YOUNG, Ella
Up the Hill, DeANGELI, Marguerite
Us, Old Fashioned Story, MOLESWORTH, Mary Louisa
Valley of Silent Men, CURWOOD, James Oliver
Vanka's Donkey, DAUGHERTY, Sonia
Velveteen Rabbit, BIANCO, Margery
Violin Detectives, LOCKWOOD, Myna
Virginia Davis Ranch Stories, NORTH, Grace May
Voyages of Jack Cartier, AVERILL, Esther H.
Wagtail, GALL, Alice
Wakaima and the Clay Man, KALIBALA, E. B.
Wally Wanderoon and His Story Telling Machine, HARRIS, Joel
Wallypug in Fogland, FARROW, G. E.
Wallypug in London, FARROW, G. E.
Wallypug of Why, FARROW, G. E.
Walter Crane's Picture Books: Volume 1, CRANE, Walter
Walter the Lazy Mouse, FLACK, Marjorie
Watch for a Tall White Sail, BELL, Margaret
Watchbirds, LEAF, Munro
Water Babies, KINGSLEY, Charles

Water Buffalo Children, BUCK, Pearl
Water Carrier's Secrets, CHAMBERS, Maria
Water People, BRONSON, Wilfrid
Watermelon Pete and Other Stories, GORDON, Elizabeth
We Couldn't Leave Dinah, TREADGOLD, Mary
We Didn't Mean to Go to Sea, RANSOME, Arthur
Wee Gillis, LEAF, Munro
Wee Men of Ballywooden, MASON, Arthur
Wee Scotch Piper BRANDEIS, Madeline
Wee Willie Winkie, KIPLING, Rudyard
Weird Islands, BOSSCHERE, Jean de
Well of the Star, GOUDGE, Elizabeth
West Indian Play Days, DALGLIESH, Alice
Westward Ho!, KINGSLEY, Charles
What Happened to Tommy, BRUCE, Mary Grant
When Lighthouses Are Dark, BRILL, Ethel C.
When Patty Went to College, WEBSTER, Jean
When Stubby Got His Start, SCHUETTE, Walter
When the Sandman Comes, KAY, Gertrude Alice
When We Were Very Young, MILNE, A. A.
Where Is Tommy?, SARG, Tony
While the Story Log Burns, BURGESS, Thornton
White Cat, D'AULNEY, Mme.
White Company, DOYLE, A. C.
White Elephant and Other Tales From India, FAULKNER, Georgene
White Fang, LONDON, Jack
White Panther, WALDECK, Theodore J.
White Plume of Navarre, CARTER, Russell Gordon
White Snow, Bright Snow, TRESSELT, Alvin
White Stag, SEREDY, Kate
Whitey Looks for a Job, ROUNDS, Glen
Whitey and Jinglebob, ROUNDS, Glen
Whitey's First Round Up, ROUNDS, Glen
Whitey's Sunday Horse, ROUNDS, Glen
Who Am I?, DOOTSON, Lily Lee
Who Goes There?, LATHROP, Dorothy
Whole Armor, GRAYHAM, Mary
Why Be a Goop?, BURGESS, Gelett
Wiggins for President, BROOKS, Walter R.
Wigwam Stories, JUDD, Mary Catherine
Wild Animals I Have Known, SETON, Ernest Thompson
Wilderness Clearing, EDMONDS, Walter
William and His Lost Kitten, FLACK, Marjorie
Willie Winkie, GOLDING, Harry
Willow Whistle, MEIGS, Cornelia

Wimp and the Woodle, POGANY, Willy
Wind in the Willows, GRAHAME, Kenneth
Winds of Deal, GRISWALD, Lotta
Windy Foot at the County Fair, FROST, Frances
Winged Girl of Knossos, BERRY, Erick
Winged Moccasins, GROSVENOR, Abbie
Wings for Per, D'AULAIRE, Ingri
Wings for the Smiths, DALGLIESH, Alice
Wings Over the Wood Shed, FRISKEY, Margaret
Winnie-the-Pooh, MILNE, A. A.
Winter Holiday, RANSOME, Arthur
Winter Noisy Book, BROWN, Margaret Wise
Winter on the Prairie, CURTIS, Alice
Winterbound, BIANCO, Margery
Wise Gray Cat, HOFMAN, Caroline
With Cap and Bells, DAVIS, Mary Gould
With Cortes the Conqueror, WATSON, Virginia
With Spurs of Gold, GREENE, Frances
Wizard of Oz, BAUM, L. Frank
Woe Begone Little Bear, BURGESS, Thornton
Wonder Book and Tanglewood Tales, HAWTHORNE, Nathaniel
Wonder Book for Boys and Girls, HAWTHORNE, Nathaniel
Wonder Book, THOMPSON, Ruth Plumly
Wonder Clock, PYLE, Howard
Wonderful Adventures of Nils, LAGERFELD, Selma
Wongo and the Wise Old Crow, MOON, Grace and Carl
Wooden Willie, GRUELLE, Johnny
Woodland Elf, EVANS, Florence
Would Be Goods, NESBIT, E.
Wynken, Blynken and Nod and Other Verses, FIELD, Eugene
Yankee Doodle's Cousin, MALCOLMSON, Anne
Yankee Thunder, SHAPIRO, Irwin
Yann and His Island, BRANN, Esther
Yearling, RAWLINGS, Marjorie
Yonie Wondernose, DeANGELI, Marguerite
You Can't Pet A Possum, BONTEMPS, Arna
You Make Your Own Luck, SINGMASTER, Elsie
Young Aunts, DALGLIESH, Alice
Young Fu of the Upper Yangtze, LEWIS, Elizabeth
Young Trajan, MILLER, Elizabeth C.
Your Manners are Showing, BETZ, Betty
Zodiac Town, TURNER, Nancy Byrd
Zuni Indian Tales, NUSBAUM, Aileen

Back to Buckeye, HALL, Esther Greenacre
Backward Day, KRAUSS, Ruth
Backward Swing, TUCKER, Charlotte
Bad Little Rabbit and Other Stories, BIGHAM, Madge A.
Ballads for Little Folk, CARY, Alice and Phoebe
Banana Tree House, GARRARD, Philip
Bandit Jim Crow, BANCROFT, Laura
Barney and the Donkey, CASSERLEY, Anne
Barney's Adventure, AUSTIN, Margot
Baron Munchausen's Narrative of His Marvelous Travels and Campaigns in Russia, MUNCHAUSEN, Baron von
Bastable Children, NESBIT, E.
Battalion Captain, WYMAN, L. P.
Battle Lanterns, ALLEN, Merritt Parmelee
Beasts and Men, Folk Tales Collected in Flanders, DeBOSSCHERE, Jean
Beauty and the Beast, BOYLE, Eleanor
Bee in Her Bonnet, KRISTOFFERSEN, Eva M.
Being Little in Cambridge When Everyone Else Was Big, ABBOTT, Eleanor Hallowell
Belinda Balloon and the Big Wind, HONNESS, Elizabeth
Belle's Pink Boots, MATHEWS, Joanna
Bells of Amsterdam, HOLBERG, Ruth
Bengal Fairy Tales, BRADLEY-BIRT, F. B.
Benny and His Birds, EVERS, Helen and Alf
Benny and the Penny, LENSKI, Lois
Beth's Wonder-Winter, a Story, TAGGART, Marion Ames
Betsy Goes A-Visiting, QUIGG, Jane
Betsy Leicester's Christmas, JEWETT, Sarah Orne
Big Aviation Book for Boys, FRENCH, Joseph Lewis
Big Brown Bear, DUPLAIX, Georges
Big World, KRAUSS, Ruth
Billy Robin and His Neighbors, JUDSON, Clara Ingram
Billy Stories, LOVETT, Eva
Billy's Picture, REY, Margaret and H. A.
Bimbi, Stories for Children, OUIDA
Birch and the Star, THORNE-THOMSEN, Gudrun
Bird Book, PEAT, Fern Bisel
Birds' Christmas Tree, BROCK, Emma
Birthday of Obash, CHALMERS, Audrey
Birthdays for Robin, SEWELL, Helen
Black Gull Rock, GERARD, Morice
Black Rain, ALLEN, Merritt Parmelee
Black Tales for White Children, STIGAND, Capt. Chauncey H.
Blackbeard Buccaneer, PAINE, Ralph D.
Blackfellow Bundi, HARRIS, Leila and Kilroy
Blacky, BARTRUG, C. M.

Blossoms by the Wayside, VanNORSTRAND, Frances
Blowing Weather, McINTYRE, John T.
Blue Barns, SEWELL, Helen
Blue Bonnet Keeps House, JACOBS, Caroline E.
Blue Dowry, UPDEGRAFF, Florence Maule
Blue Horizon, THOMPSON, Mary Wolfe
Blue Nets and Red Sails, PRESTON, Helen Bradley
Blue Poetry Book, LANG, Andrew
Blue Ridge Billy, LENSKI, Lois
Blue-Eyed Lady, MOLNAR, Ferenc
Blueberry Corners, LENSKI, Lois
Blueberry Muffin, THOMPSON, Mary Wolfe
Bluebird House, JOHNSON, Ida Lee
Bluebonnets for Lucinda, SAYERS, Frances Clarke
Boat Children of Canton, WARD, Marion B.
Boat Club, OPTIC, Oliver
Boat for People, POLITI, Leo
Bob Hazard, Dam Builder, BRANDT, Carl
Bob Son of Battle, OLLIVANT
Bonnie May, DODGE, Louis
Bonnie Prince Fetlar, SAUNDERS, Marshall
Book for Children, RICHARDSON, Frederick
Book of Cheerful Cats and Other Animated Animals, FRANCIS, J. G.
Book of Christmas Carols, GRAHAM, Mary Nancy
Book of Dragons, FULLER, O. Muriel
Book of Elves and Fairies, OLCOTT, Frances Jenkins
Book of Myths, BULFINCH
Book of Nah-Wee, MOON, Grace
Book of Pirates, PYLE, Howard
Book of Ruth, CHASE, Mary
Boom Town Boy, LENSKI, Lois
Boots of the Holly-Tree Inn, DICKENS, Charles
Border Girl, FOX, Genevieve
Both Sides of the Border, HENTY, George Alfred
Bottle Imp, TAGGART, Marion Ames
Box with Red Wheels, PETERSHAM, Maud and Miska
Boy and His Box, LEE, Mrs. Frank
Boy Artists: Sketches of the Childhood, FOA, Eugenie
Boy Editor, KIRKMAN, Winifred
Boy Emigrants, BROOKS, Noah
Boy Heroes in Fiction, McFEE, Inez
Boy Knight of Reims, LOWNSBERY, Eloise
Boy Knight, HENTY, George Alfred
Boy of the First Empire, BROOKS, E. S.
Boy Scouts of Black Eagle Patrol, QUIRK, Leslie W.
Boy Scouts on the Trail, GARTH, John
Boy Settlers, BROOKS, Noah
Boy Who Used to be Scared of the Dark, LEAF, Munro
Boy's Life of Edison, MEADOWCROFT, William

Boy's Vacation Abroad, KING, C. F. Jr.
Boyhood of Lincoln, BUTTERWORTH, Hezekiah
Boys' Book of Airmen, CRUMP, Irving
Boys' Book of Cowboys, CRUMP, Irving
Boys' Book of Mounted Police, CRUMP, Irving
Boys' Book of Exploration, JENKS, Tudor
Breaking Away, OPTIC, Oliver
Brian of the Mountain, CASSERLEY, Anne
Brian's Victory, PHILLIPS, Ethel Calvert
Brier Rabbit Stories From Uncle Remus, HARRIS, Joel Chandler
Brimful Book, PIPER, Watty
Brother Jonathan, BUTTERWORTH, Hezekiah
Brownie Flat Tail Builds a House, CHAFFEE, Allen
Brownie Numbers Combine Work and Fun, NIELSEN, Martin
Brownies and Rose-Leaves, WHITE, Roma
Brownies Around the World, COX, Palmer
Brownies Hush Fair, ADSHEAD, Gladys L.
Brownies Through the Union, COX, Palmer
Brushwood Boy, KIPLING, Rudyard
Bubbles, NEWBERRY, Fannie E.
Buckboard Stranger, MEADER, Stephen
Bud, MUNRO, Neil
Builder of Bridges, STEWART, Anna Bird
Building a House in Sweden, CAUTLEY, Marjorie
Bunny Tales, BLAND, R. Nesbit
Burial of the First Born, a Tale for Children, ALDEN, Joseph
Burning Daylight, LONDON, Jack
Burro of Angelitos, CHURCH, Peggy Pond
Butter-Scotia, or A Cheap Trip to Fairy Land, PARRY, Judge
Butterfly Hunters, MURRAY-AARON, Dr. Eugene
Buttons, ROBINSON, Tom
By the Christmas Fire, CROTHERS, Samuel McChord
By Wagon and Flatboat, MEADOWCROFT, Enid
Calico, PHILLIPS, Ethel Calvert
California Fairy Tales, SHANNON, Monica
Camp in the Foothills, CASTLEMON, Harry
Campfire Stories, CHELEY, F. A.
Candy Box, STEWART, Anna Bird
Canoemates, MUNROE, Kirk
Canterbury Tales, CHAUCER, Geoffrey
Captain Bayley's Heir, HENTY, George Alfred
Captain January, RICHARDS, Laura
Captain Jinks, Hero, CROSBY, Ernest
Captain June, RICE, Alice Hegan
Captain Juniper, HUBBARD, Margaret Ann
Captain's Toll-Gate, STOCKTON, Frank
Captured Santa Claus, PAGE, Thomas Nelson
Carcajou, MONTGOMERY, Rutherford
Cardigan, CHAMBERS, Robert W.

Careless Chicken, KRAKEMSIDES, Baron
Carl and the Cotton Gin, BASSETT, Sara Ware
Carlotta: A Story of the San Gabriel Mission, FOX, Frances Margaret
Carrot Seed, KRAUSS, Ruth
Carrots, Just a Little Boy, MOLESWORTH, Mrs.
Castaway Island, NEWBERRY, Perry
Casting Away of Mrs. Lecks and Mrs. Aleshine, STOCKTON, Frank
Castle Inn, WEYMAN, Stanley J.
Catcher Craig, MATTHEWSON, Christy
Catching Up with the Circus, CROWNFIELD, Gertrude
Cats for Kansas, LE GRAND, Henderson
Catty Atkins Riverman, KELLAND, Clarence Budington
Cecily (Elf Goldihair), HELM, Clementine
Cedar Deer, BURBANK, Addison
Cedar's Boy, MEADER, Stephen
Cedardale, or, the Peacemakers, ARTHUR, T. S.
Century of Kate Greenaway, MOORE, Anne Carroll
Century World's Fair Book for Boys and Girls, JENKS, Tudor
Champion, CRADDOCK, Charles Egbert
Chaplet of Pearls, YONGE, Charlotte
Charles and His Lamb, SAUNDERS, Marshall
Charlie and His Kitten, MAXWELL, Violet
Chatterlings in Wordland, LIPMAN, Michael
Chaucer for Children, HAWEIS, Mrs. H. R.
Cherrystones, FARJEON, Eleanor
Chi-Wee of the Desert, MOON, Grace
Chicken Little Count-to-ten, FRISKEY, Margaret
Chico's Three-Ring School, BURKE, Stella M.
Child Stories from the Masters, MENEFRE, Maud
Child's Book of Abridged Wisdom, HAROLD, Childe
Child's Book of Modern Stories, SKINNER, Ada
Child's Book of Myths, PRICE, Margaret
Child's Book of Old Verses, SMITH, Jessie Willcox
Child's Garden of Verses, STEVENSON, R. L.
Child's Garden of Verses, PEAT, Fern Bisel
Child's History of the World, HILLYER, V. M.
Childhood of Ji-Shib the Ojibwa, JENKS, Albert Ernest
Children Make a Garden, JENKINS, Dorothy H.
Children of Ancient Rome, LAMPREY, L.
Children of Dickens, CROTHERS, Samuel McChord
Children of Japan, BURKE, Stella M.
Children of the Castle, MOLESWORTH, Mrs.
Children of the Covered Wagon, CARR, Mary Jane
Children of the Desert, DODGE, Louis
Children of the Forest, YOUNG, Egerton R.
Children of the Soil, BURGLON, Nora
Children of the White House, CAVANAH, Frances
Children on the Top Floor, RHOADES, Nina

Diddie, Dumps, and Tot, PYRNELLE, Louise Clarke
Dig Here!, ALLEN, Gladys
Dixie School Girl, JACKSON, Gabrielle
Dobry, SHANNON, Monica
Dog of Flanders, OUIDA
Doll House at World's End, KNIGHT, Marjorie
Doll Land Stories, BYINGTON, Eloise
Doll who Came Alive, TREGARTHEN, Enys
Doll's Family Album, KING, Edna Knowles
Dolly Dimples and Billy Bounce, DRAYTON, Grace
Dombey and Son, DICKENS, Charles
Don Quixote of the Mancha, PARRY, Judge
Donkey from Dorking, NEILSON, Frances Fullerton
Donkey Goes Visiting, LYNCH, Patricia
Dorothy and Her Friends, KIRK, Ellen Olney
Dorothy Deane, KIRK, Ellen Olney
Dorothy Q, HOLMES, Oliver W.
Dotty Dolly's Tea Party, WHEELER, Marguerite and Willard
Dove in the Eagle's Nest, YONGE, Charlotte
Down the Bright Stream, WATKINS-PITCHFORD, Denys
Down the Mountain, CREDLE, Ellis
Down the Ravine, CRADDOCK, Charles Egbert
Dozen Dogs or So, ALDIN, Cecil
Dragon and the Raven, HENTY, George Alfred
Dragonfly of Zuni, MALKUS, Alida Sims
Dream Children and Child Angel, LAMB, Charles
Dream Fox Story Book, WRIGHT, Mabel Osgood
Dreamland Shores, AULT, Norman
Duck and the Kangaroo and Other Nonsense Rhymes, LEAR, Edward
Dude Ranch, PEET, Creighton
Dulce's Promise, SCANNELL, Florence and Edith
Dunderpate, BAKER, Margaret
Dutch Cheese, DeLaMARE, Walter
Dutch Courage and Other Stories, LONDON, Jack
Early Adventures of Peacham Grew, HELTON, Roy
Early Lessons, EDGEWORTH, Maria
Early Life of Mr. Man, SMITH, E. Boyd
East O' the Sun and West O' the Moon, RASMUSSEN, Margrete
East o' the Sun and West o' the Moon, THORNE-THOMSEN, Gudrun
Eastward Sweeps the Current, MALKUS, Alida Sims
Eddie and the Fire Engine, HAYWOOD, Carolyn
Edith Prescott, MARSHALL, Emma
Editha's Burglar, BURNETT, Frances
Edra of the Islands, MEDARY, Marjorie
Egbert and His Marvelous Adventures, GILBERT, Paul
Eight Little Indians, LOVELL, Josephine
Eight O'Clock Stories, ANDERSON, Robert Gordon

Elephant's Child, KIPLING, Rudyard
Elephants, ROBINSON, W. W.
Elfin Songs of Sunland, KEELER, Charles
Elin's Amerika, DeANGELI, Marguerite
Elmer Buys a Circus, GILBERT, Paul
Enchanted Admiral, PRICE, Edith Ballinger
Enchanted Castle, NESBIT, E.
Enchanted Castle, HARTWELL, James
End of Black Dog, MOORE, David William
Engines and Brass Bands, MILLER, Olive Beaupre
Enid Blyton's Treasury, BLYTON, Enid
Eric, or Little by Little, FARRAR, Frederic W.
Eternal Masculine, ANDREWS, Mary
Every Dog Has His Say, ANTHONY, Edward
Ezekiel, GARNER, Elvira
Ezra the Elephant, BARROWS, Marjorie
Fabulous Flight, LAWSON, Robert
Fair Play, LEAF, Munro
Fairies Up-to-Date, ANTHONY, Edward
Fairy Alphabet as Used by Merlin, MacKINSTRY, Elizabeth
Fairy Babies, SMITH, Laura Rountree
Fairy Flowers, NEWMAN, Isadora
Fairy Tales from India, PYLE, Katherine
Fairy Tales that Never Grow Old, PIPER, Watty
Fairy Tales Told by Seven Travelers, BELASCO, David
Fairy Tales, MARTIN, John
Falconer's Son, MAYER, Albert
Family at Misrule, TURNER, Ethel
Famous Fairy Tales, PIPER, Watty
Fancy Be Good, CHALMERS, Audrey
Fannie Farmer Junior Cook Book, PERKINS, Wilma Lord
Fanny Grant Among the Indians, OPTIC, Oliver
Far Over the Sea, BIALIK, H. N.
Farm Book: Bob and Betty, SMITH, E. Boyd
Farm Boy, STONG, Phil
Farm Stories, JACKSON, K. and B.
Farmer Brown and the Birds, FOX, Frances Margaret
Fatapoufs and Thinifers, MAUROIS, Andre
Father Gander's Melodies, SAMUELS, Adelaide
Father's Big Improvements, EMERSON, Caroline
Favorite Stories of Famous Children, WILLSON, Dixie
Favorite Tales of Long Ago, GALE, Leah
Feather, HUEFFER, Ford H. Madox
Fiddlers Fair, JUSTUS, May
Field and Forest Friends, HAWKES, Clarence
Fife and Drum at Louisbourg, OXLEY, J. MacDonald
Fight for the Pueblo, CANNON, Cornelia James
Financie and Other Stories from Real Life, CORSELIUS, Cornelia
Fire Eye, LINDMAN, Maj
Firelight Fairy Book, BESTON, Henry

First Thanksgiving, BARKSDALE, Lena
First the Flower, Then the Fruit, LUCAS, Jannette May
Five Little Finger Stories, WARNER, Lucy
Five Little Playmates, a Book of Finger-play, GAY, Romney
Five on a Merry-go-Round, McSWIGAN, Marie
Flamingo Arrow, MOON, Carl
Flamingo Feather, MUNROE, Kirk
Flight of Fancy, HONNESS, Elizabeth
Flock of Girls and Boys, PERRY, Nora
Flock of Girls, PERRY, Nora
Flop-Eared Hound, CREDLE, Ellis
Flying Blackbirds, BURTIS, Thomson
Flying Carpet, ASQUITH, Cynthia
Flying Locomotive, DuBOIS, William Pene
Flying Scotsman, CROCKFORD, Doris
Flying Ship, FAULKNER, Georgene
Folk Tales of Flanders, DeBOSSCHERE, Jean
Folly for the Wise, WELLS, Carolyn
Forest Friends, PEAT, Fern Bisel
Forest Friends, PEAT, Fern Bisel
Fork in the Road, PRICE, Edith Ballinger
Fortune of the Indies, PRICE, Edith Ballinger
Forty Good-Morning Tales, FYLEMAN, Rose
Four Aces, BURTIS, Thomson
Four and Twenty Blackbirds, FISH, Helen Dean
Four Cousins, ZWILGMEYER, Dikken,
Four Stories that Never Grow Old, PEAT, Fern Bisel
Four Times Once Upon a Time, BAKER, Margaret
Four Young Explorers, OPTIC, Oliver
Fraidy Cat, BARROWS, Marjorie
Franconia Stories, ABBOTT, Jacob
Frank Wildman's Adventures on Land and Water, GERSTAECKER, Frederick
Free River, LOCKWOOD, Myna
French Canada: Pictures and Stories, BOSWELL, Hazel
Frenzied Prince, COLUM, Padraic
Freshman Dorn, Pitcher, QUIRK, Leslie W.
Friends from My Garden, PRATT, Anna
Friends in Strange Garments, UPJOHN, Anna Milo
Friends of Diggeldy Dan, NORWOOD, Edwin
Frills and Thrills, GALLAGHER, Louise Barnes
From Boston to Baltimore, Patty Gray's Journey, DALL, Caroline
From the Horn of the Moon, MASON, Arthur
From Now to Adam, LANGSTAFF, John Brett
Fruits of the Earth, LUCAS, Jannette May
Fugitive Freshman, PAINE, Ralph D.
Fun With Music, NELSON, Mary Jarman
Fun With Paper Dolls, LEE, Tina
Funny Noise, GAY, Romney
Fur-Seal's Tooth, MUNROE, Kirk

Fuzzy Wuzz Meets the Ranger, CHAFFEE, Allen
Fuzzy Wuzz, CHAFFEE, Allen
Gabby Gaffer, JUSTUS, May
Galopoff, the Talking Pony, JENKS, Tudor
Garth, Able Seaman, PRICE, Edith Ballinger
Gaston and Josephine in America, DUPLAIX, Georges
Gaston and Josephine, DUPLAIX, Georges
Gay, a Shetland Sheepdog, JOHNSON, Margaret
Georgina Finds Herself, WATKINS, Shirley
Gerrit and the Organ, VanSTOCKUM, Hilda
Get-A-Way and Hary Janos, PETERSHAM, Maud and Miska
Ghost Gables, WIRT, Mildred
Ghost Town Adventure, MONTGOMERY, Rutherford
Giant Mountain, NEILSON, Frances Fullerton
Gift of the Golden Cup, LAWRENCE, Isabelle
Gigi, FOSTER, Elizabeth
Gilbert the Page, KYLE, Elizabeth
Gingerbread Boy, Fairy Tales from the World Over, FAULKNER, Georgene
Gingerbread Man, PEAT, Fern Bisel
Girl Can Dream, CAVANNA, Betty
Girl Heroines in Fiction, McFEE, Inez
Girl Without a Country, POSTON, Martha Lee
Girls in Africa, BERRY, Erick
Give Me a River, PALMER, Elizabeth
Gloomy the Camel, PAULL, Grace
Gloucester Boy, HOLBERG, Ruth
Go, Champions of Light, OLCOTT, Frances Jenkins
Gold for the Grahams, FULLER, Alice Cook
Gold He Found, CLAUDY, Carl. H.
Gold of Glenaree, LAVERTY, Maura
Golden Almanac, BENNETT, Dorothy
Golden Basket, BEMELMANS, Ludwig
Golden Boys Rescued by Radio, WYMAN, L. P.
Golden Flash, McNEER, May
Golden Hair, ARASON, Steingrimur
Golden Star of Halich, KELLY, Eric
Golden Trumpets, THOMPSON, Blanche Jennings
Golden Windows, RICHARDS, Laura
Goldsmith of Florence, GIBSON, Katharine
Golliwog in War, UPTON, Bertha
Golliwog's Bicycle Club, UPTON, Bertha
Golliwog's Polar Adventures, UPTON, Bertha
Good Fairy, STEWART, Grace Bliss
Good Luck Horse, CHAN, Chih-Yi
Good Stories for Great Holidays, OLCOTT, Frances Jenkins
Good Wind and Good Water, OSBORNE, Nancy Cabot
Gooseberry Jones, GERBER, Will
Gourd Fiddle, COOKE, Grace MacGowan
Grandpa and the Tiger, HEWARD, Constance

Granny Goose, RAE, John
Granny's Story Box, LUCAS, Marie Seymour
Granny's Wonderful Chair, BROWNE, Frances
Gray Lady and the Birds, WRIGHT, Mabel Osgood
Gray Nosed Kitten, MASON, Miriam
Great Geppy, DuBOIS, William Pene
Great Jug, RAPHAEL, Arthur M.
Green Cockade, ALLEN, Merritt Parmelee
Green Treasure, FOX, Genevieve
Greylock and the Robbins, ROBINSON, Tom
Grimm's Fairy Tales, OLCOTT, Frances Jenkins
Grocery Mouse, CLYMER, Eleanor
Growing Story, KRAUSS, Ruth
Gypsy's Sowing and Reaping, PHELPS, Elizabeth Stuart
H. M. S. Pinafore, WHEELER, Opal
Half Past Seven Stories, ANDERSON, Robert Gordon
Hand in the Picture, KELLY, Eric
Handel at the Court of Kings, WHEELER, Opal
Hans Brinker, DODGE, Mary Mapes
Hans Christian of Elsinore, KRISTOFFERSEN, Eva M.
Hansel and Gretel and Other Stories, GRIMM Bros.
Happy Children, PRATT, Ella Farman
Happy Day, KRAUSS, Ruth
Happy Days Out West, CRANE, Edith
Happy Heart Family, GERSON, Virginia
Happy Hours, DANIELS, Elizabeth
Happy Little Family, CAUDILL, Rebecca
Happy Mannikin in Manners Town, SMITH, Laura Rountree
Happy Time Fancies, BENEDICT, Emma
Happy Venture, PRICE, Edith Ballinger
Harding's Luck, NESBIT, E.
Harry and Lucy, Concluded, EDGEWORTH, Maria
Hat-Tub Tale, EMERSON, Caroline
Haunted Mine, CASTLEMON, Harry
Haven for the Brave, YATES, Elizabeth
Haverhill Herald, HALL, Esther Greenacre
Hawaiian Yesterdays, MYHRE, Ethelyn
Head Coach, PAINE, Ralph D.
Heartsease, or the Brother's Wife, YONGE, Charlotte
Heavenly Tenants, MAXWELL, William
Helen in the Editor's Chair, WHEELER, Ruthe S.
Helping the Weatherman, KAY, Gertrude
Helter Skelters, DAULTON, George
Hen That Kept House, BROCK, Emma
Henner's Lydia, DeANGELI, Marguerite
Hepatica Hawks, FIELD, Rachel
Herbert the Lion, NEWBERRY, Clare Turlay
Here-to-Yonder Girl, HALL, Esther Greenacre
Herman the Brave Pig, MASON, Miriam
Hero of the Lake, LIVINGSTONE, W. P.
Heroes and Holidays, CUNNINGHAM, Virginia
Hickory Lane, QUIGG, Jane

High Timber, NELSON, Rhoda
High Up in a Penthouse, ANDREWS, Virginia
Highway Past Her Door, THOMPSON, Mary Wolfe
Hilda's Mascot, IRELAND, Mary E.
Hildegarde's Home, RICHARDS, Laura
Hindu Fables for Little Children, MUKERJI, Dhan Gopal
His Lordship's Puppy, ELMSLIE, Theodora C.
History Can be Fun, LEAF, Munro
History of the United States, BUTTERWORTH, Hezekiah
Ho-Ming, Girl of New China, LEWIS, Elizabeth Foreman
Hole in the Wall, HARNONCOURT, Rene d'
Holly Boughs, WEATHERLY, Fred E.
Holly-Tree, DICKENS, Charles
Hominy and the Blunt-Nosed Arrow, MASON, Miriam
Honey on a Raft, PALTENGHI, Madalena
Honey the City Bear, PALTENGHI, Madalena
Hoosier School Master, EGGLESTON, Edward
Hootie the Owl, McKENNA, Dolores
Hop, Skip and Jump, Three Little Kittens, LEET, Frank
Horse That Takes the Milk Around, STERLING, Helen
Horses are Folks, ANDERSON, C. W.
House in the Wood, BROOKE, L. Leslie
House of the Misty Star, LITTLE, Frances
House on the River, BAKER, Charlotte
House the Pecks Built, EVERS, Helen and Alf
House Without Windows, FOLLETT, Barbara Newhall
How Bessie Kept House, DOUGLAS, Amanda
How Mr. Dog Got Even, PAINE, Albert Bigelow
How Sammy Went to Coral-Land, ATWATER, Emily Paret
How the Animals Came to the Circus, GALE, Elizabeth
Huffy Wants To Be A Pet, DEIHL, Edna
Hundreds of Pancakes, CHALMERS, Audrey
Hunting of the Snark, CARROLL, Lewis
Hurricane Yank, MONTGOMERY, Rutherford
Hurricane's Children, CARMER, Carl
Hurry-Skurry and Flurry, BUFF, Mary and Conrad
I Discover Columbus, LAWSON, Robert
I Go by Sea, I Go by Land, TRAVERS, P. L.
I Had a Penny, CHALMERS, Audrey
Iceblink, MONTGOMERY, Rutherford
Illustrated Bible Story Book, LOVELAND, Seymour
In and Out, ROBINSON, Tom
In Assyrian Tents, PENDLETON, Louis
In Colonial Times, WILKINS, Mary E.
In Kimono Land, YULE, Emma
In the Brave Days of Old, HALL, Ruth

In the Child's World, POULSSON, Emilie
In the Days of Audubon, BUTTERWORTH, Hezekiah
In the Days of Han, JAGENDORF, M.
In the Days of the Guild, LAMPREY, L.
In the High Valley, COOLIDGE, Susan
In the Land of Diggeldy Dan, NORWOOD, Edwin
In the Mist of the Mountains, TURNER, Ethel
In Wink-A-Way Land, FIELD, Eugene
Incarnation of Krishna Mulvaney, KIPLING, Rudyard
Incubator Baby, BUTLER, Ellis Parker
Indian Captive, LENSKI, Lois
Indians of Yesterday, GRIDLEY, Marion
Inger Johanne's Lively Doings, ZWILGMEYER, Dikken
Irrepressibles, HABBERTON, John
Isla Heron, RICHARDS, Laura
Jack and Jill, ALCOTT, Louisa May
Jack Archer, HENTY, George Alfred
Jack O'Health and Peg O'Joy, HERBEN, Beatrice Slayton, MD
Jack O'Lantern Twins, McCAULEY, Anne M.
Jack-O-Lantern, FORRESTER, Izola
Jamaica Johnny, HADER, Berta and Elmer
Jamie and the Dump Truck, JOHNSTON, Eileen
Jamie and the Fire Engine, JOHNSTON, Eileen
Jan and Betje, HALL, May Emery
Jane Lends a Hand, WATKINS, Shirley
Jane Withers, Her Life Story, JANE WITHERS Books
Jane, Joseph and John, BERGERGREN, Ralph
Janey, FOX, Frances Margaret
Janie Belle, TARRY, Ellen
Jeanne-Marie Goes to Market, SARI
Jerry and the Pony Express, TOUSEY, Sanford
Jerry Jake Carries On, JUSTUS, May
Jewel Story Book, EVANS, Florence A.
Jeweled Toad, JOHNSTON, Isabel M.
Jim Davis, MASEFIELD, John
Jim of Hellas, RICHARDS, Laura
Jimmy and Jemima, SEWELL, Helen
Jo's Boys and How They Turned Out, ALCOTT, Louisa May
Joan and the Three Deer, MEDARY, Marjorie
Joan's Door, FARJEON, Eleanor
Joan: Just Girl, GARIS, Lilian C.
Jobie, GARRETT, Helen
Jock Barefoot, LINDSAY, Maud
Jock the Scot, ROSMAN, Alice Grant
Joey and Patches, a Tale of Two Kittens, JOHNSON, Margaret
Johnny Gruelle's Golden Book, GRUELLE, Johnny
Johnny Blossom, ZWILGMEYER, Dikken,
Johnny Cake, JACOBS, Joseph
JoJo, BARROWS, Marjorie

Jolita of the Jungle, PETERSON, Alice F.
Jolly Book for Boys and Girls, OLCOTT, Frances Jenkins
Jolly Jingle Book, JACKSON, Leroy
Jolly Old Shadow Man, KAY, Gertrude
Journey in Search of Christmas, WISTER, A. L.
Juanita, POLITI, Leo
Judy's Journey, LENSKI, Lois
Julian Mortimer, CASTLEMON, Harry
Jumping Lions of Borneo, DUNNE, J. W.
Jumping-Off Place, McNEELY, Marian Hurd
Jungle Babies, KAIGH-EUSTACE, Edyth
Jungle Man and His Animals, WELLS, Carveth
Junior Cup, FRENCH, Allen
Just Being Happy, GROVER, Edwin Osgood
Kamaiwea, the Coeur d'Alene, McGEORGE, Alice Sutton
Kate Douglas Wiggin as her Sister Knew Her, SMITH, Nora A.
Katie's Work, MARSHALL, Emma
Katy No-Pocket, PAYNE, Emmy
Kees and Kleintje, KING, Marian
Kees, KING, Marian
Kelp, Story of the Isles of Shoals, ALLEN, Willis
Kersti and Saint Nicholas, VanSTOCKUM, Hilda
Key to Betsy's Heart, IVES, Sarah Noble
Kiddie Rhymes, HAYS, Margaret
King Charles, CHEEVER, Harriet
King Tom and the Runaways, PENDLETON, Louis
Kings and Queens, FARJEON, Eleanor
Kipling's Stories for Boys, KIPLING, Rudyard
Kitten's Tale, CHALMERS, Audrey
Kittens and Puppies, NEWTON, Ruth E.
Knight of Liberty, BUTTERWORTH, Hezekiah
Knuckles Down, MARTIN, Fran
Kobboltozo, Sequel to Last of the Huggermuggers, CRANCH, Christopher
Kristie and the Colt And the Others, BROCK, Emma
Ladder of Rickety Rungs, O'DONNELL, T. C.
Lady Jane, JAMISON, Mrs. C. V.
Ladybug! Ladybug!, FRY, Rosalie K.
Lances of Lynwood, YONGE, Charlotte
Land and Sea Tales for Boys and Girls, KIPLING, Rudyard
Land from the Sea, POTTER, Edna
Land of Long Ago, HALL, Eliza Calvert
Land of Pluck, DODGE, Mary Mapes
Land of Whatsit, WHITE, Billy
Last of the Huggermuggers, CRANCH, Christopher
Last of the Thundering Herd, NEAL, Bigelow
Lazaro in the Pueblos, CANNON, Cornelia James
Least One, SAWYER, Ruth
Legends of Number Nip, LEMON, Mark

Legends of the Seven Seas, PRICE, Margaret Evans

Leo's Whaling Voyage, HOFFMAN, F.

Let's Do Better, LEAF, Munro

Let's Go Outdoors, HUNTINGTON, Harriet E.

Let's Go Round the World with Bob and Betty, SOWERS, Phyllis Ayer

Let's Go to the Desert, HUNTINGTON, Harriet E.

Let's Go to the Seashore, HUNTINGTON, Harriet E.

Let's Make Believe We're Soldiers, GARIS, Lilian C.

Let's Play Fireman, LOWE, Edith

Let's Play Postman, LOWE, Edith

Let's Play Store, LOWE, Edith

Let's Read About Australia, HARRIS, Leila and Kilroy

Let's Read About Canada, HARRIS, Leila and Kilroy

Letters to Channy, WASHBURNE, Heluiz

Letty's Good Luck, GRIFFITH, Helen

Level Land, DeJONG, Dola

Life and Adventures of Peter Wilkins, PALTOCK, Robert

Light-House Children Abroad, CROWNINSHIELD, Mrs. Schuyler

Lin Foo and Lin Ching, SOWERS, Phyllis Ayer

Linsey Woolsey, TUDOR, Tasha

Lion of St. Mark, HENTY, George Alfred

Lions 'n' Elephants 'n' Everything, SMITH, E. Boyd

Little Appaloosa, HADER, Berta and Elmer

Little Aunt, TAGGART, Marion Ames

Little Auto, LENSKI, Lois

Little Black Eyes, KENT, Karlene

Little Black Hen, DEIHL, Edna

Little Black Sambo, PEAT, Fern Bisel

Little Book of Bedtime Stories, BROWN, Jeanette Perkins

Little Book of Tribune Verse, FIELD, Eugene

Little Boy with the Big Apples, MOESCHLIN, Elsa

Little Brown Jug, NICHOLSON, Meredith

Little Carolina Blue Bonnet, PUGH, Mabel

Little Champion, RIGGS, Ida Berry

Little Chap, ANDERSON, Robert Gordon

Little Cockney, a Story for Girls, GAYE, Selina

Little Duke, YONGE, Charlotte

Little Eddie, HAYWOOD, Carolyn

Little Elephant, WILLIAMSON, Hamilton

Little Engine that Could, LENSKI, Lois

Little Fanny's Journal, TYTLER, M. Fraser

Little Fire Engine, LENSKI, Lois

Little Firemen, NEWTON, Ruth E.

Little Folk in Green, WRIGHT, Henrietta Christian

Little Folks from Etiquette Town, SMITH, Laura Rountree

Little Folks of Other Lands, PIPER, Watty

Little Freckled Person, DAVIES, Mary Carolyn

Little Gardeners, MORGENSTERN, Elizabeth

Little Girl at Capernaum, BLYTON, Enid

Little Girl of Nineteen Hundred, LENSKI, Lois

Little Girl Who Curtsied, BAKER, Margaret

Little Gold Nugget, COOPER, Frederick Tabor

Little Goody Two Shoes, PEAT, Fern Bisel

Little Gorky of the Black Swans, BRADDELL, Maurice

Little Green Cart, McNEIL, Marion

Little Grey Rabbit and the Weasels, UTTLEY, Alison

Little Grey Rabbit's Party, UTTLEY, Alison

Little Hannibal, BAILEY, Carolyn

Little Herder in Spring, CLARK, *Ann Nolan*

Little Heroes of Hartford, CROSS, Genevieve

Little House in the Woods, HUNT, Clara Whitehall

Little House on Wheels, HAYES, Marjorie

Little Jonathan, MASON, Miriam

Little Kitten That Would Not Wash Its Face, DEIHL, Edna

Little Knight of Labor, COOLIDGE, Susan

Little Knight of the X Bar B, MAULE, Mary K.

Little Ladies, MILMAN, Helen

Little Lost Sioux, RAABE, Martha

Little Lulu and Her Pals, MARGE

Little Magic Horse, ERSHOFF, Peter

Little Match Man, BARZINI, Luigi

Little Mermaid, ANDERSEN, Hans Christian

Little Minister, BARRIE, James

Little Miss Ducky-Daddles, McCANDLISH, Edward

Little Miss Wardlaw, GRAY, Louisa M.

Little Moo and the Circus, STERLING, Helen

Little Mossback Amelia, FOX, Frances Margaret

Little Mr. Thimblefinger and His Queer Country, HARRIS, Joel Chandler

Little Mr. Van Vere of China, CHEEVER, Harriet

Little Old Woman Carries On, NEWELL, Hope

Little Old Woman Who Used Her Head, NEWELL, Hope

Little Peachling, FAULKNER, Georgene

Little Pierre and Big Peter, OGDEN, Ruth

Little Plays for Little Players, BLAIR, Matilda

Little Postman, NEWTON, Ruth E.

Little Princess in the Wood, OLFERS, Sibylle

Little Princess, BURNETT, Frances

Little Queen of Hearts, OGDEN, Ruth

Little Rabbit that Would Not Eat, DEIHL, Edna

Little Rag Doll, PHILLIPS, Ethel Calvert

Little Red Riding Hood and the Big Bad Wolf, DISNEY Studios

Little Red Riding Hood, FRIEND, Esther

Little Robinson Crusoe of Paris, FOA, Eugenie

Little Robinson Crusoe, FOX, Charles Donald

Little Rosebud, HARRADEN, Beatrice

Little Rough Rider, JENKS, Tudor

Little Sally Dutcher, PROCTOR, Beth

Little Sally Waters, PHILLIPS, Ethel Calvert

Little Shepherd of Kingdom Come, FOX, John Jr.
Little Sister, MALOT, Hector
Little Skipper, FENN, G. Manville
Little Storekeepers, NEWTON, Ruth E.
Little Tee-Hee's Big Day, KETO, E.
Little Tommy Stuffin, TINSLEY, Henry
Little Tooktoo, PEARY, Marie
Little Town, HADER, Berta and Elmer
Little Travelers, NEWTON, Ruth E.
Little Ugly Face and Other Indian Tales, COOLIDGE, Florence Claudine
Little Union Scout, HARRIS, Joel Chandler
Little White Chief, NIDA, William Lewis
Lively Adventures of Johnny Ping Wing, PHILLIPS, Ethel Calvert
Liz'beth Ann's Goat, PROVINES, Mary Virginia
Lob Lie-by-the-Fire, EWING, Juliana
Log Schoolhouse on the Columbia, BUTTERWORTH, Hezekiah
Lona of Hollybush Creek, FOX, Genevieve
Long Eared Bat, PEAT, Fern Bisel
Loon Feather, FULLER, Iola
Lost Baron, FRENCH, Allen
Lost Children of the Shoes, NEVIN, Evelyn C.
Lost Indian Magic, MOON, Grace
Lost Log Cabin, FURLONG, May
Lost Prince Albon, PENDLETON, Louis
Lost Slipper, JOHNSON, Ida Lee
Love's Enchantment, FERRIS, Helen
Loyal Hearts and True, OGDEN, Ruth
Loyal Little Red-Coat, OGDEN, Ruth
Lubber's Luck, PRICE, Edith Ballinger
Lucian Goes A-Voyaging, VAUGHN, Agnes Carr
Luck and Pluck, NOLEN, Barbara
Lucky Mrs. Ticklefeather, KUNHARDT, Dorothy
Lucky Orphan, MOORE, Ida Cecil
Lucy's Christmas, MOLLOY, Anne
Lull-aby Land, FIELD, Eugene
Macaroni Tree, AMSDEN, Dora
Madam How and Lady Why, KINGSLEY, Charles
Madam Mary of the Zoo, WESSELHOEFT, Lily
Made-to-Order Stories, LATHROP, Dorothy
Maggie McLaneham, ZOLLINGER, Gulielma
Magic Clothes Pins, LYNCH, Maude Dutton
Magic Doll of Romania, MARIE, Queen of Romania
Magic Ink-Pot, EDITH, Marchioness of Londonberry
Magic Ring and Other Stories, LANG, Andrew
Magic Rug, D'AULAIRE, Ingri and Edgar
Magic Slippers, BLODGETT, Mabel F.
Magic Wand, JENKS, Tudor
Magician for One Day, JENKS, Tudor
Magpie Lane, TURNER, Nancy Byrd
Magyar Fairy Tales, POGANY, Nandor
Making Good, NICHOLS, W. T.

Making Up With Mr. Dog, PAINE, Albert Bigelow
Man Elephant, HARTWELL, James
Manoel and the Morning Star, PECK, Anne Merriman
Manuel's Kite String, AUSTIN, Margot
Marco, the Gypsy Elf, PATTESON, Madge
Margaret Tarrant's Christmas Garland, HEATH, Marian Russell
Maria Rosa, KELSEY, Vera
Mario's Castle, FORBES, Helen Cady
Marjorie and Her Papa, FLETCHER, Robert
Mark Seaworth, KINGSTON, William
Mark Tidd in Sicily, KELLAND, Clarence Budington
Marta Finds the Door, CAVANAH, Frances
Marta, VANCE, Marguerite
Marta, the Doll, LOWNSBERY, Eloise
Martin Hyde, the Duke's Messenger, MASEFIELD, John
Mary and Marcia, Partners, FORBES, Helen Cady
Mary and Sue, STEPHENS, Ruth
Masha, a Little Russian Girl, MAZER, Sonia
Master Roley, HARRADEN, B.
Masterman Ready, MARRYATT, Captain
Matilda and Her Family, MASON, Miriam
Max and Moritz: a Story of Seven Tricks, BUSCH, Wilhelm
Maxims to Music, SPAETH, Sigmund
Melody, Mutton Bone and Sam, DAVIS, Lavinia
Memoirs of a Baby, DASKAM, Josephine
Memoirs of a London Doll Written by Herself, FAIRSTAR, Mrs.
Men of Iron, PYLE, Howard
Men, Maidens and Mantillas, BURKE, Stella M.
Merry Animal Tales, BIGHAM, Madge A.
Merry Go Round, WINDSOR, Mary
Merry Matchmakers, KRISTOFFERSEN, Eva M.
Merry Pranks, JAGENDORF, M.
Merry Shipwreck, DUPLAIX, Georges
Merry-Go-Round of Modern Tales, EMERSON, Caroline
Merry-Go-Round, WELLS, Carolyn
Metropolitan Mother Goose, WATSON, Elizabeth C.
Middle Five, LA FLESCHE, Francis
Middle Sister, MASON, Miriam
Midget and Bridget, HADER, Berta and Elmer
Midnight Folk, MASEFIELD, John
Midnight Revels, DESCH, John
Midsummer-Night's Dream, SHAKESPEARE, William
Mikado, GILBERT AND SULLIVAN
Miller's Wife, COBB, Bertha
Mince Pie Dream and Other Verses, ELTON, Emily D.
Miranda is a Princess, STERNE, Emma Gelders
Miss Bobbie, TURNER, Ethel
Miss De Peyster's Boy, BARRY, Ethelred

Miss Flora McFlimsey's Christmas Eve, MARIANA
Miss Granby's Secret, FARJEON, Eleanor
Miss Muffet's Christmas Party, CROTHERS, Samuel McChord
Miss Navy Junior, MILLER, Jean Dupont
Miss Pert's Christmas Tree, FREDERICKS, J. Paget
Miss Santa Claus of the Pullman, JOHNSTON, Annie Fellows
Mitty and Mr. Syrup, HOLBERG, Ruth
Mitty on Mr. Syrup's Farm, HOLBERG, Ruth
Mixed Pickles, FIELD, Mrs. E. M.
Modern Story Book, WADSWORTH, Wallace
Mog, the Mound Builder, CRUMP, Irving
Mongrel Puppy Book, ALDIN, Cecil
Monkey-Do, PRICE, Margaret Evans
Monty Marine, MacNEIL, Marion Gill
Moral Alphabet, BELLOC, Hilaire
Moral Tales For Young People, EDGEWORTH, Maria
More About Copy-Kitten, EVERS, Helen and Alf
More Tales of the Arabian Nights, OLCOTT, Frances Jenkins
Morgan Dennis Dog Book, DENNIS, Morgan
Mota and the Monkey Tree, PRICE, Margaret Evans
Mother Goose Health Rhymes, BARTRUG, C. M.
Mother Goose Parade, GRUELLE, Justin
Mother Goose, CORY, Fanny
Mother Goose, NEWTON, Ruth E.
Mother Goose, RICHARDSON, Frederick
Mother Goose, GROVER, Eulalie Osgood
Mother Goose, PEAT, Fern Bisel
Mother Goose, TUDOR, Tasha
Mother Stories and More Mother Stories, LINDSAY, Maud
Mother's Hero, DOW, Ethel C.
Mother's Little Girl, TURNER, Ethel
Mother's Little Man, BRINE, Mary D.
Mother's Song, BRINE, Mary D.
Mother-Play and Nursery Songs, FROEBEL, Friedrich
Moufflou and Other Stories, OUIDA
Mountain Born, YATES, Elizabeth
Mountain Girl Comes Home, FOX, Genevieve
Mountain Girl, FOX, Genevieve
Moved Outers, MEANS, Florence
Mr. Billy Buttons, LECKY, Walter
Mr. Blue Peacock, DEIHL, Edna
Mr. Rabbit's Big Dinner, PAINE, Albert Bigelow
Mr. Rabbit, HARRIS, Joel Chandler
Mr. Twigg's Mistake, LAWSON, Robert
Mr. Widdle Waddle Brings the Family, McKENNA, Dolores
Mr. Wind and Madame Rain, MUSSET, Paul de
Mrs. Mouse and her Boys, MOLESWORTH, Mrs.
Mrs. Tree, RICHARDS, Laura

Mrs. Wiggs of the Cabbage Patch, HEGAN, Alice Caldwell
My First Library, EULALIE
My Land and Water Friends, BAMFORD, Mary E.
My Mother is the Most Beautiful Woman in the World, REYHER, Becky
My Village, SMITH, E. Boyd
Mystery of the Laughing Mask, WIRT, Mildred
Name for Obid, PHILLIPS, Ethel Calvert
Nan in the City, HAMLIN, Myra
Nancy Herself, BERRY, Erick
Nancy of Paradise Cottage, WATKINS, Shirley
Nancy Rutledge, PYLE, Katherine
Nancy the Joyous, STOW, Edith
Napoleon Jackson, STUART, Ruth McEnery
Narcissa, or Road to Rome, RICHARDS, Laura
Nearby, YATES, Elizabeth
Needles and Pins, WEATHERLY, Fred E.
Negro Folk Tales, WHITING, Helen Adele
Never No More, LAVERTY, Maura
New Bed-Time Stories, MOULTON, Louise
New Illustrated Book of Favorite Hymns, TENGGREN, Gustaf
New Land, LEVINGER, Elma Ehrlich
New Swiss Family Robinson, WISTER, Owen
New Town in Texas, JOHNSON, Siddie Joe
New Year's Bargain, COOLIDGE, Susan
Nicholas and the Golden Goose, MOORE, Anne Carroll
Nicholas, MOORE, Anne Carroll
Night Before Christmas, NEWTON, Ruth E.
Nightingale House, PALMER, Elizabeth
Nikita, a Story of Russia, PHELPS, Frances Brown
Nils, D'AULAIRE, Ingri and Edgar
Nim and Cum, and the Wonderhead Stories, YALE, Catharine Brooks
No School Friday, MARTIN, Fran
No School Tomorrow, ASHMUN, Margaret
No-Sitch, the Hound, STONG, Phil
Noah and the Rabbit, McKAY, Herbert
Nobody's Girl, MALOT, Hector
Nonsense ABCs, LEAR, Edward
Nonsense Nonsense! JERROLD, Walter
Noodle, LEAF, Munro
Norman and the Nursery School, YOUNG, W. Edward
North Window and Other Poems, FLEXNER, Hortense
Not Really!, FROST, Leslie
Now Open the Box, KUNHARDT, Dorothy
Now or Never, Adventures of Bobby Bright, OPTIC, Oliver
Nurnberg Stove, OUIDA
Nursery Tales Children Love, PIPER, Watty
Nutcracker of Nuremberg, COOKE, Donald

Oh Susannah, HOLBERG, Ruth

Oh, Little Lulu!, MARGE

Ola and Blakken, D'AULAIRE, Ingri and Edgar

Old Fashioned Fairy Tales, WASHBURNE, Marion Foster

Old New York For Young New Yorkers, EMERSON, Caroline

Old Old Tales Retold, RICHARDSON, Frederick

Old Rough the Miser, WESSELHOEFT, Lily

Old Woman and the Sixpence, HADER, Berta and Elmer

Oliver and the Crying Ship, DURANT, Nancy Miles

Oliver Optic's New Story Book, OPTIC, Oliver

On a Rainy Day, FISHER, Dorothy

On Christmas Day in the Morning, RICHMOND, Grace S.

On to Oregon, MORROW, Honore

Once Around the Sun, GRUELLE, Justin

Once in the Year, YATES, Elizabeth

Once There Was a Little Boy, KUNHARDT, Dorothy

Once Upon a Time in Egypt, GERE, Frances Kent

Once Upon a Time, CRAIGIE, Mary

One Hoss Shay, With Its Companion Poems, HOLMES, Oliver W.

One Hundred Animal Stories, CUNNINGHAM, Virginia

One Hundred Best Poems for Boys and Girls, BARROWS, Marjorie

Ood-Le-Uk the Wanderer, LIDE, Alice Alison

Ootah and His Puppy, PEARY, Marie Ahnighito

Orange Winter, MEDARY, Marjorie

Organ Grinders' Garden, BARROWS, Marjorie

Oswald Bastable and Others, NESBIT, E.

Other People's Children, PECKHAM, Betty

Other Side of the Circus, NORWOOD, Edwin

Otherside Book, MITCHELL, Edith

Our Alphabet of Toys, GRUBB, Mary B.

Our Friendly Animals and Whence They Came, SCHMIDT, Earl

Our Little Men and Women, BABYLAND Editors

Our Little Swedish Cousins, COBURN, Claire M.

Our Vegetable Food, MARKS, Edward N.

Out of the Flame, LOWNSBERY, Eloise

Outcast Warrior, MUNROE, Kirk

Outcasts, FRASER, W. A.

Outdoor Handicraft for Boys, HALL, A. Neely

Outdoor Primer, GROVER, Eulalie Osgood

Over the Andes, BUTTERWORTH, Hezekiah

Over the Hill Stories, ANDERSON, Robert Gordon

Overheard in Fairyland, BIGHAM, Madge A.

P-Penny and His Little Red Cart, STONE, Amy Wentworth

Pa Flickinger's Folks, HOOVER, Bessie

Paddy's Christmas, MONSELL, Helen A.

Page Story Book, PAGE, Thomas Nelson

Painted Moccasin, MOON, Carl

Painted Pig, MORROW, Elizabeth

Painted Shield, WIRT, Mildred

Pan and His Pipes and Other Tales for Children, CATHER, Katherine Dunlap

Pancakes for Breakfast, PAULL, Grace

Pandora, NEWBERRY, Clare Turlay

Pansies and Water Lilies, ALCOTT, Louisa May

Parade of Obash, CHALMERS, Audrey

Park Book, ZOLOTOW, Charlotte

Parsifal, ROLLESTON, C. W.

Partners of the Forest Trail, CLAUDY, Carl. H.

Party Twins and their Forty Parties, SMITH, Laura Rountree

Pat the Bunny, KUNHARDT, Dorothy

Patch Pants the Tailor, CHRISTIAN, George

Pattern for Penelope, THOMPSON, Mary Wolfe

Patterns on the Wall, YATES, Elizabeth

Paul and the Printing Press, BASSETT, Sara Ware

Paul Laurence Dunbar and His Song, CUNNINGHAM, Virginia

Paula Goes Away to School, VANCE, Marguerite

Paula, VANCE, Marguerite

Pedie and the Twins, BRYANT, Bernice M.

Pedro, the Angel of Olvera Street, POLITI, Leo

Pee-Gloo: A Little Penguin from the South Pole, DUPLAIX, Georges

Peep-in-the-World, CRICHTON, F. E.

Peeps, the Really Truly Sunshine Fairy, COX-McCORMACK, Nancy

Peggy and the Pony, SEWELL, Helen

Peggy Stewart at Home, JACKSON, Gabrielle

Peggy's Playhouses, HUNT, Clara Whitehall

Pegs of History: A Picture Book of World Dates, FISH, Helen Dean

Penny and Peter, HAYWOOD, Carolyn

Penny Show, DAVIES, Mary Carolyn

Perez the Mouse, COLOMA, Padre Luis

Perhappsy Chaps, THOMPSON, Ruth Plumly

Peter by the Sea, MEADE, Julian R.

Peter on the Min, CLARK, Dorothy

Peter Peppercorn, PHILLIPS, Ethel Calvert

Peter Piper's Pickled Peppers, HUNT, Mabel Leigh

Peter Rabbit and His Ma, FIELD, Louise A.

Peter Rabbit and His Pa, FIELD, Louise A.

Peter Rabbit and the Little Boy, ALMOND, Linda

Peter Rabbit and the Little Girl, ALMOND, Linda

Peter Rabbit and the Tiny Bits, ALMOND, Linda

Peter Rabbit Goes A-Visiting, ALMOND, Linda

Peter Rabbit, NEWTON, Ruth E.

Peter Rabbit, Ruth Newton's Chubby Cubs, NEWTON, Ruth E.

Peter Teeter Stories, SCHWETZKY, Prof. Otto H. L.

Peter the Whaler, KINGSTON, William

Peter, Patter and Pixie, KAY, Gertrude
Pets, PHILLIPS, Henry W.
Phantom of the Forest, HARK, Ann
Phantoms of the Foot-Bridge and Other Stories, CRADDOCK, Charles Egbert
Phoebe Fairchild, LENSKI, Lois
Photography for Young People, JENKS, Tudor
Piccino and Other Child Stories, BURNETT, Frances
Piccino and Other Child Stories, BURNETT, Frances
Piccolo, RICHARDS, Laura
Picnic, TIPPETT, James
Picture Book of Poems, GAY, Romney
Picture Story of Holland, DeJONG, Dola
Picture Tales from the Japanese, SUGIMOTO, Chiyono
Pierre Pidgeon, KINGMAN, Lee
Pigtail of Ah Lee Ben Loo, BENNETT, John
Pilot of the High Sierras, LITTEN, Frederic Nelson
Pilot of the Mayflower, BUTTERWORTH, Hezekiah
Pilot of the North Country, LITTEN, Frederic Nelson
Pilots, Man Your Planes, MASON, Frank W.
Pinafore Picture Book, GILBERT
Pinocchio in Africa, CHERUBINI
Pinocchio Under the Sea, MONGIARDINI-REMBADI
Pint of Judgment, MORROW, Elizabeth
Pioneer Girl, JUDSON, Clara Ingram
Pirate Treasure, WILKINS, Harold T.
Piskey Folk, TREGARTHEN, Enys
Pit Pony, BANNING, Nina
Pitcher Pollock, MATTHEWSON, Christy
Pixy's Holiday Journey, IRELAND, Mary E.
Play Lady, a Story for Other Girls, PRATT, Ella Farman
Playmates in Egypt, LEVINGER, Elma Ehrlich
Poems for Christmas, Easter and New Year's, BUTTERWORTH, Hezekiah
Pointed People, FIELD, Rachel
Polly Peters, QUIGG, Jane
Polly Tucker, Merchant, PENNOYER, Sara
Polly's Secret, NASH, Harriet
Pony Dexter, CHEEVER, Harriet
Pop-Corn and the Peppermint Sticks, CROSS, Genevieve
Popo the Hippopotamus, DUPLAIX, Georges
Poppadilly, CHALMERS, Audrey
Portrait of Jennie, NATHAN, Robert
Pot of Gold, WILKINS, Mary E.
Prairie Anchorage, MEDARY, Marjorie
Prairie Song and Western Story, GARLAND, Hamlin
Pran of Albania, MILLER, Elizabeth
Prayer for Little Things, FARJEON, Eleanor
Presents for Lupe, LATHROP, Dorothy
Pretend Puppy, HATHAWAY, Cynthia
Pretzel, REY, Margaret and H. A.

Prince Yellowtop, PATCH, Kate Whiting
Prince and the Dragons, JENKS, Tudor
Prince and the Page, YONGE, Charlotte
Prince and the Pauper, TWAIN, Mark
Princess and Curdie, MacDONALD, George
Princess of Cozytown, THOMPSON, Ruth Plumly
Princess Rags and Tatters, COMSTOCK, Harriet
Princess Yucatan, LIDE, Alice Alison
Private Pepper, CAVANAH, Frances
Privateers of '76, PAINE, Ralph D.
Prize to the Hardy, WINTER, Alice
Prize Winners' Book of Model Airplanes, CLAUDY, Carl. H.
Pronto and Tonto, KETO, E.
Proud Roxanna, DOW, Ethel C.
Pueblo Girl, CANNON, Cornelia James
Pug Invades the Fifth Column, COOKE, Donald
Puppet Parade, CHIESA, Carol Della
Puppy Dogs and Pussy Cats, NEWTON, Ruth E.
Puritan Adventure, LENSKI, Lois
Purr and Miew, LEET, Frank
Pussy Tip-Toes' Family, SANFORD, Mrs. D. P.
Q-Boat, MASON, Frank W.
Queen Dora, KNOX, Kathleen
Queen Hildegarde, RICHARDS, Laura
Queen Nature's Fairy Helpers, EDGERTON, Alice Craig
Queer Stories About Queer Animals, COX, Palmer
Quest in the North-land, YATES, Elizabeth
Quest of the Golden Condor, KNIGHT, Clayton
Quest of the Sea Otter, CONNOR, Sabra
Rabbit's Nest, MORROW, Elizabeth
Race for a Fortune, HOLLAND, Rupert Sargent
Raft in the Bush, TURNER, Ethel
Raftmates, MUNROE, Kirk
Rag-Doll Jane, PEAT, Fern Bisel
Ragamuffin Marionettes, WARNER, Frances Lester
Raggedy Ann, see GRUELLE, Justin
Railroad Book, Bob and Betty, SMITH, E. Boyd
Rainbows End, HADER, Berta and Elmer
Ranch and Ring, MEANS, Florence
Randolph, the Bear Who Said No, NELSON, Faith
Raspberry Patch, PAULL, Grace
Read to Me Story Book, LENSKI, Lois
Real Fairy Folks, MEYER, Lucy Rider
Rebellion Dixie, CASTLEMON, Harry
Recollections of a Drummer-Boy, KIEFFER, Harry
Rectory Children, MOLESWORTH, Mrs.
Red Caboose, PEARY, Marie Ahnighito
Red Cap Adventures, CROCKETT, S. R.
Red Hat, NEWCOMB, Covelle
Red Head, LLOYD, John
Red Horse, MOESCHLIN, Elsa
Red Man's Wonder Book, KENNEDY, Howard

Red Pepper's Patients, RICHMOND, Grace S.
Red Tassels for Huki in Peru, BARRIS, Anna Andrews
Rescue Syndicate, JENKS, Tudor
Reynard the Fox & Other Fables, TROWBRIDGE, Larned
Rhymes of the Golden Age, BRILL, George Reiter
Rich Little Poor Boy, GATES, Eleanor
Riders of the Gabilans, DEAN, Graham
Riley Fairy Tales, RILEY, James Whitcomb
Rings on the Fingers, LOWREY, Janette Sebring
Ringtailed Rannyhans, COBURN, Walt
Rip Darcy, Adventurer, O'BRIEN, Jack
Road to Enchantment, FAULKNER, Georgene
Robert Francis Weatherbee, LEAF, Munro
Robert Louis Stevenson: Teller of Tales, GROVER, Eulalie Osgood
Robert Royalton and His Covered Wagon, LEIGHTON, John Jay
Robin's Recruit, PLYMPTON, A. G.
Roderick Taliaferro, COOK, George C.
Roller Skates, SAWYER, Ruth
Rollo in Society, CHAPPELL, George S.
Romance of a Christmas, WIGGIN, Kate Douglas
Romance of the Moon, MITCHELL, J. A.
Roseen, CASSERLEY, Anne
Rosemary, LAWRENCE, Josephine
Rough Riders Ho!, MONTGOMERY, Rutherford
Round Dozen, COOLIDGE, Susan
Round the Mulberry Bush, McNEIL, Marion
Round-About Rambles, STOCKTON, Frank
Rout of the Foreigner, ZOLLINGER, Gulielma
Roweny in Boston, POOL, Maria Louise
Rujub the Juggler, HENTY, George Alfred
Runaway Sardine, BROCK, Emma
Runaway Shuttle Train, FULLER, Muriel
Runner for the King, BENNETT, Rowena
Running Away With Nebby, GARRARD, Philip
Rupert Cabell and Other Tales, ALDEN, Joseph
Ruth Lovell, or Holidays at Home, MAY, Carrie L.
S.W.F. Club, JACOBS, Caroline E.
Sabu, the Elephant Boy, FLAHERTY, Frances
Safety Can be Fun, LEAF, Munro
Sailing Orders, GLADSTONE, Mrs. George
Sailor Jack, MacNEIL, Marion Gill
Sally Ann's Experience, HALL, Eliza Calvert
Sam Pig at the Circus, UTTLEY, Alison
Sand for the Sandmen, DeJONG, Dola
Sandman's Forest, DODGE, Louis
Sandy of San Francisco, CAVANAH, Frances
Sanford and Merton in Words of One Syllable, GODOLPHIN, Mary
Santa Claus Brownies, PHILLIPS, Ethel Calvert
Santa Claus's Partner, PAGE, Thomas Nelson

Santa Fe's Partner, JANVIER, Thomas A.
Sara Faith Anderson: Her Book, GARNER, Elvira
Sarah Deborah's Day, JACKSON, Charlotte
Saucy Betsy, PHILLIPS, Ethel Calvert
Savings Book, a Trip to Golden City, SARG, Tony
Scatter the Chipmunk, COBLENTZ, Catherine
School Boy, HOLMES, Oliver W.
School Days in Disneyville, EMERSON, Caroline
School Keeps Today, ASHMUN, Margaret
School on the Steep, JUDD, Alfred
Schoolhouse in the Woods, CAUDILL, Rebecca
Scotch Circus, the Story of Tammas who Rode the Dragon, POWERS, Tom
Scuttlebutt Goes to War, FRISKEY, Margaret
Sea is Blue, LAWSON, Marie
Sea Magic, BEAUMONT, Cyril W.
Seabird, HOLLING, Holling C.
Seashore Book: Bob and Betty, SMITH, E. Boyd
Seaside and Fireside Fairies, WISTER, A. L.
Second Jungle Book, KIPLING, Rudyard
Secret Mission, COOK, Canfield
Secret of the Buried Tomb, KNIGHT, Clayton
Secret Railway, MEADOWCROFT, Enid
See and Sew, KARASZ, Mariska
Seven Peas in a Pod, BAILEY, Margery
Shannon, MORROW, Elizabeth
Ship of Dreams, PRICE, Edith Ballinger
Ship's Monkey, MORROW, Honore
Shipmates in White, MILLER, Jean Dupont
Ships Across the Sea, PAINE, Ralph D.
Shoes and Ships and Sealing Wax, CHAMBERLIN, Ethel C.
Shoes for Sandy, MURRAY, Gretchen Ostrander
Shoo-Fly Pie, JORDAN, Mildred
Shooting Star Farm, MOLLOY, Anne
Shores of Adventure, McNEIL, Everett
Side Show Studies, METCALFE, Francis
Sidney Martin's Christmas, PANSY (Isabell Alden)
Sign of the Anchor, NEVIN, Evelyn C.
Sigurd and His Brave Companions, UNDSET, Sigrid
Silver and Gold, BLYTON, Enid
Silver Buckle, CRUMPTON, M. N.
Silver Crown, RICHARDS, Laura
Silver Lama, MALKUS, Alida Sims
Silver Saddles, NEWCOMB, Covelle
Silver Shoal Light, PRICE, Edith Ballinger
Simple Songs for Little Singers, TUCKER, Anna B.
Simple Susan and Other Tales, EDGEWORTH, Maria
Sing a Song of Journeys, BIANCO, Pamela
Sing for America, WHEELER, Opal
Singing Around the Clock, MENDEL, Marcella
Singing Around the Seasons, MENDEL, Marcella
Singing Farmer, TIPPETT, James

Singing Sands, MOON, Grace

Singing Twins, SMITH, Laura Rountree

Sir Alymer's Heir, EVERETT-GREEN, Evelyn

Sister Jane: Her Friends and Acquaintances, HARRIS, Joel Chandler

Sister Sally, FOX, Frances Margaret

Sitka the Snow Baby, CHAFFEE, Allen

Sitter Who Didn't Sit, PUNER, Helen Walker

Six Bold Babes, or the Adventures of a Perambulator, ADAMS-ACTION, Mrs.

Six Girls, IRVING, Fannie Belle

Skippy Rambles, CROSBY, Percy

Sky Bed, a Norwegian Christmas, THORNE-THOMSEN, Gudrun

Sky Movies, JOHNSON, Gaylord

Sky Racers, WIRT, Mildred

Sky Trail, DEAN, Graham

Skyline Trail, DAVIES, Mary Carolyn

Skyrocket, HADER, Berta and Elmer

Sleepy Time Picture Book, TAYLOR, Cathryn

Sleepy-Time Stories, BOOTH, Maud Ballington

Slovenly Peter, HOFFMAN, Dr. Henry

Sly Mongoose, POLLOCK, Katherine

Small Child's Book of Verse, DOANE, Pelagie

Smiling Road, RION, Hanna

Smiths and Rusty, HADER, Berta and Elmer

Snippy and Snappy, GAG, Wanda

Snow Baby's Own Story, PEARY, Marie

Snow Baby, PEARY, Josephine D.

Snow Before Christmas, TUDOR, Tasha

Snow White and the Seven Dwarfs, GAG, Wanda

Snowboot, Son of Fire Eye, LINDMAN, Maj

Snowdrop and Other Tales, GRIMM Bros.

So Long Ago, SMITH, E. Boyd

Soap and Bubbles, WINDSOR, Mary

Soldier Boy, LEFEVRE, Felicite

Son of the Danube, PETROFF, Boris

Sondo, a Liberian Boy, JOSEPH, Alfred Ward

Song of Robin Hood, MALCOLMSON, Anne

Song of the Swallows, POLITI, Leo

Song Stories and Song for Children, BREWSTER, Frances Stanton

Songs for Johnny-Jump-Up, FARRAR, John

Songs for Little Children, STEPHENSON, T. W.

Songs of A Little Child's Day, POULSSON, Emilie,

Songs of History, BUTTERWORTH, Hezekiah

Sonny Elephant, BIGHAM, Madge A.

Sons O' Cormac, DUNBAR, Aldis

Sorcerer's Apprentice, ROSTRON, Richard

South and East, MASEFIELD, John

Sparks and Little Sparks, FREEMAN, Ruth and Harrop

Sperli the Clockman, NEUMANN, Daisy

Spin Top Spin, EISGRUBER, Elsa

Splendid Buccaneer: A Tale of the Atlantic Coast in Pirate Days, HOLLAND, Rupert Sargent

Spotty, REY, Margaret and H. A.

Spunk the Donkey, STEARNS, David

Squash for the Fair, PAULL, Grace

St. George and the Witches, DUNNE, J. W.

St. Nicholas Anthology, COMMAGER, Henry Steele

Stagecoach Sam, TOUSEY, Sanford

Star for Hansi, VANCE, Marguerite

Star People, JOHNSON, Gaylord

Star Stories, WARNER, Gertrude

Starlings, BRONSON, Wilfred

Steamboat Billy, TOUSEY, Sanford

Steel Horse, or Rambles of a Bicycle, CASTLEMON, Harry

Stephen, a Story of the Little Crusaders, MADDEN, Eva

Steve and the Steam Engine, BASSETT, Sara Ware

Stonewall, DAVIS, Julia

Stories Children Like, PEAT, Fern Bisel

Stories from an Indian Cave, BAILEY, Carolyn

Stories from Famous Ballads, GREENWOOD, Grace

Stories of Animals, CUNNINGHAM, Virginia

Stories of Enchantment, MYERS, Jane Pentzer

Stories of the Blue and Gray, SWEET, Frank H.

Stories of the Pilgrims, PUMPHREY, Margaret B.

Stories of the Quin-Puplets, HAWLEY, Katherine

Stories of Today, LOWE, Samuel E.

Stork Book, NEWKIRK, Newton

Story of a Happy Doll, MAYOL, Lurline

Story of Ancient Civilization, PEATTIE, Donald Culross

Story of Delicia, NEWMAN, Gertrude

Story of Idles of the King, McFEE, Inez

Story of Little Black Quasha, BANNERMAN, Helen

Story of Little Konrad: the Swiss Boy, CAMPBELL, Helen L.

Story of Milk, WATSON, Elizabeth C.

Story of Nancy Hanks, PHILLIPS, Ethel Calvert

Story of Noah's Ark, SMITH, E. Boyd

Story of Old Dolls and How to Make New Ones, MILLS, Winifred

Story of Pancho the Bull with the Crooked Tail, HADER, Berta and Elmer

Story of Pioneers, MYERS, Marcelline Flora

Story of Puss and Boots, SWEET, Frank H.

Story of Simpson and Sampson, LEAF, Munro

Story of Sir Launcelot and His Companions, PYLE, Howard

Story of Switzerland, POTTER, Edna

Story of the Amulet, NESBIT, E.

Story of the Canterbury Pilgrims, DARTON, F. J.

Story of the Faerie Queene, BROOKS, Edward

Story of the Great Lakes, GILCHRIST, Marie
Story of the Great Plains, McNEER, May
Story of the Mikado, GILBERT
Story of the Pennsylvania Dutch, HARK, Ann
Story of the Red Cross, JOHNSTON, Annie Fellows
Story of the Southwest, McNEER, May
Story of Tonty, CATHERWOOD, Mary Hartwell
Story of Waitstill Baker, WIGGIN, Kate Douglas
Story-Telling Ballads, OLCOTT, Frances Jenkins
Strange Search, FOA, Eugenie
Strawberry Girl, LENSKI, Lois
Strawberry Roan, LANG, Don
Struggle for a Fortune, CASTLEMON, Harry
Stuff and Nonsense, DeLaMARE, Walter
Sube Cane, PARTRIDGE, Edward Bellamy
Such Nonsense, WELLS, Carolyn
Sugar Mill House, HARK, Ann
Sugar Plum Tree, PEAT, Fern Bisel
Sukey, You Shall Be My Wife and Other Stories, BARROWS, Marjorie
Sully Joins the Circus, CHAFFEE, Allen
Summer Day with Ted and Nina, DeANGELI, Marguerite
Summer in a Canyon: a California Story, WIGGIN, Kate Douglas
Sun-Egg, BESKOW, Elsa
Sunbonnet Babies A B C Book, GROVER, Eulalie Osgood
Sunbonnet Babies in Mother Goose Land, GROVER, Eulalie Osgood
Sunshine Annie, GATES, Josephine
Supply at Saint Agatha's, PHELPS, Elizabeth Stuart
Surprise on Wheels, FRISKEY, Margaret
Surprising Adventures of Sir Toady Lion, CROCKETT, S. R.
Susan Clegg and a Man in the House, WARNER, Anne
Susan of the Green Mountains, FOX, Genevieve
Susi, FILOSA, Dorothea
Swift Flies the Falcon, KNOX, Esther Melbourne
Swift Thunder of the Prairie, MALOY, Lois
Swords and Iris, STRACK, Lilian Holmes
Swords and Sails in the Philippines, SOWERS, Phyllis Ayer
Swords and Statues, STRATTON, Clarence
Syndicate And Other Stories, CARRYL, Charles E.
T-Bone the Baby-Sitter, NEWBERRY, Clare Turlay
Tag-Along Tooloo, SAYERS, Frances Clarke
Takamere and Tonhon, ARNETT, Anna Williams
Taktuk an Arctic Boy, LOMEN, Helen
Tale of Benjamin Bunny, POTTER, Beatrix
Tale of Corally Crothers, GAY, Romney
Tale of Peter Rabbit, POTTER, Beatrix
Tale of Squirrel Nutkin, POTTER, Beatrix

Tale of Tai, YOUNG, Evelyn
Tale of the Peninsular War, HENTY, George Alfred
Tale of Tom Tiddler, FARJEON, Eleanor
Tale of Two Bad Mice, POTTER, Beatrix
Tales Come True, WALKER, Margaret Coulson
Tales from Shakespeare, LAMB, Charles and Mary
Tales of an Old Lumber Camp, HAMLIN, John
Tales of Poindi, MARRIOTTI, Jean
Tales of the Wind King, LABORDE, E. D.
Talking Dolls, MILLS, G. R.
Talking Pony, JENKS, Tudor
Tallie, Tillie, and Tag, KUTZER, Ernst
Tambalo, LIDE, Alice Alison
Tap-A-Tan!, LOWREY, Janette Sebring
Tar Baby, HARRIS, Joel Chandler
Tartan Tales from Andrew Lang, LANG, Andrew
Tawny Goes Hunting, CHAFFEE, Allen
Ted and Nina Go to the Grocery Store, DeANGELI, Marguerite
Ted and Polly, HAEFNER, Ralph
Ted and the Telephone, BASSETT, Sara Ware
Teddy's Sailboat and Other Stories, BENNETT, Rowena
Teen Age Boy Scout Stories, CRUMP, Irving
Teenie Weenie Town, DONAHEY, William
Teeny and the Tall Man, MEADE, Julian R.
Teepee Tales, EL COMANCHO
Tell Me Why Stories, CLAUDY, C. H.
Tell-Me-Why Stories About Animals, CLAUDY, C. H.
Ten Saints, FARJEON, Eleanor
Tenggren Tell-It-Again Book, TENGGREN, Gustaf
Tents in the Wilderness, LIPS, Julius E.
Texas The Land of the Tejas, JOHNSON, Siddie Joe
Texas Tomboy, LENSKI, Lois
That Country Called Virginia, BARKSDALE, Lena
Then Came Adventure, BROCK, Emma
There Really Is a Father Christmas, FLINTAN, Douglas L.
They Go Out to Sea, DUVOISIN, Roger
Things Will Take a Turn, HARRADEN, Beatrice
This is Freedom, NELSON, Rhoda
This Way to Christmas, SAWYER, Ruth
Thord Firetooth, LIDE, Alice Alison
Thornton Burgess Animal Stories, BURGESS, Thornton W.
Thoroughbreds, ANDERSON, C. W.
Those Brewster Children, KINGSLEY, Florence
Thrall of Leif the Lucky, LILJENCRANTZ, Ottilie J.
Three Boys in the Wild North Land, YOUNG, Egerton R.
Three Brown Boys and Other Happy Children, HAILE, Ellen
Three for an Acorn, BAKER, Margaret

Three Golden Apples, HAWTHORNE, Nathaniel
Three Little Daughters of the Revolution, PERRY, Nora
Three Little Indians, LEAVITT, Ann H.
Three Little Maids, TURNER, Ethel
Three Little Pigs, PEAT, Fern Bisel
Three Little Pigs, NEILL, John Rea
Three Ring Circus, BROCK, Emma
Three Tall Tales, SEWELL, Helen
Through the Sikh War, HENTY, George Alfred
Through Russian Snows, HENTY, George Alfred
Through the Cloud Mountain, BERNARD, Florence Scott
Thumper, DISNEY Studios
Thy Servant a Dog: Told by Boots, KIPLING, Rudyard
Ti, a Story of San Francisco's Chinatown, BAMFORD, Mary E.
Tibby's Venture, HOLBERG, Ruth
Tiddly Winks Primer, SMITH, Laura Rountree
Tidewater Tales, LOCKLIN, Anne Littlefield
Tiger's Mistake, SKEAT, Walter
Tigers and Things, KAUFFMAN, Andy
Time for Bed, BERTAIL, Inez
Time Was, WOODWARD, Hildegarde
Timmy Rides the China Clipper, NAY, Carol
Timothy Has Ideas, MASON, Miriam
Timothy Tiger, BARROWS, Marjorie
Timothy's Magical Afternoon, JENKS, Tudor
Ting-Ling and Mee-Too, KETO, E.
Tiny Tots, Simple Objects, MALVERN, Corrine
Tiny Tots: Their Adventures, DRAYTON, Grace
Tippytoes Comes to Town, FORSTER, Frederick
Tita of Mexico, MOON, Grace
Tito the Pig of Guatamala, JACKSON, Charlotte
To Be a Farmer's Boy, STOKES and HARNETT
Toby's House, MALOY, Lois
Toinette's Philip, JAMISON, Mrs. C. V.
Tommy and Jane and the Birds, PEAT, Fern Bisel
Tommy and the Wishing Stone, BURGESS, Thornton W.
Tommy Apple, LAVER, James
Tommy Trot's Visit to Santa Claus, and Captured Santa Claus, PAGE, Thomas Nelson
Tommy with the Big Tents, ROOT, Harvey W.
Tommy-Anne and the Three Hearts, WRIGHT, Mabel Osgood
Tomorrow's Champion, ANDERSON, C. W.
Tony and His Pals, CHRISTESON, H. M
Tony Sarg's Book of Marionette Plays, SARG, Tony
Tony Sarg's Magic Movie Book, SARG, Tony
Tony Sarg's Surprise Book, SARG, Tony
Top of the Morning, CARR, Mary Jane
Toplofty, KEYES, Mary Willard
Topple's Wish, CHALMERS, Audrey

Topsy-Turvy Circus, DUPLAIX, Georges
Topsy-Turvy Family, BROCK, Emma
Tortilla Girl, McELRAVEY, May F.
Tower or Throne, COMSTOCK, Harriet
Town Mouse and the Country Mouse, HAYS, Ethel, illustrator
Toy Maker, ENCKING, Louise F.
Toys and Toy Makers, TIPPETT, James
Toys, BEAUMONT, Cyril W.
Trains at Work, ELTING, Mary
Traitor's Torch, CROWNFIELD, Gertrude
Tramp, the Sheep Dog, LANG, Don
Transatlantic Pilot, LITTEN, Frederic Nelson
Transplanted Tree, VanDOREN, Mark
Traveler's Candle, UPDEGRAFF, Florence Maule
Travels of a Snail, HOFFMAN, Eleanor
Treasure Bag Stories and Poems, BARKSDALE, Lena
Treasure Book of Best Stories, CLINTON, Althea
Treasure Book of Best Stories, PEAT, Fern Bisel
Treasure of the Incas, HENTY, George Alfred
Treasure Twins, SMITH, Laura Rountree
Treasures of the Darkness, CLAUDY, Carl. H.
Treasury of Play Ideas for Tiny Tots, HOROWITZ, Caroline
Treasury of Plays for Children, MOSES, Montrose
Tree Boys, NIDA, William Lewis
Trigger John's Son, ROBINSON, Tom
Trixsey's Travels, ATWATER, Emily Paret
Trolley Car Family, CLYMER, Eleanor
True Story Book, LANG, Andrew
True to his Home, BUTTERWORTH, Hezekiah
Trusty, Story of a Police Horse, BECHDOLT, Jack
Tuftoo the Clown, GARIS, Howard
Twenty Little Pets from Everywhere, DITMARS, Raymond
Twilight Fairy Tales, BOOTH, Maud Ballington
Twistum Tales, AMES, Esther Merriam
Two and Two are Four, HAYWOOD, Carolyn
Two Boys in Eskimo Land, MURRAY, Martin
Two Bridgets, HATHAWAY, Cynthia
Two Girls of Old New Jersey, SAGE, Agnes Carr
Two Gray Girls, HAILE, Ellen
Two Little Confederates, PAGE, Thomas Nelson
Two Little Pilgrims' Progress, BURNETT, Frances
Two Logs Crossing: John Haskell's Story, EDMONDS, Walter D.
Two Penniless Princesses, YONGE, Charlotte
Two Ways of Becoming a Hunter, CASTLEMON, Harry
Two Young Corsicans, STEWART, Anna Bird
Ugly Duckling, PEAT, Fern Bisel
Uncle Remus and his Legends, HARRIS, Joel Chandler
Uncle Terry, MUNN, Charles Clark

Under Blue Skies, BRIGHAM, S. J.
Under Drake's Flag, HENTY, George Alfred
Under the Little Fir, YATES, Elizabeth
Under Three Flags, PUMPHREY, Margaret B.
Unicorn with Silver Shoes, YOUNG, Ella
Universal Station, BROWN, Beth
Unknown to History, YONGE, Charlotte
Up and Down the Brooks, BAMFORD, Mary E.
Up and Down the River, CAUDILL, Rebecca
Up Creek and Down Creek, HALL, Esther Greenacre
Up Hill and Down Dale, NICHOLS, Laura
Up the River to Danger, PALMER, Elizabeth
Us Kids and the Circus, KAY, Gertrude
Vagabond in Velvet, NEWCOMB, Covelle
Valley of the Larks, PURDON, Eric
Vanishing Hounds, BECHDOLT, Jack
Viking Prince, MacKAYE, Arthur
Village that Learned to Read, TARSHIS, Elizabeth Kent
Visit to London, Verses by Edward Verrall Lucas, BEDFORD, Francis
Voyage of the Martin Connor, KENDALL, Oswald
Voyage of the Mary Adair, CROMPTON, Frances
Wabeno the Magician, WRIGHT, Mabel Osgood
Waggles, BARROWS, Marjorie
Wagon Train West, NELSON, Rhoda
Waif Maid, McNEER, May
Walk in the City, DAWSON, R.
Walter and the Wireless, BASSETT, Sara Ware
Wampum Belt, BUTTERWORTH, Hezekiah
Wanda and Greta at Broby Farm, PALM, Amy
War Wings for Carol, O'MALLEY, Patricia
War-Time Handbook for Young Americans, LEAF, Munro
Water Elf and the Miller's Child, BAKER, Margaret
Waterboys and Their Cousins, LEWIS, Charles D.
Watling Green, PANTER-DOWNES, Mollie
Way Down in Tennessee, GARNER, Elvira
Way to Glory, McNEELY, Marian Hurd
We Are Seven, BIRLEY, Caroline
Weather House People, McSWIGAN, Marie
Wee Ann, a Story for Little Girls, PHILLIPS, Ethel Calvert
Wee Brigit O'Toole, HOLBERG, Ruth
Wee Willow Whistle, AVERY, Kay
Wee Winkles at the Mountains, JACKSON, Gabrielle
West We Go, LORING, Jules
What Happened Then Stories, DYER, Ruth O.
What Happened to Inger Johanne, ZWILGMEYER, Dikken
What Miranda Knew, ADSHEAD, Gladys L.
What the Wind Told to the Treetops, BROTHERTON, Alice Williams
What to Do Now, LEE, Tina

What'll You Be When You Grow Up?, HADER, Berta and Elmer
When All is Young, MACK, Robert Ellice
When Grandma Was a Little Girl, KOEHLER-BROMAN, Mela
When Little Thoughts Go Rhyming, KNOBEL, Elizabeth
When Our Ship Comes In, FOLEY, Dorothy C.
When the Root Children Wake Up, OLFERS, Sibylle
When Toys Could Talk, PEAT, Fern Bisel
When We Were Wee, YOUNG, Martha
Where Did Your Garden Grow?, LUCAS, Jannette May
Where is Adelaide?, WHITE, Eliza Orne
Where It All Comes True in France, LAUGHLIN, Clara
Where the Blue Begins, MORLEY, Christopher
Where the World Folds Up at Night, WILLSON, Dixie
Whins of Knockattan, CASSERLEY, Anne
Whispering Walls, WIRT, Mildred
White Bunny and his Magic Nose, DUPLAIX, Lily
White Elephant, or Hunters of Ava, DALTON, William
White Mare of The Black Tents, HOFFMAN, Eleanor
White Ring, TREGARTHEN, Enys
White Stars of Freedom, ISASI, Mirim
White Tail, SMOCK, Nell Stolp
Who Knows? a Book of Puzzle Stories, COBB, Bertha
Who's Who in the Zoo, WPA
Who's Who in Tony Sarg's Zoo, SARG, Tony
Wider Wings, O'MALLEY, Patricia
Wigwam Wonder Tales, THOMPSON, William
Wild Animal Homesteads, MILLS, Enos A.
Wild Animals of the World, BRIDGES, William
Wild Lone, WATKINS-PITCHFORD, Denys
Wild Men and Wild Beasts, CUMMING, Lt. Col. Gordon
Wilding Princess, FOX, Frances Margaret
Will Shakespeare's Little Lad, CLARK, Imogen
Willamette Way, AUSTIN, Margot
Winged Arrow's Medicine, CASTLEMON, Harry
Wings for Carol, O'MALLEY, Patricia
Winifred West, CHANNING, Blanche M.
Winter-Telling Stories, MARRIOTT, Alice
Wisdom of Professor Happy, GOLDSMITH, Cliff
Wish on an Apple, GARST, Shannon
Wishbone Children, BYINGTON, Eloise
Wishing Window, FLEXNER, Hortense
Witch Demonia, JACBERNS, Raymond
With Cochrane the Dauntless, HENTY, George Alfred
With the Allies to Pekin, HENTY, George Alfred
With Wolfe in Canada, HENTY, George Alfred

Within the Capes, PYLE, Howard

Within the Gates of Oxford, WILSON, Eleanore

Within the Silver Moon, BIGHAM, Madge A.

Wonder Book and Tanglewood Tales, HAWTHORNE, Nathaniel

Wonder Book of Beasts, DARTON, F. J.

Wonder Book of Myths and Legends, FORBUSH, William Byron

Wonder Book, THOMPSON, Ruth Plumly

Wonder Garden, OLCOTT, Frances Jenkins

Wonder Garden, WINTER, Milo

Wonderful ABC Book, WINTER, Milo

Wonderful Chair and the Tales It Told, BROWNE, Frances

Wonderful Fan, AUNT ELLA

Wonderful World of Being, SQUIRE, Charles

Wood Magic, JEFFRIES, Richard

World in a Barn, WARNER, Gertrude

World of Animals, FARJEON, Eleanor

Wreck of the Wild Wave, HURD, Edith

Wrecking Master, PAINE, Ralph D.

Wu and Lu and Lee, YOUNG, Evelyn

Wynken, Blynken and Nod, PEAT, Fern Bisel

Wynken, Blynken and Nod, FIELD, Eugene

Yama Yama Land, BOYLAN, Grace Duffie

Yankee Doodle's Cousins, MALCOLMSON, Anne

Yankee Ships in Pirate Waters, HOLLAND, Rupert Sargent

Yasu-Bo and Ishi-Ko, SOWERS, Phyllis Ayer

Year's Best Days for Boys and Girls, THORPE, Rose H.

Yellow Eyes, MONTGOMERY, Rutherford

Yellow Star, EASTMAN, Elaine Goodale

Yen-Foh, a Chinese Boy, ELDRIDGE, Ethel J.

Yes, Virginia!, GRIFFITH, Helen

Yinka-Tu the Yak, LIDE, Alice Alison

Young Andy, a Story of a Hundred Years Ago, AMES, Esther Merriam

Young Audubon, Boy Nauralist, MASON, Miriam

Young Carthaginian, HENTY, George Alfred.

Young Folk's Book of Polar Exploration, ELIAS, E. L.

Young Folk's Uncle Tom's Cabin, BOYLAN, Grace Duffie

Young Folks History of America, BUTTERWORTH, Hezekiah

Young Folks History of Boston, BUTTERWORTH, Hezekiah

Young HIckory, YOUNG, Stanley

Young Ice Whalers, PACKARD, Winthrop

Young Man of the House, HUNT, Mabel Leigh

Young McKinley, BUTTERWORTH, Hezekiah

Young Mountaineers, CRADDOCK, Charles Egbert

Youngest Camel, BOYLE, Kay

Zauberlinda, the Wise Witch, GIBSON, Eva

Zeke, OVINGTON, Mary White

COLLECTOR BOOKS

Informing Today's Collector

For over two decades we have been keeping collectors informed on trends and values in all fields of antiques and collectibles.

DOLLS, FIGURES & TEDDY BEARS

4707	A Decade of **Barbie** Dolls & Collectibles, 1981–1991, Summers	$19.95
4631	**Barbie** Doll Boom, 1986–1995, Augustyniak	$18.95
2079	**Barbie** Doll Fashion, Volume I, Eames	$24.95
4846	**Barbie** Doll Fashion, Volume II, Eames	$24.95
3957	**Barbie** Exclusives, Rana	$18.95
4632	**Barbie** Exclusives, Book II, Rana	$18.95
4557	**Barbie**, The First 30 Years, Deutsch	$24.95
4847	**Barbie** Years, 1959–1995, 2nd Ed., Olds	$17.95
3310	**Black Dolls**, 1820–1991, Perkins	$17.95
3873	**Black Dolls**, Book II, Perkins	$17.95
3810	**Chatty Cathy Dolls**, Lewis	$15.95
1529	Collector's Encyclopedia of **Barbie** Dolls, DeWein	$19.95
4882	Collector's Encyclopedia of **Barbie** Doll Exclusives and More, Augustyniak	$19.95
2211	Collector's Encyclopedia of **Madame Alexander Dolls**, Smith	$24.95
4863	Collector's Encyclopedia of **Vogue Dolls**, Izen/Stover	$29.95
3967	Collector's Guide to **Trolls**, Peterson	$19.95
4571	**Liddle Kiddles**, Identification & Value Guide, Langford	$18.95
3826	Story of **Barbie**, Westenhouser	$19.95
1513	**Teddy Bears & Steiff** Animals, Mandel	$9.95
1817	**Teddy Bears & Steiff** Animals, 2nd Series, Mandel	$19.95
2084	**Teddy Bears, Annalee's & Steiff** Animals, 3rd Series, Mandel	$19.95
1808	Wonder of **Barbie**, Manos	$9.95
1430	World of **Barbie** Dolls, Manos	$9.95
4880	World of **Raggedy Ann** Collectibles, Avery	$24.95

TOYS, MARBLES & CHRISTMAS COLLECTIBLES

3427	**Advertising Character** Collectibles, Dotz	$17.95
2333	Antique & Collector's **Marbles**, 3rd Ed., Grist	$9.95
3827	Antique & Collector's **Toys**, 1870–1950, Longest	$24.95
3956	Baby Boomer **Games**, Identification & Value Guide, Polizzi	$24.95
4934	**Breyer Animal** Collector's Guide, Identification and Values, Browell	$19.95
3717	**Christmas** Collectibles, 2nd Edition, Whitmyer	$24.95
4976	**Christmas** Ornaments, Lights & Decorations, Johnson	$24.95
4737	**Christmas** Ornaments, Lights & Decorations, Vol. II, Johnson	$24.95
4739	**Christmas** Ornaments, Lights & Decorations, Vol. III, Johnson	$24.95
4649	Classic Plastic **Model Kits**, Polizzi	$24.95
4559	Collectible **Action Figures**, 2nd Ed., Manos	$17.95
3874	Collectible Coca-Cola Toy **Trucks**, deCourtivron	$24.95
2338	Collector's Encyclopedia of **Disneyana**, Longest, Stern	$24.95
4958	Collector's Guide to **Battery Toys**, Hultzman	$19.95
4639	Collector's Guide to **Diecast Toys & Scale Models**, Johnson	$19.95
4651	Collector's Guide to **Tinker Toys**, Strange	$18.95
4566	Collector's Guide to **Tootsietoys**, 2nd Ed., Richter	$19.95
4720	The Golden Age of **Automotive Toys**, 1925–1941, Hutchison/Johnson	$24.95
3436	**Grist's** Big Book of **Marbles**	$19.95
3970	**Grist's** Machine-Made & Contemporary **Marbles**, 2nd Ed.	$9.95
4723	**Matchbox** Toys, 1947 to 1996, 2nd Ed., Johnson	$18.95
4871	**McDonald's** Collectibles, Henriques/DuVall	$19.95
1540	**Modern Toys** 1930–1980, Baker	$19.95
3888	**Motorcycle** Toys, Antique & Contemporary, Gentry/Downs	$18.95
4953	**Schroeder's** Collectible **Toys**, Antique to Modern Price Guide, 4th Ed.	$17.95
1886	**Stern's** Guide to **Disney** Collectibles	$14.95
2139	**Stern's** Guide to **Disney** Collectibles, 2nd Series	$14.95
3975	**Stern's** Guide to **Disney** Collectibles, 3rd Series	$18.95
2028	**Toys**, Antique & Collectible, Longest	$14.95
3979	**Zany Characters** of the Ad World, Lamphier	$16.95

FURNITURE

1457	American **Oak** Furniture, McNerney	$9.95
3716	American **Oak** Furniture, Book II, McNerney	$12.95
1118	Antique **Oak** Furniture, Hill	$7.95
2271	Collector's Encyclopedia of **American** Furniture, Vol. II, Swedberg	$24.95
3720	Collector's Encyclopedia of **American** Furniture, Vol. III, Swedberg	$24.95
3878	Collector's Guide to **Oak** Furniture, George	$12.95
1755	Furniture of the **Depression Era**, Swedberg	$19.95
3906	**Heywood-Wakefield** Modern Furniture, Rouland	$18.95
1885	**Victorian** Furniture, Our American Heritage, McNerney	$9.9
3829	**Victorian** Furniture, Our American Heritage, Book II, McNerney	$9.9

JEWELRY, HATPINS, WATCHES & PURSES

1712	Antique & Collector's **Thimbles** & Accessories, Mathis	$19.9
1748	Antique **Purses**, Revised Second Ed., Holiner	$19.9
1278	Art Nouveau & Art Deco **Jewelry**, Baker	$9.9
4850	Collectible **Costume Jewelry**, Simonds	$24.9
3875	Collecting Antique **Stickpins**, Kerins	$16.9
3722	Collector's Ency. of **Compacts, Carryalls & Face Powder Boxes**, Mueller	$24.9
4854	Collector's Ency. of **Compacts, Carryalls & Face Powder Boxes**, Vol. II	$24.9
4940	**Costume Jewelry**, A Practical Handbook & Value Guide, Rezazadeh	$24.9
1716	Fifty Years of Collectible **Fashion Jewelry**, 1925–1975, Baker	$19.9
1424	**Hatpins** & Hatpin Holders, Baker	$9.9
4570	Ladies' **Compacts**, Gerson	$24.9
1181	100 Years of Collectible **Jewelry**, 1850–1950, Baker	$9.9
4729	**Sewing Tools** & Trinkets, Thompson	$24.9
2348	20th Century Fashionable Plastic **Jewelry**, Baker	$19.9
4878	Vintage & Contemporary **Purse Accessories**, Gerson	$24.9
3830	Vintage **Vanity Bags & Purses**, Gerson	$24.9

INDIANS, GUNS, KNIVES, TOOLS, PRIMITIVES

1868	Antique **Tools**, Our American Heritage, McNerney	$9.9
1426	**Arrowheads** & Projectile Points, Hothem	$7.9
4943	Field Guide to **Flint Arrowheads & Knives** of the North American Indian	$9.9
2279	**Indian Artifacts** of the Midwest, Hothem	$14.9
3885	**Indian Artifacts** of the Midwest, Book II, Hothem	$16.9
4870	**Indian Artifacts** of the Midwest, Book III, Hothem	$18.9
1964	**Indian Axes** & Related Stone Artifacts, Hothem	$14.9
2023	**Keen Kutter** Collectibles, Heuring	$14.9
4724	Modern **Guns**, Identification & Values, 11th Ed., Quertermous	$12.9
2164	**Primitives**, Our American Heritage, McNerney	$9.9
1759	**Primitives**, Our American Heritage, 2nd Series, McNerney	$14.9
4730	Standard **Knife** Collector's Guide, 3rd Ed., Ritchie & Stewart	$12.9

PAPER COLLECTIBLES & BOOKS

4633	**Big Little Books**, Jacobs	$18.
4710	Collector's Guide to **Children's Books**, Jones	$18.
1441	Collector's Guide to **Post Cards**, Wood	$9.
2081	Guide to Collecting **Cookbooks**, Allen	$14.
2080	Price Guide to **Cookbooks** & Recipe Leaflets, Dickinson	$9.
3973	**Sheet Music** Reference & Price Guide, 2nd Ed., Pafik & Guiheen	$19.
4654	**Victorian Trade Cards**, Historical Reference & Value Guide, Cheadle	$19.
4733	**Whitman Juvenile Books**, Brown	$17.

GLASSWARE

4561	Collectible **Drinking Glasses**, Chase & Kelly	$17
4642	Collectible **Glass Shoes**, Wheatley	$19
4937	Coll. **Glassware** from the 40s, 50s & 60s, 4th Ed., Florence	$19
1810	Collector's Encyclopedia of **American Art Glass**, Shuman	$29
4938	Collector's Encyclopedia of **Depression Glass**, 13th Ed., Florence	$19
1961	Collector's Encyclopedia of **Fry Glassware**, Fry Glass Society	$24
1664	Collector's Encyclopedia of **Heisey Glass**, 1925–1938, Bredehoft	$24
3905	Collector's Encyclopedia of **Milk Glass**, Newbound	$24
4936	Collector's Guide to **Candy Containers**, Dezso/Poirier	$19
4564	**Crackle Glass**, Weitman	$19
4941	**Crackle Glass**, Book II, Weitman	$19
2275	**Czechoslovakian Glass** and Collectibles, Barta/Rose	$16
4714	**Czechoslovakian Glass** and Collectibles, Book II, Barta/Rose	$16
4716	**Elegant Glassware** of the Depression Era, 7th Ed., Florence	$19
1380	Encylopedia of **Pattern Glass**, McClain	$12
3981	Ever's Standard **Cut Glass** Value Guide	$12
4659	**Fenton** Art Glass, 1907–1939, Whitmyer	$24
3725	**Fostoria**, Pressed, Blown & Hand Molded Shapes, Kerr	$24
4719	**Fostoria**, Etched, Carved & Cut Designs, Vol. II, Kerr	$24
3883	**Fostoria Stemware**, The Crystal for America, Long & Seate	$24
4644	**Imperial Carnival Glass**, Burns	$18
3886	**Kitchen Glassware** of the Depression Years, 5th Ed., Florence	$19

COLLECTOR BOOKS
Informing Today's Collector

5	Pocket Guide to **Depression Glass**, 10th Ed., Florence	$9.95
5	Standard Encyclopedia of **Carnival Glass**, 6th Ed., Edwards/Carwile	$24.95
6	Standard **Carnival Glass** Price Guide, 11th Ed., Edwards/Carwile	$9.95
5	Standard Encyclopedia of **Opalescent Glass**, 2nd ed., Edwards	$19.95
1	**Stemware Identification**, Featuring Cordials with Values, Florence	$24.95
6	**Very Rare Glassware** of the Depression Years, 3rd Series, Florence	$24.95
2	**Very Rare Glassware** of the Depression Years, 5th Series, Florence	$24.95
6	**Westmoreland Glass**, Wilson	$24.95

POTTERY

7	**ABC Plates & Mugs**, Lindsay	$24.95
9	**American Art Pottery**, Sigafoose	$24.95
0	**American Limoges**, Limoges	$24.95
2	**Blue & White Stoneware**, McNerney	$9.95
8	So. Potteries **Blue Ridge Dinnerware**, 3rd Ed., Newbound	$14.95
9	**Blue Willow**, 2nd Ed., Gaston	$14.95
8	Ceramic **Coin Banks**, Stoddard	$19.95
1	Collectible **Cups & Saucers**, Harran	$18.95
9	Collectible **Kay Finch**, Biography, Identification & Values, Martinez/Frick	$18.95
3	Collector's Encyclopedia of **American Dinnerware**, Cunningham	$24.95
1	Collector's Encyclopedia of **Bauer Pottery**, Chipman	$24.95
5	Collector's Encyclopedia of **Blue Ridge Dinnerware**, Newbound	$19.95
2	Collector's Encyclopedia of **Blue Ridge Dinnerware**, Vol. II, Newbound	$24.95
8	Collector's Encyclopedia of **Brush-McCoy Pottery**, Huxford	$24.95
2	Collector's Encyclopedia of **California Pottery**, Chipman	$24.95
1	Collector's Encyclopedia of **Colorado Pottery**, Carlton	$24.95
1	Collector's Encyclopedia of **Cookie Jars**, Roerig	$24.95
3	Collector's Encyclopedia of **Cookie Jars**, Book II, Roerig	$24.95
9	Collector's Encyclopedia of **Cookie Jars**, Book III, Roerig	$24.95
8	Collector's Encyclopedia of **Dakota Potteries**, Dommel	$24.95
0	Collector's Encyclopedia of **Fiesta**, 8th Ed., Huxford	$19.95
8	Collector's Encyclopedia of **Figural Planters & Vases**, Newbound	$19.95
1	Collector's Encyclopedia of **Early Noritake**, Alden	$24.95
9	Collector's Encyclopedia of **Flow Blue China**, Gaston	$19.95
2	Collector's Encyclopedia of **Flow Blue China**, 2nd Ed., Gaston	$24.95
3	Collector's Encyclopedia of **Hall China**, 2nd Ed., Whitmyer	$24.95
1	Collector's Encyclopedia of **Homer Laughlin China**, Jasper	$24.95
6	Collector's Encyclopedia of **Hull Pottery**, Roberts	$19.95
2	Collector's Encyclopedia of **Lefton China**, DeLozier	$19.95
5	Collector's Encyclopedia of **Lefton China**, Book II, DeLozier	$19.95
0	Collector's Encyclopedia of **Limoges Porcelain**, 2nd Ed., Gaston	$24.95
4	Collector's Encyclopedia of **Majolica Pottery**, Katz-Marks	$19.95
8	Collector's Encyclopedia of **McCoy Pottery**, Huxford	$19.95
3	Collector's Encyclopedia of **Metlox Potteries**, Gibbs Jr.	$24.95
7	Collector's Encyclopedia of **Nippon Porcelain**, Van Patten	$24.95
9	Collector's Ency. of **Nippon Porcelain**, 2nd Series, Van Patten	$24.95
5	Collector's Ency. of **Nippon Porcelain**, 3rd Series, Van Patten	$24.95
2	Collector's Ency. of **Nippon Porcelain**, 4th Series, Van Patten	$24.95
7	Collector's Encyclopedia of **Noritake**, Van Patten	$19.95
2	Collector's Encyclopedia of **Noritake**, 2nd Series, Van Patten	$24.95
7	Collector's Encyclopedia of **Occupied Japan**, 1st Series, Florence	$14.95
8	Collector's Encyclopedia of **Occupied Japan**, 2nd Series, Florence	$14.95
8	Collector's Encyclopedia of **Occupied Japan**, 3rd Series, Florence	$14.95
9	Collector's Encyclopedia of **Occupied Japan**, 4th Series, Florence	$14.95
5	Collector's Encyclopedia of **Occupied Japan**, 5th Series, Florence	$14.95
1	Collector's Encyclopedia of **Old Ivory China**, Hillman	$24.95
4	Collector's Encyclopedia of **Pickard China**, Reed	$24.95
7	Collector's Encyclopedia of **R.S. Prussia**, 4th Series, Gaston	$24.95
4	Collector's Encyclopedia of **Roseville Pottery**, Huxford	$19.95
5	Collector's Encyclopedia of **Roseville Pottery**, 2nd Ed., Huxford	$19.95
6	Collector's Encyclopeida of **Russel Wright**, 2nd Ed., Kerr	$24.95
3	Collector's Encyclopedia of **Salt Glaze Stoneware**, Taylor/Lowrance	$24.95
4	Collector's Encyclopedia of **Van Briggle** Art Pottery, Sasicki	$24.95
3	Collector's Encyclopedia of **Wall Pockets**, Newbound	$19.95
1	Collector's Encyclopedia of **Weller Pottery**, Huxford	$29.95
6	Collector's Guide to **Lu-Ray Pastels**, Meehan	$18.95
4	Collector's Guide to **Made in Japan** Ceramics, White	$18.95
4	Collector's Guide to **Made in Japan** Ceramics, Book II, White	$18.95
5	Collector's Guide to **Rockingham**, The Enduring Ware, Brewer	$14.95
9	Collector's Guide to **Shawnee Pottery**, Vanderbilt	$19.95
5	**Cookie Jars**, Westfall	$9.95

3440	**Cookie Jars**, Book II, Westfall	$19.95
4924	Figural & Novelty **Salt & Pepper Shakers**, 2nd Series, Davern	$24.95
2379	Lehner's Ency. of **U.S. Marks** on Pottery, Porcelain & China	$24.95
4722	**McCoy Pottery**, Collector's Reference & Value Guide, Hanson/Nissen	$19.95
3825	**Purinton Pottery**, Morris	$24.95
4726	**Red Wing Art Pottery**, 1920s–1960s, Dollen	$19.95
1670	**Red Wing Collectibles**, DePasquale	$9.95
1440	**Red Wing Stoneware**, DePasquale	$9.95
1632	**Salt & Pepper Shakers**, Guarnaccia	$9.95
5091	**Salt & Pepper Shakers** II, Guarnaccia	$18.95
2220	**Salt & Pepper Shakers** III, Guarnaccia	$14.95
3443	**Salt & Pepper Shakers** IV, Guarnaccia	$18.95
3738	**Shawnee Pottery**, Mangus	$24.95
4629	Turn of the Century **American Dinnerware**, 1880s–1920s, Jasper	$24.95
4572	**Wall Pockets** of the Past, Perkins	$17.95
3327	**Watt Pottery** – Identification & Value Guide, Morris	$19.95

OTHER COLLECTIBLES

4704	Antique & Collectible **Buttons**, Wisniewski	$19.95
2269	Antique **Brass & Copper** Collectibles, Gaston	$16.95
1880	Antique **Iron**, McNerney	$9.95
3872	Antique **Tins**, Dodge	$24.95
4845	Antique **Typewriters & Office Collectibles**, Rehr	$19.95
1714	**Black** Collectibles, Gibbs	$19.95
1128	**Bottle** Pricing Guide, 3rd Ed., Cleveland	$7.95
4636	**Celluloid Collectibles**, Dunn	$14.95
3718	Collectible **Aluminum**, Grist	$16.95
3445	Collectible **Cats**, An Identification & Value Guide, Fyke	$18.95
4560	Collectible **Cats**, An Identification & Value Guide, Book II, Fyke	$19.95
4852	Collectible **Compact Disc** Price Guide 2, Cooper	$17.95
2018	Collector's Encyclopedia of **Granite Ware**, Greguire	$24.95
3430	Collector's Encyclopedia of **Granite Ware**, Book 2, Greguire	$24.95
4705	Collector's Guide to **Antique Radios**, 4th Ed., Bunis	$18.95
3880	Collector's Guide to **Cigarette Lighters**, Flanagan	$17.95
4637	Collector's Guide to **Cigarette Lighers**, Book II, Flanagan	$17.95
4942	Collector's Guide to **Don Winton Designs**, Ellis	$19.95
3966	Collector's Guide to **Inkwells**, Identification & Values, Badders	$18.95
4947	Collector's Guide to **Inkwells**, Book II, Badders	$19.95
4948	Collector's Guide to **Letter Openers**, Grist	$19.95
4862	Collector's Guide to **Toasters** & Accessories, Greguire	$19.95
4652	Collector's Guide to **Transistor Radios**, 2nd Ed., Bunis	$16.95
4653	Collector's Guide to **TV Memorabilia**, 1960s–1970s, Davis/Morgan	$24.95
4864	Collector's Guide to **Wallace Nutting Pictures**, Ivankovich	$18.95
1629	**Doorstops**, Identification & Values, Bertoia	$9.95
4567	Figural **Napkin Rings**, Gottschalk & Whitson	$18.95
4717	**Figural Nodders**, Includes Bobbin' Heads and Swayers, Irtz	$19.95
3968	**Fishing Lure** Collectibles, Murphy/Edmisten	$24.95
4867	**Flea Market Trader**, 11th Ed., Huxford	$9.95
4944	**Flue Covers**, Collector's Value Guide, Meckley	$12.95
4945	**G-Men and FBI Toys** and Collectibles, Whitworth	$18.95
5043	**Garage Sale & Flea Market Annual**, 6th Ed.	$19.95
3819	**General Store** Collectibles, Wilson	$24.95
4643	**Great American West** Collectibles, Wilson	$24.95
2215	Goldstein's **Coca-Cola** Collectibles	$16.95
3884	Huxford's Collectible **Advertising**, 2nd Ed.	$24.95
2216	**Kitchen Antiques**, 1790–1940, McNerney	$14.95
4950	The **Lone Ranger**, Collector's Reference & Value Guide, Felbinger	$18.95
2026	**Railroad** Collectibles, 4th Ed., Baker	$14.95
4949	**Schroeder's Antiques** Price Guide, 16th Ed., Huxford	$12.95
5007	**Silverplated Flatware**, Revised 4th Edition, Hagan	$18.95
1922	Standard **Old Bottle** Price Guide, Sellari	$14.95
4708	**Summers' Guide to Coca-Cola**	$19.95
4952	**Summers' Pocket Guide to Coca-Cola** Identifications	$9.95
3892	**Toy & Miniature Sewing Machines**, Thomas	$18.95
4876	**Toy & Miniature Sewing Machines**, Book II, Thomas	$24.95
3828	Value Guide to **Advertising Memorabilia**, Summers	$18.95
3977	Value Guide to **Gas Station** Memorabilia, Summers & Priddy	$24.95
4877	**Vintage Bar Ware**, Visakay	$24.95
4935	The **W.F. Cody Buffalo Bill** Collector's Guide with Values	$24.95
4879	**Wanted to Buy**, 6th Edition	$9.95

is is only a partial listing of the books on antiques that are available from Collector Books. All books are well illustrated and contain current values. Most of these books are available from your local bookseller, antique dealer, or public library. If you are unable to locate certain titles in your area, you may order by mail from COLLECTOR BOOKS, P.O. Box 009, Paducah, KY 42002-3009. Customers with Visa, Discover or MasterCard may phone in orders from 7:00–5:00 CST, Monday–Friday, Toll Free 1-800-626-5420. Add $2.00 postage for the first book ordered and $0.30 for each additional book. Include item number, title, and price when ordering. Allow 14 to 21 days for delivery.

Schroeder's ANTIQUES Price Guide

. . . is the #1 best-selling antiques & collectibles value guide on the market today, and here's why . . .

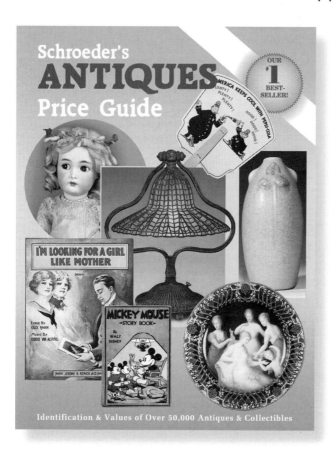

8½ x 11, 612 Pages, $12.95

- *More than 450 advisors, well-known dealers, and top-notch collectors work together with our editors to bring you accurate information regarding pricing and identification.*

- *More than 45,000 items in almost 550 categories are listed along with hundreds of sharp original photos that illustrate not only the rare and unusual, but the common, popular collectibles as well.*

- *Each large close-up shot shows important details clearly. Every subject is represented with histories and background information, a feature not found in any of our competitors' publications.*

- *Our editors keep abreast of newly developing trends, often adding several new categories a year as the need arises.*

If it merits the interest of today's collector, you'll find it in *Schroeder's*. And you can feel confident that the information we publish is up to date and accurate. Our advisors thoroughly check each category to spot inconsistencies, listings that may not be entirely reflective of market dealings, and lines too vague to be of merit. Only the best of the lot remains for publication.

Without doubt, you'll find
SCHROEDER'S ANTIQUES PRICE GUIDE
the only one to buy for
reliable information and values.

COLLECTOR BOOKS
A Division of Schroeder Publishing Co., Inc.